BLOOD OF EMPIRES
Trilogy - Volume II
A Novel

JOHN LAWRENCE BURKS

Copyright © 2019 by JOHN LAWRENCE BURKS

BLOOD OF EMPIRES Trilogy - Volume II
A Novel
by JOHN LAWRENCE BURKS

Printed in the United States of America.

ISBN 9781545660195

All rights reserved solely by the author. The author guarantees all contents are original and do not infringe upon the legal rights of any other person or work. No part of this book may be reproduced in any form without the permission of the author. The views expressed in this book are not necessarily those of the publisher.

Unless otherwise indicated, Scripture quotations taken from the King James Version (KJV) – *public domain.*

Scripture quotations taken from the New American Standard Bible (NASB). Copyright © 1960, 1962, 1963, 1968, 1971, 1972, 1973, 1975, 1977, 1995 by The Lockman Foundation. Used by permission. All rights reserved.

Scripture quotations taken from the Holy Bible, New International Version (NIV). Copyright © 1973, 1978, 1984, 2011 by Biblica, Inc.™. Used by permission. All rights reserved.

www.xulonpress.com

PROLOGUE

Rome – One in the morning on the 2nd day of September (the 9th month as adopted by Julius Caesar's Julian Calendar and the 2nd year of Rome's Adoptive Emperor, Marcus Ulpius Traianus Trajan. Sixty-seven years since the crucifixion of Jesus of Nazareth. (100 AD)

"Death may be the greatest good that can happen to man: but we fear it as if we knew quite well that it was the greatest of evils."   Socrates

Two hours after midnight seems to be the eerie time of quietness, even with the sounds of wagons slowly rolling over Rome's stone-paved streets. With vacantness of animal sounds, including the thousands of dogs in the Imperial City, I feel somewhat *pax* (peaceful) in my cold prison cell on this 131st anniversary since the Battle of Actium. Augustus designated this slightly forgotten successful event, which always falls on the 4th day before the Nones in September; and a smile arises from deep within my soul as I realize this date marks my 91st year in this world. Ironically, today shall be the day of my death – happening sometime this afternoon at the amphitheater Coliseum, which was constructed by Emperor Titus. My scribe is still resting his head on his small wooden writing table. He has been in that position for the past hour, but I need to wake him because every moment is now precious as my life is dripping away like an old, cracked water clock. My old friend has been writing for many hours before I allowed him this one break. Until he awakes I shall pick up his pen and tell a little of my story.

During the last hour, I could not find sleep but instead wondered why I never wholly processed my long-ago feelings after Messina dismissed me for someone else. In my mind's eye, I can still see her waiting for me at the far edge of the pool at Bethesda; but I always try to forget her plans concerning my arch enemy Demos. Honestly, my initial response was to end my own life after learning of her decision. Those evil thoughts were interrupted by the strange man named Jesus. After he and I had spoken, I witnessed the healing of the lame man who had been afflicted for 38 years. Today I am now confident that this one miracle helped vanquish my inner pain that now has silently returned after all these years. How strange our minds work and what they remember and choose to forget. Besides witnessing the miracle of the lame man of 38 years, there was a second miracle, which was just for me. Jesus gave me the news concerning my upcoming meeting with John the Baptist. It to me was a divine moment. As prophesied, I did talk with the Baptist, which is where I ended my story and allowed my scribe a short nap. I shall continue writing for just a little longer before waking him. Only with him sleeping can I experience this strange sadness that is now overtaking me. My mental state is caused by my reflection of that long ago event before the healing when Messina rejected me at the Pool of Bethesda. How could she spend her life with such a snake of a human as Demos Treverorum? Why would she want such a fate? My chest ached as I realized that great loss so many years ago. Now I understand why that ancient protuberance did not overwhelm me until tonight. Well, enough of this sadness; I must wake my scribe, and return to my story on the morning after my most glorious time with John the Baptist. Little did I know he was going to be beheaded in a few days by Herod Antipas, the man I served as a mercenary.

JOHN LAWRENCE BURKS

BOOK II

BLOOD OF THE BAPTIST

PART FIVE

CHAPTER ONE

Machaerus – Nisan 15. Tiberius's 17th year as Rome's emperor. Pontius Pilate's 5th year as Prefect of Judaea. Jesus of Nazareth ends his 2nd year of Public Ministry. John the Baptist's last days after one-and-a-half years in prison at Machaerus in the province of Peraea. Herod Antipas's 35th year as Tetrarch of Peraea and Galilee.   *Nisan 14 (March 27, 31 AD)*

There is no witness so dreadful, no accuser so terrible as the conscience that dwells in the heart of every man.   Polybius, a Roman freedman

The Herodian messenger waited while Amcheck and I tried to finish our morning meal in the soldiers' dining room. Learning of the summons to appear before Herod Antipas caused me to lose my appetite. Both Amcheck and I were to appear in Machaerus's throne room on the quick. I stuffed dry bread in my mouth and softened it with watered-down red wine. Amcheck looked at me instead of eating, and I saw a strange look cross his eyes. I wondered if stuffing my mouth took away his appetite. It couldn't be because he had to stand in front of Herod Antipas. I knew he had appeared before Herod in the past, and was it not I who had to tell Herod what I witnessed when Jesus of Nazareth healed the lame man at the Pool of Bethesda? Maybe Amcheck felt guilty for revealing my meeting with Jesus at the pool of Bethesda. I concluded he was a hard man to read.

We both followed the messenger up some stairs and down several long halls to the entrance door that led to Herod Antipas's elegant throne room that doubled as a banquet hall. Reaching a large closed ornate wooden door, we were waved to sit on a stone bench. Since becoming a mercenary, I learned a soldier's most celebrated adage: hurry up, and wait. Here we sat for over an hour. During that time we were visited by the soldier with the missing hand, the guard at the pit that held John the Baptist. Seeing us caused him to smile as he approached us and asked me before addressing Amcheck: "What did you say to the prisoner last evening?"

"Why do you ask?" was my befuddled reply.

"He has not been the same since you left. He started singing and yelling praises to his God. Not many survive a year and a half in that hole without losing their minds. I have been worried about him. He fell into a gloomy state about six months ago until you arrived and spoke with him. He is now full of hope and even – *agape*." I was taken back when the old guard used the Greek word *agape* on top of the Aramaic he had been using. *Agape* is the word that describes a specific one-way love someone has for another, even if the other is about to kill him or her. It is often used in connection with Yahweh's love for mankind. We humans dismiss the ever presence of the Creator all because it is hard to understand the magnificence of God's love, an undeserved love. Regarding John, God's prophet, I was touched that I was perhaps used in some mysterious way to help him return to the idea that instead of blaming or grumbling against God he has accepted what God has allowed. Besides, wasn't that what he told me last night when I visited him in his hole?

I began to believe that there must be a spiritual war raging all around us that involves both good and dark spirits all battling for our souls. It is incredible to me to realize that it is possible for one idea to lock us back in step with God granting us also the ability to demonstrate *agape*. A rare smile warms my face; and I looked at the old soldier with the missing hand and said, "I heard this stated a few years back: 'Hope is the home where love grows high.'"

"What does that mean?" asked the smelly soldier after looking over to Amcheck with his eyebrows arched up in a look of confusion. Amcheck touched his own head in a jester showing I had been out in the sun too long. They both laughed at my expense; and the man left, not even aware he needed a serious bath. I wondered if he could ever get the smell out after all these years of guarding prisoners down in the deep basement of this palace-fortress.

Once he was gone, Amcheck turned to me with a stern look and said, "Do not do that again!"

"Do what?" I asked with confusion.

"Showing off your vast learning and using obscure quotes that simple men, especially soldiers, do not understand. Do we want to be found out? You talk like that in front of Herod Antipas; and, in the time it takes to kill a fly in this blasted land, he will know who you are if he hasn't already guessed."

"You are right; I am sorry. I believe it was Cicero who said, 'Just as a ship captain must stay away from rocks, we, too, should never use lofty language or large words.' From now on, I will keep my mouth shut." After a long period of silence, Amcheck's concerns flew from my mind like a large carrion bird circling around riding the high winds above me. His words were still with me but far away.

The silence was finally broken by Amcheck. "When we stand before Herod, I will do all the talking. Remember you are supposed to be a stupid youth who works for one of the most influential men in the Empire. People are looking for someone your age who studied at that high and expensive school in Greece. Saying things like 'captains and rocks' will mark you – do you understand?"

"I understand and rest your mind concerning my words. I will work at keeping my thoughts to myself." Amcheck let out a sound like that was not going to happen. I said nothing, and we both again sat quietly for a long time. I soon returned my thoughts back to John. I was delighted to hear that John was now filled with a hope that must have come from God through me. A good feeling overcame me that went beyond understanding. Something glowed deep within at the realization that the God of Israel must still love me. Why else would He use me to help the Baptist in John's time of need?

Three more hours slowly crawled by. Amcheck and I just sat silently like the simple soldiers we were supposed to be. I would have been happier doing something other than sitting but remained passive and submissive just waiting on the tetrarch's summons. Near the end of the third hour, Amcheck broke the silence by telling about two previous occasions he had stood before Herod Antipas. Both included lavish banquets, which he was allowed to attend. Amcheck attested to sordid details of these two wild parties. I concluded that on both occasions Amcheck was being rewarded because of his work with the *sicarius*. I began to feel sick in my spirit realizing I had helped Amcheck in two previous assassinations, and I wanted nothing to do with any wild parties before we left Machaerus. If a thing like that happens tonight, I decided to secretly exit any festivities and try to visit the Baptist once again.

It was now mid-morning, and we both stood stiffly to stretch when a guard finally opened the door and waved for us to enter the great hall. Amcheck and I smiled at one another and then entered a huge, ostentatious throne room. At the far end, I saw Herod Antipas. This was the second time in my life to have placed my eyes upon him. The first was from a distance when he was sitting next to Emperor Tiberius at the gladiatorial game in Rome when Marius the gladiator won the wooden sword for the third time. Seeing him sitting alone on a high stage at the rear of the room seemed surreal; yet, what I saw did not impress me one *iota*. Studying him as we moved slowly toward his dais, I saw that he was on the wrong side of middle age, tilting beyond corpulent with his massive neck dropping straight into his golden robe, which made him look like a giant, golden worm. Draped over a plush golden robe was a scarlet-purple cloak about the same color as the Spartan robe returned to me by Messina and now hidden in my room back in Jerusalem. His hair was thin on top and gray on the sides. It looked as if he were trying to grow it long to comb it over to hide the sizeable balding plat on top. He looked ridiculous, and I wondered why he did not just shave it all off and admit the inevitable. On top of the sparse head, he wore a strange, ray-type crown. I quickly recognized it as a copy from the one I saw Tiberius wearing in the amphitheater nearly a dozen years back. All of a sudden, this picture reminded me of my father the night I killed Claudia and when I also tried to kill him. On that stormy night, he was wearing a laurel wreath attempting to hide his baldness. My final opinion of Herod Antipas after hours of waiting was he was one of the most overdressed actors I would ever meet. Herod, along with my father were cut from the same hypocritical, deceiving block of wood. I was confident both men would become close associates if they ever met.

As we approached his throne, the tetrarch did not eye me but instead smiled upon Amcheck. The ornate wooden chair on which Herod Antipas sat had several steps with cat-sized lions flanking the throne. Counting two on each level there were 12 identical lions in all. Perhaps this was reminiscent of King Solomon's throne; but Solomon's lions were made of ivory, not wood. Herod's lions were all carved out of olive wood showing the dark and unique, stringy wood grain. I am sure Tiberius in Rome did not have anything as elegant as this; and, if Tiberius were ever to visit, I am sure he would have one made for himself. The only difference would be Tiberius would have his lions covered in gold.

The tetrarch clapped his hands signaling we could stop once we reached his throne platform. Amcheck bowed his head in homage, but I held back any show that gave tribute to another human. After my encounter with Caiaphas the high priest, I was ready to lose my life over showing devotion to anyone. While Amcheck was bowing, I slid back a step or two and tried to be invisible. "Tell me, Amcheck; what brings you to Machaerus?" Herod then made

Chapter One

a quick hand jester to someone to my left. Looking over I noticed a rotund, bald chamberlain approaching from the far side of the room. He walked like an effeminate eunuch using dainty steps. When he looked at me as he glided along, I noticed black lines painted on his lower eyelids and his lips were made up in bright red grease. I almost laughed aloud watching this eunuch approach us with those mincing steps. I noticed he was able to make this forward movement by using only his toes and not the balls of his feet. Amcheck did not seem perturbed by the chamberlain's approach and only handed the strange man a tightly rolled scroll he had been holding all morning.

"Is this message different from what I received yesterday on your arrival?" inquired Herod after the eunuch gave it to him.

"Yes, my lord."

"I beg you; do not address me as lord. I'm just a lowly tetrarch," he said sniggering under his breath while he took the papyrus and unrolled it. Lifting it to his left he began reading it by the light streaming in through long, narrow air vents near the ceiling. I watched while his lips pursed outwards while he read to himself. When he finished, he looked up. "Most fascinating. Now tell me in your own words about the incident with the Romans and the Jews at the Castle of Antonia. And do not forget that the 'Pilum Man' and I do not see eye to eye."

The eunuch tittered a strange cackle after the "Pilum Man" comment, which also caused Amcheck to guffaw as well. I just stood quietly acting disinterested. This was the first time I had heard of this name for Pontius Pilate. Apparently, Pilate was not his family name but a nickname. I did learn later that his family name was Pontius, but the story was he was an expert with the Roman spear called a pilum during his time in the legions. He must have earned the name "Pilum Man" in the legions with his expert ability to throw a pilum further and on target over any other Roman soldier. Today, almost seventy years later, many think Pilate is his family name when, in fact, it is Pontius. I am sorry to report that I never did learn his first name.

Perhaps I should again explain the Roman endocentric practice regarding Roman names. A Roman citizen usually held three designates. The first was the personal name, the second was the clan name, and the third was typically a nickname. For instance, the father of the Roman Empire was Gaius Julius Caesar. Gaius was his personal name given at birth; and Julius was his family name, which is the origin of the Julian or Julio Dynasty. The third name Caesar was Gaius Julius's nickname. From his reign of consul for life, up to the present, all emperors use his nickname for themselves, such as Augustus Caesar, Tiberius Caesar, and so forth. It is believed that Gaius Julius adopted the original nickname, Caesar, from some grandfather who was cut from his mother's belly when she could not give birth the normal way. Thus, the word *caesar* just means to "cut out." This practice was known as having a *caesarean* delivery. Gaius Julius was not born this way; but, like others in his clan, he used this unique cognomen that today has become a title of rulership. A note concerning females in the Roman world. Most never were given a personal name at birth and only used the family name. For instance, in the ruling Julian Dynasty, many women were just given the name Julia, the feminine pronunciation of Julius. Where there were more than one Julia the term elder or lesser were added to their names. Thus, Julia the elder, Julia the lesser, Julia the younger, and so forth.

My name, on this day in front of Herod Antipas, would be Venustus Vetallus Cata. My father, Gaius Vetallus Crassus, was given "Crassus" as his nickname. The name came from Marcus Licinius Crassus, who had been one of Rome's First Triumvirate members as well as the wealthiest man in the world. Crassus was also famous for leading eight legions that brought down the slaves under the runaway Thracian gladiator Spartacus years before *triumvir* Crassus's shocking death in his sixties at the Battle of Carrhae. Over ten thousand mounted archers of the Parthian king Orodes II encircled his eight legions on the plains of Parthian Mesopotamia, between the Euphrates and Tigirus Rivers, shooting arrows from horseback as they rode around the foot-bound Romans. At the end of the day, those who were not dead suffered painful wounds from iron-barbed arrows. The Parthian horses carried two men: one facing forward to control the horse and the archer sitting backward firing missiles into the cracks of the Roman shields. There was a rumor I heard from a reliable source that Crassus was captured alive and had molten gold poured down his throat because of his thirst for wealth. Ironically, the Latin word *crassus* means someone who is rude. This term fits my father very well when one refers to his personal behavior.

A few moments after the Pilum Man comment, Amcheck started to relate in vivid details of all he and I observed from the roof of the Jew's house near the western *agora* in front of the Castle of Antonia. Herod slapped his leg several times during the narration saying he wished he had been there to watch. Herod then fingered a couple of silver coins from a purple leather coin bag before giving them to the chamberlain who minced his way down from the lion-flanked stairs and obsequiously brought them down to Amcheck.

After Amcheck bagged the coins, Herod asked with a sly smile. "Who is the soldier behind you who does not laugh at our wit?"

Chapter One

"He is a friend, an earnest mercenary, and upcoming spy, my tetrarch. He was the soldier who stood at my side and witnessed the slaughter by Pilate. He has also assisted me on several assignments."

"A promising spy you think? What story does he bring me?"

"He witnessed the Nazarene heal a man at the waters of Bethzatha in Jerusalem just a few days ago," stated Amcheck with a concealed smile as he looked back toward me.

"Now that is a story I would want to hear," implored Herod like a child asking his mother for something sweet. He waved me to come and stand beside Amcheck. I complied with his request feeling sick in my stomach perhaps due to the fact he was the one who had the holy man in a hole below us.

"He is young but fierce-looking," Herod observed openly. "He reminds me of Achilles from the Iliad," he continued as he studied me further. I was feeling uncomfortable until Herod focused on something from the back of this vast hall. I turned to look at what captured Herod's attention; and entering through the large door, I saw two women walking next to one another. It had to be Herodias and her daughter Salome, who was close to my age in years. Both were exotic beauties coddled in the most expensive gem-embedded robes I had ever seen. They were almost copies of each other, except the girl was slightly taller than the mother. Both the mother and daughter had beautiful dark, cat-like eyes; except the younger's feline eyes had more of a vacant stare. Both of their lips were full and painted red in the Egyptian style; and their eyes were colored with blue and black eye paint, much more exotic than the eunuch had his eyes outlined. The young girl seemed to be eyeing me as she came closer and then strangely transformed into a leering creature that did not hide her coquettish thoughts. Both Amcheck and I could be clearly seen since our helmets were cradled in our left arms. My hair was freshly washed and falling slightly over my shoulders. This was because I had bathed in a hipbath last night after visiting John the Baptist. Soon the mother and daughter passed. Amcheck and I both watched the two slowly mount the lion-lined steps to sit on two small cushioned stools that were stationed to the right and left of Herod.

"My dear," remarked Herod Antipas to his wife after she had settled herself comfortably. "This young soldier witnessed the Nazarene heal a man in Jerusalem just a few days ago."

Herodias smiled at her husband with what looked like affection and then gazed over at me for the first time. The daughter, I noticed from the edge of my vision, was still flashing her strange, lascivious smile in my direction. It reminded me of the smile the slave girl gave me in Rome at the tavern when I had beer and *garum* with Felix the Praetorian.

"Achilles, tell us your tale from the beginning," ordered Antipas with a playful, upward movement of his head.

I lowered my eyes to the floor and swallowed deeply before I began. "I was in the Sheep Market last Sabbath…"

Herod gave out a loud grunt and lifted his hand for me to stop. "Why were you at the Sheep Market on the Sabbath? Is that not a strange place for a soldier of mine to be on the Sabbath? And this Jesus performed a miracle on the Sabbath? Well, this is very instructive as well as inflammatory."

"I was not in uniform," I quickly added realizing I had stepped into a potential trap. I wondered what question Herod wanted me to answer. I quickly decided the only direction was to keep to the facts. I began to understand that, with John the Baptist in prison here at Machaerus, it was possible Herod wanted Jesus in that second hole. I did not want Jesus arrested, so I decided to pull the story onto myself. I repeated that I was in disguise, but now I gave the reason: "I was meeting a woman."

"Oh, I knew there was more to this story," said Herod clapping his hands and glancing over at his wife who smiled back at his delight. I felt as if I were providing some kind of deviant, vicarious entertainment to these wasted, pretentious prisoners of their own isolation in this barren land. It all seemed very strange; yet, it was evident that money and abundant leisure do not necessarily bring happiness.

"At what hour was this assignation?" asked Herod before he winked at his wife.

"The arrangement was to meet at Bethesda in the middle of the day or the twelfth-hour Roman time."

"Was she there?" asked Antipas.

"She was waiting for me at the back of the enclosed structure, not the open aired-pool."

"You must tell us why you had to meet this woman secretly," asked Herodias speaking for the first time with a tone that was innocent enough; but her expression was suggestive. For some reason, I liked her voice. It was sweet and soothing, not matching her makeup and clothing. Maybe in a different life, she would have been an ordinary, kind person. I noticed Salome was no longer smiling and was acting bored, which I was unwilling to ignore. I decided to try to titillate Salome with a slight twist away from the truth. Today I would call "slanting the truth" nothing more than out-and-out telling falsehoods but back in my mercenary days, I was an expert at slandering as well as lying. Lying is not telling the truth where slandering is telling the truth but out of context. My motives at this moment were very base, and today I am ashamed of myself as I recount these details. I should also say that slandering and lying are both a waste of mental energy because of all the false stories one must remember and inevitably come unraveled at one's great embarrassment.

"The woman is engaged to someone else," I said. "So we had to meet secretly where people do not generally flock for such reasons. Yet, it had to appear innocent should we be discovered." I realized Amcheck knew I was now fabricating. I heard him softly clear his throat to warn me of my foolishness. I understood Amcheck's disapproval and that I was now on dangerous ground. He was entirely correct, so I returned to giving an emotionless narrative and jumped to the heart of the story regarding Jesus. "The teacher named Jesus arrived with one of his disciples when I was leaving the pool. He approached a man lying on his stretcher near the water's edge and asked him if he wished to be healed." I purposely left out my personal conversation with Jesus.

"And what did the crippled man say?" inquired a sober Herodias obviously intrigued by my story by the way she was leaning forward.

"The man speaking from his mat said something about angels stirring the water, and he had no one to put him in. Jesus just told him to stand and take up his pallet and carry it away. The man who had been like this for the past thirty-eight years obeyed. He stood as if he never had a problem and picked up his wooden stretcher and walked with it under his arm. To be completely honest, it looked at first as if the whole thing had been staged."

"Staged?" questioned Herod, now sitting back in his chair. "And he told him to carry his pallet on the Sabbath?"

It was difficult communicating with Herod Antipas since he was always asking multiple questions, and any wrong response could threaten my own safety. I decided to only answer the first inquiry. "Well, the man looked perfectly healthy when he stood up; but I did ask him after Jesus left how long he had been in his crippled condition.

Herod interrupted by asking, "So you actually spoke with the crippled man? How amazing!"

"Well, yes, and he told me with wonder on his face that he had been like that for thirty-eight years ever since the time around his birth. Several bystanders murmured agreement to the man's statement. That is when I believed it was not staged."

"Simply fascinating. And this was just last Sabbath?" probed Herod again.
"Yes."

Herodias with all her pretension evaporating asked, "You actually went up to the man and asked if he really was healed?" Then looking at her husband with a look of horror, she asked, "Could this be one of those your father tried to kill about forty years ago in Bethlehem, a few years before the famous earthquake? I am talking about the earthquake a year or so before your father died."

Antipas scratched his chin filled throat and then said, "No, this Jesus is from Galilee, not Judaea." Then Herod looked over to his chamberlain. "Am I not right? Is not this Jesus from the town of Nazareth, not Bethlehem?"

The chamberlain nodded; Herod Antipas turned and asked me to continue. "As I said, I wanted to know what actually happened." I certainly was not going to breach the story of the killing of children in Bethlehem knowing there was a chance Herod would have Amcheck and me find Jesus only to murder him. This was the first time I realized Jesus had to be the same age as the healed lame man, and I needed to keep this thought out of Herod's mind. "The man seemed genuinely sincere. No actor could have delivered a performance as convincing as this cripple. He was as radiant as the sun because of what this Jesus had done. If a man could glow with genuine elation, it was this man. What I witnessed is unexplainable by any knowledge I have ever encountered. I believe I indeed saw a miracle."

Herod waved a hand toward Herodias. "I believe it as well. My spies tell me this miracle worker named Jesus is heading back to Galilee perhaps returning to Capernaum on the Sea of Tiberius. The last report I received stated that Capernaum is now Jesus's new adopted home. Apparently, all of Nazareth and including his family have rejected him." Looking back to Amcheck and me, he said, "Now what I want you both to do is very delicate. I want both of you to go to Galilee and find this Jesus. I also want a report from Nazareth to see why his loved ones have rejected him. You will leave today, and I do not care if it is the Passover or a Sabbath. If Jesus is telling people to carry pallets on the Sabbath, then it is no crime to ride horses on a rest day," he said with a hearty laugh. "I want you to find Jesus and observe him without his knowledge. See if he does any more miracles; and listen to anything he teaches, if possible. You both will have to wear clothing other than your uniforms. You must question those who have seen him do any unexplainable works. Afterward, return to Jerusalem; and have one of my scribes write a report. Give it to Saben, the captain of my palace guard, who will send it here to me. In the meantime, I will relay a message to Saben telling him you both are on a particular assignment and will be away for possibly a couple of months. However, I want your report in my hands before the Feast

Chapter One

of Pentecost. That will give you about 50 days to find Jesus and have your story in my hands. Can you do this, soldiers?"

"Yes, tetrarch," said Amcheck. I just nodded and stepped back to where Amcheck stood.

"My chamberlain will give you supplies and money for your journey. Now he will see you out," and he waved us away as if he were now bored with us.

While we were following the mincing eunuch, Herod called out to a guard at the far end of the hall standing at the door. "Send in the Romans and that legendary gladiator!" The chamberlain stopped and asked in a high, reedy voice if we both would wait a moment; for he wanted to see the famous gladiator. He directed us to sit against the back wall on a stone bench next to some potted palm plants.

Amcheck quickly turned to me and asked, "Are you thinking what I am thinking?" I slowly nodded my head. "Do we have your knives handy?" he whispered. Again I nodded, and we both watched the door to our right peering through the long leaves from the palm that was planted in a large clay pot.

It was not long before the massive door opened; and in came Lentulus, Marius, and Messina. My heart skipped a beat as I recognized Messina. She was more beautiful than Salome could ever dream, and this without all of Salome's makeup. Messina had on the same powder-blue *stola* she had on in Jerusalem, and my breath became labored just seeing her again. I now knew I was in love with this woman and cared about her more than I did my own life. However, it was tormenting to see her because of what she told me at the pool; and now I was unable to speak to her in order to change her mind. Marius, on the other hand, looked monstrous with his nose laid over and one shut swollen eye. Besides being puffy, his face was black and blue along with dark bruises ringing each eye. I almost laughed when the image of a highway robber wearing a mask flew through my mind. Following up was Mayus Lentulus limping with the aid of his cane and wearing a black leather eye patch that covered his left eye. All three moved past without looking in our direction as we just sat frozen in the shadows of the bushy palm plant. This moment felt irrational or dreamlike, but it was real. Here I was close enough to smell a whiff of rosewater coming off Messina, and the three passed without noticing us as they were looking toward Herod Antipas's throne.

After the three Roman guests reached the front of the dais, Herod asked with a genuine smile, "Tell me; which one of you is the famous gladiator?"

"I am," answered Marius in a gravelly voice with his head lowered. Salome put her hand to her mouth to conceal a laugh. I clearly understood her surprise because it was somewhat humorous since it looked like the famous hero had been severely beaten at his own game.

"You, the one who looks like he ran into a charging bull?" posed Herod with a disarming look showing he meant no offense. Standing not far from me was the chamberlain giggling like a girl, which caused others in the hall to openly snicker. After no answer came forth from Marius, Herod asked, "What was the name of the bull that did this to you?"

Marius lifted his head and in a defiant voice said, "The bull was one of your guards in Jerusalem."

"What was his name?"

In his strange, hoarse voice, he said, "I do not know; but, if I run into him again, you will be minus one guard."

Herod peered over everyone's heads looking down the hall and waved toward his corpulent, mincing attendant. "Bring Achilles forward so this gladiator can identify him with his good eye."

My stomach dropped as if I were being pushed violently off a high cliff. What was this all about? Herod must have known all along I was the one and set this up for his own entertainment. Did he want me dead, or did he want me to follow Jesus? The chubby administrator put his hand on my now-uninjured arm and forced me to stand. I realized I did not have my falcata with me, but I did have my two knives on the sides of my cuirass. I had not forgotten to replace them after I had scrubbed the smelly leather last night. They were difficult to see unless one was looking intently for them as both handles were covered with the same dark-black leather as the cuirass. Amcheck stood and said into my ear that he did not have anything to do with this. I did not know if I should believe him or not. My eyes caught Messina's eyes, and her hand went to her mouth in shock. She just as rapidly dropped her hand and eyes to hide her visible recognition. I was not sure she was able to disguise her acknowledgment until she turned away making a slight cough; and her acting scene looked quite natural, even if someone were carefully watching. Lentulus apparently was not listening to Messina's cough, nor was Marius. Mayus Lentulus quickly pulled his gladius and handed it to the unarmed Marius, who was wearing his green tunic. Marius snatched the sword, and I noticed once again his strange top ponytail sticking up like a cap on his head giving him an aberrant, ghoulish look.

"He is the one!" remarked Herodias showing her part in this obscene drama.

"Is that right?" inquired Herod. "Did my Achilles beat the famous arena fighter fairly in wooden swords? Was it a fair fight, Amcheck?" questioned Herod loud enough for us both to hear from the back of the hall.

Chapter One

"It was an honorable encounter," replied Amcheck diplomatically. "But I suggest you ask your quests; they also witnessed the contest, my lord," stated Amcheck waving his arm toward Messina and Lentulus.

Herod looked over to Lentulus. "Was it fair?"

"Honorable enough for children's games. But wooden splinters are childish mocking compared to honed edges of iron," commented Lentulus.

"Shall we have a rematch? Tomorrow is my birthday, and it could be the highlight of my party. Wouldn't you agree, Achilles?"

It was peculiar and unnerving the way Herod kept calling me Achilles, but I knew this was only for his amusement. "Honor would be uncertain, my tetrarch," I called out in a loud voice. "The man is half-blind. Let us reschedule a rematch at your next birthday after the famed gladiator has had time to heal."

"What say you, Marius?" queried Herod sympathetically. "I believe he is showing you some honor by alluding to your reputation."

"He is a coward! I will fight him right here, right now! And why is your left arm not swollen and bruised, soldier? I hit you in that arm just as hard as you struck my face!"

He was correct for it was useless until my time with John the Baptist last night. Someway during my visit, it was healed, but I wasn't going to tell them what happened. Instead I spoke in a brash, provoking way, calling out for all to hear, "There is no problem with my arm because I guess you hit like a girl!"

With that, Marius projected a gob of yellow-blood goo from his mouth firing it up and out in my direction. A strange peace came over me as I realized his hatred toward me put him at a disadvantage. He then foolishly charged toward me holding Lentulus's sword outstretched to impale me on the run. Amcheck stepped aside with his hand pulling the eunuch with him, and I took a few steps toward this charging fool before I stopped and stood stationary. I wanted to give him room to run past me at full charge when I stepped quickly to my right. Then at the last moment before a collision with Marius, I moved to the side of his bad eye. Just like I calculated, Marius's rage affected his sword thrust that barely missed my throat. As he passed me with his good eye trying to turn and look into mine, I grabbed a handful of his straight-up ponytail with my left hand. With his hair in my hand, I slightly pulled his head back as his feet kept moving. Once he lost his footing, he let out a yelp; and I smelled something under his breath that reminded me of fly ointment and sour wine. His roaring growl was instantly muted as his back slammed hard onto the stone floor. Before the horrible thud of his impact stopped echoing in the vast hall, I had my knee on his chest and a dagger at the hollow spot below his throat. Amcheck pulled out his long, curved *sicarius* and efficiently dissuaded Lentulus from coming to Marius's aid. I next stood and put my booted foot onto Marius's hand that still held his sword. I looked up and asked if Herod wanted to give thumbs up, the signal to send him up to the gods. Herod quickly gave the thumb down sign and said, "Let's keep him here a while longer with us mortals. Nevertheless, you were right; he is half-blind. Maybe a rematch next year would be in order," he mused but letting everyone hear what he thought.

Amcheck grabbed me by the cuirass and yanked me abruptly away from Marius, who was still gasping for air. We left the hall suddenly listening for any footsteps in pursuit. Once we reached the outside of the palace in the welcoming sunlight, Amcheck ordered me to get the horses and meet him at the front gate and do it on the run. He said he would pack our gear from the barracks and get what we needed from the eunuch, who was the only one who had exited the hall with us and was now standing near us with fear in his eyes. Amcheck's entire demeanor was urging quickness; and he barked, "Make it now!"

Once at the stalls, I saddled our two horses and fetched two skins of water since we were going north through desert lands. I thought I was alone in the stables until a young girl of ten or so came up to me holding a snowy-white puppy with a black nose and eyes. In the dim light, I noticed unique black markings around both eyes, which gave the pup a more fashionable look than Queen Cleopatra herself. The little girl held out the animal for me to take. In Aramaic she said, "Please, Master, you must take this puppy; or my father will drown it." Tears began to pour as she pleaded again for me to save its life. I did not want the whimpering creature but took it to appease the little girl. Taking the dog seemed to work as she stopped her sobbing.

"Don't worry; I will give your puppy a good home." Understanding what I said, she turned and ran from the stables bereft at losing her pet but somewhat comforted that it would now live. After she was gone, I realized she had not given me any instructions or the dog's name. I held the dog up by the scruff of its neck and checked its sex. It was a male, and the poor thing looked too young to be away from his mother. I placed the white cur in a cloth bag with only his head protruding and lashed the furry package to the front of my saddle.

Just as I finished tying up the puppy, a second visitor entered the stables. I turned with a throwing knife in hand should it be Marius but, instead, saw a woman in a sky-blue *stola*. It was Messina. She stopped inside the doorway, turned quickly to see if she had been followed, and then ran toward me placing a soft kiss on my mouth. The little dog started to yelp thinking maybe

I was being attacked by this strange woman. Messina laughed, and I told her about the little girl giving me the dog.

"What is her name?" she asked.

"It is not a she, and he is now waiting for you to give him his name."

She looked intently at the furry white head sticking out of the bag with the strange black-outlined eyes. She put her finger on its muzzle, and the dog sniffed and then licked her finger affectionately. "The little thing looks to be only a few weeks old. We could call him Achilles, but he does not have a scar under his eye," she laughed with a disarming smile. "Since you have given this dog life, we should call him Zoe. Isn't the Greek word for life, *zoe*?"

"Zoe it will be since I have given him *zoe*," I said hiding the fact I did not think Zoe was a fitting name for a male dog. I would have picked Ajax, Hercules, or perhaps Samson since this was the land where Samson did his heroic exploits. However, Zoe was going to have to do since the woman I loved named him at my suggestion. Messina turned again toward the entrance to the stables. I realized she was worried and was risking much by coming to find me.

"How did you know I was in here?" I queried.

"Your friend who holds your sword told me. I went to the barracks after you left." She then moved closer, and I could now smell the rose attar that wafted from her clothes and skin. "Venustus, I am glad I found you. I deeply regret what I said to you at the pool back in Jerusalem. The truth is I have been bonded to you since that day in the alley at Ostia. Our destinies keep crossing, and it would be foolish to deny that for the sake of only worldly comfort."

"You do not need to say these things," I said trying to ease her pain.

Looking down she said very sweetly, "But I do love only you. It would only torture me more than I could bear if I were to marry Demos. I now understand it would work out better for me to be with you, or I will die waiting."

"Are you saying you would give up this world's wealth for a fugitive on the run?"

"Lentulus and Marius are looking for some Carnalus Scroll more than for you. Your father fears it more than he enjoys his pleasures. That scroll would destroy all his plans to ascend your brother Julius to the throne of the Empire."

"How do you know about this scroll?"

"Zeno was tortured before he died. I told you all this that night you saved Eli's life."

I dreaded the mentioning of Eli's name; the pain was still fresh as Eli had died only a year and a half ago. I felt like I saved Eli's life only to get him killed. Then the words of Jesus came back to me reminding me not to worry about

Eli because of his faith in the Messiah. Messina pulled back; perhaps seeing I was not listening to her. I apologized and asked her again about the scroll.

"Zeno told your father about it and that you someday would produce it to his destruction. That is what you must do, Venu. Use the scroll to destroy your father, and then maybe we can escape this horrible world to find some shreds of happiness. I asked Lentulus just yesterday why the scroll was necessary. He said the contents from Senator Carnalus would topple your father if it found itself in the hands of Tiberius. Do you not see? If you could get the scroll into the emperor's hands, your father's plans would be crushed; and we could be free of him to marry."

A horrible thought flashed before me. Could Messina be working for my father? Was this a ploy to get me to reveal where I had secreted the scroll?

"Venustus, what are you thinking?" she asked with pained vehemence. "You think I want you to tell me where the scroll is? If that is on your mind, it is not true. I do not want the scroll, but you can use it to expose your father for the man he really is."

She had correctly guessed my suspicion. Now she was scaring me. How did she know what I was thinking? I reached out and took her left hand in my right. She did not resist. I felt a softening overtake me, and she looked intently into my eyes. I gently pulled her closer to me at the same moment Amcheck entered the stables.

"You were supposed to be waiting at the gate!" he blurted out before he realized what he had walked into. "Oh! We are sorry, but we must go now. Marius is raging like a bull back at the barracks looking for you. Someone is going to be dead if we do not *exodus* now."

Amcheck tossed me my falcata, which caused me to release Messina. The sword was still in its scabbard. Holding it in my left hand, I looked back to Messina. She was still looking deep into my eyes. All I could see was terror and it was heart-wrenching. Her eyes were bottomless blue pools that reminded me of someone drowning. What should I say? I finally murmured softly, "I must go, but I will find you; and together we will bring my father to justice."

"Venu, there is one more problem."

"What?"

"Demos is coming to Judaea to help hunt you. He is the only person who could confidently recognize you, and your humiliation of both him along with Marius has set a death-seal upon your future."

"Do not worry; I can deal with Demos just as I did with Marius."

Chapter One

"I do not think so, Venu. Did you deal with Marius? He is still alive; you should have killed him when you had your chance. Three times in my presence you have allowed him to live."

She was right; I had given *zoe* three times to Marius. The first was on the wall in Rome when I only cut his hand. The second was a few days ago in Jerusalem on the exercise grounds, and today was the third. "You mean I should have killed him like I did Claudia?" I asked wishing I had not.

"Killing Claudia was different, and you know it. Besides, killing Claudia has complicated your life a hundredfold. Yet, if anyone needed killing, it was Claudia."

This last statement surprised me, and I wanted to change the subject. "Are you going to marry Demos?"

"No!" she beseeched with great pain in her voice as she pushed away from me. "I will give up everything just to have you! I told you I will wait for you. Did I not just tell you I love you? Just find me when you can, and I will go with you. We will escape to India or beyond just like you said at the pool in Jerusalem."

Amcheck now grabbed my sleeve. "We must be off. That one-armed gladiator will soon find us here. This love talk is going to get us killed."

"Messina," I said with finality in my voice. "Find the preacher named Jesus. Find refuge with him and his followers. He has the power to protect you."

"Jesus of Nazareth?"

"Yes, go to him into Galilee; and I will find you by finding him."

"Come on!" implored Amcheck pulling on the reins of the two saddled horses. The two animals whinnied as they stepped out of the stables, apparently happy to be out of their small, dark confinements.

Standing alone again with Messina I said, "I must go now; but I love you too, more than life itself."

"Venu, please find it in your heart to forgive me. I have been faithful to you since Ostia. Demos has never touched me, nor will he. Now go with Yahweh's protection."

I kissed her gently on the mouth, then released her, and ran out into the midday sunlight. Amcheck was waiting near the arched stone gate astride his horse. I leaped up at a run and pulled myself onto the wood and leather Roman-styled saddle, all in one move. The wetness of Messina's kiss was still present on my lips, and it was the most memorable occurrence I had ever experienced to that day. It may not have been as grand as the kiss I had with her in my old room in Rome on the night I rescued Eli, but it was close.

"What in the name of Horus is in that bag next to our leg?" Amcheck demanded after seeing the dog's head for the first time. "And when did your left arm heal?"

"Never mind; let's be off," I said with a bit of urgency in my voice.

An old Jewish man standing outside the gate picked up a rock, perhaps to throw at us for riding horses on this holy day. I looked up at the sun and concluded it was past noon when no work was to be performed. Amcheck glared at the Jew with such fierceness the old man just dropped the fist-sized rock and lowered his head. I felt the man's zeal, but it was in his best interest to do as he did. Besides, I concluded that Amcheck and I had enough excitement for one day. Now with little Zoe in his bag next to my right leg, we rode away without any further incident, not knowing that neither of us was ever going to return to this aberrant and forgotten fortress that also served as the Baptist's prison.

Chapter One

A READING GIVEN AT THE GREAT LIBRARY OF ALEXANDRIA BY EPAPHRODITUS

Given in the year of the four emperors or the Year of the Four Legates. Soon after Emperor Nero committed suicide, a new civil war began in the Roman Empire, actually the first civil war since the Republic died in the year of the Battle of Actium, which caused the birth of the Empire.

Legate Galba (governor of Hispania) took the throne for seven months after the suicide of Nero, the last of the Julio-Claudian Dynasty. Galba was executed in the Roman Forum near the base of Capitoline Hill by members of his Praetorian Guard. On that very day, the Roman Senate proclaimed Legate Otho with the name Augustus. During the next three months, Germanium legions proclaimed their governor, Legate Vitellius, as emperor. Vitellius sent half of his army to march on Rome, which defeated Legate Otho at the Battle of Bedriacum. Otho committed suicide after he had realized his forces had been defeated. During all of this turmoil, the troops of Syria and Judaea proclaimed their legate, General Vespasian, as emperor. General Vespasian had been fighting in the Great Jewish Revolt for over two years when his troops proclaimed Vespasian as the next emperor. In response to this declaration, Vespasian relocated his new throne to Alexandria while preparing to send troops taken from Syria and Judaea to secure his bid for the throne in Rome.

Before the Syrian and Judaean troops could be sent, Danubian legions loyal to Vespasian fought Legate Vitellius's legions at the Battle of Cremona. With a victory in this battle and Emperor Vitellius's demise, Vespasian was able to return to Rome and end the year-long civil war.

During this turbulent time of internal fighting, a great fire broke out in Rome and consumed all the major structures on Capitoline Hill, which, sadly, destroyed much of Rome's archives. Due to this loss, the scholars and librarians of Alexandria's Great Library requisitioned anyone with past knowledge to recreate the history of Rome and its Empire. Scholars and others delivered many lectures on the afternoons of the seventh day of each week for about a year after the great fire. A generous fee of 25 denarii was paid to anyone who provided information that could replace any history of Rome. I decided to supplement my financial situation at this time by contributing several lectures. I have chosen a few excerpts from my lecture readings to coincide with this story. **69 AD**

HEROD THE GREAT AND HIS YOUNGEST SON HEROD ANTIPAS

To understand Herod Antipas, one needs to go back to the beginning of the Herod Dynasty and recall the old Cathay-Sinica adage: "The apple does not fall far from the tree." It all began with the wealthy great-grandfather of Herod Antipas for whom he is named. This great-grandfather was Antipater or Antipas the Idumaean, governor of this land before the Romans arrived. As time went on, one of the sons of Antipater the Idumaean was also named Antipater or Antipas. He, too, was called an Idumaean and became the grandfather of Herod Antipas. The Romans and Greeks used the word Idumaeans or Idumaeas in place of the Hebrew word Edom or Edomites. The Edomites were the descendants of Esau, twin brother of Jacob, who were sons of Isaac; and Isaac was the second son of Abraham behind Ishmael. It was this Antipater who became the father of Herod, who later took the title "the Great " and was the father of Herod Antipas, the man I served for several years in my youth as a mercenary in Palestina.

It was the second Antipater, or grandfather of Herod Antipas who befriended Julius Caesar, and his reward was the rulership of all Palestina. After Antipater was poisoned one year after Julius Caesar's assassination, his second son, known today as Herod the Great, seated himself on the dynastic throne. Soon war broke out with the Parthians, one of many of the Parthian Wars, which led to a siege of Jerusalem. Not only was there war with the outsiders, but there was also a bloody civil war between the different Jewish factions at that time. During this period in history, Herod the Great was able to make an escape with his remaining troops to the fortress atop Masada, which is located west of Machaerus and adjacent to the Dead Sea. From Masada, Antipas's father found it necessary to escape to Petra, the capital of the Nabataea kingdom.

The Parthians, people from the ancient empire of the Persians and the Medes, were pillaging Jerusalem and other parts of Judaea. The Nabataea king at this time asked Herod the Great to leave Petra, fearing the Parthians would attack his city. Herod the Great had no choice and made his escape to Egypt and from there to Rome. It was in Rome where Herod was able to secure a Roman patron. His new patroni was none other than Mark Anthony, who was able to arrange the Senate into giving Herod a confirmation to the title "King of Judaea." It should be remembered that the Parthians at this time were the archenemies of Rome; and, at this period in

Roman history, Licinius Crassus entered onto the world stage as one of the first triumvirates in Rome. The First Triumvirate was a triple dictatorship made up of Pompey, Caesar, and Crassus. Crassus perished during one of the Parthian Wars at the Battle of Carrhae near the Tigris River, perhaps the second worst defeat in Rome's history just after Hannibal's victory at Cannae. It should be remembered that during Rome's Punic Wars with Carthage, the Battle of Cannae took place in Southern Italia where over 50,000 Romans died in one day. At Carrhae, I believe more than 20,000 Roman soldiers, including Crassus, died. To put Cannae or Carrhae into context, perhaps 40,000 Persians drowned at the Battle of Salamis; and maybe 10,000 Persians killed at the three-day Battle of Thermopylae.

Rome hated the Parthians since the Parthians fought from horseback shooting arrows as they circled around the Roman cohorts. The only defense was the breeding of Anatolian Shepherds that had long legs, which allowed them to jump upon the Parthians and drag them off their horses. When I served Herod Antipas, I inherited one of these dogs, which was half Anatolian Shepherd and half some other type of shepherd. He grew to be somewhere around 100 pounds. The first Anatolian Shepherds grew to around 150 pounds. These ancient dogs were first bred by the Hittites who disappeared from history's stage about a thousand five hundred years ago. Apparently, these people, like their dogs, interbred with others. Perhaps some of the Parthians had Hittite blood and were the only ones to never be defeated by Rome. In the hope Herod the Great might conquer these hated people of ancient Persia, he was able to garner favor from the Senate of Rome with money, titles, and soldiers. Therefore, the timing was perfect for Herod, son of Antipater II, to visit Rome and ask for military and monetary help. Rome gladly gave it to Herod along with the title King of the Jews.

With this new-found Roman aid and armies to fight the Parthians, Herod could secretly fight his own fellow citizens who also hated Rome. What Rome did not understand was Herod was not a full-blooded Jew, and the vast majority of Hebrews rejected him. They would never accept a king of the Jews being half-Jew and half-Idumaean. Just like my dog would never win any dog prizes as a full-blooded Anatolian Shepherd, he was in many ways smarter than any full-blooded dog of his breed. It was three years after Herod had been proclaimed king of Judaea by Rome that he put a siege on Jerusalem with his collected troops of mercenaries, Jews, and Syrian auxiliaries, along with many Roman cohorts. During this long siege, Herod made a significant political move: he married Mariamne, the niece of Antigonus, the sitting Hasmonaean king still reigning in Jerusalem.

Jerusalem finally fell with the Romans wanting to plunder all the wealth of the second Jewish Temple, rebuilt centuries earlier with Persian funds provided by Cyrus the Great. This was the substandard Zerubbabel Temple but still a prized Jewish Temple on Mount Moriah. Herod shrewdly bribed the soldiers and officers of Rome from his own money to not pillage the gold in the Temple after the city was captured. This was a wise move to win over the different Jewish factions, the ones who held the Temple of Yahweh as the only common ground to their faith. After the bribe had worked, Herod left for Rome with Antigonus in chains. At Herod's insistence Mark Anthony ordered Antigonus to be put to death by an ax. Thus ended the Hasmonaean rule of almost one hundred thirty years. Herod, via his Hasmonaean wife Mariamne, now claimed to be the legitimate king of the Jews.

It was slow in coming, but Herod I or Herod the Great did achieve all his desires. Later, this dubious, cynical, and incredulous ruler removed all connections to the Hasmonaean line. This included the murder of Mariamne and her two sons. Herod the Great became very fearful of everyone, including his own children. Just a few days before he died in Jericho and surely knowing his days were numbered did he still murder another son. This left only Herod and his few remaining part-Jewish sons to inherit the Herodian Dynasty. After the fall of Jerusalem, Herod the Great, king of the Jews, fortified the city with the construction of the Castle of Antonia, where all the future Roman procurators/governors would hold court during Jewish religious festivals. The fort was named in honor of Herod's patron, Mark Anthony, with his Latin name, Marcus Antonius.

Perhaps this is an excellent time to tell another story about Herod the Great. I learned of this event 38 years after it occurred; and I remember the incident because just a few days after it happened I was officially introduced to Herod the Great's youngest son, Herod Antipas. This unique story involves Jesus of Nazareth and his strange birth. Herod the Great first learned of the birth of Jesus when he received a small delegation of Zoroastrian Magi priests from the region that once was the Persian Empire. These priests from the East were looking for a child king of the Jews and perhaps believed Herod had just fathered this child. Herod had not recently fathered any children prior to the visit. After further questions to his newly arrived quests, he learned they had sighted a bright star in the section of the sky assigned to Pisces, which they said according to their numerology and astral predictions represented the House of Israel. Apparently two planets, Jupiter and Saturn – the Royal Star and the Anointed Star, respectively had formed this sign-star within the past year. After hearing about the birth of a king, Herod remembered a prophecy from the Scriptures. It came from Israel's ancient prophet Micah who wrote about the Messiah, stating this child was going to be born in Bethlehem, the town of the famous King David. Once Herod the Great feared a possible fulfillment of this prophecy, his wicked and depraved mind came up with a solution. Before the Magi left to look for this child, Herod the Great requested that they return to him once they found him. When it was apparent they were not going to return, Herod the Great ordered his soldiers to kill all the males in the town of Bethlehem two years or younger. When a human thinks he can take on God and His Word, this says volumes about the character of Herod the Great.

I should point out a second concern Herod may have had concerning these Persian Zoroastrian priests, who could also be called Parthians. These magi priests would have had many soldiers with them for protection; and Herod, who was now over seventy years old at this time, could have seen this as a spy mission to be followed by a new invasion of the Parthians. What Herod did to the innocent children in Bethlehem was definitely callous, but I am sure Herod did not want to spend his last years in a new war with the Parthians. This is just my opinion, and I might be wrong about Herod's true motives. But the foremost fear of Herod was the possibility of a king coming from his own land, which might threaten his legacy.

It is important to remember that Herod the Great almost lost his kingdom as a young man to the Parthians. Decades before the visit by these Parthian holy men, Herod had nearly lost his kingdom to the Roman Octavius after the battle of Actium. Two years after Actium, Octavius celebrated his victory over Mark Antony and Cleopatra with a triple-triumph parade in Rome. Rome was mesmerized by this young man, who in a short period, was able to produce three military victories. One was in the Balkan Mountains; second, the waters near Actium; and third, a daring triumph over Egypt. All three events put together led to Octavius's new title of Augustus. The title would become permanent in just two years after Octavius's triple-triumph parade. Soon after Octavius would forever be known as Augustus Caesar, Herod the Great made peace with Octavius through several envoys sent to Rome on his behalf. In time Augustus Caesar allowed Herod to maintain the title of King of the Jews and rulership of the region of the Galilee, Samaria, Peraea, and Judaea. Herod the Great, as he wished to be remembered, remained loyal to Augustus until his dying day. Herod the Great was the ultimate politician and man-pleaser. He could well distinguish the pulp from the peel. Early in his reign, he publicly observed the Mosaic Laws in order to please the Jews. He then dismantled

Zerubbabel's Temple in Jerusalem and rebuilt a magnificent third Jewish temple to Yahweh, which today bears his name: Herod's Temple. His argument to construct a new temple was that the aging Zerubbabel Temple had been standing for almost half a millennium and was not as glorious as Solomon's Temple. Herod only hoped to ingratiate himself with the Jews, especially the Pharisees and those who attended synagogues each Sabbath in the two hundred or more towns and cities of Palestina. Trying to present himself as a Jew was a problem when it was well known in Palestina that his ancestry was to Edom, a tribe consistently hostile to the Jews since the days of Jacob and Esau. Once again, it should never be forgotten that the Edomites are the decedents of Esau, the twin brother who was cheated of his birthright and his father's promises deceptively taken by Jacob, Esau's younger twin. Since Esau was the elder of the twins, he had the rightful claim to the full inheritance from his father according to Semitic practice and even the tenants of the Torah in the Scriptures.

The later years of Herod the Great showed his true nature. It wasn't until the entire Promised Land had been turned over to paganism and philosophical ideas of the Greeks and Romans that the Jews saw all the twisted personality fractures surfacing. By then it was too late because the Promised Land permeated a Hellenistic stench beyond anything the Syrian kings had established before the Maccabean Revolt. Now on a daily rotation, there were well-staged gladiatorial games, chariot racing, and other indecent spectacles. Secretly or not, it was well known that Herod the Great encouraged and financially supported most of these events. The building of bathhouses and open nudity of men was also promoted. Soon a Jewish political party for these new liberal developments rose up and called themselves the Herodians. These Herodians were not religious but only political in nature. They naturally supported the dynasty of Herod and the rule of Rome because of the financial gains to be made by standing with the winners of the world, the Roman Empire. Many of the Jewish tax collectors emerged from this Herodian political organization and funneled a significant percentage of their collections to Herod the Great. Today the sons of Herod still receive a substantial portion from Jewish tax farmers.

Herod the Great, who reigned for 34 years, had at least ten wives and many children, the youngest being Herod Antipas, the only Herod I knew personally. The mother of Herod Antipas was Malthace of Samaria, which further diluted his Jewish heritage. In the end, Herod the Great became a raving lunatic, a word that comes from the Latin word for the moon goddess Luna, which is still slang in the Empire for a prostitute. Since the moon appears unpredictable, coming and going at whim, the word lunatic is now synonymous with anyone rising and living an unpredictable life. Herod the Great was such a person. Besides being known for his numerous infidelities and unconcern for Jewish laws, he became well known as a man of violence. For instance, he had personally ordered the murder of more than one hundred people during his life, including many close friends, several of his own offspring, and his favorite wife all because of delusional beliefs amid fits of jealousy. His final testament bequeathed his vast empire to Herod Antipas and three other sons. The death of Herod the Great mirrored that of the Roman dictator Sulla. Both men died almost identically: a painful death of worms eating from the inside out, apparently brought on by a lifestyle of decadence and debauchery. As a physician and reading closely about his death, I would conclude that his kidneys giving out was most likely the cause of his final demise.

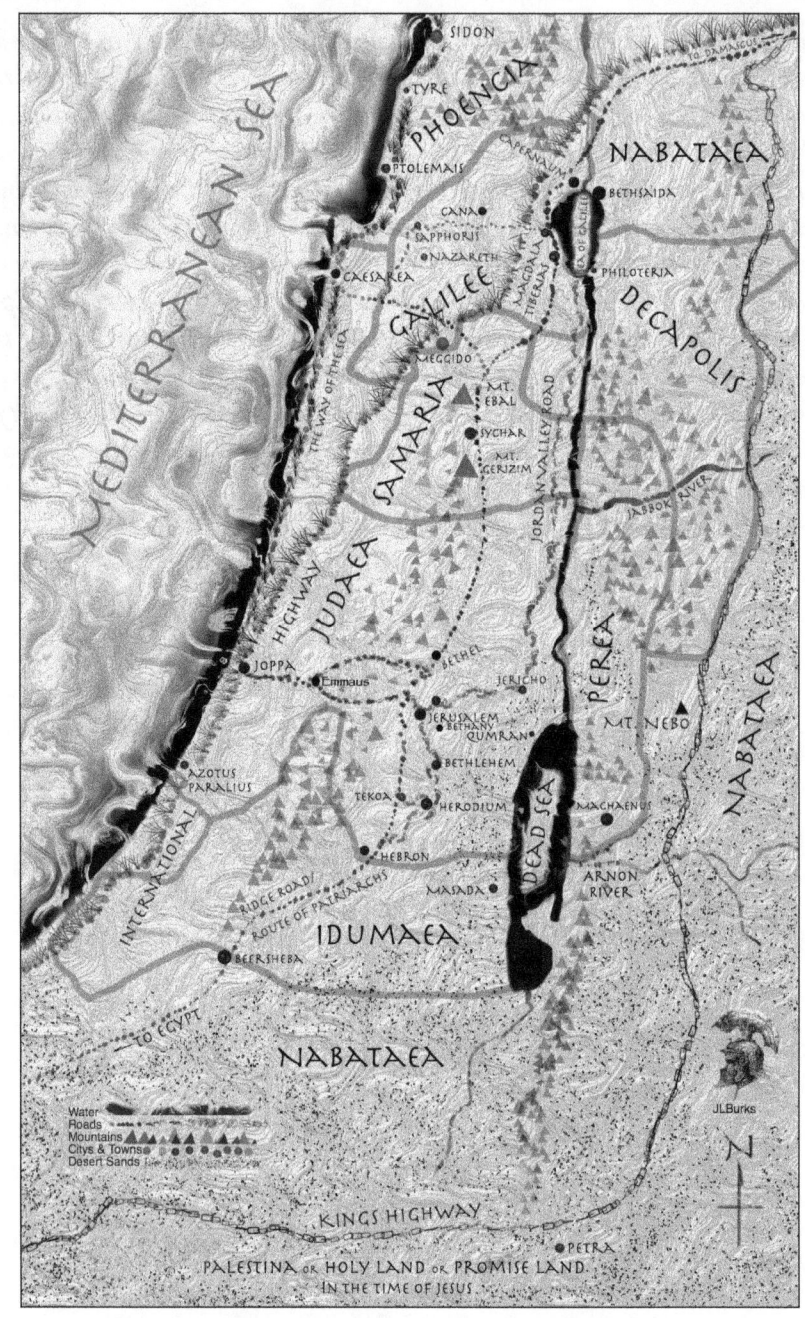

PALESTINA or HOLY LAND or PROMISED LAND
(in the time of Jesus)

CHAPTER TWO

The Land of Moab to Galilee – The Feast of Passover and Unleavened Bread, which marks the start of Jesus of Nazareth's 3rd year of public ministry.   *(31 AD)*

"What lies in our power to do, it lies in our power not to do."   Aristotle

During the hottest time of day, Amcheck and I descended on horses the narrow track down into the valley of Siddim and turned toward the Jordan River. The air was hot and thick making every breath an effort. My chest was aching, and lungs were burning with each gasp. Dizziness swept in and out while each drop of sweat evaporated as fast as it formed. Apparently, I was not acclimating to this harsh environment while we plunged deeper toward the Dead Sea. My tongue felt more like fabric than flesh. When I tried to spit, only white, cottony spittle came forth. I willed myself to stay on my horse hoping this creature was accustomed to this arid land, for I was not. He continued to carry me and kept moving forward. It seemed much hotter than yesterday when we came up this way. I was astounded by the fact this hairy creature was not stumbling through the same trauma I was experiencing. Amcheck, riding ahead of me, appeared unaffected by this land of dry heat; and I pondered about this. I tried to keep up a good act, not wanting to betray my weakness in this hellish and bottomless region. Part of the problem was the time of day. It was utter foolishness to travel at this hour near the lowest spot in the Empire of Rome or perhaps the earth. Yet, our only alternative was blood and iron if we had lingered any longer at Machaerus. Not that it mattered; I could quickly take my daggers and permanently stop both Lentulus and Marius, but the result would have revealed my identity. There was also the problem that Messina and I would not be able to escape if I had killed those two *thags*. Besides, if Messina and I were to run, my only small amount of money was back in Jerusalem; and I am sure I would never be able to reach it without being caught by Saben and the other guards once Herod Antipas discovered who I was.

When we finally came to where the Jordan River flowed into the Dead Sea, the sun was dropping down toward the jagged hills to the west. I took Zoe out of his bag, and carried him after dismounting my horse to the river's edge. Zoe lapped at the cold, fresh water with his little tongue. I followed Zoe's example, except I used my hand as a cup. We both drank from the slow flowing river before it became fouled forever in this stinking, unfathomable body of water that spread out beyond us. This river was a refreshing treat I have never forgotten. Amcheck stood over us drinking from his refilled water skin smiling at Zoe and my aggressive slurping. After my thirst had been slaked, I placed my head under the cold waters trying to lower the temperature in my aching head. The trick soon worked, and I began to feel better.

When our short break was over, we started traveling again. I had dipped Zoe's bag in the river so he would be cool with only his head sticking out looking at the world like any four- or five-week-old pup. He looked healthy and had to be a few weeks older than Messina had guessed. He seemed happy enough, but the heat sapped any play out of him. Most of the time he spent sleeping with the natural rocking rhythm of the horse, which must have been soothing to him. It was not long before we passed Jericho off in the distance to our left, shimmering in muted colors making it look almost like a glimmering opal in a golden ring bracketed by the cliff-like walls in the distance, which stood guard behind the desert city. The view was quite pleasing while I watched the sun making its way down toward the high cliffs looming over Jericho.

Little Zoe would whimper with a sad cry about once an hour, and I would stop to let him stretch his legs and relieve himself. Before returning to the bag, I would give him a little water in my hand from my waterskin. We continued north along the winding Jordan River until the sun completely dropped over the wall-like hills and bathed the west in various shades of red to orange and finally dark purple. I noticed a strange stand of palm trees clustered in the middle of barren land, and they appeared to be dancing in the evening breeze. Amcheck pointed toward the sight to our left. He explained that the palms marked the first base camp of Joshua after the Children of Israel crossed the Jordan into the Promised Land. "That is Gilgal, and this is the plains of Moreh. The ancient Israelites camped out there during the war years against the Canaanites. This all happened after Moses died up on Mount Nebo even though no one could find his final resting place, somewhere only the God of the Jews knows."

A few hours later a full Passover moon climbed up into the eastern night sky painting the landscape in subdued blue tones. We could see almost as well had it been early morning. Everything became silent until a cold wind began to blow, and the temperature eventually dropped to a comfortable condition as the night completely vanquished the heat in this desolate land. Amcheck decided to push on because of the mild traveling conditions, and we needed to put time and space between Marius and us if Herod had revealed our direction of travel. I ultimately agreed this was a wise action since Herod the *Luna* could have betrayed us.

Several hours later into our night travels we reached the Jabbok River where it joined with the Jordan. I looked eastward to the spot I envisioned where the patriarch Jacob had his encounter with an angel or perhaps the human manifestation of Yahweh himself. Eli told this story to me on the grain galley when we traveled to this land. This event ended with Jacob receiving a blessing, but he limped forever after he was touched at his hip by the supernatural being he was wrestling with all night. Part of his blessing was a new name, "Israel," meaning "Prince of God." Today the Jabbok side of the river is covered with dense vegetation, which is undoubtedly a marked contrast to the barrenness of everything else stretching out beyond in every direction. Maybe that was why no one built a shrine to record this event in Jewish history, or perhaps Jews did not do such things as the Romans with an arch or a tall monument. Years later I read in the Scriptures that my conclusions were faulty because Joshua had 12 stones carried out of the Jordan River where the Children of Israel crossed centuries earlier and made a memorial with the piled rocks in a heap. I would have liked to have hunted for this monument to see if the stacked stones still existed. This was something I never discovered.

Once we had stretched and filled ourselves with water, I noticed the Passover moon was much higher in the sky. Amcheck commented, "We are now at the halfway point between the Dead Sea and the Sea of Tiberius. We will keep on riding until we reach Herod's Palace on the Sea of Tiberius. We should be there by noon at the latest."

"Are we going to have trouble riding horses on a Sabbath?" I asked realizing this was now the Feast of Unleavened Bread and a Sabbath.

"No problems – all the little villages between here and Tiberius are Gentile towns, and no one will bother us. Remember we are soldiers of Herod Antipas, and we can do no wrong."

"'I see,' said the blind man to his deaf daughter, who said, 'I hear,'" I added with a little mirth in my voice.

"School Boy, didn't we talk about you spouting off about such things?" After a long silence, Amcheck changed the subject. "Since we are out here alone, tell me, School Boy, why is the moon only up at night."

After his query, I remembered reading about the Buddha on the Ganga River who said to answer any matter if you have the answer. "The moon can also be up in the sky during the day, but you cannot see it because of the brightness of the sun."

"You are telling me the truth?" he asked looking like I was having fun with him. When I did not smile back or break out in laughter, he looked up at the moon thinking. "You are smart for being so young." I did not answer but looked behind us to see if we were being followed. There was no sign of human or animal movement from our rear. Had there been men on horses, we would have been able to see a plume of dust rising from those chasing us. A good portion of the old Rift Road, or the Jordan Valley Road, was not paved or if so, it was covered by blowing sand and dirt.

Amcheck started talking again but was now changing the subject. Perhaps I had this influence upon him. Menander, the ancient Greek playwright, said, "Bad morals will corrupt good behavior." I am sure it applies to any relationship. I have seen people take on another's hand jesters or walking patterns after they had been together for even a short time. Many times this can be undoubtedly noticed in married couples.

Amcheck seemed to have gained a second wind as he rode on and talked. "Herod Antipas has been demanding the Lake of Galilee be renamed the Sea of Tiberius. This is only to ingratiate himself with the Emperor. Such vain measures pushed upon the populace sours the stomachs of especially the Jews as well as the rest of us living in this dried-up land."

Regarding the new name of the Sea of Galilee, I discovered that every time I heard the emperor's name being mentioned, I was only reminded of that sad day in Rome when my mother died. Hearing the name Tiberius always pictured in my mind an ugly, oozing man sitting in his pomp and grandeur watching gladiators killing each other in Rome's biggest amphitheater.

"You know the Jews will never refer to that body of water other than the Sea of Galilee," I said to get my mind off the emperor's name, and the memory of my mother's death.

"I have no problem with that." I assumed he was taking a sarcastic position thinking I was not actually listening to him ramble on. Or maybe he was right because I wasn't paying much attention. Grillius, back in Athens, did warn me to not trust even the man that holds your sword. I was still mad about his mouth that could very well be behind my third encounter with Marius. It could not have been by accident we were both in the throne room at the same time, but I just could not shake the feeling that Amcheck and Saben were behind that little charade. I wanted to believe that Saben's written report was the source, the written message handed to the captain of Machaerus on the eve of Passover when we first arrived. I wanted to confront Amcheck on this issue, but a new problem was now haunting me. Not that having Marius as an enemy wasn't a problem, but soon Demos would be in this land looking for me. And there it was, another reminder of that day my mother died. Thinking about the amphitheater, I remembered Demos sitting a row above my father. All my enemies were present at one moment in time. In the arena was Marius and seated with the emperor was Saben and a beautiful woman. She had to be Herod's stolen wife Herodias. I definitely recognized Herod Antipas as the one next to her, for he had not changed much in 11 years. In my mind's eye they were all there. Standing at the arena rail, I witnessed this bad omen that would forever haunt me. What was the Creator doing with me? Was He pre-warning me on that horrible, hot day about all the enemies of my future? I realized Amcheck had stopped talking; and I, too, stayed quiet. My only concern was to periodically look back to see if we were being followed.

Almost true to Amcheck's words, it was noon when we reached the shore of the southern edge of the Sea of Galilee but not yet at the city of Tiberias. Amcheck said, "It was that useless dog that slowed us down. We will be in the new city soon. You can see it if you look hard over there in the distance." Sure enough out and over across the left side of the lake, I could see what had to be Tiberias. "Over to your right is Philoteria. You can see two Greek towns in the land of the Jews. I am guessing that Philoteria was named after one of the sons of Herod the Great."

"Didn't he have two sons named Philip?"

"Maybe when you have ten wives, you might have to start reusing names. Don't the Romans give the same name to all their daughters, or is it they don't name them?"

"Philoteria could be named after Philip of Macedonia, the father of Alexander the Great," I replied with Amcheck giving that look again when I showed my knowledge. To further irritate Amcheck, I said, "Or maybe Philoteria comes from one of the Greek words for love, *philos*."

"I told you to stop it, and I will not tolerate your spouting off one more time," barked Amcheck before he put his heels to his horse and struck out toward the big, blue lake. I sat for a moment realizing that this was one of the most beautiful bodies of freshwater I had ever seen. It looked almost like an ocean because it was so large. Never before had I seen a lake this size.

I soon followed Amcheck toward the seaside town of Philotera where he bought some provisions. We then rested outside of town under a shade tree for over an hour. It was late afternoon when we finally reached the newly built Gentile city Tiberias. Antipas had constructed an enormous citadel in the center of this town and also several pagan temples over the past ten years. My guess was Tiberius was trying to honor the emperor of the world in which we lived. It was plain to me that Herod Antipas was making a Gentile island amid a Jewish sea. It looked out of place in this land; and, apparently, Antipas was spitting into religious sensitivities by building this city on the lake he was trying to rename after the emperor. Flaunting a magnificent secular city in the midst of the land given to the children of Abraham, Isaac, and Jacob by Yahweh was his way of erasing the prophecies of the Promised Land. Yet, the Prophet Daniel in the Scriptures explicitly stated there would be a coming time of the Gentiles; and, if it were not now, it would soon start.

When I walked my horse into the palace stables in Tiberias, I realized little Zoe was not faring well. I asked an old slave cleaning out a stall if there was a dog with a litter that would take an orphaned pup. By the loose skin of his neck, I held up a handful of white fur; and the old man smiled broadly showing all his upper teeth were missing. Little Zoe had at times sucked on a rag soaked in water during our trip, but he needed something more than I could give him. I followed the old slave's lead to a back stall where there was a female cur lying on her side with four mongrel pups sucking away. I placed Zoe in the square booth full of fresh straw, and the nursing mother allowed Zoe to snuggle up and partake as if he had been hers all along.

The old slave smiled and then spoke with a lisp through his toothless grin, "She lost one of her pups a week ago, and maybe she thinks it has returned."

I thanked the stableman and placed a silver *denarius* in his palm for his troubles. "I should be back in in a few days," I said actually thinking it might be longer. "I will give you another coin when I return if you keep a careful eye on him. This dog means a great deal to me."

He grinned and shook his head up and down indicating that he would take good care of the pup.

When Amcheck and I found the barracks, we joined the other soldiers who were eating supper at several long wooden tables. Soon after the meal, we slept what was left of that day until the next. When we arose, Amcheck checked with the guards to determine whether anyone from Rome had been looking for a Herodian mercenary from Jerusalem. He discovered no one had been asking for anyone. Amcheck seemed delighted and spent the rest of that day in a dark tavern throwing dice with mercenaries who had the day to themselves along with other bottom dwellers. I went to the stables and played with Zoe and the other puppies. Afterward, I walked around the Gentile city; and when I returned to the barracks, I found Amcheck had lost most of our money the eunuch at Machaerus had given him. Even the silver coins Herod Antipas gave us after Amcheck told about Pilate slaughtering the Jews in front of the Castle of Antonia was missing. I figured this was normal for Amcheck but wondered what we were going to do for money. I could have been angry with him but felt it was a waste of time since he would never change.

The next morning after more sleep Amcheck ordered me to leave my armor and uniform in the stall with Zoe and change into peasant garb. He did the same, and we surprised ourselves in how we looked the part; yet, I do not think we fooled too many people, especially with my long hair and high boots marking me as something other than a Jew. Amcheck declared we were going to travel to Magdala until I told him it was now the weekly Sabbath. Amcheck grunted out a disgusting sound and proclaimed that we would leave tomorrow even though it was going to be the Feast of First Fruits. There were no official travel restrictions placed on anyone according to this feast, which always fell on the first day of the week. However, like any Mosaic feast, most Jews took it for a rest day. The next morning before sunrise Amcheck hired a Gentile fisherman to sail up to Magdala if we helped with his nets once we reached deep waters. Being once a fisherman, I found this not as a burden. In all the years as a fisherman off the coast of Greece, never did I fish in the dark. Those who did fish at night always used torches to attract bugs and, I am guessing, fish. The Gentile fisherman had a crew of one boy, and we did use torches but did not catch one fish until after sunrise.

Once we arrived at the little Jewish town of Magdala, it was in the middle of the day. Amcheck suggested I spend the rest of the afternoon at the shoreline sleeping since I did most of the work with the nets in the morning dark. I agreed; and near the shore I found a big, flat rock nestled in a patch of bulrushes and tall grass. After a few hours of sleep, I swam in the cold, refreshing lake. I had learned to swim like most children in Rome, thanks to the many bathhouses and the pools provided for this purpose. The water was transparent in the shallows and became dark blue in the deep areas. When looking across the lake to the other side as I swam, I could see heat waves distorting the distance. I watched small fishing boats throwing nets in spots where the waters were dark and cold.

By late afternoon, when the temperature reached its zenith, I left to find Amcheck. Once again I found him in a tavern sampling the local wines. I asked how he was able to pay for his wine, and he placed his empty moneybag on the table and said, "I have been waiting for you since you owe me a jug since the first day we met." I wagged my head in disgust and handed him a silver coin. I tried to be civil and sat with him drinking a cup of wine. About an hour later a warm glow came to visit, and I thought of my enjoyable time in the Rome tavern with the soldier Felix. I would have been happy to buy a second jug of wine if the man across from me were Felix and not Amcheck. The only subject Amcheck could talk about was what he learned while I sat around on the shoreline of the Sea of Galilee.

"This is what I now know. Most people wanted to talk about this prophet named Jesus. There is a wide range of opinions of who they think he is. Some say he is the promised Messiah, others think he is just like the other false prophets of the past, and a few even say he is demon possessed. The only consensus is most believe he has gone back to his hometown of Nazareth. So we now go to Nazareth."

"What happens if he is at his newly adopted home of Capernaum? That town is not that far north of here on this lake."

"I have decided that we go west tomorrow and find this village of Nazareth."

"What are we going to use for money?"

"Worry no more. I hired us out as guards for a caravan from Damascus that arrived here at Magdala a few hours ago. Tomorrow about a thousand camels head to Sepphoris, Meggido, and then will reach Caesarea tomorrow night. I told the leader of the caravan we would go all the way to Egypt. Little does he know that we are leaving when we get near the village of Nazareth after passing through Sepphoris. We might not get paid; but we don't have to walk, and we will be able to eat."

Early the next morning we joined the large caravan we were to guard. There were more camels loaded and ready than I cared to count. This group of traders had come out of Mesopotamia and not Damascus. Amcheck had been correct in that the convoy was heading to Sepphoris and would pass near Nazareth before dropping down into the Jezreel Valley and ending at

Caesarea for the night. It would rest a few days while goods were sold and then continue to Egypt by next week.

The leader of the caravan showed us our camels, and this was the first time I had ridden one of these strange creatures. I found the experience bone jarring. The conventional way to ride was to sit in front of the hump and cross the right leg over the left side with your left foot. You control a camel with a long stick and use different commands and clicks over what one uses on a horse. The most important command is *"hut"* in a loud but aberrant grunt, which causes the camel to step out for you. If you want to go faster, you say *"hut-hut"* with a tap of a stick on the neck. After I adjusted to the rocking motion, the ride became extraordinarily uncomfortable and something I would never enjoy. My backside was already distressed from the long horse trip from Machaerus to Tiberias making the shifting back and forth on the camel an added misery that was moving into wretchedness. Once we reached Sepphoris later that morning, the traders sold goods for a good hour while we stood around guarding the wares. During that time I wandered off and found the famous bathhouse and remembered Felix's story over *garum* and beer. I looked carefully at the bathhouse and checked to see if the wooden beams were made of a red-colored wood. Sure as the sun comes up every morning, I counted three sandalwood beams forming the lintel and two door supports. They were polished into a beautiful, red oiled wood color and were excellent and squared perfectly. Felix had told me the truth; and that meant we were fewer than a few hours away from Nazareth, the hometown of John the Baptist's cousin. I was filled with a new feeling of anticipation when I returned to the caravan market and found Amcheck holding a bowl of *garum* and some bread. He told me where to get mine and to eat up, for this was our free mid-day meal and maybe the only meal for today. When the camels were being reloaded, I ate as much as I could hoping I didn't meet Messina with my breath fouled with this rotten fish goo.

The caravan finally set out again; and within an hour of riding the spitting, grunting camels, we found ourselves at a single fork in the road. One way went south toward the little Jewish town of Nazareth, and the other headed west. From where I could see, the caravan had already started down the way that bypassed Nazareth. When I pointed this out to Amcheck, he told me the people of Nazareth were Jews and not like the Hellenized people of Sepphoris who were happy to purchase faraway products. Amcheck had me stay with him until the old leader arrived in his litter carried by eight Nubian slaves. Amcheck announced to the corpulent man in the silk litter that this was the end of the road for us. Amcheck explained that he had a carbuncle on his backside that needed to be lanced by some physician. The caravan leader was not happy; but when he learned from Amcheck that we would not take any money, he seemed to calm down. No one seemed delighted that we were leaving including my camel who spat on me as I walked away. I do not mind horses; but these nasty, snorting beasts are not to my liking. To my surprise, when I was wiping my tunic of camel spit, the old leader tossed two silver *denarii* into the dust near Amcheck's feet. I just stood there and watched Amcheck smile and pick up the coins and place them into his own money bag.

Once we reached the outskirts of the little Jewish town, Amcheck began talking like he was going to get drunk on our newly earned wages. To my surprise, Amcheck declared he really had an abscess that needed attention; and he had to get drunk first before he had it lanced. I did not believe him, so he bent over and pulled up his peasant robes showing me an ugly boil. It did look painful, and he said it felt like a hot piece of metal. I never experienced that type of pain; but years later I was struck by a viper behind my knee, and that oddly felt like I had a hot piece of metal under the skin.

I wagged my head with some sympathy for Amcheck's situation and said, "Be my guest and get good and drunk. I am sure I will find you later in the best tavern this fine town offers."

"And you thought I was a great *hypocrite* when I was talking to the old camel merchant?"

I just slapped him on the shoulder wondering what Amcheck meant by the Greek word *hypocrite*. The common term for a man performing in a theater with a mask was known as a hypocrite. Whatever Amchek meant by this word, he was honestly a great actor. Here was the first time I began to entertain the idea that Amcheck was smarter than he tried to let on. I realized I had to watch Amcheck, for at times he used double meanings to make jokes. Only a sharp individual could think faster than others with this kind of humor. I was taught at the Lyceum that someone who made plays on words, especially when creating jokes, was engaging in a higher form of thinking or reasoning. Filing away those thoughts, I decided to show some empathy for Amcheck because of his boil. I told him I would question the populace of Nazareth about Jesus and see if he were actually present in his hometown. Amcheck gave me a lop-sided smile and told me I knew where to find him after the sun was down.

"If you can't find anyone to lance that boil, I will do it free of charge," I said jokingly and winked trying to make it look somewhat lascivious. Amcheck dismissively waved me away with his hand.

Chapter Two

Watching Amcheck amble off toward the center of town, I began looking around. I first crossed the village up to a steep bluff that looked down upon the Jezreel valley. Staring down below and stretching far out to the west was the vast plain of Megiddo, the most contested spot on earth. Besides that fact, Nazareth seemed to be a quaint and quiet place nestled in hills above steep cliffs and bluffs. There were groups of pines and other trees scattered among vast, open expanses of rock groups providing an isolated, quiet location. It took only an hour of asking in Aramaic to discover the rumors of Jesus returning to Nazareth were not true. It was conveyed to me more than once that the people of this village doubted Jesus would ever return to Nazareth. One man told me even Jesus's mother and brothers were away looking for him believing he would never come back on his own. Further questions revealed that Jesus's family also wanted to take custody of him because they thought he was under the influence of his popularity or possibly was no longer in his right mind. One man told me the residents of Nazareth had applied pressure to the family to prevent any further embarrassment of their peaceful village. I guessed the people of Nazareth desired no trouble from Antipas or the Romans. Most of those with whom I spoke would not even give me a cup of water, let alone information about their local embarrassment. Grunts and sneers were a frequent response to any of my questions.

It was not until late in the afternoon when I finally found someone willing to converse in depth far beyond what others had offered. I discovered an old man sitting outside Nazareth's one synagogue under the shade of a huge, gnarled sycamore tree. Without asking permission, I sat next to him on the wooden bench that was positioned to the left of the main entrance to the town's worship center. I had not seen Amcheck all day thinking he must have found a wine shop. I was hoping he had enough money to feed me once I found him, or I would have to pay using my own money.

"You are here to ask about Yeshua, I presume," said the old man in a thick Galilean accent that reminded me of Jesus's speech from the two times I spoke with him.

"Is it that obvious?"

"It is a small village; a visitor's words travel more quickly than the visitor. Besides, no one comes to Nazareth these days unless to inquire about Yeshua. You see, young man, high up here on the cliffs above the Jezreel Valley there are no main roads running up to us. This little village has been bypassed for years, if not centuries. Even those coming from the Greek city of Sepphoris do not stop but take the cutoff that misses us completely. I believe you and your friend appeared shortly after that thousand-camel caravan made the very same cutoff toward the sea. Besides, who would journey here unless to learn about our famous stonemason-turn-teacher-miracle-worker?"

I was stunned into silent wariness. I had not anticipated this old Jew resting on this wooden bench with his back leaning against the wall of the synagogue would be so forthcoming to a stranger. I was completely taken off guard as I had prepared myself for another brief outburst of suspicious conduct, such as all the other town's people had given me. Yet, to my amazement, here was a man without murmurings and slits for eyes. "Why does Yeshua's family think he is mad or mentally cracked in some way?"

"What family?"

"His mother, brothers, and sisters, to be precise."

"Oh, them," he said revealing little sympathy for their situation. "They do not trust at this time. I am sure they will understand and will become ardent followers later. Today they are ashamed of what they do not comprehend. Yeshua definitely has turned everyone's life upside down here at Nazareth," the old man said with a particular tittering laugh. Since Aramaic is littered abundantly with figurative idioms, it was difficult catching all his humor.

"What led to this doubt by his own kinsmen?" I asked dangling the question in the hope he would elaborate. It felt like the times I sat in a fishing boat off Piraeus with bait on a fishing line. You never knew when or if anything would bite. The old man remained silent and thoughtful. While waiting, I watched several sparrows pick at something substantial out in front of us. It may have been a hard piece of dried bread or a wooden stick. At least six birds were trying to get the same object. Soon one larger bird was able to get an edible part from the hardened object. Once he flew away, his friends pecked at what remained. I smiled while I watched the birds' heads pop up and down poking and tapping before swiveling their heads around several more times before jabbing at the object again. It was almost like watching the old man. Was he going to feed me or not? I had to admit, in a perverse way, I enjoyed this quiet, conspicuous wait. Then all of a sudden, the old man hit the bait and ran with my question.

"It could have started years ago when Yeshua went to the Temple with his parents when he was 12 years old. The family traveled together to Jerusalem to fulfill their religious obligations. Afterward, they headed back to Nazareth. On that first night in their camp down on the Jordan River, they realized Yeshua was not with them. Can you believe it? His entire family walked a full day toward home before realizing Yeshua was not with the group. Well, you could imagine their plight. Both adults were out of their minds that night and the next day walking back to Jerusalem – all uphill, mind you. Another day of angst came upon them as they wasted most of it scouring the city. Shortly before sunset, they found little Yeshua in the Temple courtyard talking with elder teachers and conversing most proficiently. When his mother chastised him in front of the men, Yeshua said without malice that he had only been at his father's house. Joseph, the boy's adopted father, obviously had nothing to say. Joseph, you see, told all of this to me after the family had returned. He and I used to be best friends before he passed away a few years back. Joseph had married Mariam, the daughter of Heli, when she was just a young girl going into her teenage years; and Joseph was already middle age. Well, anyway, the birth of Yeshua, I must add, remains under a strange cloud. Yeshua was not born here in Nazareth but in Bethlehem, the Bethlehem south of Jerusalem, home of the famous King David. It was during the first Roman census that caused Joseph to be there in the first place along with his unconsummated bride Miriam. I know he paid the girl's father the marriage fee, but the marriage was still not sealed with the two becoming one. Do you understand what I am saying?"

He must have noticed a quizzical look on my face and assumed I did not understand the Semitic customs. Before I could answer, he began to explain. "You see, most marriages with the Hebrew people are arranged shortly after birth. Mariam or Mary, the Latin form of Mariam, was promised to a young boy who fell out of a tree at age 12, broke his neck, and died. Joseph ben Jacob was a widower without any children and in need of a female to help feed him and clean his house. Since Mariam was no longer promised to the dead boy, Joseph purchased Mariam as his bride. Joseph was middle age, and Mariam had not reached puberty. In cases like this, a promise is made before the elders of town not to violate the young girl sexually until she passed through puberty. Our Semitic customs allow an old, widowed woman to witness the coming together after puberty begins; and the sheet with the blood mark is given to her parents. Some of this is explained in the Torah. However, this did not happen; for Mariam became pregnant shortly after the wedding ceremony but before it was consummated by Joseph. You see, my friend Joseph swore an unusual oath in Yahweh's name that he was not the father and offered to return the money, which is an act of divorcing the young girl. Does that help you understand?"

"Somewhat, I guess. Anyway, tell me about when Joseph and Mariam found Yeshua at the Temple when he was 12."

"Yeshua did leave and returned with Joseph and Mariam. But I tell you his family looked at him a little differently ever since that day they found him conversing with the elders at the Temple."

"How did you look at him?" I asked trying to be sensitive to his feelings.

The old man looked over at me and smiled. After looking into my eyes for just a moment, he moved his gaze to something off in the distance. I noticed his smile leaving as if he were lost in another world. I wondered if I would become like this when I became old. I can tell you today that I move and think slower than when I was younger, but I have learned that being hesitant to speak is a sign of wisdom. On this day in my youth, I just patiently waited for his vicarious spell to pass. When the smile returned, I smiled inwardly as well knowing he was going to speak. He looked back at me and then lifted his chin up before he said, "I liked the boy, the most brilliant scholar of the Holy Writings I have ever encountered. He always answered all my questions with a gracious simplicity. Listening to him always made my heart jump. He never asked me what the Scriptures meant, it was as if he knew everything."

I could feel the old man wanting a reaction to what he just said. When I did not respond, he asked, "Can you understand that?"

I knew exactly what he meant but did not comment; instead, I was quiet before asking him a hard question. "His family is rejecting him because of his knowledge?"

"Not true. It is not so simple. Consider what took place at Cana when the wine ran out. I remember it happening exactly two years ago, right before Passover. It was right before Yeshua cleansed the Temple according to the prophecy of Malachi, which very few want to acknowledge. Oh, yes, the Temple cleansing was the second major embarrassment for the family; and that happened shortly after the wedding at Cana. But I should start with the wedding. When the wine was all consumed, Yeshua's mother told him to do something because she did, to a degree, believe in who he was."

"His mother expected Yeshua to do something?" I asked.

"Maybe I should explain. A bride's family is required to supply all the food and drink, and the bride was the half-sister of Yeshua. This was a year or so after Joseph's death making Yeshua the eldest male in the family. Yeshua responded by saying, 'Woman, what do I have to do with you? My hour has not yet come.' You see, the prophecy of the Messiah is he must first appear at the Temple and cleanse it, which had not occurred when his mother expected a miracle. Like I said, his mother always had faith in him as the Messiah; but she did not understand everything about the Messiah. Most Jews only believe what they want to without looking at the full counsel of the Word of Yahweh. Besides, there are many interpretations from all the different factions here in Israel. For example, the Zealots want the Messiah to be a warrior-king who will kill all the Romans. The Sadducees don't want the Messiah to come because he would be against Roman rule and that would take away their high positions in Jerusalem. Well, anyway, Yeshua turned about one hundred and eighty gallons of water into the best wine I have ever consumed."

"You were there?"

"Almost the entire village of Nazareth was present. Like I said, Yeshua's sister was the bride; but Cana is her husband's village."

"You actually witnessed the water being turned into wine?" I asked again making sure I heard him correctly.

"Absolutely; your hearing is healthy, young man," he replied acutely aware of my astonishment. "It was the opposite of Moses's first miracle. You see, Moses turned water into undrinkable blood. Yeshua turned water into drinkable wine; and the wine on that late afternoon, come to think of it, was the color of blood. That I remember with vivid clarity," he said with a grin of delight overtaking his countenance. His manner stilled as if savoring the reminiscence. His eyes were looking up again, and he looked out into the far distance; but this time the memory was apparently joyful. I looked at the ground noticing more birds looking for something in the dirt. It was not long before he continued.

"There was the incident right here at this synagogue soon after the Baptist was arrested by Herod Antipas. That would have been a year, no, a year and a half ago. Yes, that poor fellow has been imprisoned for a year and a half by that 'old fox' Herod and his sorceress wife. Just after the Baptist was arrested is when what I am saying happened. Yes, it was right here at this synagogue about a half year after the Temple cleansing and the wine miracle at Cana."

"Right here where we sit? And wouldn't that place the event around the time of the Feast of Atonement?" I acutely remembered the day Eli told me John the Baptist had been arrested by Herod Antipas, which was on the Day of Atonement. That was also the last day of Eli and the day Amcheck and I killed the captain of the Temple.

"You must be right about it being near the Day of Atonement," he nodded. "It was late fall when Yeshua came back to Nazareth after John was arrested. The crowds from nearby villages swarmed around when he came home because of his new fame in Judaea. Yeshua walked through these doors," said the old man waving his left hand toward the ornately carved wooden doors. "He sat in the very front row right in front of the unrolled scroll that was ready for that morning's reading. It was a section from that week's assigned reading from the words of the Prophet Isaiah. The attendant purposely allowed Yeshua to read the scroll. Do you know the Scriptures?" asked the old man, who was continually changing the subject, which was driving me senseless, until I realized I was guilty of the same practice. I lowered my head in shame.

"I am a proselytized Jew but familiar with Isaiah."

"Good! Well, Yeshua stood; and, with his head covered in his *simlah*, he pronounced only a small portion and then stopped mid-sentence. He returned the scroll to the attendant and sat quietly. Those in attendance were aghast. First of all, if you are a proselytized Jew, you might not know that what I just said was strange, indeed. When I observed Yeshua, he held the scroll in both hands; but his eyes never looked at what was in his hands. You see, he did not need the scroll at all. Actually, his eyes were looking up toward the far ceiling. He quoted by heart as if he were personally talking to the Creator of the Universe. Second, he had not completed the final sentence when he handed the scroll back to the attendant and sat. No one in my long memory had ever stopped in mid-sentence and sat down after reading the Scriptures."

"Why would that be a problem?"

"Not completing a sentence in the unchangeable script is always an issue."

"I see your point. Any abrupt stop could alter the context as it is originally written. How could anyone change the very words of God? Go on please; what happened next?" I asked amazed at what I just heard. Taking any passage out of context was very serious.

"It is a little complicated. You must understand the procedure after someone reads the prescribed passage on the Sabbath. The reader is to provide commentary for the reading before sitting. You see, Yeshua had not commented nor completed the entire text for that morning's reading. It was the correct passage that was designated for that Sabbath, but what was most disturbing and highly irregular was he did not give comment to what he just read. Yeshua just sat there while the room of men with the women in the rear began to murmur among themselves. Finally, Yeshua stood and faced the crowded room, which included his mother and brothers. As I have already said, Joseph ben Jacob had passed away some years earlier leaving Yeshua in the role of patriarch of the ben Jacob family. Remember that was why his mother turned to him at Cana to deal with the wine shortage. She was embarrassed since custom requires the week-long wedding to be a joyful event and the bride's family is expected to supply all the food and drink."

Wanting the old man to stay on topic, I said, "What happened at the synagogue when Yeshua turned and the room became silent?" I wanted desperately for this old man to stay focused, and I hoped I had not offended him.

The elderly man smiled showing me he was not offended. I decided to remain quiet and let him go wherever he wished. When I smiled back, he started talking again. "Mariam, his mother, was in the section for women; and his brothers sitting by age were near the front. That I remember vividly. When the room became silent, Yeshua said the reading he had just read had been fulfilled as of this moment. The crowd gasped in amazement knowing this passage to be a famous Messianic prophecy. Then Yeshua said, 'No doubt, you will quote this proverb to me: *Physician, heal yourself!* Whatever we have heard done in Capernaum, do also here in your hometown as well.' Then he continued with great authority saying, 'Truly, I say to you, no prophet is welcomed in his hometown. But I say to you in truth, there were many widows in Israel in the days of Elijah when the sky was shut up for three years and six months when a great famine came over all the land; and, yet, Elijah was sent to none of them but only to Zarephath in the land of Sidon to a woman who was a widow. And there were many lepers in Israel in the time of Elisha the prophet, and none of them was cleansed but only Naaman the Syrian.'"

"Yeshua actually said all of this?"

"I witnessed it all, and I can tell you I have never seen this synagogue in such a rage. Elijah and Elisha were prophets to the northern tribes hundreds of years past. Referencing these well-respected prophets was very insulting to the crowd that day. I tell you Yeshua really knows how to kick up the dust. To be more precise, the prophets Jonah, Hosea, Amos, and Nahum were also from Galilee or at least to the north of Judah. Then to my utter amazement, a man jumped up near the back and quoted the very proverb Yeshua said someone would say: 'Physician, heal yourself!' That was the breaking of the dam, and all restraint evaporated. The crowd rushed to take hold of Yeshua in their rage. Someone yelled, 'Let's throw him from the brow of the hill!' Out of these very doors, the crowd disgorged like a living fountain of human flesh. When the synagogue crowd reached the precipice over thereabouts, Yeshua was not in their midst. They searched among themselves and became somewhat addled due to the fact Yeshua was nowhere to be found. After that event, Yeshua was reported to be teaching and healing in the city of Capernaum. It was at this time and from there that Yeshua selected his closest disciples, known as 'The Twelve.' Capernaum now appears to be his new, adopted home; yet, some influential men do not want him there either."

"So did Yeshua ever come back here after the incident at the brow of the hill?"

"Oh, but he did – one other time. The last was just a few weeks ago when literally thousands followed him here from Lake Galilee. You see, his popularity is growing everywhere except here in Nazareth; for he was correct in saying a prophet is welcomed everywhere except his own home. I am afraid he will never again return home."

I felt as if two times was not significant to this old man. I decided to help him see the importance of two times. His head was hanging low when I began to ramble out my thoughts. "Julius Caesar states in his Gallic Wars, which lasted 8 years, that he crossed the ocean to Brittany two times. There was also in two years when Caesar was in Gaul that he bridged the river Rhine and crossed over with his army two times. You see, two times is significant."

The old man wagged his head after I spoke. Perhaps he didn't understand a word I said. When he began to talk, I was sure he didn't understand, so I just let him be. "It was after the first visit and before the second return to Nazareth that Miriam found her son at Capernaum. The crowds down at that fishing village prevented her and her children from getting close to him. That is when Mariam and her children first came to take custody of him, but the crowd unwittingly prevented them because of their numbers."

The old man stopped, and after a moment, I said, "I am interested in what happened. Do you know?"

He looked up and smiled before he resumed. "Miriam, the mother of Yeshua, had no other option other than sending word to him by a well-respected man from Capernaum. You see, this man is the one who told me this story. Anyway, she was outside and not able to get in because of the crowds. Interestingly enough, this all happened at the same time prominent officials arrived from Jerusalem, who were vainly primping to give their official edict of the power behind the miracles that Yeshua had been performing. Perhaps, this was the very thing Miriam was afraid of happening."

"I don't mean to stop your story, but what miracles?"

"Many miracles."

"Such as?"

"Such as the healing of a centurion's slave boy in Tiberias when the Roman had sent representatives to ask Yeshua in Capernaum if he would heal his slave. That had to have been a healing that covered at least twenty-five miles away from where the Roman representatives had asked for Yeshua's help. In Capernaum one of the mothers-in-law of the twelve was bedridden with a fever, and Yeshua went to her and healed her. Then there was a paralytic lowered through the roof of a home where Yeshua was teaching, and Yeshua first forgave the man's sins before he healed him. I have heard of at least two people being brought back from the dead. One was a widow's son at Nain. The town's people were carrying him out to be placed in a tomb; and Yeshua touched him at the gate and commanded him to rise, which he did, instantly.

The second was the daughter of Jairus, a synagogue official at Capernaum. Oh, and I must not neglect to mention the notorious, demon-filled man who lived in the tombs at Gergesa over on the eastern shore of Lake Galilee, where the bank to the sea is quite steep. The story told to me by one of his disciples was there were literally thousands of demons in one man. When Yeshua ordered them all to depart the man, the horde of demons entered a herd of swine, which immediately plunged over the steep bank into the lake and perished. The people from that side of the lake demanded Yeshua leave the area because of the financial loss to some of the town's wealthy. You see, a man was freed from evil spirits; and the people were more concerned about their filthy pigs. Can you believe it? I cannot understand it. What have we become? Sometimes I think we are in the last days. And why were Jews raising pigs in disregard to the Torah? Perhaps they were not eating them but selling them to Gentiles at the southern end of Lake Galilee as well as the Roman city named after the Roman emperor," he said making that tittering laugh again. After a long moment, he began to moan as if he had smashed his big toe and then became silent. I thought he now might weep if I did not get his mind off the ills of this world.

"Why was Jerusalem concerned about the miracles?" I was hoping my question would redirect him to the story of the Jewish delegation, which arrived at the Capernaum synagogue from Jerusalem. I was also wondering how I was going to remember all that I was hearing. It was like being back at the Lyceum listening to a distinguished lecturer, and I began employing my old memorization tricks to plant all the different stories in my mind. If I could hold every story for just a short time, I could write them down tonight. Writing is truly man's greatest invention because any type of script preserves one's thoughts and later allows one to transmit those ideas, even after death.

"What do you believe about these miracles, young man?" came the response to my question. He was now looking again and probing my eyes apparently not taking my baited hook to return to the delegation.

I looked away in frustration by this elderly man, who was entertaining himself at my expense. I was also somewhat embarrassed at my own thoughts and sense of transparency. I shrugged off my unease by remembering the miracle I had witnessed in Jerusalem the day I met Messina. I finally smiled to myself thinking that would be my deflection. "I witnessed Yeshua healing a lame man at the waters of Bethesda in Jerusalem right before the last Passover. It was a miracle as far as I am concerned. There was no trickery involved that I could detect."

"Have you asked yourself by what power Yeshua performed that miracle you witnessed? Do you realize there are only two possibilities that exist: one being Yahweh's power; or power coming from Lucifer, the leader of the fallen sons of gods?"

"God or the Devil?" I asked before I understood the extremeness of the question. Then the subtlety of it came to me. "I saw no evidence of Lucifer, but only the Lord Himself could and would have done such an act. Now, please tell me about the other works of Yeshua?"

"I heard of a leper being cured as well as the Jerusalem healing you witnessed at the two pools with the five porticos, the one you called Bethesda."

"Yes, the pool with the colonnades that is spring fed, not the one that is open and rain filled. You mentioned two people coming back from the dead. How dead were the two?"

"From what I remember, one was a widow's son in Nain who had died earlier that day and was brought back to life near the city gate as he was being carried out to be buried. By only a word and touch from Yeshua did the young man come back to life. Jarius's daughter had just expired and was also restored by a word after he had taken her hand. I was told by one of his disciples that Yeshua had merely said in Aramaic, *'Talitha kum,'* which means 'little girl, I say to you arise.' On that day before the raising of the little girl, a miracle occurred out in the streets of Capernaum. When Yeshua was walking toward Jarius's home, a woman with a bleeding illness had secretly touched Yeshua's robe; and she, too, was healed. Yeshua must have felt something leave him when the woman touched his clothing, for he had questioned who had touched his robe. I would count perhaps two dozen miracles have been performed by Yeshua in the past two years. These are wonders never performed before, even by Moses, Elijah, or Elisha all put together."

This information was too overwhelming for my mind to process. I had not expected this outpouring of details. I wanted to get back to the day Jesus's mother and brothers rejected him; so I asked, "What about the day the religious leaders arrived in Capernaum from Jerusalem, and don't forget to tell about when Mariam could not get into the synagogue?"

"Oh, yes. These leaders were using the name Jesus over his Hebrew name Yeshua. They declared that Jesus was doing all the miracles in the power of *Beelzebub*. It was a calculated way of saying Yeshua was demon possessed by the ancient god of the flies."

"Flies?"

"Well, you must understand that during the summertime here in the Galilee, especially on the western side of Lake Galilee, there is a plague of flies. It actually becomes unbearable at times as black clouds of these little pests fly around and land on everything. To make things even worse, they often inflict a murderous bite. So, calling Yeshua *Beelzebub* strikes a sensitive spot to all of us who have suffered the fly plague over the years."

"What was Yeshua's response?"

"Quick and devastating. He declared that any belief that the leader of the fallen angels was behind his miracles would be a sin against the Holy Spirit. He was openly saying that the power of all his works came from the Holy Spirit, and a sin against the Holy Spirit could never be forgiven once it was committed."

"An unforgivable sin? You mean like murder?"

"Oh, no! Murder can be forgiven, but sinning against the Holy Spirit is unforgivable. Therefore, saying the miracles are from the hand of Satan means one commits the unpardonable sin. Because of that statement on that day, Yeshua became the most controversial person in the entire world and, for that matter, possibly all of history. No one has made such a declaration. His statements have a life in themselves like a tremor in the earth. Remember he forgave the paralytic his sins, the one lowered down to him by his friends in Capernaum. Was it not enough to say stand and walk? No, this preacher from this town says, 'Your sins are forgiven.' You see, the problem is only God can forgive sins. Now, my young listener, do you understand the situation, especially here in Nazareth? Are we to think Yeshua is making himself equal to Yahweh himself? Moreover, what most will not admit, but it is in the Scriptures, is that God Himself will walk among us in the last days."

"You mean like Alexander the Great stating he was Zeus or the son of Zeus?"

"No, of course not. That was a demonic counterfeit. Alexander was a classic anti-Messiah. And if there is a Zeus, it is Satan who has been very busy over the years. What I am talking about is when the true and only God walked with us humans in the past. He walked in bodily form with Adam in the Garden of Eden each afternoon. Yes, the Creator walked and talked with the first man every day. Abraham spoke and walked with God on a few occasions, and father Abraham even fed the Creator a meal under an oak tree where he lived in tents near Hebron. It is recorded in the Scriptures that this happened before the destruction of Sodom and Gomorrah and the other cities down on the plain where the Dead Sea is now located. None of those cities abides any longer, and that area is now a warning of what happens when evil goes un-repented."

"Well, I do believe Moses talked to the burning bush on Mount Sinai, which spoke to him and said, 'Take off your sandals; you are on holy ground.'"

"True enough. When asked by Moses what the Creator's personal name was, the bush responded with the Hebrew word YHWH or Yahweh. Joshua, Moses's lieutenant and successor of the descendants of escaped slaves from Egypt, spoke face to face with the Captain of the Host. This happened just after the Children of Israel crossed the Jordan River before the fall of Jericho. The Captain of the Host spoke the same words as the burning bush: 'Yeshua, take off your sandals; you are on holy ground.'"

There was a long silence before I asked to confirm what I just heard. "Are you telling me Jesus and the lieutenant of Moses hold the same name?" The old man looked at me and smiled with his head going up and down a couple of times to agree with what I just asked. I wanted to reject Jesus; but, on the other hand, I wanted to believe. This was to be my personal dilemma; yet, this quandary is what all humans struggle with at different times before they die. Finally, I asked, "What about his family at the synagogue in Capernaum? What was Jesus's response to them since they wanted to take custody of him?"

He tittered again and then sank into a short silence before he answered. "Could anyone anticipate his words? I heard his response was something for the recorders of history to behold. Word came to him inside the synagogue that his kin, unable to get through the throng, was outside to see him. Well, Yeshua answered as if he knew the very intents of their hearts, which were not entirely obvious to all. He asked, 'Who are my mother and brothers? Behold my mother and brothers!' he declared waving his hand around the crowded room. It was obviously a rhetorical question, which he answered himself. 'For whoever does the will of God, he is my brothers and sisters and mother.'"

I leaned back against the synagogue wall in mental fatigue as I digested these words and tried to condense all of this before it faded from my mind and heart. It was at this moment I noticed that the sun was setting, and people were lighting oil lamps that were glowing out of a few windows down the street.

"Do you know where Yeshua is now?" I inquired without any malice in my voice. With the sun setting, I knew my time with this old man was now short.

"Still down around Capernaum, I would guess. Like I said, I doubt he will ever come back here since Nazareth has rejected him two times and even tried to kill him on the first rejection."

We sat in silence for a long time as if we both had all the time in the world to enjoy a beautiful sunset. Daylight faded into gray, broken by a few flickering oil lamps casting busy shadows on windowsills and outside walls. After processing all that the old man said, I repeated in my mind everything so that

I would be able to write it down later that night. I then decided to ask a final question. "Who do you say Jesus, or I mean, Yeshua is?"

The old man smiled broadly before turning to me with a twinkle in his eyes. "I will answer it with a question to you. As a proselyte Jew, have you made any sacrifices at Herod's Temple for any of your sins?"

"Well, yes, but no. I mean I intended to offer a sacrifice; but something happened, and I was not able. To be honest, my faith in the Temple system is waning. I am not an Essene; nor was John the Baptist, who could have been a priest like his father but stayed away from Jerusalem. But how does that answer my question to you?"

"Well, if you were to learn more about Yeshua, you will find he also has never offered a sacrifice at the Temple in Jerusalem. Never! Not one burnt offering, grain offering, peace offering, sin offering, or guilt offering. Nothing! You see, I would know because I am the leader of this synagogue. I have witnessed this young boy grow into a man, and I know everything about him. I have never seen him sin. Never! What is your answer to that?"

"What does that mean? And why does it matter?" I asked in my ignorance.

"When you have an answer to why and what, then you have answered your own questions."

The perfunctory nature and the implication of what this old man was saying inexplicitly numbed my mind. I had no answer. While the evening shadows were embracing the village of Nazareth into a slow darkness, my own comprehension was slipping into a similar shadowy vagueness. I caught myself yawning and shook my head to try to regain some alertness. My knowledge of the Scriptures at this time was, indeed, lacking even though I thought it wasn't. Words such as *"The people perish because they do not know my words"* would later be a direct rebuke to me. Ignorance of the truth can send someone to Hell just as quickly as bad behavior. If I had only known, it would have made all the difference in the *cosmos*. Knowledge does not save a man, but it is instrumental when one is making certain life-altering decisions.

The old man leaned forward and began speaking more quickly than previously. "Our choices truly determine our destiny. Those who sit in the middle are sentenced to be cast into oblivion for eternity according to the words spoken by Yeshua when He said, *'You are either with me or against me.'* No one who has walked the face of this world has ever been this divisive, dissenting, or inflammatory. Yeshua has given everyone only one of two options, and that is the only reason we are alive. Believe in him, and follow; or go the other way, and ultimately die. Each human is on the same quest, going down the same road. This life is nothing more than a search for the narrow path that is not well traveled."

"My mother said the same on my tenth birthday. 'Find the Messiah, and follow him.'"

"This Messiah you look for is Yeshua," he emphatically said without blinking. "Believe by faith, and make the step to accept this truth. This will make you either a son or daughter of God through adoption."

After the old man sat straight and turned his head looking off into the night, I thought about my father, Gaius Vetallus. He was my biological father; yet, he adopted me because of my mother being a slave. I wondered if all humans understood that we all are born into this world as fallen slaves to our sinful impulses and desires. Only a transformation from above can alter the curse we find ourselves enslaved under. Once the truth is accepted, then the war begins. Breaking my concentration, the old Jew started talking as if he could read my mind.

"I heard Yeshua once say, *'For I have come to set a man at conflict against his father, and the daughter against her mother, and the daughter-in-law against her mother-in-law. And a man's foes shall be those of his own household.'* Certainly, the truth can and will separate families just as it has mine. My young friend, understand this: to add complications to complexity is one result of the coming of Yeshua. Yet, this is not the reason he came. He came to this world to fulfill ancient prophecies that were pronounced by angels and humans hundreds of years previously, and he is also doing miracles. He has healed the blind, lame, and lepers; raised the dead; walked on water; cast demons out of people; and commanded authority over storms. He has healed people from dozens of miles away, can read people's thoughts, and forgives sins. Is it not true that you have witnessed one of these miracles?"

"You left out the miracle of water into wine."

"But Jesus turned water into wine, perhaps one of the most incendiary events that started happening shortly before Yeshua cleansed the Temple. It was not long after that when the religious leaders of Judaea could not brush away the miracles. They are now officially saying Jesus did them by the power of *Beelzebub*, the god of flies and the prince of devils."

"But you told me Jesus has drawn a line in the sand – if anyone today says the miracles are in the power of *Beelzebub*, this is now an unforgivable sin."

The old Jew looked at me before he spoke. "Understand this, my new young friend; this sin against the Holy Spirit places a person in danger of eternal damnation. I do not jest. Just proclaiming that Yeshua has an unclean spirit and that this is the source of his power to speak and perform miracles leads a person to someday wish he or she were never born. Yeshua's life and works have brought with it an unending controversy that has polarized the world against him and has ushered in division or devotion. Now here is wisdom: a few chosen ones embrace Yeshua while the rest are enraged. You see, if Yeshua is who he claims to be, Yeshua deserves worship. I believe only a few are offering the devotion and adoration he deserves, and then there are those who give only a false adulation. From this point forward until the end of time, the bulk of humanity will blasphemy Yeshua's name openly along with vile profanity. Until the end of this age, the majority will spit in the face of the one who created us. Yes, you heard me correctly. Someday you will understand that the Creator Himself is walking with us humans."

I was numbed by his declaration while the old man went silent after his prophetic prediction. I looked back at only one bird still pecking at the ground. When did birds do such a thing in the dark? I smiled to myself as if down on the ground was a living, divine metaphor that God was allowing me to see. There I was nipping at what I did not understand. And we humans sometimes don't even realize what is being observed could give us eternal life. Did I know what I was biting at? If I did, would I use my wings and fly to the highest peak and proclaim devotion to the one who put me here in the first place? Why not invite the Creator to take me back to Him? Why do we humans try to exist in our own power by fighting over the little things when there is so much more for our true *zoe*? Didn't the Jews, or was it the high priest, who proclaimed that one man should die or the nation would perish? In some strange way, could this one man be Yeshua? Yet, only God could save the world. Could Yeshua be God in a human body? If this were true, this knowledge would turn the known world upside down. How could this ordinary time become so momentous? What kind of a historical episode was now befalling the *cosmos,* shaping time and eternity, along with the course of my life?

Sitting in my cell in Rome, I am technically 91 years old. I am to die in the Colosseum in Rome because of my decision made so long ago. My conversation with the old man at the Nazareth synagogue was one of those first steps of that long-ago journey. Now, almost seventy years since, everything I have experienced depended on the few questions that I asked in Nazareth as the sun fell below the horizon. To put it very simply, everything depended on the precise identity of the man from Nazareth named Yeshua or Jesus. I can now tell you it would still be several more years before I was ready to make my decision concerning Jesus. When I did make my declaration to follow this sinless man, it became a resolution that set the pillars of my life into eternity.

Sitting in my jail cell in Rome, I can honestly say I am not afraid of my death. I finally understand what the ancient Jewish King Solomon meant when he recorded, *"The day of your death is better than the day of your birth."* However, I do ask forbearance and understanding in my role in the death of Jesus of Nazareth; for I believe I was placed in Palestina at that time as a witness. Yet, as a witness, I became one of the ugly actors, still filled with some shame. But, as a witness, I do not believe Jesus was afraid of death even though it came much too early in his life and how it happened was completely unjust. Just so that you might understand, I petition whoever reads this or hears these words for serenity and kindness as I present how I went from onlooker to participator in my offense toward Jesus of Nazareth. I am trying to give a complete testimonial of what I saw and did as a witness during those ominous last years, days, and hours of the fateful events of the Nazarene's life. Understand one thing: I was not a hero when it came to the suffering and death of Jesus.

How I came to the point where I participated in the Nazarene's distress was a complete reversal from when I first met him at the Jewish Temple in Jerusalem. The first time I heard him speak my heart burned to hear more. When I asked him who he was, he told me he was *Christos*. I heard him while I had a burning rage toward Judaism and the Temple cult. There is no excuse for the role I played in Jesus's suffering and death but just a fact of my spiritual collapse – a collapse that Jesus told me at that first meeting would occur. How he knew this tells me all I need to know about this innocent and righteous man. The old Jew at the synagogue of Nazareth was correct when suggesting that Jesus, or as he called him Yeshua, was without sin. Why else would he have never sacrificed under the law of Judaism? To be perfect and sacrifice would be a sin. The only sacrifice Jesus made was himself. From the time of that sacrifice, I started on a new path, about which I have never been ashamed.

While you read this confession, comprehend one thing: tomorrow in the Colosseum my life literally ends and begins, all because my sins are removed by the sacrifice *Christos* did on that lonely tree on Golgotha. Yet, the awful events of Christos's death were still two years away from that late afternoon I sat with the old Jew in Nazareth.

After the little bird flew away, I realized the old man was tired. Maybe it was his time for bed. The quiet moment was about to end and I was about to leave when down the main street came another elderly Jew. He was approaching the synagogue from out of the darkness, and I placed a gentle elbow into the old man's side to alert him of the intruder. When he looked up, I noticed his body went tense. I pondered this as we both waited quietly for the visitor to approach. The approaching Jew in peasant garb addressed the old man sitting next to me as Eli. He may have said Heli in his thick Galilean accent, but it sounded like Eli to my ear. There was respect in the man's voice along with subservient manners. I did not pay much attention to the man's words while I began thinking of my dear friend Eli, who died on the day of Atonement as I tried to sacrifice my two birds. The memory was still painful, and I began to associate this old man with an elderly version of my dead friend. The same feelings and sensations of sitting under the teaching of the younger Eli during the long days on the grain galley came flooding back.

"Tell us what news you hold so dearly?" asked old Eli to the man before us.

"Can I tell you privately?" he asked looking at me.

"This young man is a brother of ours; you can speak freely."

The man before us seemed to relax and said, "A traveler who was with that camel caravan that passed by Nazareth this afternoon is sitting at Lev's wine shop."

Hearing about the camel caravan, I began to wonder if Amcheck had seriously injured or maybe killed someone in the wine shop. I finally asked, "Is someone dead?"

The stranger looked at me with a puzzled look. "How did you know?"

My heart dropped as I began to work out several avenues to take in order to rescue Amcheck. I put those thoughts aside to hear the details of the dead man. The visitor stated very plainly, "The man who is dead is the Baptist."

"What did you say?" I demanded. Just hearing what he said split open my mind and placed it in a state of dread and horror. Maybe my urgency caused the gentle stranger to cringe, for he stepped away from me saying he thought I knew. I asked for forgiveness for my rudeness, and he still just looked at me before he answered. "The Baptist was murdered a few days ago at Machaerus by King Herod. It happened at the king's birthday celebration, and he had John beheaded for his stepdaughter's delight as well as for the enjoyment of all his other guests."

"The Baptist cannot be dead," I said not wanting to believe the news. "That cannot be; he was alive just…" and I stopped midsentence as Jesus must have when quoting the reading of Isaiah in this very synagogue.

"That is what the traveler said," commented the stranger. "Maybe he is wrong; I do not know. I just thought Heli would want to know since John is a relative."

"Who is this traveler?" I asked remembering it was Antipas's birthday a few days ago. Perhaps it was true that John was dead; but I wondered about Amcheck, for I thought he would be in the same wine shop. The traveler wouldn't be Amcheck I concluded.

"A stranger like yourself. I think he is a seller of papyrus scrolls. He may still be at the wine shop down the street. Go talk to him yourself."

I got up and thanked old Eli, or Heli, by taking his hand into both of mine to show him I appreciated all he had told me about Jesus. I turned and apologized again to the old messenger for my impoliteness and then left for the wine shop. The messenger graciously forgave me, which I would not have done if I were he.

"I have just one last question," I asked the old man still sitting on the wooden bench.

"What is it, young man?"

"You are a kinsman to John the Baptist?"

"Yes, my wife and John's mother are sisters. You see, I am the father of Miriam, the mother of Yeshua. That is how I know about Yeshua's unusual birth. Joseph was not only the husband of my daughter, but he was perhaps my best friend. He told me the story of the angel Gabriel who came to Miriam and who also spoke to Joseph in his dreams. I am the one who sent Mariam to John's mother when she was pregnant with Yeshua to protect her from harm here in Nazareth."

"Thank you again, and perhaps we will meet again," I said trying to digest all that I had learned about Jesus. I tried to shake my head to understand something and again noticed the huge sycamore tree standing majestically near the door of the synagogue. This was the tree in the story told by Felix, the tree which stood in front of the largest building in Nazareth. Could this be the old man the Praetorian told me about at the tavern in Rome? "Forgive me, but I have one further question. A little over ten years ago around noontime on a warm Sabbath Eve, did you ask Yeshua a question from the Scriptures? It all happened on a day Yeshua and his brothers were dragging three trees they cut from the Jezreel Valley. It would have been a question about King David saying something like '*The Lord said to my Lord*.' Do you remember?"

"Are you talking about the three sandalwood beams for the bathhouse in Sepphoris?"

"Yes," I answered with a new excitement in my voice.

"A day I will never forget. That was when I knew Yeshua was more than the Messiah. But how would you know that story? Are you an angel?"

"I am far from being an angel, but I would enjoy telling you someday how I learned of that story." I turned away from the open-mouthed old man staring at me and went to find Amcheck and the papyrus seller.

Chapter Two

When I walked into the wine shop, a large crowd had gathered around the middle-aged papyrus vendor. Sitting in a corner with a large clay vessel on his table and a smirking grin on his face was Amcheck.

I worked my way toward him. "Sit down, Falcata; I have a jug of wine with gall mingled inside. You are going to need most of it when you learn of the news this scroll seller is pushing about your bug-eating friend back at Machaerus."

I sat only to take a long drink before I went to question the stranger. His evidence about the Baptist's death and his answers to my questions spawned more unwelcomed grief. After I was satisfied he was telling the truth, I returned to drink more with Amcheck. I stayed until the clay jug was empty.

I do not remember much until the next day when I awoke alone and sweating under the midday sun in a courtyard that served as a sleeping area for travelers. I looked at the scroll of papyrus that I had purchased from the manuscript dealer at the tavern the previous evening. I had also paid for ink and a stylus-quill made from a feather. With these items I began to scribble all that I remembered what old Eli, or Heli, had told me before I learned of the death of John. Just as I finished, Amcheck entered the courtyard and declared that we had better get back to Jerusalem since the populace was breathing fire against Herod Antipas, including his mercenaries. I agreed, and Amcheck said we were going to have to walk to Tiberias. "We will retrieve our mounts from there and ride the rest of the way to Jerusalem." After noticing my scroll-work, he said, "I believe you can write something interesting for Herod unless that is what you are doing."

"Just notes about what I learned about the Jew named Jesus. However, from these notes I will be able to compose something interesting for our tetrarch to read. Yet, why do we need to report on Jesus considering Herod has just beheaded the Baptist?"

"We are not to question but do as ordered. Understood?"

I nodded my head in submission, which cloaked my sickness and grief over the death of the desert preacher. His death was utterly senseless and sealed for me the fact that I worked for an evil lunatic. This new revelation concerning Herod hit me hard. Even the deaths of my mother and my friend Eli paled in comparison with my depression at the news of the brutal and callous execution of John. For some mysterious reason, the death of John hit me like a sword blow to the heart. If John had only taken my offer, I would be dead, not John. Moreover, John seemed like such a good, decent, and innocent person not deserving captivity in a pit for a year and a half along with a beheading because of the whims of a silly, bored girl. I became sick to my stomach thinking I even cared what Salome thought of me. I was just as much of a fool as everyone in this insane drama. Thus, I found myself falling into a brutal depression that went beyond words. I could not imagine seeing the Baptist's head on a silver platter at a dinner party as the papyrus dealer described in the wine shop. "A good man died because an erotic dance was performed by Salome for her uncle's birthday."

Amcheck limped the entire way to Tiberias from Nazareth. It was the next day when we finally arrived at the lakeside city dusty and tired. On the outskirts of Tiberius, we had encountered thousands of people, mostly ordinary peasants but some well-dressed nobles, mostly trying to board fishing boats going toward Capernaum. The death of John the Baptist had spread like a virulent plague, and the Jews were now looking for spiritual direction. The source for this was Jesus, the miracle worker. It was rumored that he was up around the northeastern shore of the Sea of Galilee. Amcheck and I debated about joining the mass of people looking for Jesus since Herod Antipas gave us a month to gather information. However, my heart was dead at this point; and Amcheck was tired of the spy mission and in great pain due to the boil that had been lanced in Nazareth.

In surprising simplicity, Amcheck summed up the enigma we were facing. "This many people going north to find Jesus will soon find themselves starving from the scarcity of food. Even if we all have money, how are we all going to find anything to buy? Second, what would we do if someone recognizes us as Herod's mercenaries? Finally, I refuse to sleep any more nights on the hard ground until my boil is healed. What I really need is to spend some time in a bathhouse soaking my behind."

Amcheck was resolved on returning to Jerusalem, which meant I wasn't going to find Jesus. In many ways, my heart was broken to the point I did not care if I lived or died. Like all the pilgrims looking for Jesus, I, too, wanted to go find him. But I reluctantly agreed to return to Jerusalem with Amcheck. I convinced myself that I could collect my savings and return to Galilee and find Jesus. Sooner than later Messina would show, and we could leave this wretched land. In the meantime, I would have to write a report for Herod Antipas. My source being Jesus's grandfather should be acceptable. If he didn't like my report, he might have Amcheck and me flogged. When I asked Amcheck about his thoughts about Herod, he said, "Herod is like the moon; he is up during the day, but we cannot see him. Does that make any sense to you?"

"It makes profound sense, something beyond your ability to understand, let alone say." I touched his shoulder just as Jesus had done to me at Bethesda while we walked looking for a bathhouse. After I had left Amcheck to soak his wound, I went and found the stables. The cute, little, plump furball recognized me by smell and wanted to play. He was twice his size since the little girl gave him to me.

The next morning Amcheck said he felt better and wanted to travel. He also said, "If we take two days, we should make Jerusalem before the next Sabbath begins." I paid the stable man the other *denarius* I had promised, and we started back to Jerusalem with the white puppy in his bag tied to the front of my saddle. We used the same Jordan Valley road until we turned toward Jericho. We spent one night at Jericho drinking with Amcheck's friends before heading uphill a little later the next morning. We used the Old Jericho route that bypassed the little village of Bethany that ran south of the Mount of Olives. When reaching the northern crest of the Mount of Olives, we found ourselves passing from desert into a thick forest. The road atop the Mount of Olives gave us the sight of Jerusalem that always enthralled my eyes and other senses.

Our horses carefully picked their steps down the steep way that led over the western side of the Mount of Olives onto the northern end of Jerusalem. It was late afternoon when we neared this side of the city walls. With the city walls in sight, I heard some horrible screams to my right. At first, I did not understand until Amcheck turned to me and said we were next to the Skull of Golgotha. Looking up toward the sounds, I saw the top part of one man hanging by nails driven in behind his hands in the wrist area. The scream came again from the top of this little rocky knob of a hill. I realized this was where the Romans carried out their executions, located just north of the city walls. There were several cave holes on the sheer escarpment, which formed eyes and a mouth. Growing below the step cliff was a grove of tall sycamore trees. A new cry could now be heard from atop the hill, and I concluded there had to be more than one man being crucified. Again I looked up at the one man I could see. Blackened blood covered his wet, dusty body. Amcheck must have realized I was disturbed by what I was looking at. "The first crucifixion that we have witnessed?"

After I nodded, he let out a hideous laugh. "You better get used to it. Drink in the vision, for we will see hundreds more before our days are ended. Do we see the eye and nose holes on the side of this hill? This place is called *Golgotha* in Aramaic and Greek. In the language of the priests, it is *Gulgoleth*. Both *Golgotha* and *Gulgoleth* mean bald, round, skull-like, or just bald skull. The Latin name is *Calvarius*. Most Jerusalemites just called it 'The Skull.'"

Looking back toward the city walls, I realized we were just about two stones' throw from the Sheep Market and the two pools of Bethesda. I later learned the Romans liked to crucify their victims near a main road as a warning to all. This way running next to The Skull was one of the leading routes to the junction of the Ridge Road that would take travelers north toward Samaria and Galilee or south toward Hebron and Beersheba. This crucifixion spot was the perfect place to send the Roman message to the people of *Palestina* to follow Roman rules.

"What a sight, men dying on a skull," I said mostly to myself. "Leave it to the Romans' dark art to have discovered this spot to carry out their executions." Looking toward the southwest, I saw the towers of the fortress of Antonia and the edge of the golden roof and top edges of the white walls of the Jewish Temple. Hearing a loud crack sound and a wretched cry from one of the crucified victims, I looked to Amcheck for understanding.

When he stopped laughing he gave me the answer. "Today the Sabbath begins at sunset. The Jews have a rule that no man can hang on a tree once the Sabbath begins. The Romans break the criminals' lower legs to speed up their deaths."

"How does this barbaric act speed up their deaths?"

"I not sure, but it has something to do with the ability to breathe properly."

I began to think on this quandary before asking, "How does a man breathe when he is crucified?"

"A man pushes up by his feet to breathe out and hangs by his hands to breathe in," answered Amcheck. "When his legs are broken, a man cannot blow out anymore. Normally a man has the strength to move up and down for a couple of days before death. Actually being crucified on Frigg's Day is a blessing, in my opinion," answered Amcheck before making a clicking noise with his tongue against the roof of his mouth to get his horse walking again toward the city. I noticed Amcheck leaning slightly to his right trying to keep his weight off his carbuncle wound.

"I believe it has something to do with the diaphragm," I finally said to no one but myself.

Amcheck stopped, turned, and asked, "What is a *dia* what?"

When I rode next to him, I explained. "A thin membrane of skin below the lungs. Remember my telling you about hitting Marius in my father's villa in Rome with only my knuckle. Well, I was trying to rupture his diaphragm."

"I am sorry we asked the schoolboy," hooted Amcheck. "Maybe when my backside is not hurting us so much you can explain again."

Once inside the city, I definitely felt the mood of the people; and it was not friendly. A rift had occurred over John and Jesus versus the religious leaders, including the political power that swirled around the city. The leaders of the Sadducees and some Pharisees were openly discussing Jesus as being demon possessed. A few days after our return to Jerusalem, I became concerned that Herod Antipas would send his soldiers out to arrest Jesus so he could kill him next. I wanted no part in any of this. As the days dragged on after our arrival back to Herod's Jerusalem palace, I found my only cessation of pain at Amcheck's wine shop in the lower city. My plan of escaping to Athens and finding Hector was going to have to wait. I could not leave this land until I found Messina, which meant I would need to run into Jesus at least once more. Sooner or later, Jesus was bound to visit this ancient city of prophets and kings. Until then I would remain drunk whenever I had a chance. I was medicating my dark mood with the poison of gall. This period of my life became one of the foolish points of my entire existence.

As the days grew in number, I became more and more dependent on wine and gall, the favorite drink of my father. In my spirit during this time, I become as dead in the heart as my father. The cycle was now complete. My state of mind became incredibly dark, to the point no one wished to be around me, including Amcheck. He stopped drinking with me, and now I just drank alone with a jug of wine and gall in my room in the lower level of Herod's palace. I had plenty of coins from my savings and winnings from when Amcheck collected on the day I beat Marius with wooden swords.

Besides wine and gall, all I had was little Zoe, who was growing into a beautiful, lean, snowy-white, long-legged dog, whose ears flopped when he ran and who always wanted to play. If it had not been for the companionship of Zoe, I might have fallen on my own falcata seeking the darkness provided by a hewn heart. The name Zoe or "Life" became the only reason I did not end it all. Also, I wanted to see Messina again and escape with her; that is, if she had not changed her mind once again. If she were to see me now, she most certainly would abandon me to my own depravity and return to marry Demos. And if that happened, I would not blame her at all for being a fickle female.

A READING AT THE GREAT LIBRARY OF ALEXANDRIA GIVEN BY EPAPHRODITUS

The year of the four emperors. During this year of civil war, the great fire broke out on Capitoline Hill destroying much of Rome's archives. Due to this loss, the scholars of Alexandria's Great Library requisitioned anyone with past knowledge to recreate the history of Rome. These short lectures were delivered on the afternoons of the seventh day of the week for a fee of 25 denarii. I have incorporated several lecture readings that I personally gave during this pivotal year.   **69 AD**

CALENDARS

The Essenes, a Jewish sect living down near the Dead Sea, claim that the Day of Atonement always had to fall on the sixth day of the week since that was the day God created the first man named Adam. Out of all the creation of Yahweh, this man Adam and all his offspring were going to need and would someday receive atonement. To the Romans, the sixth day of the week is called Venus Day, which many Barbarians in Rome call Frigg's Day or Friday. (Frigg is the chief Barbarian sex goddess.) I believe the Romans are the most eclectic people in this world. All the emperors I have known are interested in only two things: first, taxes being paid; and second, foreign people remaining submissive to Rome. Beyond this, the provinces could be somewhat free with their own laws and customs except for the death penalty. For a death sentence, all foreign nations had to get Rome's permission to execute anyone. Any type of atonement would mean death, and only Rome could facilitate the death of the one who could provide this complete blood compensation.

If people wanted to use different calendars, so be it; Rome did not care. Whoever maintained the greatest control and held the ultimate power was allowed to set any calendar as far as Rome was concerned. For example, consider the Sadducees, the Jewish sect that controlled the Temple complex in Jerusalem. If the Sadducees wanted to observe the Day of Atonement on the tenth day of Tishri, which might fall on any day of the week, this was acceptable to Rome. Yet, the holiest day of the year and what day it was observed caused most of the high divisions and arguments among many religious sects within the Promised Land and beyond. To a Jew, when the sun sets each day, that day ends. I first arrived in Jerusalem on the second day of Tishri or the last day of the Feast of Trumpets. It was a thrilling moment hearing all the horns and trumpets blaring away until sunset. The Essenes at Qumran always celebrated the Feast of Trumpets on one day and not two, which was always on the fourth day of the week (or Wednesday), because Yahweh created the lights of the moon and sun on the fourth day of the week of creation; thus, the celebration of the beginning of counting time by sunsets and sunrises. As the Torah prescribes, ten days after the Feast of Trumpets is the Day of Atonement. This day (Atonement) to the Essenes would always be on the sixth day of the week (or Friday) because the Feast of Trumpets is on the fourth day (Wednesday). Counting ten days from the fourth day would always land on the sixth day (or Friday). How all this works is beyond me, but I understand the reasoning.

With a seven-day calendar, the math just does not cooperate with the number of days in a solar year, especially in relation to a lunar year. To compound this debilitating mental situation, the Jews use a lunar-solar calendar that is corrected every third year with an added month to coincide with the solar year. The Romans are more practical and use a solar calendar of 365 days a year and forget the lunar year of 354 days. However, the Essenes calculate their calendar using a solar year of 364 days a year, which is divisible by seven. What the Essenes do with the missing solar day each year is anyone's guess. But, with the Essene calendar, festivals always land on the same day each year; and that is precisely what the Essenes desired.

The Essenes, that small group down in the Valley of Salt, reject the Sadducees' holy days in Jerusalem and are waiting for the Temple of Herod to fall under their control to set the days back to their original order. This is not likely to occur since only about two hundred men live at Qumran, the lowest spot on earth, who wait for their turn to correct the calendar to please Yahweh. The story goes that no women live in Qumran, which means this sect will soon die out in a few decades; and the day that happens the Essenes will no longer be a thorn in the side of the other sects. I am only guessing; but I think the Jews will always be creating factions in the future, which will only further complicate this calendar situation.

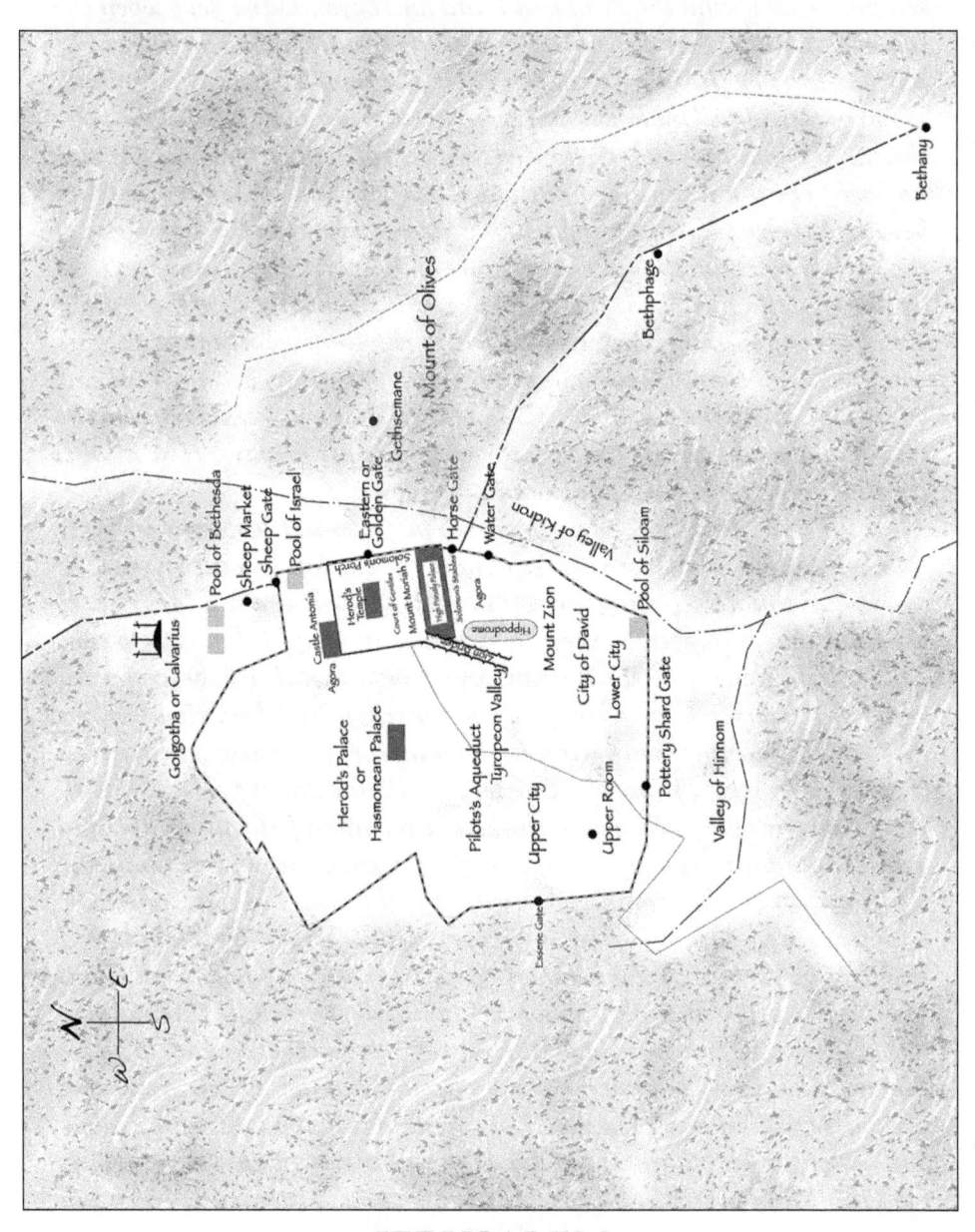

JERUSALEM
In The Times of Jesus (29 -33 AD)

CHAPTER THREE

Jerusalem – A week before Passover in Tiberius's 18th year. Pontius Pilate's 6th year as Prefect of Judaea. Jesus of Nazareth's 3rd year of his public ministry is about to end. This is the prophetic year of the coming of the Jewish Messiah to set up his Kingdom according to the calculations as written by the Prophet Daniel.   *(32 AD)*

To go into battle with people who have not been properly trained is to forsake them.   The Analects of Confucius

The year after the death of John the Baptist passed like sand in an hourglass. The days in Jerusalem felt like there was some malignant force lurking in the shadows just biding its time. Events in Rome were also far from peaceful, and the entire world seemed to know something was about to come and change it forever.

In *Italia,* Tiberius came close to losing his grip as ruler of Rome and its Empire. Even though I gave little attention to international events, I, being a mercenary in Jerusalem, did hear bits and pieces of the collapse of the conspiratorial stratagems of L. Aelius Sejanus, *prefect* of the Praetorian Guard. Sejanus was still ruling Rome while Tiberius was living on his pleasure island of Capri, located south of Neapolis and just a little northwest of Pompeii, out in the ocean away from everything in *Italia*. To the southeast of Capri, on the mainland was the ancient Greek city-state Paestum, now just a ruin with old temples marking its former grandness. The bloodshed that took thousands of lives in the days of Sulla, Marius, Pompey, and Caesar was not slowly being forgotten in most Roman's minds. Yet, it is important to remember that Caesar had won six major military campaigns after crossing the Rubicon with himself in the vanguard of eventually 12 legions. These victories are important because it took only five years, and once again the treasure houses of Roman exploded with more loot and slaves.

If Tiberius lost his grip on Rome, I believe Spain, Gaul, Asia, Egypt, Greece, Syria, and all of *Palestina* would rise up in revolt. I wondered what role my father would play if a new civil war broke within the Empire if Tiberius were to die prematurely. At first, I considered that these rumors concerning Rome were merely imperial gossip and mostly false stories meant to deceive. Due to my spiritual sickness during this year in Jerusalem, I was not interested in thinking about my father because my only goal in life was numbing my heart and mind with wine and gall. I had put on over thirty pounds of fat by doing nothing but drinking and eating sweet bread. If I kept up this habit, I would look like my father the day I tried to kill him with my dagger. A year of anguish and disappointments can inevitably stalk a man to death in a short time. Looking at me, anyone could say I was not a glad participant in life. The loss of my friend Eli and the senseless beheading of John the Baptist still haunted me with a thick heaviness of heart. Whenever I thought about the man-made traditions of the Temple system, my anger pulled me down like a bronze anchor tossed over the side of a small fishing boat.

I even wondered what role Amcheck played in these events that were spilling over into Judaea and what Rome called *Palestina*. Weeks went by when Amcheck did not speak and when he did it was to play the stupid-comic role. I wondered whose side he was supporting. Mostly he was supporting Herod Antipas because of his love of money. If he had been my friend, it was hard to tell by his deliberate absence. I felt vulnerable because Amcheck knew my secrets, except he knew nothing of the whereabouts of the Carnalus Scroll. I had now entered the realm of not trusting him. Actually, our relationship had grown into something dangerous. I had opened the door to entertaining the thought that I might have to kill him before he put a knife in my back.

Only two subjects gave me hope. One was Messina, and the second was Jesus. Was Messina really going to give up all the riches of this world for a runaway fugitive? I was hoping she would, but I was preparing myself for the worst. The second strand of hope was when I would listen to bits and pieces about Jesus of Nazareth. These tidbits of news became like light drying and killing a deadly foot fungus. Had Amcheck and I been ordered on any more journeys to "keep watch, and obtain information on Jesus," I would have been much happier than I was now; but nothing like this occurred. Herod Antipas continued as his own prisoner at Machaerus, mostly due to the continued threat of King Aretas. Rumors said the king of Petra was gathering an army of mercenaries. Only the might of Rome could save Herod Antipas if a war did break out between him and the Nabateans. The Jews, as well as the Samaritans, hated Herod Antipas for his beheading of the only prophet to appear in the Promised Land in 400 years. All who had claimed to be a prophet during these past centuries were all put to death for being false prophets. Allowing Jesus of Nazareth to openly preach was keeping the people at bay, but the authorities in Jerusalem were planning on killing him on the grounds that led to the death of all the so-called prophets over the past 400 years. Oddly, according to some reliable sources, Herod Antipas was seriously entertaining the thought that Jesus was John the Baptist back from the dead. I suppose, if I were Herod, this might be a significant dread and horrible torment, which I could not carry for very long. All our deeds over time bear some kind of fruit, may it be good or bad; and Herod's fears were well-founded.

Now many decades later, it is clear to see I was switching my anger from Rome and my father toward Herod Antipas. His dreams of becoming "king of kings" was evident with each passing day, all magnified by his wife and her daughter's sick game at his last birthday. Whenever I thought of the Baptist, I realized my visit on Passover Eve may have been the last time the prophet-preacher had a normal conversation before his time ended in this world. I might add, 70 years later, I still remember every word he spoke. When thinking about the details of the wilderness preacher's death, I hoped Messina had not been present at this so-called party-orgy at Machaerus. If she had witnessed this event and agreed with its entertainment elements, well, let's say, that would be the end of my relationship with her; and she was welcomed to marry Demos. With the next Passover looming on the Sanhedrin calendar, every conceivable, twisted thought and scenario passed through my now-damaged mind, a state I was entirely responsible for creating.

Since the last Passover, which marked John's death, had been a most dangerous year for me personally. Being a mercenary guard for Herod Antipas marked me as an enemy of the Jews, who made up the majority of people living in Jerusalem. On top of that, was my fear of the potential war looming with King Aretas. My fear mostly concerned being ordered to kill helpless civilians. I never wanted to find myself secretly stabbing anyone in the back in a crowded square if ordered by Herod Antipas. When I heard he might appear in Jerusalem this coming Passover, there was a genuine chance of trouble between the Jews and his soldiers. I was hoping the hated tetrarch would stay put at Machaerus and prepare for the war against the Nabateans. However, if war did come, Amcheck and I would most likely be sent to fight in the desert of Perea. For some reason, this possibility did not scare me the least. If it happened, I almost hoped I would be killed by an arrow to the neck, or better yet, escape in some confusion before or after a battle. Both scenarios seemed fine with me.

Due to my deep slide into darkness during this murky year, Jerusalemites left me alone when I was in or out of uniform. I had apparently developed a look that at times could startle even Zoe, a dog that ran the streets of Jerusalem scaring everyone because he had become a copy of me, with his scowling looks and low growls at the slight movements of people or things. My right eye had become half-closed most of the time giving me a squinty, critical look. My added weight, placing me over two hundred pounds, further slitting my eyes that resembled a snake. My growing had stopped by this time, and I was a good head taller than the majority of men, adding to the fear most seemed to possess when around me.

Zoe grew to be about half my weight as he was part Hittite Shepherd and something else from Anatolia or some other lands of the Barbarians. He undoubtedly had a war-dog temperament in him, which must have been bred into his being. His long legs enabled him to take an ankle of a man and pulling him off any horse or drag him to the ground. Never was there a dog more protective. No one wanted this beast of a dog near him or her, especially when Zoe was tagging along beside me. One man accidentally moved his hand near me on a crowded street, and Zoe about took the man's arm off. There was much blood, but the man apologized as he ran once I pulled Zoe from him. It was almost comical to watch women snatch up their children and lock their doors when they spotted the two of us coming down a narrow street when I was in or out of uniform. The two of us became a feared sight and considered by most as underworld fiends. The only physical encounter that required extreme violence was when six Zealots tried to attack me on a narrow street one evening. Two died instantly with iron daggers; and two perished at the teeth of Zoe, who had quickly ripped out their throats before they knew what was upon them. After this attempt on one of Herod's soldiers, there was no more trouble directed toward the white dog and me or any other Herodian mercenary for that year. I am guessing the remaining two Zealots ran for their lives and spread the word to leave the white dog and his master alone.

Still, the only solace for my heart was when I would hear of Jesus's display of miracles. I wondered about the old man at the synagogue in Nazareth. It took me many weeks before I totally understood or even believed I had spent the late afternoon with Jesus's grandfather and the man who had been in Felix's story as told in the Rome *popina*. I wondered whether Jesus's grandfather, Ol' Heli, now thought this year's miracles were becoming more spectacular than the ones he had relayed to me that late afternoon in Nazareth.

One miracle that occurred this third year of Jesus's ministry was an event that Amcheck and I could have witnessed ourselves had we not returned to Jerusalem after reaching Tiberias. This was the feeding of thousands with only a few fish and loaves. This event had occurred in northern Galilee shortly after the death of John. In a barren area northeast of the Sea of Galilee, thousands of people, the very ones Amcheck and I witnessed hiring boats to Capernaum, were most likely the witnesses of this supernatural feeding. It was not long after Amcheck and I had returned to Jerusalem from Tiberias when we first learned of the details of the feeding of the thousands. Jesus, with his closest followers, was looking for solitude due to the horrible news concerning John the Baptist when the crowds found them above Capernaum and the Sea of Galilee. Jesus had shown great compassion for the thousands who had traveled so far without provision. It became similar to the feeding of the children of Israel after leaving Egypt, who also were in the wilderness without food. Moses had given them food from heaven called "what is it" or in Hebrew *"manna."* Yet, what Jesus had accomplished by multiplying a few fish and loaves of bread was real, earthly food leaving several baskets of leftover scraps. Reports stated that maybe ten thousand men, women, and children were fed after Jesus prayed and broke the few pieces of bread and fish. Afterward, Jesus spoke until dark to the multitudes. When he finished, the people slept where they sat in groups of 50.

On the following day, the people could not find Jesus. Word spread that he had returned to Capernaum in the night walking a good part of the way across the lake, literally on top of the water. The story also had Jesus's disciples sailing in a large fishing boat when he climbed aboard for the rest of the trip to Capernaum. The news of Jesus walking on water and showing he could feed them caused the multitude to find him again to make him a king. Many thousands swarmed around the lake by foot until they converged on the synagogue at Capernaum where they found Jesus. Learning of the people's plan of making him a king, Jesus began to test them with his words. He understood they only wanted to make him a king because he fed them. Jesus was in the direct lineage of King David and since he could feed them, surely, he should be their king. Apparently their motives were not pure. Perhaps they thought that they would never have to work again and that he could order with his words the death of all Romans. Whatever, Jesus knew what was in their hearts; and he dealt with their sins by speaking troubling words. After his lengthy discourse in Capernaum, he said that, if the people wanted eternal life, they must eat his flesh and drink his blood. As his words were being repeated from the synagogue to people out in the streets and in and around Capernaum, a spiritual earthquake occurred that compared with a physical blasting of a volcano right in the center of the Sea of Galilee. What he had said would have been less disruptive if the thousands had understood his words figuratively and not literally. Hearing this, the Jews were stunned; for it is forbidden in the Mosaic Law to eat human flesh and consume any blood, especially human blood. Open rejection of Jesus was the result. Eating human flesh was inordinate and a boundless abomination, if not outright blasphemy. Even though Jesus was speaking figuratively, this was lost on most Jewish ears. After that day in Capernaum, the horde of followers turned away from him. Even most of his closest, adherent, supporting disciples abruptly abandoned him, no matter what miracles he had performed before or even after these offensive words.

Jesus's response to this lack of faith was to depart from the Galilee and travel north into Syria. Only his inner circle of a dozen disciples and a small band of women accompanied him out of the Galilee. He remained unseen for the rest of the summer and into the fall. The rumor that spread all the way to Jerusalem was that Jesus now resided in the region of Sidon or maybe Tyre. No one seemed to be sure; yet, strangely, Jesus's lack of appearance paralleled that of the ancient prophet Elisha, who traveled up to that area due to a famine in his days. Perhaps this, too, was a famine; but to the words of Jesus, which were causing a scarcity of belief.

Actually, there were many parallels in the Jewish Scriptures if one compared them with Jesus. When he was a child, he lived for a time in Egypt just as the Children of Israel did in antiquity. Then Jesus as a child came out of Egypt just like the Children of Israel escaped slavery from Egypt under Moses. There were also the 40 days in the wilderness of fasting after John baptized him, similar to the 40 years in the wilderness after the Israelites left Egypt. What was certain was that Jesus was now unwilling to walk in Judaea. Maybe it was because of the Pharisees, scribes, Sadducees, and lawyers who had all joined in an exclusive unification of sanctimony against Jesus. All past differences, deep enmity, and hatred that had separated these groups melted away because of Jesus; and the leaders formed a poisonous consensus to kill him. These groups chanted this threat of death, together and separately. Jesus had to die because he was just another false prophet sent to test them. Some leaders of the Jews went beyond the accusation of Jesus being a false prophet and began saying Jesus claimed that he was God Himself, which provided an explicit justification for this evil conspiracy of enemies demanding the death of this simple man from Nazareth. The final disturbing blow came when Amcheck confided to me that, on two occasions since our return from Galilee, he had been contacted by the Weasel to kill Jesus if the miracle worker ever returned to Jerusalem. Amcheck assured me he would not do the job because of my feelings for the Baptist. I felt the Jewish leaders' deep hatred of Jesus was merely a matter of professional envy, especially after the great feeding. Their resentment of Jesus festered as a swelling boil that I was sure would soon come to a head requiring surgical lancing, much like Amcheck's carbuncle in Nazareth.

Then, during the days before winter began at the last Mosaic feast of the year, the Feast of Tabernacles, Jesus mysteriously showed up without warning to the Temple in Jerusalem. I personally did not learn of his visit until after he had slipped back to the Galilee or beyond. I was on guard duty at the Hasmonaean Palace during those few days Jesus was in Jerusalem. I, along with the other Herodian Guards, had been ordered not to leave Herod's Palace during this fall festival. Over the next few weeks, after this restriction was lifted, I learned what happened by using Aristotelian logic and subtle stealth when interrogating witnesses. Actually, I discovered an easier way to get people to talk: the power of a silver *denarius*. This trick never failed when I uncovered an eyewitness to what Jesus did and said at the Temple. One coin was more than enough to get a Jew to tell all he remembered. Some would sing like birds, and suddenly many would return my *denarius* as if they would lose some kind of spiritual reward after they first took my money. I must emphasize I am only reporting what came to me by more than one person.

On the first day of the feast, Jesus stood near the northeastern porch at the Temple adjacent to the Castle of Antonia. He preached a few words and then asked why the Jews wanted to kill him. The crowds answered that he had a demon; yet, no one was seeking to kill him. The Pharisees and the chief priests of the Sadducees did at one time send the Temple Guards to seize him, but the crowds had grown to such a size by the time the guards arrived they had to stand back fearing a riot. The Romans had warned the Sadducees who controlled the Temple area, if they suspected any suspicions of an uprising, they would enter from the tunnels out of the Castle of Antonia to quell the people with force. With Jesus teaching outside the walls of the Roman fort, the Jewish authorities could do nothing to stop this rabbi from Galilee. After the religious police had backed away, the Romans did not enter the Temple compound. The people whom I interviewed enjoyed hearing Jesus openly talk about the religious leaders' murderous intent. He said, "He who believes in me, as the Scriptures said, from his innermost being will flow rivers of living water." In response, heated debates erupted throughout the Temple courts over the true nature of Jesus. Was he a prophet or a false teacher? Was he the one Moses had predicted would come, or was he the evil one of the last days as taught by the Essenes? The leaders at the religious schools located at the Temple proclaimed that no prophet had ever ascended out of Galilee. It was an underhanded way of condemning him to the uneducated because famous prophets did come from the north such as Elijah and Elisha, two of the most celebrated prophets of the Jews. Both men did many miracles like Jesus, but not as spectacular as the ones Jesus had performed.

Hearing that the religious leaders wanted to kill Jesus burned a deeper hole in my heart against them. They were afraid of this uneducated stonemason from Galilee. I understood why they could not openly accept him as the promised Messiah; for, if they accepted Jesus, their lives would change; and they would lose a great deal of social and financial prestige.

On the second day of Tabernacles, Jesus once again arrived early at the Temple. He was once again teaching at the backcourt under the shadow of the Castle of Antonia with the Romans looking down from the parapets and towers. The scribes and the Pharisees brought a woman who was caught in adultery to Jesus while he was writing something in the dirt with his finger. Apparently she was a well-known woman in *Palestina*; she was half-dragged and then thrown at Jesus's feet amid a large group of listeners. A Sanhedrin spokesperson called out in a loud voice, "Teacher, this woman has been caught in adultery in the very act! The Law of Moses instructs we stone such a woman. What then do you say?"

The religious leaders' deceit was well hatched. It was a simple but crafty trap. Known for his compassion, Jesus would wish for this woman to be freed; but the law was clear. If he said, "kill her," then Jesus would be in conflict with the Roman overlords and their laws, which ruled all Jews in Judaea, especially when it came to the death penalty. Had the woman been taken to any Roman judge in the Empire, not one would sentence her to death for adultery. Adultery in the Empire was as common as drinking a cup of cheap wine. If Jesus even suggested the woman be put to death, he would be arrested by Rome and charged with inciting murder. Yet, does a Jew follow the teachings of Moses and disregard the law of Rome? That was the dilemma. What law overruled what statute? This was a contest between God's rules and the government's guidelines. The Scriptures taught that God Himself controlled everything, including mighty empires that were no more than a drop of water in a bucket.

The leaders persistently demanded a ruling from Jesus, who in reply continued writing in the dust. When I questioned those who could read what Jesus wrote, I was shocked to learn that it was the opening verse of the very psalm John the Baptist had quoted to me from his prison at Machaerus: "Praise Yahweh, O my soul." After long heckling by the Pharisees, Jesus finally left the words in the dry dust and slowly stood to look each man in his eyes before he said, "He who is without sin among you, let him be the first to throw a stone at her."

This was a brilliant and righteous ruling that stunned everyone. The religious men's spiteful bluster evaporated like shadows when the sun appears from behind the covering of a dark cloud. Jesus had won, but then he took the issue to a higher level. Squatting down again and using his finger, he wrote in the dirt above the words from the psalm previously etched in the dust. Consequently, the first word was that of a woman. After he had written the name, Jesus looked up into the eyes of the eldest Pharisee. The Pharisee lowered his eyes before turning away leaving the crowd. Jesus had written in reverse so that the name was all too visible for the Pharisee and others to read. Those present told me it was an eerie moment, much as it must have been for Moses on Mount Horeb watching the finger of God writing the first commandment in stone. Jesus wrote again and eyed the next eldest religious leader. He repeated the silent communication down through the ranks of those who wanted Jesus to rule on having the woman stoned for her sin. The witnesses said this process continued one by one until each accuser turned and left and all had departed. I was wondering where the man, with whom the woman was caught could be, but never asked any of those interviewed. Once all the woman's accusers had left, Jesus stood and walked up to the woman who was still sitting in the dust where she had been thrown. With Jesus's helping hand, she stood alone in the center of the court with her head bowed before Jesus and several of his disciples along with a few witnesses I had questioned. He asked, "Woman, where are they? Did no one condemn you?"

She said, "No, my Lord."

Jesus then said, "I do not condemn you either. Go; and from now on, sin no more."

On the final day of the feast, which was a Sabbath, a miracle occurred at the exact time a Temple priest poured a large pitcher of water from the pool of Siloam over the Altar of Burnt Offerings extinguishing the flames from the previous year. While the water was being gathered at the pool located in the Lower City, Jesus sent a blind man with mud on his eyes to the same spot. Jesus had applied mud made from his own spittle and dirt. This miracle was unusual because the blind man standing before Jesus with mud on his eyes was instructed to go wash in the pool of Siloam, much like Elisha of old told Naaman the leper, captain of the king of the Arameans, to go and wash in the Jordan. Once Naaman did as instructed, he was healed. The pool of Siloam was initially constructed by King Hezekiah to protect Jerusalem from a long military siege. An ingenious tunnel had been chiseled through solid rock, zigzagging under Mount Zion, permitting the Kidron Valley's Spring of Gihon to flow from outside the city walls into the Tyropeon Valley that was now protected inside the city walls. This complicated tunnel system was built to provide water for Jerusalem if and when Assyria or any other power came and put a siege on the city. After the tunnel was completed, the old spring outside the walls was hidden by debris and camouflaged with wild plantings.

Why Jesus instructed this blind man to go to this pool and wash off the mud is a mystery to me; yet, it happened just as the priests were collecting their water in the gold vessel for the Great Altar in front of the Temple. Or, the obedient blind man was washing his eyes of mud just as the ceremonial vessel was being poured out on the Great Altar. Besides these events occurring at the same time, everything at the pool of Siloam was quiet since it was a rest day. There was a massive construction project waiting to start up again on the next day. The water level was high for this time of year as springs of water can be very whimsical. During the rainy season, this spring would flow and fill the pool twice a day and was plentiful. In the late summer, it would flow once in two days and would be very low. Stone steps carved into the vertical rocky sides allowed access to the water that flowed from outside the city, no matter the season. The quiet construction project was a city program of building a tall tower around the pool. It was almost finished and would have a 20-foot high domed ceiling above the once-open aired pool. Most understood the purpose of the tower was to provide the last shield of protection in the unlikelihood the city walls fell to some future enemy. This tower would be the last and final stand for the small number of chosen ones giving them plenty of water. Besides, this pool provided the secret tunnel under the pool for the elite survivors to possibly escape the city in the likelihood the tower was breached. The primary benefactor of the building of this walled-pool project was Herod Antipas. Perhaps he wanted to protect his interest in a worst-case scenario. The only power capable of such a siege would be the

Romans; and, if a war against Rome did occur, he had a way of survival. This construction project did not go unnoticed by the Romans and was one of many reasons for the enmity between Herod and Pilate.

I am sharing all these details because, a few months after the healing incident, the tower collapsed onto the workers and some women fetching water at the pool – killing 18 in all. In my opinion, the project was doomed from the start because the foundation of the tower stood atop an old foundation of brittle stones that had been standing hundreds of years from an earlier tower over the pool. To my knowledge, this was the last time a project to enclose the pool of Siloam was undertaken. I do not remember a tower standing over the pool when General Titus stormed that part of Jerusalem in the year after the four emperors. Regarding this pool when I was a mercenary, I stayed away because the tower under construction, in my opinion, did not look safe. I am not an engineer, but this project just looked faulty from the start.

Numbers seem to be relevant to the Scriptures and God; and the meaning of 18 is something I have never really given much thought until now, many decades later. The 18 people who died was ironically the same number of years a woman was suffering from her ailment before Jesus healed her. I do remember a considerable debate ensued whether this was a judgment from Yahweh or just a fatal accident. This disastrous event did happen a few months after the blind man washed his eyes in this pool. Therefore, many common Jerusalemites proffered that this was as a punishment from God because the religious leaders had rejected the healing of the blind man told to wash the mud off his unseeing eyes at the pool of Siloam. Disaster seems to visit when there is a judgment from God; yet, the entire book of Job refutes the idea of catastrophes are always the result of sin. God explicitly does not assign a cataclysm for every evil in this age. When tragedy does happen, it could be considered an act of grace for those with eyes to see. Therefore, spiritual events in the unseen element must always be understood when one reviews the world, the realm we know by our five senses, along with our minds. Yet, once again, the very place the blind man was healed was also the place 18 soon tragically died. However, the tower and the pool of Siloam and the 18 are equal if one uses what Euclid said that both are equal to a third. To me, this all seems to be an obvious connection. Other events in the Scriptures have the number 18 attached as well as events outside the Scriptures. When this all happened was the 18th year of the rule of Tiberius. It took Herod the Great 18 months to build the temple that now stands in Jerusalem, Herod's Temple. The city of Shechem was about 18 miles from the pit into which the sons of Jacob threw their brother Joseph. The connections to these numbers may be spurious, and I have no answer to their meanings if there is even one.

I later learned that, on the day of the healing of the blind man, the Pharisees held a secret meeting with the Sadducees in the High Priestly Palace located on the south side of the Temple area. The ex-blind man and his family were brought before the religious leaders, and the ecclesiastical court ruled that the healed man was to be put out of all synagogues. Their justification was that those born blind were born entirely in sin. When the man tried to defend himself, the religious leaders ruled that a sinner could not teach them.

When the Jewish festival was over, I was able to return to my wine shop and began asking and listening to anyone who actually witnessed the events concerning Jesus during his recent visit to Jerusalem. Each time I learned something new I would later return to my room and write about these secret interrogations; I kept them in my leather psalm-tube given to me by Rabbi Issachar. I also kept all the other accounts and information about other events I learned while in Nazareth. Everything was recorded from my memory as soon as possible after the events, including my conversation with John the Baptist.

After Jesus's visit to Jerusalem in the late fall, I heard nothing again through that long winter. It wasn't until about 14 days before Passover that next spring when fresh news began spreading about the return of Jesus to Jerusalem, and many believed he would proclaim himself openly as the long-awaited Messiah. A second rumor was circulating Jerusalem concerning an old, half-blind scholar of the Sanhedrin, who lived in an obscure scripture school in the lower city. Word was he had calculated, according to the prophet Daniel, that the Messiah would come to the Temple during this Passover, the 18th year of Tiberius. The city was debating the validity of these calculations; and, of course, the Pharisees, the scribes, and priests of the Sadducees rebuked any notions of these prophecies, suggesting that Jesus could not be the promised Messiah. The religious leaders' only argument was "How could a sabbath blasphemer be the Messiah?" The discussions brought back all the things my mother told me as a child on her last day in this world. About a week before the coming Passover, I decided, instead of going to my wine shop and drinking on my next day off, I was going to find this scripture school and talk to this old master who said the Messiah was coming to Jerusalem this spring.

Five days before Passover was the next day I had off. I dressed as a Jew so I could secretly visit the scripture school without any difficulty in gaining entrance. I knew where it was since I often passed it with the frequent visits to my wine shop. It was about the third hour after sunrise, and Zoe came up to

Chapter Three

me from somewhere and stood next to me as I rapped on the heavy door. Zoe stood erect like a sleek lioness-looking dog. He had pure white fur matching his teeth; his appearance was accented by his black muzzle and nose and dark markings around his eyes that made him a spectacular-looking dog. His ears still flopped but could stand erect when he was alerted to any danger. His tail curled proudly upward in a perfect bend fanning his tail hairs like the feathers of an eagle, which gave him a majestic profile. Since I was still a fugitive, I was becoming concerned that this exceptional and extraordinary-looking dog was too easily recognized in the city. Most knew the owner was a mercenary of Herod, even though the dog roamed the street of Jerusalem alone fending for himself. However, my friendship with and love for Zoe overpowered the danger he might bring upon me. He was not exactly a friendly animal to others, just to me. He would refuse all attempts of affection. Yet, when he wanted companionship, he would curl up at my feet on nights he wished to be with me, resting his head on my leg and allowing me – and no one else – to touch him. Otherwise, there was a small growl and show of teeth to any hand reaching to contact him or me. There were times he did not growl and actually attacked people when someone reached out to pet him. I was afraid someone was going to secretly kill my dog because most Jews despised dogs due to their false interpretations of the Scriptures. Some Arabs said that spirits called the jinn would not visit any human if a dog lived in the house and these and other ideas spread amongst the Jews.

As I have already stated, Zoe protected me on several occasions. One such time was during a drill in the exercise yard of Herod's palace, Zoe almost took a chunk out of a fellow soldier's leg when we were practicing with our wooden swords. I was able to get Zoe to back down and he was not allowed in the practice yard after that event. Whenever I extracted my falcata from its scabbard, Zoe, hearing the unusual singing of metal on leather, would run to protect me. This deep loyalty always made me feel safe. Zoe many times would follow me around the city and at times would disappear only to show up a half hour or so later. He must have been using his nose to locate me no matter where I would go. I also assumed others were feeding my dog, for he never seemed hungry and never begged for food from me. He was an independent soul; yet, he recognized me as his master and respected my commands. For instance, a closed fist raised signaled for him to sit. Going from a closed fist to an open palm told Zoe to attack whatever I was looking at.

"You stay!" I ordered holding up a fisted hand as the heavy door opened at the scripture school and an elderly Jew peered out with Zoe sitting perfectly straight.

"May I help you?" came an old, squawky voice.

"I wish to ask a few questions about the Messiah."

"Yes?" he said waiting to hear more before inviting me in.

"May I come in, or do we discuss it out here on the street?"

The man cocked his head out the door moving his head up and down the street without actually looking with his eyes. Zoe growled sensing there was something wrong with the man. I guessed that Zoe was only reacting to the man's strange and suspicious actions. "Are you a Jew?" he finally asked after he was satisfied with whatever he was doing.

"A proselyte Jew wishing knowledge to satisfy my soul. *Without knowledge, my people perish.*" I quoted to show I had some limited knowledge of the Scriptures. But then again, I was not sure where I read that quote. I did hope it was in the Scriptures, and he did not ask me but opened the door for me to enter.

"Come in quickly, and bring the dog. I cannot have that creature sitting at my door waiting for you."

"Why?" I queried.

"Some wicked men are looking for the owner of a white dog. Are you that dangerous man?"

"What evil men?" I asked wondering how he knew my dog was white. I guessed he was not wholly blind after all.

"Roman soldiers to be precise; at least I think they were."

He said nothing else as I followed him inside. I told Zoe to wait just inside the door; and he curled up into a big, white ball in the cold anteroom. I followed the stooped, old man to a room with a long table that looked like a scripture room adjacent to any synagogue. On the long table, an entire scroll was unrolled and the ends weighted to keep it open. Lining the walls were hundreds of rolled manuscripts organized in square holes. There were also a number of bound *biblios* or books.

"What question do you wish to ask?"

"Are you blind?"

"*Neti-neti,*" he said.

"I am sorry; I do not recognize that word," I confessed.

"*Neti-neti* is a Sanskrit word, which means yes, but no, but yes, but no. Now, what is your other question?"

I thought it odd that our conversation started out with a Sanskrit word. Dismissing *neti-neti*, I directed my question on the subject I wished information. "Do the Holy Books state the very year and day the Messiah will present himself?"

Chapter Three

The man went to the middle of the table and picked up a metal cuneiform stylus. Using it as a pointer, he stood far away, almost arm's length, before he began lecturing about the words from the scroll laid out on the table. "The prophet Daniel states right here that the Messiah will be cut off. He will come but will die a violent death – such a violent death that a psalm says the Messiah will cry out, 'My God, My God, why hast thou abandoned me?' Very sad, but it will happen just as it is written."

"I am familiar with that psalm. It is one of the early ones written by King David, the 22nd Psalm in the Jewish Canon, I believe. The 21st in the Septuagint?"

The old man turned his head toward me in a quizzical way and smiled showing me I was correct.

"When will this happen?" I inquired with a tone of wanting to know and not just wasting his time.

"And that is all you want to know?"

"That is one of many questions."

"That is one of many questions?" he repeated with a little mirth in his voice. After his inquiry, he smiled, looked back to the table, and continued. "The Scriptures that are speaking about the future are written in a very mysterious way. Most of what is written does not make sense until the event has passed; that is, if the passage is definitely prophetic. Yet, at times, what does not seem prophetic is. The Books that the Creator has given us are the most marvelous insight mankind could ever receive. Just in assigning the number of the Hebrew alphabet to numbers and then doing simple division is a study in itself. For instance, did you know everything seems to be divisible by seven? Perhaps I can show you later how this works. There are so much more than stories to the diligent and serious student of the Word, so perhaps it is possible to predict the future. For example, it is very clear the Messiah will come to Jerusalem this year on the Passover. Mysteriously, your presence here today is not by mistake. I will explain once that water clock over next to the wall tells me it is time to leave to meet him."

I looked over to the two glass vessels of water, one above the other. The glass container that was on top had water slowly dripping from a small hole from its bottom. I noticed both glass vessels had line markings indicating the slowly changing water levels. Turning my attention back to this eccentric man, accepting him as a serious and diligent student of the Word, I had only one important question. "Passover is in a week? He will come in a week?" I asked.

"Not in a week but today. Nothing happens by accident. Knocking on my door on this morning of all mornings is not by mistake. To answer your question, today is the day of the Messiah's long-awaited visitation, not in a week. It is today. I am basing my calculations on Daniel's prophecy stating when the Messiah would present himself to Jerusalem as the King of the Jews. I counted the days beginning with a decree given by the king of Persia. I am going to confess and say it was a difficult math problem to figure out the day the Messiah would present himself to Israel as its long-awaited king."

Although this was complicated and technical, I felt maybe he knew something unique. "Trust me," he said, "today is the day, glory be to God. My reasoning is based on the math; and, besides, today the Passover lamb is to be selected for the annual Passover sacrifice in a few days. Perhaps Yahweh has sent you to me on this day, the 10th day of Nisan, which is the mystery of all mysteries."

"Why is that a mystery?"

"If a man throws a rock, the rock will fly for a distance and then fall to earth. That is just like the Word of Yahweh. God tells us what will happen, just as you know the rock will fall. To some, this is a mystery; to others with understanding, it is only an act of faith. Without faith, you cannot please Yahweh. Is it a coincidence the man with the white dog, being hunted by the Romans, comes to me on this day of all days? Is this odd, or is it just a mystery? Are you a fugitive? Are you a Zealot or both? Does not Yahweh choose the weak to confound the wise?"

Not wanting or even afraid to respond to his query, I asked, "From what direction will the Messiah enter the city?"

"Are you asking because you wish to harm this man or because you believe?"

Understanding his fears, I said, "No, I seek him as you do. I do not wish to harm him. It is true I am a fugitive, but this has nothing to do with why I am here."

He stood for a while looking directly at me almost sniffing the air like Zoe would. Finally, he was convinced of my sincerity. "He will come from the same direction King David came after he fled his evil son Absalom. He will return from the same direction the glory of God left the Temple from the north gate as stated by the Prophet Ezekiel."

"I am not familiar with either event."

"The prophet Zechariah said, on the Day of Yahweh, He will stand on that day upon the Mount of Olives. You can read his prophecy near the end of his words in the Scriptures. It appears just after it mentions the feet of Yahweh touching the mount east of Jerusalem. After his foot touches the mountain, it will split into two parts. This prophecy eludes me; but, if it is for today, expect the earth to shake like never before. Yet, even if it is for another day, today is

Chapter Three

the promised day. I was getting ready to close the school and go wait for him on the Mount of Olives near the Garden of Gethsemane, which is half the distance to the top. One of my disciples was supposed to meet me, but he has failed to show. You are welcome to accompany me in his stead. You see, my eyesight is not superb; and I have been praying for someone to help guide me. Perhaps you are the answer to my prayer, the stranger with the white dog."

"You say your eyesight is bad; yet, you can read all these scrolls, and you know I have a white dog."

"Strange, isn't it? I see at times, especially up close when reading; but, beyond the length of my arms, everything is dim. I have been this way since I was a child."

"Do you know who the Messiah is?"

"I have my opinion."

"What about the man the Romans call Jesus, who healed the blind beggar on the last day of Tabernacles at the pool of Siloam?"

"Yes, I remember that day. I actually spoke on behalf of this Jesus to the Sanhedrin. The man from Nazareth proclaimed on the last day, the great day of the feast, saying, 'If anyone is thirsty, let him come to me and drink. He who believes in me, as the Scriptures says, out of his heart will flow rivers of living water.' The Sanhedrin wanted him arrested; but I said, 'Does not our law judge a man before it hears him and knows what he is doing?' From the crowd of religious leaders, the captain of the Temple rudely asked me if I were a Galilean. I am guessing he was asking if I were a secret follower of this Jesus. Between you, me, and your dog, I am a secret disciple of this Galilean; but I am afraid to tell them. The Messiah could be this Jesus you speak of, or it very well could be someone no one knows. And today, if my calculations are correct, my new friend, I will know for sure who is the Messiah. The important point is now we are going to the Mount of Olives to see for ourselves. You know, it is my duty to show the Creator there are those who study the Word of God and believe what it says. Does this make any sense to you?"

"I understand, but indulge me for a moment. Why do you think the Messiah might be Jesus?"

The old man was silent; then he smiled before he answered. "It was a year or so back when Jesus healed a man at the pool near the Sheep Gate. It was the healing at the pool on the Sabbath, which caused a considerable controversy here in Jerusalem."

I moved my head indicating I was aware of this event but did not tell him I witnessed this very miracle. Apparently the old man did not see my expression, for he continued.

"Many Jews were persecuting Jesus because he did this healing on the Sabbath. Afterward, I went to hear him teach in Solomon's Porch that stands before the Temple thinking that he was going to be arrested and that I would never get to meet him. I found him speaking freely; and Jesus answered his critics by saying, 'My Father is working until now, and I am working.' I could tell you that his words cut deep into my soul. Many Jews who were present wanted to kill him and not for just breaking the Sabbath but because he was even calling God his own Father making himself equal with God. Jesus spoke as no prophet has ever spoken in the Scriptures. Then he said something I will never forget. He said, 'You search the Scriptures because you think that in them you have eternal life, and it is they that bear witness about me; yet, you refuse to come to me that you may have life.' After he had spoken those words, I returned to this very room; and I began searching the Scriptures differently."

To let this old man know I was listening, I just muttered, "Hum."

After I noticed a slight twinkle in his eyes, he continued. "Since then I have looked at God's Word very carefully, and he was right. The Scriptures are like a sealed treasure that can be understood only if you have the code. Jesus gave me the code that day. The Scriptures are all about Him. You see Adam, you see the Messiah. He is Abraham. He is Jacob and Joseph. He is Moses, and he is the Son of the blessed one. Jesus has to be the Messiah. He is the son of David, which is another prophecy of the Messiah. He is the mighty counselor. He is God with us. He is David, who was rejected by the Jews under his own son Absalom. David returned by coming from the east over the Mount of Olives, so Jesus will come back from that direction. It is all straightforward, really, once you understand the code. Now, on this very day, the Messiah is prophesied to enter Jerusalem; and He will come over the Mount of Olives. I believe this Jesus is the one who is coming today as foretold hundreds of years ago by the prophet Daniel. I go today, not to improve my eyes, but to be among those who study the Word of God and believe what it says. Do you understand?"

"What assistance do you require?"

"Let me hold onto your arm, and you can be my eyes. Perhaps we both will meet the Messiah today, whoever he may be."

"Let's say I am curious enough to investigate your calculations." The old scholar smiled at my declaration.

I left with this man holding onto my arm and Zoe following silently at a distance. I felt a little ridiculous, but why not humor this old Jew in his quest. Either he was right, or his mind was with the pixies and fairies. I had to admit to myself that going with this old scholar was better than getting sadly inebriated at my wine shop.

We left the city by the Water Gate where the spring of Gihon had once stood but was now covered over, and its location today remains a hidden mystery. We walked down a well-worn path into the Kidron Valley toward the retaining wall next to the eastern side of the Temple compound, which from where we stood to the northern corner is about the same length of one side of the Circus Maximus in Rome. Once we reached the juncture of the road leading toward the Golden Gate and the other way going up to the Mount of Olives, the old scholar said that he needed to rest. We sat for a while on some flat stones that made up a crude structure that was circular in fashion with only one entrance. I asked the old man about the structure, and he told me it was a sheep pen; and the door was where the shepherd would sleep at night while guarding his flock. The shepherd and his sheep were apparently out looking for food and water and would be back at evening.

The old scholar's breathing was labored, and I wondered how he was going to climb up the Mount of Olives. The grade of the hill was quite steep. After a while, the redness in his cheeks receded, and his breathing leveled out. I did not want to rush him, and he did not seem to be in a hurry. He began looking around, and a smile came to his face along with a twinkle in his blue eyes.

"What is it you are thinking about?" I queried.

"King Josiah is whom I was thinking about. Are you familiar with him?"

"Never heard of him," I confessed realizing again there was much I still needed to learn about this land and its history. Even Amcheck knew more than I did about ancient stories of this country and its people. "Tell me about this king," I requested wanting to learn. I experienced a warm feeling deep in my chest as if I were back at the Lyceum. A strange peace came upon me, and I'm sure my old companion detected my sense of learning from the eagerness in my voice.

"King Josiah was the 17th descendant of the Davidic Dynasty, one of the very few good kings from the loins of Judah. Hilkiah, the high priest at that time, discovered the Book of the Law in the House of Yahweh, hidden and forgotten in the Holy of Holies, the room beyond the thick curtain. When King Josiah learned of the discovery, he became excited; but, soon after the words of the lost books were read to him, especially the last book of the Torah called Deuteronomy, he ripped his clothes from top to bottom. No one had heard these words for many years, and they spoke of the judgment of God when His words were not obeyed. It had to have been the covenant curses and the threat of exile that disturbed the king because he understood how his people, the people of God, had forgotten Yahweh. King Josiah sent a delegation to seek a word from a renowned prophetess named Huldah, who lived in the Second Quarter of Jerusalem, over in the northwest part of this walled city. When she learned what happened, she explained that her answer came directly from Yahweh. 'The Lord was not happy, and what was read to King Josiah from the lost books of Yahweh would come to pass. The inhabitants of the land had forsaken God and had burned incense to other gods. Yahweh's wrath burned against Jerusalem and all the surrounding regions, and this wrath would never be quenched.' Am I boring you, young man?"

"Quite the opposite – this is all very fascinating." Even Zoe had sat at my feet with his tongue hanging out as he looked up at the old man; Zoe looked like he had an enormous smile on his face as the old man spoke. Maybe Zoe was confused by the old man's eyes that matched the color of the sky that was behind his head. I know I am projecting my own thoughts onto my dog, but it was an odd sensation that appeared like looking through his eyes and seeing the blue sky beyond. I decided to direct the old man's thoughts back to his story. "What happened next in response to the prophetic words?"

"The great reforms of Josiah came next. The king gathered all the elders of Judah and Jerusalem. All the people, the priests, and the prophets, great and small, gathered at Solomon's Temple in the area known as Solomon's Porch, which is just above where we now sit. The lost books of Moses were read for all to hear. Afterward, King Josiah ordered to be burned all the vessels that were made for Baal; for Asherah; for the sun, moon, and all the constellations; and for the many hosts of heaven. The ashes of the fires were dumped into the Kidron Valley landing right where we now sit. Later the ashes were gathered up and carried to the town of Bethel and scattered there. Josiah took all the Asherah poles, statues of the naked goddess Asherah, and burned them right here as well in the Kidron. Those ashes were spread on those tombs of the common people you perhaps can see over there. Then the house of the male cult prostitutes, which was also up above us near the House of Yahweh, was destroyed. Those stones were also tossed down here where we sit. Perhaps the very stones we are sitting on were part of those evil places. Josiah also tore apart the altars atop the Temple and on the tops of the surrounding buildings. The high places upon the Mount of Olives that King Solomon had erected for some of his wives from the Sidonians, who worshipped the goddess Ashtoreth; the Moabites, who worshipped Chemosh; and the Ammonites, who worshipped the god Molech, were turned to rubble. Do you know the Valley of Hinnom where the city burns its refuse?"

I indicated I did but said that I had never seen it. Before the next year was to end, I would become well acquainted with this valley of perpetual fires.

"Josiah even destroyed the ovens in the Valley of Hinnom, the valley to the south beyond the City of David. In those days the Hebrews, instead of circumcising their sons on the eighth day, were burning their first-born males on the eighth day to the god Molech by placing their sons in the hands of the bronze statue of the god Molech that was heated from the inside with fire. King Josiah had the ovens of Molech destroyed, and the practice of child sacrifice was forbidden."

"What about the child sacrificing that occurred for centuries in the Phoenician city of Carthage?"

"That is an interesting observation. Child sacrificing is so evil that even the heartless Romans were used by Yahweh to destroy Carthage a few hundred years ago, for Carthage practiced the same abomination. Was not Carthage razed to the ground and the land sowed with salt hundreds of years ago? Did you know tens of thousands of graves still exist on the plains of Carthage and are filled with the bones of infant children who were sacrificed to the Phoenician god Dagon? I have been told the graves go underground for several levels. Child sacrificing is one of the great sins we humans commit against our Creator of the Universe. In His wrath, Yahweh will even use an evil people to overwhelm another corrupt society, which is immersed in such corruption. The prophet Habakkuk teaches as much."

"Perhaps you are correct. I, too, believe Yahweh used the Romans to destroy evil Carthage; and maybe Yahweh will use the Romans again to destroy this city. The question is, who is going to destroy the Romans?"

"It is all unfortunate. It would make sense if Yahweh used the Romans like he used the Babylonians against Jerusalem. Just like a bowl cleaned and turned upside down, it will happen again here in Jerusalem. And God will deal with Rome, but Daniel indicates that Rome will change over time and still be present in a different form at the end of time."

"Did Yahweh punish Josiah when he showed such repentance?"

"Josiah did die an early death – another sorrowful mystery."

"Was it because he returned to the ancient gods like Solomon?"

"He died for a different failing. Josiah was told by Yahweh not to interfere with the Egyptian army that was marching along the International Highway to fight the Babylonians. Josiah's sin was he had an alliance with the Babylonians. Because of that alliance, he felt obligated. He was trusting in arms of flesh and blood, not in Yahweh. Consequently, Josiah died in judgment at the hands of the Egyptians on the plains of Megiddo. After Josiah's death, Yahweh used those very same Babylonians to punish Judah just like Habakkuk predicted. Many survivors from Judah and Jerusalem were deported to regions around the Euphrates River. Yet, the good news was the prophet Daniel wrote his prophecies from that foreign land that brings us here today." Standing up without any help, the old man declared, "We should be on our way lest we miss the Messiah."

Halfway up the hill was as far as the old man could go. He stopped to get his breath at the familiar gate that led into the Garden of Gethsemane. I felt a quick sting of sadness as I thought of Eli standing at this spot but it flew away when I realized the old scholar was panting with visible trouble and looking extremely flushed. When I asked if he was having difficulty breathing, he said he was fine. "We will wait for the Messiah here. The main road passes by this garden, and my hope is the Messiah will stop here so we can speak with him." I looked around; and I could not see anyone waiting for anyone, let alone the Messiah. A camel caravan of about fifty camels came down the road and kicked up a lot of dust – but no Messiah. There were other people, mostly pilgrims coming down the narrow way for the Passover, Feast of Unleavened Bread, and First Fruits. I did the math in my head and calculated that Passover would begin in five days. Goatskin tents were standing off the road, and some children were playing on some boulders not far from us; but no one looked like he or she expected a king to be marching by at any moment. I felt embarrassed had someone asked me why I was here.

The old man found an excellent rock to sit upon, and Zoe was sniffing around some bushes when all of a sudden his head furrowed and his ears stood erect. I looked up toward where his long nose was pointed; and all I could see was a group of women coming over the ridge from the direction of Bethpage, a small village just beyond the crown of the hill. The time of day had to be at least four hours since the morning sacrifice, and there was not a cloud in the sky. A sharp horn blast came from the Temple area and my attention shifted toward the city. Not knowing what it meant I turned my attention back toward Zoe, and noticed his eyes were still fixed on the group of female travelers. Then abruptly, for no apparent reason, he let out a short, heartfelt cry and bolted like a runaway horse toward the women. He was whining as he ran. I called after him, but he did not obey. When he reached the startled group, one woman put out a hand; and Zoe began licking it. I had feared he was going to bite someone, but his tail was wagging happily. The woman was bent at the knees in a most graceful movement, and Zoe began licking her laughing face. The woman's hood, which had been hiding her face, fell back; and I was startled to recognize Messina. I froze in shock and felt my heart pounding like the heart of a little boy finding a beloved lost toy. Zoe turned and ran back toward me yelping and still wagging his tail. How he remembered her, I had no idea. He had only been a young pup of a few weeks when Messina last saw him and that was one year ago. Reaching my side, Zoe pranced around me throwing his long legs up and out like a dancing horse. I finally heard Messina let out a loud gasp from where she was up above me. She apparently recognized the owner of the white dog. She left the group and moved somewhat unladylike toward me, also laughing with delight.

I just stood with my stomach feeling like it was up in my throat while I watched Messina running. Frozen in a strange sensation, I felt like someone who had just won a fortune at the Circus Maximus in an impossible wager. When she reached Zoe and me, she wrapped her arms around my neck nearly knocking me down. Her hair smelled of spring air touched with jasmine. I was taken over by sensations of joy, the likes I had never thought possible. After I had spun her around in a couple of circles, she let go and just smiled up at me. We just looked at each other smiling until the other women in her group arrived.

"Who is this?" asked an older woman who seemed to be the leader of the rest.

Messina turned with a playful smile and made a declaration that unnerved me. "This is the man I will marry someday."

"Does he believe in the Master?" asked the same woman in a disbelieving tone.

Messina turning back to me said, "Venu, this is Miriam, the mother of Jesus, the man who is from Nazareth, the man you told me to find and follow."

I looked at the woman who had asked the question and tried to fathom what I had just heard. There was a strange, incommodious silence before the woman spoke again. I looked for a resemblance to her father, the old man with whom I had talked in Nazareth next to the old sycamore tree in front of the synagogue; and I did not see any resemblance, except perhaps in her chin and forehead. "I am glad to meet the future husband of Messina, but do you believe in my son?" she asked again.

Unpleasant thoughts began to flood my mind after hearing, now twice, her abrupt question. Didn't Messina just tell her I sent her to find and follow her son? But I knew why I had not answered her; it was because of what I knew about her. Her own father told me she was standing against her son thinking he had lost his senses. I found myself reaching into my "ugly bag" to throw something back at her. I seemed to have acquired a much bigger "black bag" of insults ever since John the Baptist was murdered and my somewhat unpleasant visit to Nazareth. Grillius had taught me how to kill or maim a man in the blink of an eye, but who taught me how to hurl poisonous darts that would sink deeper than my throwing knives? I knew Grillius would disapprove of my tongue these days, but for some reason I told myself that I did not care what he thought. At the thought of Grillius, a strange sadness came over me as I realized I missed him and Hector. The deaths of my mother and Claudia flashed before me along with the death of the man I had killed with my dagger on the lane leading to my father's villa and the two Zealots in the streets of Jerusalem. A whispered memory momentarily glinted in my mind about the chopping away of Marius's forearm, and I relived what I perceived to be the last moments of John the Baptist before the executioner delivered his head to Herod Antipas on a silver platter. My flaring emotions ended with my words from the "ugly bag" being whipped at the mother of Jesus. "Maybe you should ask yourself the same question. Do you believe? Last I heard; you thought your son had lost his senses and had gone to bring him home."

"Venu!" cried Messina stepping away from me. "What is this cruelness that has come over you? Did you not tell me to find the man from Nazareth?"

"No, Messina, he is right," said the mother of Jesus as she lowered her eyes. With her 50-something head now bowed, she told me she had repented for that; but I had a right to ask. She then slowly lifted her eyes with a new boldness and posed the same question but in a much softer tone. "But you still have not answered my question, and then I will answer yours."

She was a brave and intelligent woman, and I now noticed more of a resemblance she shared with her son. The long face and the eyes were the same. Only the nose was different.

"Was he really virgin born?" I inquired.

"Venu, please!" blurted out Messina now standing next to Miriam.

"No, Messina, an honest question," said Miriam. "And the answer is yes. Gabriel, the angel, visited me when I was just a young girl; and he told me I was going to be with child. I thought this was an odd statement coming from an angel. You see, at that time I was the wife of Joseph, the son of Jacob; but the marriage had not been consummated since I was too young to reproduce. Joseph had been a widower, an older man who had purchased me from my father's home. I am now guessing that you were the one who spoke to my father in Nazareth, the day the news arrived of the death of our beloved John. My father told me about you. He was impressed because you had a profound interest in my son."

"Yes, I enjoyed my time with your father; how is he?"

"He is back in Nazareth and doing fine. Thank you for asking."

"Regarding your original question, I have twice spoken with your son. I want to believe, and I do thirst for the 'living water' only Yeshua says he can give."

"When the man I was betrothed discovered I was with child, he knew he had not known me. He was a good man and tried to return the marriage fee back to my father. But an angel had visited him in a dream and said to keep me and raise the child. The angel also instructed that the child was to be named Yeshua, who is now called Jesus."

"A fascinating story if true," I said. "I've heard of your son's great works and even witnessed one. I do not think he does this in the power of Satan. But will your son present himself today as the Anointed One, the Messiah? I'm waiting here with this old man for no other reason than to see the promised Messiah."

"He is coming now over the crest of the hill with his disciples. Maybe you should ask him yourself," she said looking over her shoulder.

Looking to where she was facing, I noticed for the first time our conversation drew condemning glances from those passing nearby. Men did not usually speak freely with women, especially outside their own families; and here we were talking on a public road.

I turned to this older, assertive woman and openly apologized for being ill-mannered. I said in a broken and low voice, "I have been rude and I am sure rudeness is not love. Besides, the Scriptures say there will be a king who will reign righteously, and no longer will a fool be called noble. Perhaps this is that time. Please forgive me for my hasty words."

"If you have repented as you say, I will forgive you," she said very sweetly. "But, it seems like you changed the subject."

"My repentance is genuine," I said with heartfelt sincerity that even surprised me. I then looked up once again toward the approaching group of men using the road that would pass next to the Garden of Gethsemane. After a few moments of looking, I turned and said to Miriam, "But allow me to say this. If he is the long-awaited Messiah-king and only this old man and I are the only ones from this great city waiting for him, then Jerusalem is cursed, yes cursed, even more so than after the days of King Josiah when the Babylonians came and destroyed Solomon's Temple."

The old, half-blind scholar spoke up for the first time. "You are right. Judgment is not far away and rightfully so; for this is the long-awaited day of visitation, and who is ready?"

No one answered, and everyone became quiet. I moved toward the old sage guiding him off the road toward the gate at the small garden. Waiting next to the old man, I recognized Jesus in the center of his students looking like he did that day at the pool called Bethesda. He was wearing a simple homespun robe, a purple sash at the waist, and sandals. Over his robe, he wore a brownish cloak that had a beautiful design weaved into the borders. They were geometric designs that I had never seen before on anyone's robe or cloak. I thought for a moment that this could be a popular item in Rome. Little square patterns stood out because of the use of darker threads, with more extensive diagonal lines, producing six-sided stars. These skillfully embroidered motifs looked like two pyramids turned up and overlapping each other. His beard was a little longer than last time, and his hair was now resting on his shoulders. I recognized more graying at the temples or maybe more silver over gray. His expression was mournfully sober, even though his disciples were in a happy mood on this beautiful morning. When I took my eyes off Jesus and found Messina, she was looking intently at the man in the white homespun robe with purple sash and uniquely designed darker outer coat. She, like his disciples, seemed convinced that he was the promised Messiah; and this was a historic moment. Standing next to Messina was Miriam, also proud; but I wasn't sure she understood the serious dilemma that awaited Jerusalem or her son. I then remembered the old man at his scripture school saying something about the Messiah being "cut off." I looked toward the old man; and he looked at me, perhaps understanding the evil implications of Jesus's fate.

As we waited, I leaned toward the semi-blind scholar and described what Jesus looked like. He smiled at my detailed description. When Jesus and his students arrived, the master first addressed the women with a kind word and a smile. Then he turned and looked toward the old man, walked over, and put his right hand on the scholar's shoulder. "Are you the only one waiting on this day of visitation?"

"I believe it is just I and this young man with me, my Lord."

I was shocked by his use of the word *Lord*, for this was consistent with a divine title. Actually, it was the same title told to me about the woman caught in adultery when she, too, had addressed Jesus as *Lord* after she was asked, "Where are those who condemn you?"

"Where is the rest of the city?" asked Jesus as if he did not hear the old man's declaration.

I kept my mouth shut but wanted to say something like "They all lack faith." My own conscience convicted me since my heart was just as hard as the rest of Jerusalem. I was here only because of curiosity, not faith. Maybe this was what Miriam detected. She seemed to love Messina and only wanted to protect her from this hard-hearted man Messina had just declared she was

Chapter Three

going to marry. Nevertheless, seeing Messina gave me great joy and hope. If Jesus were the Messiah, this was a moment in history that would be talked about forever. Realizing this, I began memorizing every line on Jesus's face. For a moment, I teased with the idea that maybe it was not a coincidence I was here, that he was the long-awaited Messiah, and that I was chosen to be here. It was at this point my many thoughts were interrupted and I moved towards Messina just to be near her.

"Rabbi, Rabbi!" cried out a voice from an old man in the midst of a small group of boys, climbing quickly from the direction of Jerusalem and the Golden Gate that exited out of the Temple complex. We all grew quiet as this group neared. The clothes and grooming revealed they were Jewish students, and the older man must be their teacher from one of the temple schools. Perhaps they were out on an outing. "Rabbi! Please wait!" said the teacher once again.

When they reached us, we all listened, including Jesus's disciples, who were now gathered around their teacher. Jesus's disciples were much older and a motley group compared with the temple students who had come with their teacher. "Rabbi, we came to warn you. Just a few hours ago at the morning sacrifice, some Galileans were murdered by Pilate's troops near the North Gate of the Temple. It happened without warning, and the Romans butchered everyone waiting to sacrifice. It was a repeat of what happened a year ago during the aqueduct protest in the *agora* area in front of the Castle of Antonia. It was unbelievable, the blood and the screaming. The Romans claimed there was a riot, but it is all a lie. The atmosphere right now is extremely dangerous at the Temple. It is especially treacherous for you; do not enter the Temple compound today. Please listen to me. These boys and I are witnesses. We left the Court of Gentiles and spotted you coming down from the direction of Bethpage. You, I believe, are the miracle worker from Nazareth, which makes you a Galilean."

I was stunned by this report and looked over the deep valley toward the Temple compound; and, contrary to the rabbi's testimony, all appeared peaceful. Smoke was ascending from the Great Altar into the morning sky, just like any other morning.

All eyes returned to Jesus to see his response to this disturbing news. He waved his arm toward the Temple and asked the teacher and his students, "Do you think that these Galileans were sinners above all others because they suffered this way? No, I tell you; but, unless you repent, you will all likewise perish." He pointed to the Kidron Valley toward the city of David that was down below us and over a little to the south and continued. "Or those 18 on whom fell the tower in Siloam. Do you suppose they were guiltier than all the others living in Jerusalem? I tell you, no! But, unless you repent, you, too, will perish." His sweeping gaze stopped on me. I lowered my head; having no strength to look at him because I sensed he knew my heart and shame. I had previously concluded the 18 died because they were all sinners deserving what had happened. Now I wondered why I was not among the dead. Wasn't I just as much a sinner?

When I did raise my eyes, Jesus was no longer looking at me. He was staring toward the Temple. Lifting his hands in what looked like a troubled man praying, he said in a loud and commanding voice, "Now this is the great day of visitation – and only if the city knew. Nevertheless, I shall show compassion. Listen, and remember. A certain man had a fig tree planted in his vineyard and came seeking fruit in it and did not find any." Jesus was now pointing off to the south to a lone fig tree all leafed out growing on the side of another route from Bethpage running down toward the Horse Gate. "And he said to the vineyard keeper, 'Behold, three years I have come looking for fruit on this fig tree without finding any. Cut it down! Why should it use up the soil?' But the vinedresser answered saying to him, 'Lord, leave it also this year until I may dig around it and put in dung; and, if, indeed, it makes fruit next year, fine; but if not, cut it down.'"

What a strange but simple story. I wondered what it meant. Looking at each disciple they all looked muddled, also seeking to understand. I noticed Jesus had again used the word *Lord* in his story. He said nothing more and turned back toward the direction from where he had come. His disciples seemed somewhat puzzled, but they also said nothing and began following their teacher going back up the hill back toward Bethpage and beyond. The schoolmaster, wagging his head in bewilderment, also turned and quickly returned to Jerusalem with his young disciples in tow. Messina said something to her group of women as if to wait, for they all stood silently; and she came over to face me. With tearful eyes and her voice filled with sadness, she asked, "Venu, do you understand what he just said?"

"I need to repent or end up like my friend Eli, whom I rescued in Rome, but only to see him murdered a couple of years ago right where the Galileans were slaughtered this morning. I will be honest with you; I did not comprehend a word he just said," I confessed. "I feel thoughtless when I am around that man in his white priestly robe with the beautiful embroidery around the neck."

"Fear not, this is what I understand," she said with genuine conviction. "I joined Jesus one year ago as you instructed just after John the Baptist was murdered. Yes, I was present when the Baptist died, and it was horrible; and I don't believe he died because he was a sinner. The morning after his death I secretly arranged to travel from Machaerus with a caravan going north along the Jordan Valley Road. I left without the knowledge of Lentulus or Marius, and I did as you said; I found Jesus with a mass of people north of the Sea of Galilee. Everyone was starving, all those who had traveled to hear Jesus speak. Everyone was like me, stunned by the news of the death of John. Then a great miracle occurred. With just a few fish and some bread, almost ten thousand people ate their fill. Some woman told me that this event marked the second year of Jesus's public mission. It had officially started two Passovers earlier in Jerusalem when Jesus cleansed the Temple of the moneychangers and presented himself to the Hebrew religious system. When the Passover arrives in a few days, Jesus's public ministry will end its third year."

I looked at Messina with stunned silence. When she asked me if I now understood the parable, I nodded my head that I might. When she asked me to explain it, I had trouble finding my tongue; but when I did speak, Messina just smiled at my understanding. "Jesus is the gardener. For three years Jesus has been looking for fruit. Israel as a nation must be the fig tree?"

"And the house of Israel has no fruit!" explained Messina.

"I see what you are saying," blurted out the old scholar who was listening as well as the group of women, who began to confirm Messina's understanding. The old scholar continued, "So Jesus has given the House of Israel an extension of an extra year, one more year for the nation to repent and receive its Messiah. Next year at this time, he will return again to inspect the proverbial fig tree."

"Yes, that has to be what he means," said Miriam for the first time since her son had left with his disciples.

"But," I said, "If there is no fruit of repentance next year, the fig tree will be uprooted."

"True again," said the old scholar. "But there is always hope that will not happen. Oh, such grace Yahweh has given to the House of Israel."

"But Old Man," I queried, "can Jesus change what has been prophesied over centuries ago?"

"I know what you are thinking. You come back with me to my school, and I will show you several Scriptures that might explain this extra year extension."

"God knew there was going to be an extra year?" I asked still trying to understand how the future worked in God's prophecies.

The old scholar said with a smile, "God knows everything, and He anticipated this was going to happen. Everything that is necessary for us humans to understand has been prophesied in the Scriptures. Or, should I say, nothing happens by mistake; and fatalism does not factor into God's sovereignty."

I pressed the scholar. "Old Man, do you think Jesus is the Creator visiting His own handiwork?" I was basing this on the story Felix shared at the Rome tavern concerning Miriam's father and his question to Jesus years ago.

He smiled a broad spread of teeth only a rich man could own. He looked blankly up into the blue sky with those eyes of the same color. "The nation of Judah and Israel has for most of its history been addicted to ritualism. This obscures God's actual purpose for man. God has always wanted His Chosen Ones to defeat the god of this world, which can only be done by being obedient and showing mercy to the afflicted. Yahweh is more interested in us humans showing mercy, walking humbly with Him, and showing kindness to the weak rather than sacrificing and performing rituals. Based on what this young lady has just said, I think the world has only one more year. And, if Jerusalem does not accept this man for who he is, then this city along with the Temple and all the magnificent buildings of this city will inevitably be destroyed. Most of the citizens will be either killed or taken into captivity just as Nebuchadnezzar did to our people years ago. However, this time it will be the Romans; and it will be far worse if that is even possible. One more year – that is our hope. Now, young man, please help me back to my scrolls; and I will show you what I mean."

I turned and looked at Messina; and she said, "I will meet you here next year, and then we will decide what to do with our lives."

"Why not run away now?"

"And miss the great repentance? We will all be a witness in one year; the city will see who he is and accept him. Can you not see? God is giving the Jews incredible grace and time to understand. Next year, Venu, I will meet you right here on this day, right where we are standing at this very hour."

Without saying she loved me and showing any sign of affection, she turned and joined the women who were now only a few steps away. The combined group of women began climbing toward the crest of the Mount of Olives. I turned away and helped the old man down toward the city. I looked over my shoulder once we reached the bottom of the Kidron Valley, and I saw Zoe trotting next to the group of women. He had chosen Messina over me. My life seemed in shambles; and I, like the fig tree of Jerusalem, had only one year to work out this mysterious enigma: who was this man Jesus?

When we reached the Water Gate, many Roman soldiers were standing around looking at the people coming and going through the massive gate. I lowered my head to hide my face.

"Tribune Demos, there is the white dog we are looking for – up there near the top of that hill!" called out a Roman soldier sitting on a beautiful black stallion pointing his right hand upward. I looked at whom he was talking; and there was my old nemesis, Demos, splendid in a Roman officer's uniform sitting astride a red horse. I began to withdraw a throwing knife to kill Demos, but at least a dozen soldiers were standing around him. It would be suicide if I tried.

"Is not that the man from Galilee next to the white dog?" asked the same soldier to Demos. "Was not there a rumor the Messiah was to show today?"

"No!" yelled a Pharisee with a few scribes standing with him who were listening to the Romans at the gate. "That man up there is coming in accord with the activity of Satan. He comes with power, signs, and false wonders but wonders from the prince of the air, not heaven."

The words of the Pharisee stung me. Who really was the one coming in the power of Satan? It had to be me; for I wanted to kill Demos, the Roman soldiers, and all the religious fools! But the old blind scholar would be implicated and imprisoned for a very long time, unable to meet Jesus next year. I restored the dagger and continued through the Water Gate steering the old man with my left hand.

I turned one last time from the throat of the gate to look at the crest of the Mount of Olives. I let the old man walk on as I studied everything. Zoe seemed like a puppy again as the man with the purple sash stroked my dog's head. The small entourage of women had now reached Jesus and his disciples. The skyline briefly outlined them all before they slowly vanished behind the hill. After the group had disappeared over the rise, I felt alone as never before. An enemy stood only feet away, and I chose not to kill him. My dog had deserted me; but, by his doing so, I was now alive and free. And the woman I loved was gone for one more year. I knew that what was yet to come depended on my accepting or rejecting the one whom John the Baptist had pointed and proclaimed as the Lamb of God

JOHN LAWRENCE BURKS

THE RIDGE ROAD

PART SIX

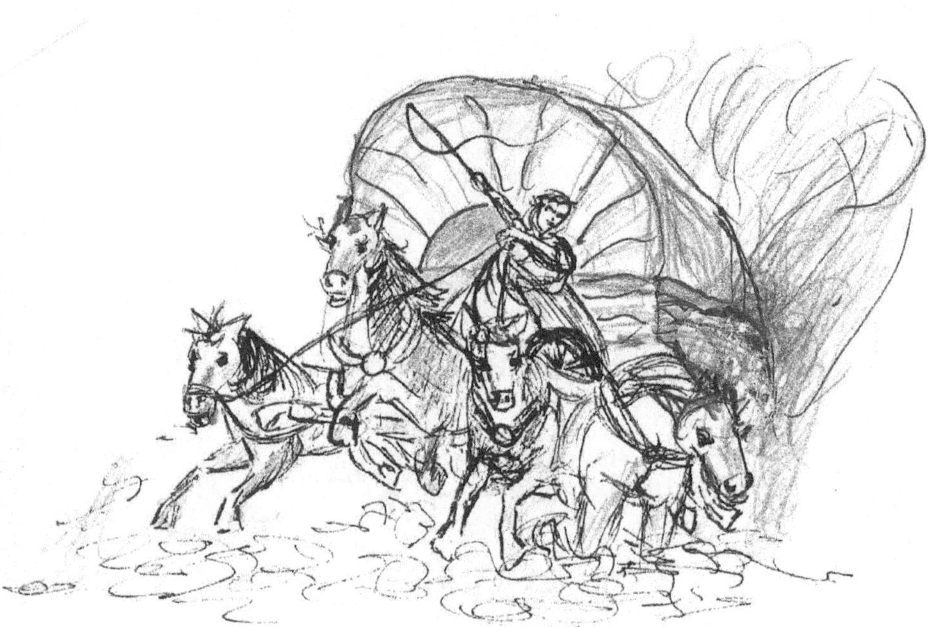

CHAPTER FOUR

Jerusalem – Mercury's Day, or the 5th day of the week to the Jews; five days before Passover. Tiberius's 18th year as Roman Emperor. Pontius Pilate's 6th year as Prefect of Judaea. Passover will mark the end of the 3rd year of the public ministry of Jesus of Nazareth. A one-year extension has been given to the nation of Israel to repent and accept its Messiah, coming five days before the start of the Feast of Unleaven Bread.   *(32 AD)*

He who fears every ambush falls into none.   Pubilius Syrus

My morning meeting on the Mount of Olives with Messina, Jesus, and his mother will always remain in my memory as one of my most glorious days; yet, what happened afterward in the early afternoon will go down as one of the darkest of my life. How, in just a few hours, two extremes went beyond my understanding. For instance, I confess that, even after meeting Jesus, talking to his mother, and touching Messina, I also wanted to kill Demos at the Water Gate. It would take more time for a man to drink a cup of water than it would for me to have struck down Demos with my knife. This prospect of extreme emotions still plagues me regarding our human feelings jumping from one excessive to the other almost simultaneously. The sight of Demos sitting smugly on his red horse boasting with his officers and preening in his Roman tribune uniform as if he were the *prefect* of Jerusalem himself still brings bile to my mouth when I recall the moment. I do not know why considering an old man's needs over my own evil desires reigned supreme that late morning and guided me away from the Water Gate, but it did. However, this kind act for an old man did alter my life in a direction I could never have predicted or even imagined.

Once the scholar and I reached his modest yet palatial domicile-school, the old man graciously invited me in. After he closed the door, I stood in the anteroom where Zoe had slept earlier. The teacher shuffled past me, and I just stood with my heart torn realizing I had lost my dog and the woman I loved. I tried to convince myself that it was for only one year and it was for my own protection that Zoe had gone with Messina. I felt a bony hand on my shoulder, and the man said he was grateful for my assistance today. I began wondering if I hurried I could run to the barracks at Herod's Palace and retrieve all my money. Then I might find Jesus, Messina and my dog. When I asked about seeing the promised Scriptures, the old Jew proceeded to tell me he had grown tired and needed to rest. I bit back my anger thinking this was an empty reward for not killing Demos. Now I was fighting a new rage wondering why I didn't leave him to fend for himself at the Water Gate and take Demos down.

"My young friend, please understand. Next time we come together, I will share all that I can with you about the Messiah. Perhaps you can return and share the Passover meal with me in a few days, and we will go over everything then. Yes, we will celebrate together right here. What do you say? I have an invitation to share the Passover meal with the high priest, but I will withdraw my invite. We will be alone and undisturbed. What do you say?"

I remained silent, which is a form of communication and not a very nice one at that. It is a rude thing to do to someone. I could see the hurt in the old man; and, in some perverse way, I was glad. However, if he were hurt, he was gracious enough not to show it. Instead, in his wisdom, he spoke about something else to alleviate the tension. "You are a young believer of the Holy Books and Scrolls. Trust me when I tell you this is what pleases God. Being young and innocent in the Word of God is not a sin. You must understand that it will take many years to grasp just a little of what it has to offer. As Jesus said, the Scriptures are all about him. Remember the code, and this entire world will pass away; but not God's Word nor the code. We have eternity to learn and understand. Now I will thank you again for your help; however, I will leave you with this one truth. Father Jacob, who wrestled with God at the Jabbok River many centuries ago, refused to stop struggling until he was disabled in his hip by only a touch from God. The only explanation was Jacob knew 'the man' with whom he was wrestling could only be God, who had taken a human form and somehow had entered into Jacob's time. With this faith, he was not going to let go until God blessed him."

"Did God bless him?" I asked.

"God did bless Jacob and changed his name to Israel, which means 'he who struggles with God'; it can also be translated 'Prince of God.' Many years before the event at the Jabbok River, Jacob, with deceit in his heart, longed for the birthright to this land and the blessing from Isaac his father, which he had stolen from his elder brother with a pot of stew. God keeps the books in Heaven, and Jacob was given to the wrong woman when he first married. She was a woman he never loved, but Jacob did not learn his lesson. God is a loving God with whom we wrestle in this short life of ours, but in the end we all end up crippled after fighting for the blessings we already have. Second, we reap what we sow. Never forget this one maxim, and it will serve you well. Here is an intimate maxim: *sin brings disgrace.* That is what God is telling you to remember: *sin brings disgrace.*"

"You used the Greek word *sin,* which means the distance from one point to another; or do you mean the Babylonian name for the moon god Sin?"

"Knowledge will never save anyone. Was not Eve looking for knowledge in the Garden of Eden? However, for the sake of your understanding of the word *sin,* both definitions would be correct; but let us stick to the Greek meaning. *Sin* is commonly associated with Euclid, the father of geometry, who referred to the distance between two points. This term *sin* describes how far away you are from God. You see, God wants everyone to cease from his or her sins; but it is difficult when we humans are separated from God. Knowing that we all have *sin,* or all standing at different distances from God's standard, should evoke *metaneon.*"

"*Metaneon,* the Greek word that means to change your thinking?"

"Correct. Did not Yahweh give us humans 613 laws to save us? Never! The law only defines *sin.* The eternal law was given to Moses to show us humans what *sin* is. Only then can people realize they need to repent or change their thinking. Repentance is the theme of the Scriptures. Unfortunately, most will not repent, even though *sin* is now defined very clearly for all to demarcate. Rationalization weaves a web around our *sins* to make them acceptable. This is called deception, and it first occurs in our minds; but, when it darkens our hearts, there is little hope."

"Was not John the Baptist's favorite word 'repent' or *metaneon*?"

He nodded in return with a weak smile hoping that perhaps he had not insulted me.

I nodded and left feeling as if I had just received a lecture from Zeno or my mother. Under my breath once I exited the old man's home, I said, "When will people stop lecturing me?" The feeling of self-pity was raising its ugly head. This was my last thought as I stepped out the door into the narrow street. I felt something hit the back of my head before I heard the sound of bones breaking. Something flat and hard had just struck me from behind. What a fool I had been. Grillius taught me well, however, I failed to secure my exit. I should have left by another way, but now it was too late. All went black, and I am not sure for how long I was unconscious. I came back to my senses when a bucket of water came washing over my face like a wave splashing against a breaker wall out of Ostia on a stormy night.

"Stand up!" yelled a strange voice as a second bucket of water splashed over me. I started to realize I was flat on my back on smooth stones in a large, dimly lit room. From the floor I noticed many burning torches in wall brackets, interspaced by tall three-legged braziers, with hot coals blazing away in metal basins. Orange and red shadows jumped up and down the walls. I struggled to stand realizing I was in Herod's main banquet room of his Jerusalem palace. Sitting up on a dais, just as I remembered at Machaerus, was Herod Antipas and his wife. They both were wearing matching purple robes and small matching golden ring-crowns. Trying not to fall over, I noticed a third person sitting along with them. It was a man wearing a simple white wool toga, which sported narrow purple borders. At first, I thought the man might be my father. Staring longer, I realized it was not my father. This person seemed to have some substantial rank but not of senatorial level. Still squinting my eyes, I looked at his footwear and hands. I did not see red sandals nor iron rings, so he was not a Roman senator. There was one gold signet ring on the middle finger of his right hand signifying some kind of high imperial rank, but he had to be from an equestrian family.

"The man you are staring at is the Roman *Prefect* of Judaea, Governor Pontius Pilate," explained Herod Antipas. "I am sure you also remember my lovely wife Herodias from your last memorable visit at Machaerus. However, you today are out of uniform; and we are all now in Jerusalem."

I looked at my wet peasant garb of an ordinary citizen of Judaea and tried to understand why I was out of uniform. Looking around the large vaulted room, I noticed Amcheck standing next to a marble bench not far from me. Resting on the stone bench was my red scabbard and falcata along with my two iron throwing knives. It was at this point I discovered the walls were decorated with many gold-coated shields. I had been in this room many times, and these shields had not been hanging on the walls. Looking back at

Amcheck, I saw that he was in his usual black and red uniform with his head lowered, not making eye contact with anyone. Then to my horror standing next to Amcheck was my nemesis, Demos. Beside him were several other Roman officers, all smirking with impish grins. They, too, were all in uniform. I challenged myself not to wobble as I tried to remain on my feet. My head was throbbing as if a horse had kicked my head from behind. Dizziness was attempting to overtake me as the room started spinning. I widened my stance feeling as if I were on top of a ship mast at sea. I felt nauseous but swallowed several times to keep from embarrassing myself.

All these thoughts and observations flew through my mind while Herod Antipas had been speaking. "This Roman tribune standing next to Amcheck is accusing you of being someone other than my soldier-gladiator Achilles. Now, on that subject, my wife and I witnessed possibly the greatest demonstration ever seen in any gladiatorial contest." I slowly moved my head back toward Herod who paused speaking and was now looking to his right toward Pontius Pilate. "I am speaking of any private or public shows in Rome or at the Hippodrome in Alexandria, Antioch, or even here in Jerusalem. It was exactly one year ago near my birthday at Machaerus when Achilles easily defeated Rome's greatest gladiator, Marius, the winner of the wooden sword three times. Perhaps I should start a *ludi*, and Achilles will be my *doctus*. With my birthday arriving soon, you, Achilles, had promised me a rematch. But thanks to this Roman tribune, I will now have to wait another year." Herodias laughed at this intended humor, but the Roman next to Herod sat silent and glared at me and then at Demos. "Now to business," stated Herod looking directly at me. I widened my stance a little more to relieve the sensation I was going to fall to the floor. "This Roman tribune says you, Achilles, are someone named Venustus Vetallus, the son of the most famous senator in Rome. Is this true?"

Herod was speaking in Latin. I spoke for the first time surprised that I could actually talk considering my painful condition and answered in Aramaic saying I needed a translation, for I did not understand Latin. Herod smiled as he waved to Demos and said, "There you see, Tribune; you have the wrong man, and we will leave it at that."

Demos stopped grinning and looked at me. "It has been a few years since I saw him last; but, without a doubt, this is the long-lost son of Senator Gaius Vetallus. He murdered the wife of Vetallus, the Varus woman, in Rome over two years ago on a rainy night in the senator's *domicilium*."

Pilate interrupted. "Was this Varus woman the grandniece of Augustus and late wife of *Legate* Varus, who shamefully lost three legions in the forest near the Rhine River in northern Germania at about the time you were born, Tribune?"

"The very same, sir," answered Demos now standing at attention.

Herod translated this accusation in Aramaic for me; and I tried to look horrified before blurting out, "I demand justice if this coward is the one who struck me from behind and now falsely accuses me of murder!"

When Herod translated my statement into Latin, Demos laughed and then stared at me with squinted eyes and a fiendish smile. Then turning his blank eyes away from me, Demos blurted out about his lost dagger like the dupe he was. "He also owes me 100 *aurei* for a dagger he threw into the sea in front of my father, Senator Treverorum. There are also other substantial witnesses as well."

Herod now answered in Greek knowing everyone present would understand. "I do not care about your dagger, but murder is something else. Does anyone have any other proof other than this Roman pup's fantasies?" Demos understood the insult and looked at the floor to hide his anger.

Amcheck stepped forward two steps in his strange, submissive posture. He spoke in slow Aramaic almost as if he had rehearsed what he was saying. "Your Majesty, this man whom you call Achilles is not a Roman; but he is a Jew. He has been a Jew ever since I have known him, and it should be noted that he has served faithfully for several years here in Judaea and Galilee as one of your own."

I noticed Demos asking anyone of his soldiers to translate, and no one admitted to knowing Aramaic, even though I am sure one of the auxiliaries should have known this common tongue.

Governor Pontius, whose slang name was Pilate, spoke to Amcheck for the first time in perfect Aramaic. "Soldier, how do you know he is a Jew? For it is well known that this Venustus Vetallus is Roman and not Jewish."

"You know all Jewish boys are circumcised on the eighth day," explained Amcheck. "The Egyptians, along with some tribes of Arabs, are the only other circumcised men in the Roman Empire and for that matter in the known world. The Arabs and Egyptians, however, circumcise their males in their 13th year. I know Achilles standing before us is neither Arab nor Egyptian, but he is circumcised; for we room together here in this palace."

"Tribune Treverorum!" said Pilate switching to Latin. "You claim to have attended the Academy in Athens with Venustus Vetallus for some years. Did you ever see him as circumcised in the exercise yard or bathhouse?"

"He never exercised in the nude like normal Romans or Greeks but wore a loincloth. He was modest of whatever little he had to prove his manhood," mocked Demos looking to see if any of his soldiers were laughing with him. All stood at attention and made no noise. Demos realized he had crossed over an invisible social demarcation in front of Queen Herodias and the Roman *prefect*.

"Tribune!" scolded Pilate. "You are to watch your tongue. This is not the brothels of Rome but the throne room of Herod Antipas, Tetrarch of Galilee. Now, once again, have you ever seen this man before as a circumcised male?"

Demos, not understanding the Aramaic spoken by Amcheck and not understanding the seriousness of Pilate's question, answered very boldly, "No! Venustus is a Roman, and he was not circumcised when I saw him in the terracotta hipbaths at the Academy. I do notice those kinds of things."

Stupid Demos smiled as a few of his soldiers snickered at his last comment. Pontius Pilate turned and whispered something into Herod's hearing only. I was surprised at this act of familiarity since the gossip was Pilate and Antipas hated each other, and there was considerable enmity between them. However, here they appeared as equals and close friends. I also wondered why they were even together on this day considering the report of Pilate killing Galileans as they waited to sacrifice perhaps this morning or yesterday as I tried to think about how long I had been unconscious. These Galileans would be subjects of Herod Antipas, and Rome had no jurisdiction over Herod's subjects. Then a year ago, Pilate had killed scores in the *agora* in front of the Castle of Antonia. Becoming nauseous once again, I stopped thinking about this oddity and clenched the muscles in my stomach.

"Exquisite!" said Herod Antipas in Aramaic understanding whatever Pilate had suggested. Turning to his wife Herodias, he whispered to her; and she put her hands to her face trying to look embarrassed, but an excited chirp in her voice revealed the opposite. Herod turned to me and said, "Achilles, remove your tunic. Strip, and make yourself naked; and do it now!" I glanced at Demos whose eyes searched for any soldier who knew Aramaic. Someone finally answered his query. When he understood the order, his eyes widened; and a grin appeared on his face, as he thought he had just won. Amcheck winked at me with a suppressed smile as he stepped back into a line with the other Herodian guards. For some odd reason, I had not noticed the Herodian Guards before this; and all were wearing the same ominous black tunics with red edging on their sleeves. Their tunics were longer than before hanging slightly below their knees. I began to wonder if there was something wrong with my mind. I did not remember a uniform change since I joined the mercenary guards two years earlier. We had always worn red tunics, not black. Maybe there had been a uniform change since Herod arrived from Machaerus.

I personally liked the red tunics, but the red edging on black did look smart and professional.

"Strip!" ordered Herod one last time.

I untied my belt and the wet neck string. With the tunic now loose, I yanked the brown Judaean cotton garment over my head. Humiliation hit me as I thought of the victory I had gained at the Academy to wear only a loincloth in the exercise yard. Now I wore nothing under my robe. Herodias put her hand to her mouth again in the act of mortification, but her eyes betrayed something else. Even though my naked body would rival any statue of Achilles, I was ashamed to stand this way in front of everyone, especially a beautiful queen.

"Well!" commented Herod with a smug line running up the left side of his face. "He looks Jewish to me; what say you, Tribune?"

Demos said nothing but stood with a shocked look on his face.

"Definitely Jewish!" answered Pilate standing to leave. "I will have my tribune flogged with ten lashes as soon as we reach the fortress, Antonia."

"No!" called out Herodias with a commanding tone I had never witnessed from a woman other than Claudia Vetallus. "Justice should be carried out immediately, here and now."

Due to the recent slaughter of Galileans, I am sure Herodias's wish was not going to be challenged. Why Herodias wanted to watch a man flogged could only mean she suffered some spiritual sickness. I remembered it was Herodias who desired the Baptist's head on a silver platter a year ago, and this statement confirmed to me her wretched condition. The Roman p*refect*, still standing and wishing to show respect for his word and authority in Jerusalem, turned to the seated tetrarch with a red face. He reminded Herod in front of his own guards that Herod was only a guest in Judaea and Pilate was governor of Judaea, not Herodias.

Herod stood quickly to defend his wife and challenge Pilate when Demos unexpectedly screamed out in a wild screech with his right hand pointing at my naked body. "It is Venustus Vetallus! It is! Do you see that scar on his right arm? I put that scar there at the Academy! Get our *paidotribes* from the Academy to verify my words. His name is Grillius the Spartan, and he will tell you I am telling the truth. As the son of a senator, I demand you summon this Spartan to Jerusalem!"

Now the trouble in the throne room had blown from the insult to Herodias to my naked body. Pilate stood looking at Demos and spoke first with a mocking tone. "Very astute of you, tribune! Behold the man before you, unless you are blind, has the mark of a Jew. Is it possible you put that scar on

Chapter Four

his face and also the one on his chest? What about the one on his stomach and his left arm? Possibly, you also placed the scar on his right thigh. I see from here many scars. When did you see this man at the Academy? Only two or maybe three years ago? Did this naked man before us have all those scars when you sat in a hipbath at the Academy? Or did you put all of those scars on him with your phantom dagger that he tossed to the bottom of some sea?" The room broke into great, hilarious laughter. Pilate remained standing until the great hall was completely terminus of all its mirth. This was the first time I realized Pilate had a quick mind along with clever wit. After a noticeable pause and still looking at Tribune Demos, Pilate called out in an authoritative voice that sounded extremely angry. "Now, son of a Roman senator, I have had enough of your arrogance; and it is only because of your father I even allowed you to serve here in Jerusalem. Now I will confess the truth. I was not going to have you flogged back at Antonia, but Herodias is right; and I apologize publicly to her and her husband. What happened at the Temple this morning was a mistake and will never happen again as long as I am governor of Judaea. The officer who was responsible for this morning's slaughter was you! Now that crime on top of your present behavior will be severely punished before I leave this palace!"

Herod graciously accepted the apology by nodding and sitting down. Pilate remained standing, but before going further in this narration, I would like to make a quick historical note. First of all, I was not sure about Pilate's complete innocence regarding the slaughter of the Galileans. Within four years of this event, Pilate's soldiers once again slaughtered innocent people; this time, Samaritans. This was the final blow; and a delegation of Jews and Samaritans complained to the Roman governor of Syria named Vitellius, who ordered Pilate to Rome to explain himself to Tiberius. By the time Pilate did reach Rome, the emperor had died; but Pilate never returned to *Palestina*.

The only person still standing on the dais was Pilate, and he pointed to Demos. "You, tribune of Rome's legion of Judaea, are going to be flogged here and now by the man you have falsely accused."

With a wave of his hand toward a Roman centurion, Pilate ordered him to have four auxiliaries restrain Demos and strip him naked. As I watched in my nakedness, Demos was pulled and cross-tied between two pillars, which were only two of many that held up the roof of the great hall. With Demos's arms stretched out by cloth torn from some slave's garment, he had his uniform removed and thrown in a heap next to one of the pillars. His back and right side could be clearly seen by those on the dais.

Pilate, now turned over to Herod, speaking in Latin with a stern voice, "Tetrarch, with your permission, may we proceed?"

Herod Antipas nodded and pointed to my wet robe on the stone floor; then with an upward flick of his hand, he indicated for me to cover myself. As I slowly and painfully tried to replace my fallen garment, Amcheck came over and helped me dress. It was at this point Amcheck turned to Antipas. "Achilles is too weak to truly administer the flogging. With your permission, may I do the honors?"

Everyone looked at me as I weakly nodded to Amcheck to take my place knowing Demos would receive the whipping of his life at the hands of Amcheck. Herod lifted his hand to signal yes, and a simple flogging whip with a wooden handle and three lengths of wide cowhide came flying through the air from one of Herod's guards for Amcheck to catch.

"Hold up!" protested Pilate still on his feet. "That whip will not do. Centurion, send someone to fetch the *phagellow* from Antonia unless there is one here?" asked Pilate looking over to Herod. Antipas shook his head in the negative. Pilate signaled the centurion who sent an auxiliary to run on the double to the Castle of Antonia. "Perhaps I will give you a *phagellow* for your birthday," said Pilate with a condescending smile. Herod nodded in what looked like an equalizing jester and just as patronizing. These men apparently hated one another and were engaged in some kind of a dangerous dance. Pilate walked over to Herod and Herodias, and whispered something only for their hearing. Herod Antipas along with Herodias both smiled with delight after hearing what secret message was given. Forgetting about this little show, I slowly shuffled to the marble bench where my falcata and daggers lay. I carefully sat, which put me on the opposite side of the hall from Demos, where he was cross-tied to the two pillars not far from two braziers and a wall. He was shaking like a leaf in a strong fall wind. Then without reason Demos stopped shaking. I watched as he turned his head to his right and yelled out to Pilate, who had just sat back down. "My father is going to hear about this!"

Pilate smiled at the insolent threat and addressed the entire room in a calm but loud voice speaking in Latin for Demos's sake. "I am sure your father will hear, and he will thank me for turning a boy into a man." Pilate then switched to Aramaic now looking in the direction of Amcheck still holding the simple whip standing alone behind Demos. "Soldier, where are you from? Are you a Jew?"

"I am not a Jew but a Parthian. The people of Rome have never taken the land of my ancestors. My father fought Herod the Great and General Crassus

Chapter Four

at Carrhae on the other side of the Euphrates, where the Romans lost perhaps ten thousand fighting Parthian arrows."

"Sorry to correct you, Parthian; but our Roman records say you are somewhat modest as 20,000 Romans died that day under Crassus with 10,000 out of 40,000 captured. To my reckoning, four out of seven legions ceased to exist after that day was over. Therefore, the Battle of Carrhae is the worst defeat in Roman history, just behind Cannae when the Carthaginian General Hannibal killed 50,000 Romans in a single day. I believe the third greatest Roman disaster in our history would be during the time of Augustus Caesar when Varus, in the forest upon the Rhine in northern Gaul, lost his three legions along with their eagles. Varus's wife, the woman murdered in her Roman villa a few years back, is whom my tribune, Demos Treverorum Asus, is accusing your Jewish friend of killing. Let the record show that Tribune Asus has also threatened his commanding officer for ordering proper punishment for a false accusation upon one of Rome's commanding officers. He should be aware that death is a possible sentence for insubordination to his superior, not a flogging." Pilate nodded to a slave writing on a sheet of papyrus apparently recording the words of each participant in this mock trial. When the slave was finished writing, he bowed to Pilate. Pilate nodded back to the recording slave. Turning away from the edge of the dais, the Roman governor slowly spun around to once again face Amcheck. "Forgive me if I digress, Parthian. Claudia Publius Quinctilius Varus received what she deserved by the hand of Mars on that stormy night several years ago because a devoted Roman wife would have at least opened her own veins like her husband Varus. Instead, the scheming coward married Senator Gaius Vetallus Crassus and his wealth. I also have it on good authority that Tiberius is satisfied that she is now dead because he feared she was going to somehow maneuver her son onto the throne of Rome."

At the moment Pilate finished his political dialogue, Herod Antipas stood and in a loud, booming voice began asserting the assembled crowd, "I agree! Publius Quinctilius Varus was a fool. Losing three legions was not forgiven because he committed suicide. Besides, Varus was no friend of anyone in this land for all the death and destruction he brought here in the years after my father, Herod the Great died. Therefore, I, too, agree that Varus's wife deserved what she received that night in Rome!"

"Tell me why Tetrarch? Was she not Augustus's grandniece?" Pontius Pilate acidly requested before sitting and turning the stage over to Herod Antipas.

The tetrarch paced the stage twice before answering. "All knowledgeable Romans know that many years ago when Varus was governor and *legate* of

Syria, he intervened on my brother Archelaus's behalf by bringing troops into Jerusalem and forever giving this realm to Roman rule. This was almost forty years ago. Am I not right, my half-brother?" asked Herod Antipas looking to a man and woman who had just stepped up from rear stairs to the dais. Herod then motioned for the two to join him on the platform where there were two empty chairs next to Herodias. The man bowed his head to Pilate, and he and a young girl about my age walked up the hidden steps. My mouth fell open when the woman dressed as a queen was none other than Salome, the daughter of Herodias. She was the same girl from the throne room in Machaerus. For some reason, after the sudden recognition of Salome, a horrible pain in my head came upon me. It was so intense I began to shake with fear that I might die or be permanently addled. Was I going to become a valetudinarian (someone whose chief concern is his ill health)? I began breathing slowly so as not to fall over. If I were not sitting, I would have fallen flat on my back.

Herod turned to look at Pilate. "*Prefect*; this is my half-brother Philip now sitting to my left who received Ituraea and the region of Trachonitis at the death of our father Herod the Great. Archelaus, my elder brother who shares the same Samaritan mother as I, received the lion's share of my late father's kingdom. I was given only Galilee and Perea. Another half-brother named Lysanias rules Abilene or also called Abila near Damascus. Am I telling you something you already know?"

"No, go on; it will occupy the time while we wait."

"Philip, Lysanias, and I were named tetrarchs along with Archelaus. However, Archelaus also became an ethnarch. He hated either title desiring the title king instead because he received Judaea with the ancient capital of King David, Jerusalem. My father told me before his death I was to be the next king of the Jews. However, the great Herod apparently changed his will shortly before his death. Now that is all in the past; and, as the saying goes, 'That water has already passed under the bridge.'"

Pilate scratched his chin before commenting at the point of pause made by Herod Antipas. "And all this happened about twenty or so years ago? I mean when your brother Archelaus was banished to Gaul by Rome?"

"Correct to a point," answered Antipas. "You are correct. The banishment occurred about ten years of ruling Jerusalem, which would have been twenty-five or so years ago. First, I should start at the beginning. After my brain-diseased father made his will, perhaps between thirty-five or forty-some years ago, and then died, the people of Jerusalem revolted against Archelaus as their king. The news of that situation in Jerusalem reached the ears of Augustus.

Chapter Four

That event led to the *legate* of Syria, the very same Publius Quinctilius Varus, to enter into this city with his troops; and that changed everything, especially after the crucifixion of over two thousand Jews. Archelaus immediately went to Rome and gave his version of events to Augustus and the Roman Senate as well as demanding the title King of the Jews. I also traveled as fast as I could to Rome and gave my version to Augustus. Shortly after my arrival in Rome, a very powerful priestly delegation appeared before Augustus giving the same story as I; but Augustus overruled all our combined efforts. Oddly, Augustus gave my brother Archelaus everything he had before, except he was not granted the title of *Rex* or king as I am sure you remember, *Prefect,* since you are known as a scholar of our history." When Pilate did not communicate that he remembered or not, Herod continued. "After ten years of Archelaus's tyrannical rule of Judaea a new delegation visited Augustus, and it was that group of Jews that led to my brother's banishment to Gaul."

Herod appeared finished with his history lesson and returned to his seat. It was now Philip, tetrarch of Ituraea and Trachonitis, who stood to talk. I later learned he had recently become the new husband to Salome. Once again, another Herodian uncle-niece marriage. Salome's marriage to her uncle Philip occurred soon after the death of John the Baptist. To complicate the absurdity, Salome's father was the other Philip, the one now called Herod Philip or Philip of Rome, who lived in Rome and received no kingdom after his father's death.

Standing alone on the stage, Philip lifted two fingers indicating he wanted to interject something into the discussion. Everyone became quiet to listen to this new potentate who had just arrived on the dais. "I believe that there is a different narrative. Tell us, Antipater, what happened after our father's death?"

This was the first time I had ever heard anyone call Herod Antipas by the name Antipater. I gathered there was a reason for his brother's use of this particular designation, but my mind could barely keep me from collapsing onto the floor from the marble bench, let alone understand all these little details. The room was spinning faster and faster while I forced myself to listen and tried to remain in an upright position. Much later I learned that Antipas was a shortened version of Antipater, his name given at birth. Antipater was the name of both brothers' grandfather; and, as to why Antipas did not use Antipater, I have no knowledge. The use of this name showed that the two half-brothers did not relish one another, something noticed by all in attendance, especially Pilate.

"Whose version?" asked an annoyed Antipas.

Philip waved his arm at his brother with a ceremonious smile. "My information comes from my spies who are following that new prophet from your district of Galilee."

"What new prophet?" queried Pilate.

"Jesus of Nazareth," answered Philip. "And just a few days ago this Jesus gave an interesting parable outside the walls of Archelaus's grand palace in Jericho. That was before he almost entered this city this very morning."

With my mind swimming in distress and pain, I still understood that he was talking about the castle where Amcheck and I spent the night in Jericho on our way to see John the Baptist and again on our return to Jerusalem from Galilee. I also now understood that I had been unconscious for only a few hours and it was still five days before Passover.

"I have never heard of this Jesus," snorted Herod Antipas, obviously lying as everyone in the room suspected. I knew he was being mendacious since Herod Antipas had Amcheck and me follow Jesus precisely one year ago.

The beautiful Salome called her uncle Antipas a fabricator. "Come, come! Who does not know of this Yeshua-Jesus and all his stories and miracles? Besides, I was present at Machaerus when you sent the man holding the whip to Galilee and his young friend to find this very Jesus."

"If you are speaking of the Galilean miracle worker, yes, I have heard of him; but I just heard about him as Yeshua, not by his Latin name Jesus." Antipas began to slouch in his chair, perhaps showing his contempt of his brother from a different mother. "Now," continued Antipas, "Salome, please tell your uncle-husband to enlighten us of Jesus's most recent story." I thought this a strange way of speaking to his niece-step-daughter who was the daughter of Herodias, also married to an uncle. It would be many years before I learned we humans often project our own failings onto others. This could be because everyone is clean in his or her own eyes. Why we do this is a mystery; but a typical occurrence, nonetheless.

Philip signaled his wife to be silent and not to answer her uncle's question. For the first time, I realized Philip was developing something he wanted to express concerning Jesus and his brother. After Salome turned her head away after the wave off, she gave a pouty look to show compliance but under protest. I believe we humans communicate much more without words than we ever can with our words. Philip did not smile but started walking back and forth on the platform indicating he wanted the stage to himself and he had what he thought was a remarkable story to tell. Maybe he saw himself as a famous orator and learned this tactic somewhere at some Hellenistic school in either Rhodes or Alexandria. Once Philip felt that he owned the dais, he stopped at his chair and picked up a silver cup. Apparently Philip must have brought the cup with him when he and Salome arrived. After swishing a mouth full of wine, he began his oration. It appeared that this, too, was a learned tactic. Whatever the purpose, I understood that he was alerting everyone to a long story since he was lubricating his throat. Those on the platform got comfortable waiting for his saga. I felt that, if we were not waiting for the *phagellow* to arrive from the Castle of Antonia, someone on the dais would have interrupted Philip to put a stop to this apparent long-winded tale.

Philip then moved to the far edge of the elevated platform and looked toward the seated dignitaries. "Well, as I said, this happened just a few days ago when this pseudo-prophet was in Jericho. My spies reported that Yeshua-Jesus was spotted again just this very morning on the Mount of Olives heading toward Jerusalem but turned around midway, never entering the city. Mind you now, that little tidbit of this mornings arrival has nothing to do with my story. Perhaps Yeshua or Jesus, as he is becoming known, turned around after learning of the killings that occurred at the Temple in the Courtyard of Galileans; and I am in no way attacking you, Governor Pontius Pilate." I cringed at Philip's use of the word Galileans instead of Gentiles. This was like sticking his finger into Pilate's eye and pulling it out very quickly. Perhaps it was also a poke into his brother's eye as well. Looking over at Pilate, I noticed he was taking the jab in stride by sipping from his own ornate goblet apparently showing he had not heard the double wordplay used by Philip.

"Come on, Philip; get to the point," demanded Antipas as he also held up a silver wine cup. I later learned Herod Antipas was quite angry this morning over the killing of his own subjects in the Temple area. However, I later discovered that Pilate had apparently appeared at this palace to publicly apologize to Herod and that is how he happened to be here when I was carried unconscious into the throne room just before buckets of water revived me. Now all seemed forgiven between Herod and Pilate. At least that is how it appeared; yet, even with my head throbbing in pain, I could see deep hostilities smoldering between Herod and the Roman *prefect*. Why Pilate was in the same room with Antipas, just hours after this horrific event at the Temple was a mystery to me. Yet, in this life, we find ourselves at times living most contradictory. I have long learned that truth is far stranger than fiction.

From the corner of my eye, I noticed Herod giving his brother a stern look, which in turn caused Philip to pause and take another sip of wine. After he had swallowed, he made a face that showed his teeth with his tongue making a slight sucking sound. "Let us return to a few days ago. This new prophet or replacement of John the Desert Man was in Jericho next to the palace our brother Archelaus had refurbished at great expense."

Antipas moved his head ever so slightly when his brother mentioned Jesus as John's replacement; it would have been missed if one had not been looking for it. With my eyes on Antipas, I noticed he lifted his right hand to indicate he wished to say something. Philip gave him a nod; and Herod asked, "Was this the day Jesus ate at Zacchaeus's home? I am sure both the Judaea governor and you, Philip, know of Zacchaeus of Jericho. He is the little man who is chief among the publicans who collects taxes at the Oasis of Palms near the Jordan River."

"See, I knew you had spies of your own, my shifty brother. Perhaps you deserve the epithet, Fox, and yes, the very day. Well, back to my story. This Jesus told a tale for all in Jericho to hear; and it was clearly directed at you, my brother. Did your spies tell you of this parable?"

"No, I have not heard his fabled story. All I know is he does not like me for killing the Baptist. He is nothing but a fake, upstart prophet who calls me names like 'Old Fox'; and I am sure he uses other appellations beyond that. Now quickly tell us the rest of your story. We are all losing patience."

"Surely," said Philip. "As I have said, this Jesus used you, my brother, as the unspoken example in his parable." Philip walked over to his silver cup resting on the ornate stand next to his chair. I was sure it was for effect more than a need for another drink. Even in my weak mental condition, I could see Philip was needling his brother with his apparent delay.

"We are waiting, Philip," squawked Antipas.

"My apologies. It went something like this: A nobleman went to a distant country to receive a kingdom for himself and then, after a long absence, returned. You see, brother, I am sure this holy man in Jericho was referring to the time when you went to Rome trying to be king of Judaea over Archelaus."

"Hold it right there, Philip. Our father, Herod the Great, went to Rome years earlier when Antony and Octavius apparently made him king of the Jews. It was after our father's death that your half-brother, Archelaus the ethnarch, went to Rome to get the same title as our father retained; but he failed."

"No, I think the Jewish holy man was referring to you because you also went to Rome after the Varus affair; but I could be wrong. Now back to the story. The nobleman, before his trip, called ten slaves together and gave them different sums of money to take care of his business while he was gone. Jesus said some of the nobleman's citizens hated him and sent a delegation after him saying, 'We do not want this nobleman to reign over us.' Was there not a Jewish delegation that went after you to Rome to convince Augustus not to give you the kingship of Judaea?"

Antipas had made an obscene noise with his mouth that sounded like wind being blown out on purpose. Everyone on the dais pretended as if they didn't hear it, but I heard many suppressed snickers from the gathering crowd. After the room grew quiet, Antipas said, "That delegation was not as large as the one that went to attack Archelaus. Besides, if Jesus was outside Archelaus's palace, is it not notable that Jesus is referring to Archelaus and not me? It was his palace that he spent a fortune refurbishing?" After this short interruption, Antipas looked away allowing Philip to continue.

"Well, as the story goes, the nobleman returned to his original kingdom, which is what Augustus ordered in your case. Once the nobleman reached his home, he dealt with his faithful and unfaithful servants with whom he left money to carry on his business, which, also I am told, happened regarding you," said Philip in a sniveling voice.

"May all pomegranates turn black!" said an angry Herod Antipas. "The same could be said of our brother Archelaus. What about the delegation that went to the faraway land? What happened to them?"

"Jesus said the nobleman called all his enemies before him who did not want him to reign over them and ordered them all to be slain in his presence. Is that not also what you did, brother? All of the men who went to Rome died early deaths. Isn't that what happened?"

Pointing a ring-laden finger at his brother, Antipas replied with spittle flying from his mouth. "It was Archelaus who killed the delegates when they returned, not I. The parable is not about me. It is clearly about Archelaus. You said this Jesus told it near Archelaus's Palace in Jericho. I have nothing to do with that palace. You are just baiting me."

"Or maybe it is about both of you. Did not some of the Jewish delegates who went after you arrived in Rome die under your orders?"

"I only kill my enemies. However, I can understand your error because that was a long time ago. Yes, I did retain all that I had before I went to Rome as did Archelaus, except he lost his title as king. Then ten years later he lost Judaea and Jerusalem to another Jewish delegation complaining about his oppressive ways. The result of all that led to Rome ruling this city. The fifth of those Judaean rulers is sitting to my right," stated an exasperated Herod Antipas while waving his hand now toward Pontius Pilate.

"So that is how Rome became the rulers of Judaea and Jerusalem," commented Pilate, thinking he was showing discernment. But, most of those on the elevated platform had to have understood that Pilate already knew this part of Jewish history. If he did not know, I had no idea what point he was trying to make with this insipid statement.

Both brothers did not answer Pontius; perhaps they both understood the point that he already knew. There was, however, awkward silence after Pilate's words until the Roman auxiliary came into the rear of the hall out of breath. He came forward holding up for all to see the unique dumb-ball whip called a *phagellow*. It had three long lengths of leather, which were attached to a single wooden handle. When he passed by me, I clearly saw the three double lead balls welded to each other with short necks. The neck was the attachment point at the end of the three long leather straps. There were six round lead balls in all, each about the size of a man's thumbnail. With each strike of this whip, the victim would receive three lash cuts from the leather along with six holes caused by the lead balls entering the flesh at the last moment of each strike. It was not a whip of punishment but an instrument of either death or permanent maiming.

"Well, I guess our history lesson is over," mocked Herod Antipas. "Now a Roman nobleman will have one of his own slain before all of us as witnesses," said Herod driving a satirical wedge into the already fractured relationship between himself and Pilate.

Pilate stood with a flushed face locked onto Herod Antipas causing a fearful Philip to return to his chair on the elevated *scaena*. "The only one telling this new story will be the boy's father, and I am sure he will do whatever to squelch the truth." Pilate now turned toward the gathered crowd standing before the five dignitaries upon this sacred-looking stage, *scaena,* otherwise known in *Roma* as a *proscaenium*. "Now for my insubordinate tribune, I will give you something to really report, even without ever opening your mouth. With three strands of leather and a double lead dumb-ball at the end of each strand, you will receive not 10 but now 20 strikes: 10 for your false accusation of this Jewish guard of Herod Antipas, and another 10 for insubordination to your commanding *prefect*. I do not want you to ever forget one thing. None of this needed to happen this way. Had you kept your mouth from running with childish rubbish, you would have not suffered what is about to be visited upon you. Now with 20 strikes, I believe that will add up to 60 blows. This will give you a scarred body that will far rival the man you have falsely accused in front of such distinguished witnesses that now sit above you – that is, if you survive. If you do live, you will maybe become a man and no longer a boy; but, that is, if the gods of Rome allow you to live. Now tell that to your father, Senator Treverorum, if you so happen to live. And if you do, I will send you back to Rome; and perhaps your father will reward me with a jeweled dagger like the one you keep blabbing about that sits at the bottom of some sea."

The room erupted into side-splitting laughter from the double meaning of the dagger statement. I was perhaps the only person besides Demos and Pilate not laughing. It was then that Pilate and my eyes locked, maybe because he noticed I was not laughing at his words. It seemed that both of us seemed to understand something for just the briefest of moments. I was the first to look away placing my eyes back on Demos. I realized he was innocent in his claim against me; but I felt he deserved every stroke he was going to receive, plus more. He had cheated when he struck me in the Lyceum's *palaestra* at the conclusion of our sword match in Athens, and I was now convinced he was the coward who smashed in the back of my head at the door of the old scholar. I looked at the long, white scar on my right arm; and I started to feel like throwing up the contents of my stomach. This involuntary feeling was not because of the scar but the movement of looking down. I slowly raised my head, and the nauseated condition subsided. Looking again at Demos, the ultimate coward, I could see and smell his fear. He again started shaking like a leaf that refused to fall at the end of the season. It was embarrassing to watch someone showing such fear for all to see. I understood why Pilate said what he did. He wanted no part of the new Roman youths filling his ranks. During the civil wars, men in the legions must have been real men compared with the sons of peace that were now coming out of the *Pax* of Augustus and Tiberius.

"Parthian!" yelled Pilate over the noise of those commenting on Demos's dreaded panic. "If you ever return to your homeland, tell them the truth. Rome will never attack your people again. The world now knows that the Romans are no longer the greatest warriors as you can plainly see for yourself. I believe it is most apparent that Rome is now producing scared, arrogant little boys. Perhaps, Parthian, you can turn this one pathetic, spoiled proprietor of *ennui* into a man for Rome. Give him 20 strokes. Hit every inch of his body except his manhood and his head. On the last strike, you may place the dumb-balls on his face but only on the last strike. Regarding his manhood, I do not want his father coming after me because I ended the line of Treverorum because his son lost his... well, you know. Besides, Parthian, saving his manhood will ensure the inevitable fall of Rome with weak, frightened little boys shaking before us all."

Again, the room broke out into uproarious laughter as no one really knew how entertaining and mockingly facetious Pontius Pilate could be, something a prominent Roman diplomat should not be. He was one of the last Romans who feared nothing, including what Demos's father was going to do to him when the boy's senatorial father learned of this scourging. I felt like taking my falcata, which was resting behind me on the stone bench, and killing Demos. It would save Pilate's career and Demos a great deal of agony, something no human should experience. But, even if I could, I wouldn't kill Demos because it would cost me my life, and he was not worth it. I just sat watching Demos shake and thought that maybe I, too, might soon die. I could barely sit without my head throbbing beyond belief. This idea of compassion toward Demos was new to me, and I wondered where it was coming from. As I scanned the large crowd, I realized it had doubled in size. Word of this kind of spectacle travels fast, and those present were laughing, except Demos, Pilate, and me. I turned to once again look at Pontius Pilate, and our eyes met for the second time. Perhaps he knew something about me that was more than he was letting on; and when he nodded ever so slightly, I was hoping it was his way of saying he respected me for some reason.

I knew Pilate had climbed the ladder of the Roman "Path of Honors" as a plebeian of the Populare Party, the same party of Julius Caesar. To be *proconsul* of Judaea, he had to have been a *consul* at one time in the past. Before that, he had to have served as a *praetor* or judge. That is where the split occurred. Pontius Pilate could never be elected as an *aedile* but, instead, had to have been a *tribute* of the *plebs* and before that a *questor* or financial administrator serving somewhere in the Empire. He also had to have spent a minimum of 20 years as a tribune in the military. If Demos survived this brutal flogging, he, too, in a few years could go the other way around the path that Pilate took because Demos came from the senatorial line. Demos could be elected first as a *questor* and then as an *aedile, praetor,* which would lead to *consulship,* and finally an appointment by the emperor as a *proconsular* in some imperial province. All these political positions, minus military tribune, were unpaid elected positions; and service was at least one year. I am sure Pontius Pilate had some rich, unknown *patroni*, whom he secretly served. His debt to this *patroni* must have been astronomical. It was only as a *prefect*-governor could Pilate have the power to amass a quick fortune to pay back his financial backer, who must have been supporting him all these years in order to be paid back at such a time as this. There were also other favors a *patroni* could gain, besides money, when a *patroni* held a *prefect*-governor in his hand. Pilate, as well as all governors of Rome's provinces, were taking for themselves a substantial percentage of the taxes owed to Rome. This was expected and was how Rome functioned. Only as a *prefect, legate, procurator,* or *proconsul* of a province could anyone pay back a *patroni* (money-backer) for all the years it took to reach this pinnacle position in the Roman Empire. Governors of either imperial or senatorial provinces were the only government officials that could amass a fortune while being a servant of Rome. *Palestina* was under imperial rule and was considered one of the more affluent provinces for governors, kings, tetrarchs, and such over a senatorial province. Judaea was the richest prize in all *Palestina*, a vast treasure house for any governor ruling this land for the Empire.

Liquid metal was considered the lifeblood of the god Mercury, and it metaphorically flowed unashamedly throughout the Roman Empire. This rare and strange metal was secretly called the *patronage system*. To comprehend it is simple. Everyone owed someone a favor and thus the picture of the god with wings on his feet and helmet flitting around here and there. A favor depended on whatever the lender wished in return for the loan. The primary lender or *patroni*, such as my father, might have thousands of people who owed him favors. A favor could be anything from supplying an extra bag of grain to a specific villa or might require the secret act of murder. Having the son of a most influential senator whipped with a *phagellow* was going to be a calculated move that could very well cost Pilate his life. All Demos's father had to do was call in one favor from one of his clients. There was also the possibility of being recalled to Rome due to the whipping of Demos, and then how could Pilate ever repay his *patroni*? The only future for the Roman governor was to go into exile; that is, if he wished to stay alive. I knew Pilate had a wife but never knew of any children. Maybe being childless in his case was best; but for some strange reason, I had compassion for Pilate's wife and all that could happen to her because of Demos. The sad truth was it really did not matter if Demos lived today or not because Pilate was going to answer to Senator Treverorum in some way after today.

Amcheck was limbering up by snapping the whip to get a feel for how the dumb-balls would do the most damage along with the leather thongs. I looked again at the Roman governor and noticed that two *lictors* had appeared from somewhere, and now they were standing behind Pontius Pilate. Each *lictor* wore a little red coat over a white tunic, and both were holding a *fascis*. Prefect/procurators were allowed up to four *lictors*. Pontius Pilate probably had only two *lictors* standing behind him today to not up-stage the *legate* of Syria to whom Pilate answered and who was allowed up to five *lictors*. I was guessing that having two *lictors* standing behind him also showed some kind of humility toward the two tetrarchs sitting with him.

I looked away from Pilate and stared at Demos's naked body. His outstretched arms made him look as if he had been crucified. It reminded me of my childhood friend Eli just before I struck down Claudia in the atrium of my father's villa. The only difference was these columns were snow white, and the ones in my father's villa were blood-red. I noticed Demos had soiled himself. Everything was running down his legs onto the mosaic floor. Several of Herod's guards stood with wrinkled noses due to the foul smell near Demos. One man picked up a water-laden bucket that was ready to revive Demos, not if but when he passed out as well as wash away the blood to show Amcheck the body parts he had yet to strike. The guard with the bucket quickly launched the water onto the floor beneath Demos, and a second bucket was splashed onto Demos's legs. I looked over at the platform or *proscaenium* where the five dignitaries sat and the two *lictors* stood. Apparently, only Pilate noticed the washing of the floor before the flogging. Antipas was busy talking to Herodias, and Philip was in the same fashion whispering something into Salome's ear. Other than Pilate, it looked like the two couples were getting each other ready for some high entertainment.

Pilate, from his seated position, lifted his right hand and barked, "Begin!" The first blow connected with Demos's back and the lead weights whipped around his right side into his stomach. This was going to be a brutal beating. When Amcheck pulled back his first hit, Demos bowels made an involuntarily obscene noise, which caused all the Roman soldiers across from me to laugh. After the noise came Demos's first scream. It was filled with unbelievable fear and sounded almost womanly. Five strokes later Demos's back and rib cage had been viciously lacerated. A bucket of water was thrown at Demos, and I could see white bones that were his ribs. Five more strokes were laid over his shoulders, and each time the leather and lead balls cut deep into his chest and stomach muscles. More buckets of water were thrown, and I noticed many onlookers leaving the throne room. Perhaps it was the smell alone, but I was sure the horror they were witnessing would drive any curious, faint-of-heart spectator away. More water splashed over Demos, who had passed out since the second whip strike. He had let out a horrible shriek and then buckled at the knees hanging only by his tied wrists. The water caused him to stand on his own power. Amcheck quickly delivered five more strokes cutting every inch of his legs from his thighs to his ankles. Water was thrown again, and more bones from his femur to his shins could be seen. Whenever Demos was conscious, his high-shrill screams cut everyone as deeply as the dumbballs cut into Demos's flesh and muscles. When he was out, the heavy thud sounds were unbearable to hear. The next four strikes, two to each arm, cut him from his shoulders to his hands. I could see that the lead weights at the ends of the leather had broken fingers and shattered his left elbow. Another bucket delivered into his face woke him for the final strike that was going to be delivered to his head and face.

Amcheck took several steps to his own left to reposition himself for this final hit. Amcheck looked visibly tired from all the work he was exerting. I could see him resting for a few moments before he executed his final strike. Then, Amcheck's right arm went up with the wooden handle in his hand. The leather thongs appeared to be moving almost in slow motion. Amcheck had positioned his wrist with a slight angle before snapping the wrist to drive the lead dumb-balls right where he wanted them. The entire hall could hear the horrible cracking sound of leather and the hollow thud of the lead tearing flesh and breaking bones. Amcheck then quickly jerked the iron balls out sideways producing the maximum damage. The leather had put three cuts to the top of Demos's head removing hair and skin right down to the skull. Each metal instrument at the end of each of the three thongs landed right where Amcheck wanted. Amchek had successfully placed all three weights into Demos's face. One had created a hole in his right check that would never fill in when healed. The second tore off the center of his beautiful, aquiline Roman beak right in the center that also would never heal leaving half of his nose forever missing. The final weight buried itself into Demos's left eye; and, when Amcheck pulled sideways, the network of nerves attached to a large round thing went flying across the room and struck one of the Roman officers in the chest causing him to fall to the floor in a faint after he saw what hit him. It took a bucket of water to wake him and more than one bucket to bring Demos back to consciousness. Like a wounded rabbit, Demos began screaming until he fell again into silent unawareness. The room of people believed he was dead, but another bucket of water awakened him as he started screaming again in horrific agony. When Demos knew it was over; he gathered himself, turned his bloodied head to the side, and shouted the best he could, "Venustus, you are dead for this!"

I looked to Pilate, and he shook his head in disgust at the poor performance of one of his own soldiers: a Roman officer fainting and screaming like a woman. I knew Demos would never be the same, and I am not sure how I would have handled such a scourging. Perhaps I would have embarrassed myself as well. He had a 50-50 chance of living. If he did live, I knew he would not be the better because of this wicked act. If I thought he was evil before this, he most assuredly would become something unbalanced and beast-like from the pits of Pluto. Hate and love live on fine lines, but Demos had already crossed over into a darkness that would leave him as the ugliest and meanest human to walk the earth. Even though Pilate spared his manhood, no woman would want him unless she was filthy drunk, completely blind, or a raving witch. The 20 blows, I also feared, would end Pontius Pilate's career or life, notably the last vicious strike to the head and face.

Pontius Pilate in no way was a nice man killing thousands of Jews in Judaea and Jerusalem. For the past six years as the fifth imperial *procurator* in Judaea, he had made a name for himself whom people feared. He started his career in Judaea by carrying the Roman standards into Jerusalem showing the Jews images of the god Tiberius. Thousands died because of that act. Golden shields were later hung in the Temple area embossed with the names of the Roman gods artfully inscribed on each one. Thousands again died at this insult before they were removed. Amcheck and I witnessed the aftermath of the temple tax being stolen and used to build an aqueduct. Then again, just this morning in the Temple, Pilate had his soldiers indiscreetly kill Galilean Jews waiting to offer their sacrifices. This morning's bloody message falls beyond what was told to Jesus and the rest of us who heard. Glancing at Pontius Pilate after the beating of the son of an influential Roman senator almost to the edge of death, I could not even guess at Pilate's future fate. Perhaps he was hard-hearted beyond understanding, or he thought he was far enough away from Rome to do whatever he wished. Maybe he believed his *patroni* was powerful enough to protect him.

Amcheck, sweating and now covered with specks of blood and pieces of skin, walked over to me and threw the bloody-handled instrument with its iron ends at my feet. "No one hurts my friend and gets away with it. You remember that when you have to cover my back. Also, remember, if anyone tries to tell you, 'Amcheck is not your friend.'" I slowly lowered my head in pain, and Amcheck ordered two guards to help me to my quarters in the lower basement of the palace. Once I was placed on my cot, I concluded my skull had to be fractured. I felt like going to sleep and never waking up. My last thoughts were about the possibility of inevitable swelling that could kill me or render me blind. I also treated the idea that I might lose the ability to speak or think correctly. Those were my last memories before I felt as if I fell off the edge of a cliff into utter darkness.

CHAPTER FIVE

Jerusalem – Passover on Moon Day. Tiberius's 18th year as emperor of the Roman Empire. Pontius Pilate's 6th year as Prefect of Judaea. End of Jesus of Nazareth's 3rd year of public ministry.   *(Nisan 14 or April 14, 32 AD)*

Men generally believe what they want to.   Julius Caesar – The Gallic Wars

It had been the darkest void I could ever remember once I gained consciousness. It took a long time for my eyes to focus on what appeared to be a high, pinkish, fluted-looking plaster ceiling. When I finally moved my eyes from side to side, I discovered I was lying on a bronze-framed bed in a large masonry room. My last memory after the scourging of Demos was being placed on my soldier's bed in the bowels of the barracks in Herod's Palace. But this was no longer the basement of the soldier's barracks. I could hear voices, and it wasn't Amcheck since they sounded like the voices of women. Maybe I was dead; and these were angels talking to each other, or perhaps the voice was of my mother. I quickly banished those thoughts because, if I were dead, why was I still in such pain? My head throbbed with every heartbeat. Sweat poured from my brow, and I could feel my body was wet and clammy. Thinking about the pain caused me to involuntarily vomit, and soft hands quickly cleaned me with damp cloths.

When I finally came to my senses, I was, indeed, in a beautiful place resting on my back in a bed only a queen would sleep in. It now seemed to be early morning based on the sounds of birds singing that came in from a large open window. From the angle of light and because the birds were singing, it had to be around daybreak. Turning my head very slowly to look out the window, I was surprised to see the rear wall and golden roof of the Jewish Temple. I was still in Jerusalem. The sound of silver trumpets floated in through the window followed by the voices of young boys singing. The morning sacrifice must have been offered to the Creator and one to Tiberius. I smiled thinking of the first sacrifice, not the second. It seemed to me that the Jews were committing a great blasphemy by offering a sacrifice to Tiberius every morning and evening. Yet, I understood the thinking of the Sanhedrin and Sadducees. This invalid token twice a day was to keep the ruler of the Empire from halting the daily services of the Temple. I watched until the sun began to touch the golden roof points of the Temple, and the room started to fill with natural light. Based on the view, I concluded that my location was still in Herod Antipas's Hasmonaean Palace; but I was up high in some room. Then two beautiful women appeared before my eyes. Neither was my mother nursing me; but I soon recognized Herodias and a younger version of herself, who had to be Salome. A third girl was also in the room holding a tray of towels and a small silver flask filled with water. She was maybe fourteen years old and wore the tunic of a slave and Herodias called her Nina.

"What day is it?" I finally asked in what sounded somewhat hoarse and weak.

"Oh, you poor thing!" said Herodias. "It has been Passover since sunset last night."

"I have been here for how many days?" I queried.

"Salome, get the physician. Tell him, 'Good news; the patient is awake and talking.' Also, inform the doctor that the patient's mind is working and is not impaired. He knows what day it is and how long he has been sick. Now go!" she ordered, and Salome hurried obediently out of the room that was quickly filling with the light from the rising sun. "Nina, go and fetch more towels and a bigger basin of water."

After the two women had left and I was alone with the wife of Herod Antipas, she asked, "Achilles, do you know who I am?"

"The wife of Tetrarch Antipas."

"Magnificent!"

"But why am I here and not in my room?"

"You are too valuable to die on us down in that pig hole," she said; and her words actually hurt my feelings. She must have noticed her words

Chapter Five

stung. "Apologies. I know you have no choice but live in the barracks, but I insisted you be carried here where I could personally care for you." I tried to smile my thanks when I noticed my head was bandaged. "My head, what is wrong with it?"

"Those horrible Romans crushed in your skull with something hard and flat. Quite a blow, indeed. My Greek physician Phoneinus had to shave your head and drill into the bone at the back to release the pressure of swelling. He also pulled out the broken pieces with his tools and then re-set the bones in the back of your skull. He replaced the larger bones and somehow mended them together with something that looked like a thin cement. Well, anyway, the bones are back in place; and your head will look satisfactory once your hair grows out." She hurried to a table, opened a drawer, extracted over a foot of brownish hair tied with something bright red at the top. It looked like a scalp whip some Barbarian riders used on their horses. I had heard about Barbarian soldiers from the far north taking a captured women and cutting only the skin in a circle on top of the entire head area with the point of a knife. Then with a swift upward yank off came the entire scalp, hair and all. Normally these violent men would do this right after they raped the woman and the hair trophy was taken while the woman was still alive. Some women died from infection and some survived with an ugly scar on top of their heads. The Barbarian soldiers would usually tie the scalps either to their belts or on the side of their horse's heads. Grillius had told me even more horrifying deeds perpetrated by these people he called the Budini of Scythia, who lived north of the Pontus Sea. He said they were mostly red-haired savages with gray-blue eyes. They loved blond-hair women to rape and scalp. I looked closer at what was in Herodias's hand and realized it was not a scalp but a good-sized ponytail of brown hair with reddish tints from the morning sun now streaming in through the eastern window. "I shall treasure this lock as a great memento of you. Have you heard of the *Manes?* You see, the spirit of the dead lives on in the tress. The Romans honor the dead at gravesites with human sacrifice or a gladiatorial fight to the death. Is that acceptable to you?"

What she just confessed was a mystery to me. In the upcoming year, I would be concerned beyond life itself when I tried to destroy what she now held in her hand. On this morning all I understood was she was carrying a whip of my hair. She looked hurt because I did not comment on her declaration of the long strand of hair being mine.

"Is it acceptable to you if I retain your long tress?"

I foolishly said, "I do not mind as long as your husband agrees." I was not thinking clearly and was confused by her comparing my hair with *Manes* or dead, deified spirits. What religion did this woman practice? All I knew was she wanted John the Baptist's head on a silver platter. Now I wondered if she had a lock of his hair in that drawer. Did she think there was some magical power with someone's hair? Maybe she believed a person's hair held the *Manes*? Yet, I was not dead. I tried closing my eyes and inside my head I heard a strange voice trying to speak to me. This was the first time this happened, and it would plague me for the next year. It sounded like the voice of a woman, but it was without question the voice of an evil spirit. At first, I just listened and it said, "This hair is just a simple payment for her saving your life. Besides, her just taking your hair and not your life should be acceptable. It is a fair swap, is it not?" Little did I know this piece of me would soon become a weapon against me. My ponytail of hair in the hands of this witch was a power I did not believe in but would before the next Passover arrived. Allowing this woman to retain my hair became a costly price to pay, and I should have demanded that she burn my hair immediately in my presence.

"That Old Fox does not care what I keep as a memento. But, if you like, I will ask," she said very sweetly. I wondered why she was acting this way; yet, I did not have much experience with her nor any other women. Many of the soldiers and even fishermen said women were stupid and horrible creatures. Most claimed women were good for only one thing. I wondered if they were right or wrong. I knew my mother to be sweet and a joy to be around. Claudia, on the other hand, was a woman who needed to go to Hades, where I hoped she was.

"You see, Achilles, my husband will do anything I tell him. He is an 'old fox' just as that holy man Jesus calls him. I wonder how this Jewish prophet knows my husband by a name I have called him for years. I tell myself there is no way he could know. But he seems to know my little secret name for my husband, so who is he? Very odd I must admit. But my Old Fox knows better than to cross me," she bragged more to herself than to me. The slave girl Nina returned holding a silver tray with little linen towels and a large clay jug filled with water on top of her head. She asked Herodias what she should do with the tray. "Put them down, and you may leave. Oh! And go tell my husband the good news about his Achilles. I am sure Salome forgot since she went after that Greek, my master healer," she said with a little laugh at her own words.

I noticed, when she spoke, she looked off to her right as if seeing something far away almost as if she were talking to someone who was not in the room. Her movements were more like a butterfly; she would not stand still as she spoke but moved toward some distant object she seemed to be looking at. Each time she did this she would turn and sidestep back, only to do it again to return to her original spot after a few moments. Perhaps she was thinking of some past event as she talked, or maybe some medicine she had taken was causing the strange movements. Whatever was going on with this woman, her bizarre behavior confirmed to me that she could very well be controlled by some invisible spirit. The thought came to me that, if she were influencing her husband in any way, this was a powerful and dangerous woman. Just like Claudia, whose beauty could turn any man's head. Besides, Herodias also had a beautiful voice that was both lovely and soothing when she spoke. It made me feel as if I were in the mountains on a warm spring day with the wind blowing through the treetops. I felt as if I were in a strange story from the *Panchatantra*, the book of fairy tales from the land of the Buddha and King Asoka. These peculiar people living in the far east beyond the Hindu Kush Mountains, where monsoon rains and heat defeated the army of Alexander the Invincible, were the most creative thinkers when it came to stories. I thought to myself that maybe the four months of each summer when the temperature reached a point where a bird egg could cook on a rock and in the constant rain, which caused the greatest western army to mutiny, must have been the catalyst for their imaginations to reach new heights. Thinking about a few stories I had read from the *Panchatantra*, I concluded that, if Herodias had given me a blue apple to eat or handed me some magical seeds to plant, I would not have been surprised at all.

"Now tell me. How do you feel?" When I made eye contact with Herodias, I at first didn't realize she asked her question in Latin although she had been speaking Aramaic up to this statement. Foolishly, I had been infatuated with this woman and answered in perfect Latin before I realized my mistake.

Her eyes went wide, but she held her beautiful and disarming smile. "So you are Venustus Vetallus as that young Roman said. You know, the young boy that was flogged by Pilate's command about five days ago?" I turned my head away from her ashamed of myself for being so easily tricked. "Don't be so hard on yourself. You are safe here, Venustus. Amcheck told my husband long ago who you were. You are more valuable to us than the reward your father is offering. I believe it is beyond three or even four million *sestertii* by now."

"What in the *cosmos* do you mean, woman?" I was angry, more so with myself than the way she had played me. Actually, it was Amcheck I wanted to kill. I knew there was something wrong with him all these years; and now I realized he was not my friend, but all along he had been spying for Herod. Once again, I had a pretend friend just like the slave boy Eli. I am sure Eli, like Amcheck, would say he did not start out as my friend but in time grew to like me. What about Felix Cornelius, the Roman Praetorian at the *popina*? Was he a friend or foe? I actually fantasized seeing Felix walk into the room for the four million *sestertii* reward. He would say he had just waited until the amount grew before turning me in.

"First of all, 'woman' will not do. I am Herodias, and I have your hair in my keeping. What does that tell you?"

"My head hurts as if a horse just back kicked me, and you are talking about my hair? And what is all that noise out the window? Is there a riot out in the streets?"

She went and closed the wooden shutters to dampen the noise. "Let me educate you, Schoolboy, on a few things before the physician and my husband arrive. That little story Philip told about the nobleman going to Rome, coming home, and killing his unfaithful subjects is all true. My husband is afraid of this Jesus more than he was afraid of John the desert preacher. That is why I had John, that sun-crazed baptizer, beheaded. It took all my wiles and my daughter to bend my husband's will to do the right thing. Actually, it was really Isis that should get the credit. Isis is my sweet goddess from Egypt who came to me in a dream the night before my husband's birthday party and told me how to accomplish the deed. Unfortunately, I thought that would solve my husband's problems. Death normally does solve all problems, but not this time."

Herodias stopped talking, stepped to the side, looked away, then stepped back, and picked up where she left off about her husband. "Fifty delegates arrived in Rome to persuade Augustus Caesar to remove Archelaus. They came taking my husband's side. Then, when Archelaus returned to this city not receiving his coveted title of king, he ordered his soldiers into the Court of Gentiles right here in Jerusalem killing over three thousand stupid Jewish worshipers waiting to offer their Passover sacrifices. This happened many years ago, and three thousand is much more than what Pontius Pilate killed a few days ago in the same area. Then 40 years ago, my husband's father, who is my grandfather, killed about the same number Pilate did when he ordered the killing of little children who were two years old or younger in the villages south of Jerusalem. I see how you are looking at me. Yes, I was alive back then; but I was just a little girl. I remember that day. Apparently the king of the Jews was not successful if that child is now Jesus of Nazareth. Next time my husband has a chance to kill this Jesus, if I have anything to do with it, he will not hesitate like he did with John, that so-called prophet. You see, why would a few Galileans killed by Pilate be noteworthy when the entire slaughter of Jews is placed in its proper totality? Besides, a new delegation will be sent to complain to Tiberius Caesar. They will demand my husband replace Pilate as king of Jerusalem. The death of the Galilean will only benefit my husband. But, of course, Tiberius will never turn an imperial province over to a local king. We are living in a new world with new rules. Now, let's return to Jesus's little story, the one he gave at Jericho a few weeks ago. A smaller but more influential delegation came to Rome and slandered my husband. Augustus Caesar did not know whom to believe, and he sent everyone back to this dried-up desert-land standing on *status quo*. But may Isis be praised, Archelaus did not receive the title as king of the Jews. Archelaus received only the title of ethnarch. Do you know what an ethnarch is?"

"Ethno means people-ruler or the people's *rex*," I surmised using Latin since there was no need to hide who I was.

"Superb. Your mind matches your bright eyes and good looks, notwithstanding your facial scars."

"What is all this about and why the compliment? I have no idea what you are trying to explain." Once again, I felt like I was in a children's fairy story. This story had the evil witch turning into a beautiful queen-mother, but I kept telling myself that behind the beauty was the heart of a *luna*.

"The delegation spoiled everything for my husband. He could have been given Judaea and Samaria; but he had to return as he was before he arrived in Rome, Tetrarch of Galilee and Perea. My husband wanted more than that birdcage at Machaerus. He didn't even get Masada, a much easier stronghold to survive any assault while you could sit and get drunk on any one of the three spectacular porches hanging out over the world. Herod wanted to be king of Jerusalem. He wanted to be a king, not a tetrarch; and he almost had it until that other delegation came after the first one. When my husband returned to this stone-ridden, dried-up land, he had every one of those evil delegates killed. It is true that Archelaus slaughtered everyone from the first commission, but my husband killed everyone in the second delegation who went against him. The only difference is how each brother completed the task. Archelaus murdered his enemies outright in one season, where my husband took his time over the period of many years. But in time, one by one and secretly, each met his end early. No one knows except you now, but my husband has been behind all of their assassinations. He didn't do it openly like his stupid brother, who ended up exiled. You, my dear, were instrumental in the death of the last delegate. Two and a half years ago you and Amcheck helped kill the captain of the Temple. That was a glorious day for my husband when that task was finally accomplished. It took over twenty years; but with his assassination completed in the Court of Gentiles, everyone from that second commission had been punished. Now this Jesus goes and tells that story in Jericho about the nobleman coming back and killing the delegates in his presence. Do you see how this Jesus is bringing all of this back upon us Herods? It is clear that Jesus was referring to Archelaus; yet, the truth is my husband and his brother of the same mother were the characters in that story Jesus told next to Archelaus's Palace in Jericho."

"I do not see it that way. How does Jesus's Jericho story cause such a problem? And I agree it sounds like Jesus was referring to Archelaus in two ways. One, the story was given next to Archelaus's refurbished palace; and Archelaus did have his enemies killed in his presence. Isn't that what you just said?"

"I hope you are right. I like the way your mind works," she said with a sweet smile. "Still, Archelaus returned from Rome as ethnarch of Judaea; and he spent a small fortune of the people's money rebuilding that palace in Jericho into something short of magnificent. He diverted half the water from the village of Neara to water those palm trees, which he had planted out there in the desert. He built a new city next to Jericho and named it Archelaips after himself. If that was not a scandal, his marriage to Glaphyra was. She had been the wife of his brother Alexander, who was the mother of three children by the brother. You see, the Jews forbid anyone to marry his brother's wife, especially when she has children by her first husband. No one said a thing about that until John the Baptist started attacking me for being the wife of Antipas's brother in Rome. You see, I am guilty under Jewish law since I had Salome with Antipas's brother, whose name is Philip. Yet, Antipas and I are not even Jews, just partially by blood. Why should the laws of the Jews single me as a sinner? My husband is maybe one-eighth Jewish, and I am less. What logic is there in demanding we follow their rules? Truth be told, these rule followers want the whole world to follow their twisted laws. The Jews have already started changing times with their rules. Does not every citizen of the Empire of Rome embrace seven days in a week, not eight like under the Republic; and that change is because of the Jews. Did you know that no Jew can serve in the legions because a Jew will not fight or work on the seventh day? The Jews all over the Empire get all the protections of Rome and do not have to fight to enjoy those privileges. The list goes on and on. Do you see how the Jews are infecting the entire world with their laws? They want everyone to bow down to their one god and throw hatred over the pantheon of Roman gods or even older established cultures, like Egypt. Why does the entire world have to be subject to the laws that were given by their precious myth of a man named Moses?"

Chapter Five

Herodias turned away and stepped to the window. After throwing open the wooden lattice shutters, she returned and picked up her lecture of vileness toward the Jews and the legacy of her family. "However, in the tenth year of Archelaus's ethnarchy, Caesar had heard enough complaints and had Archelaus exiled to Vienna, a city of Gaul. Glaphyra killed herself a few days after the order arrived from Rome. Then, instead of giving Judaea to my husband along with the title of king of the Jews, Augustus Caesar annexed all of Archelaus's treasure and palaces, except the one in which we are presently residing, including the one at Jericho, and Masada. Oh, yes, Jericho is the palace where Herod the Great died, so my husband is allowed to have soldiers there instead of Romans, but technically it belongs to Rome."

"Wasn't there a second palace; belonging to Herod the Great located at the western edge of Jerusalem?"

"Yes, my grandfather built that palace, but it now belongs to some wealthy Roman." Herodias seemed to be enjoying her trip into the past. She smiled down at me and then looked away as she continued. "Publius Sulpicius Quirinius was the Roman *legate* of Syria back again when Augustus started the second imperial census. This was about ten years after my grandfather died and fourteen years after the first Augustan census. This was at the time Judas the Galilean lead an insurrection and perished under the boot of Quirinius and his legions from Syria. To help pay his troops, Quirinius sold my grandfather's palace on the far west side of Jerusalem to the highest bidder. Some rich nobleman from Rome bought it but has done nothing with it. That was decades ago, mind you; and today that palace just sits and rots from neglect."

I lifted my hand to speak, which finally stopped Herodias's laborious history lesson. To my surprise, Herodias now seemed to be thinking of me and not herself. She wanted to listen to whatever question I wished to ask. I did not understand why she was being polite to one of her young guards but would later understand her designs. "Did you say this Quirinius was a *consul* during the start of the Empire under Augustus?"

"Yes. I believe Quirinius was one of the two yearly elected *consuls* after Augustus took his position as dictator. It was just a few years later that Quirinius was appointed as *legate* of Syria by Augustus. It was also Quirinius who supervised Judaea when that territory was annexed after Archelaus was banished. Quirinius lived at Antioch in Syria, which is another reason why he sold everything in Jerusalem that belonged to my grandfather, except this palace. He gave Rome only a fraction of the proceeds and got away with the theft of my grandfather's kingdom and properties. Today Pontius Pilate answers only to Rome via Antioch as acting governor of Judaea. Pilate has been *procurator* for almost six years now if I am not mistaken, but he lives in Judaea at the dockyards of Caesarea. And he is no different from Archelaus when it comes to how to handle the Jews. Therefore, Pilate's days are numbered; and then my husband will get his kingship. He will, you know, because he is an old fox."

I was barely able to listen to this woman as she ran around the memory pole. I finally raised my hand again to stop her. When she ceased her flight of ideas, she looked down at me with a smile. She again patiently waited until I asked my question. "What is going on out in the streets below this window? Is it not a little early for this many people to be up and screaming?" I realized I had closed my eyes after I spoke because of the unbearable pain that racked my head. It felt like a hammer blow had been delivered to the back of my head; and, every time I tried to lift my head, I became nauseous.

When I did open my eyes, Herodias stepped away and started moving back and forth leaning from her left foot to her right. I closed my eyes again; and when I opened them, she was ablating her now-circular swaying movements. When she stopped and stood looking toward the open window, she sweetly answered my query. "The noises you hear are people near the Castle of Antonia demanding the gold-covered shields be removed from my husband's throne room here in this palace. If you know your Jewish history, King Solomon had 300 golden shields, not gold-coated shields like the ones here in the throne room. You see, my darling, King Solomon took 14 years to build his palace over on Mount Zion; and his throne room was called the House of the Forest of Lebanon. And may I point out that was twice as long as it took him to build the first Jewish Temple. Solomon crafted the golden shields as a sign of his title, king of the Jews. But why can a son of Herod the Great not also in these days be the king of the Jews? Rome refused to give my husband that title; but here in this palace hangs counterfeit shields as Rome's symbol that my husband is rightfully the king of the Jews but not in name, only in a vain gesture of symbolism. Rome wants to make it look like my husband is the king of the Jews without giving him the title. Well, that is not going to work. Out there in the street at this very moment, my husband and three of his brothers are staging a mass protest before Pontius Pilate demanding that the shields be removed. The Herod brothers are threatening to send a letter and a delegation to Tiberius if he does not. Now do you understand why that Jesus story in Jericho is such a thorn under everyone's skin? Did you not see the gold shields hanging on the walls when that Roman boy with such an Adonis body was whipped?"

Chapter Five

Herodias must have noticed I had my eyes closed, but she mistook it for disinterest and not because of my sickness and pain. "Well, since you do not understand the politics of Rome, why am I telling you all of this?"

Realizing she misunderstood my closed eyes, I replied with them open, "I understand Roman politics well enough. I know that my father, the Roman senator, and Claudia Varus murdered my mother and tried to kill me as well because of Roman politics. Yes, I am the son of Senator Vetallus; and my real name is Venustus Vetallus. But understand one thing; I am just a little fish in a pond of man-eating creatures."

My emotional reply to this scheming woman prompted Herodias to explain something that would forever make me a student of Roman politics. "Well, my poor injured darling, I will explain." Trying to keep my eyes open, I focused on Herodias's aquiline nose as she babbled on. "Oh, yes! Amcheck perhaps has told you he assassinates people from time to time for the Zealots. Well, the truth is Amcheck does not work for the Zealots. He works for my husband and the Herodians. The Herodians are a small but powerful group of men who want to see my husband on the throne as his grandfather Antipater and my grandfather and my husband's father, Herod the Great. The Herodians are not against Rome because, you see, it was Rome who gave my grandfather, Herod the Great, his kingship of all this land. The Herodians just want to go back and be rid of a Roman governor ruling over them."

"What did you say about Amcheck?" I asked still confused.

"Amcheck is our best assassin, and you are being trained to take his place. Claudia Pulchra Varus was despised by my husband because she also sided with the delegates when her husband Varus was governor of Syria. You see, General Varus marched his army into Jerusalem with the Old Fox's brother Archelaus's blessings. When you threw a knife into Claudia Varus, the war-god Mars finally blessed my husband. Don't you believe in the gods of Rome? Is it not obvious that the god Mars brought you to us to protect us as one of our guards? Since Amcheck is getting up in years, my husband has decided Amcheck needs someone to replace him. Amcheck did not like the idea at first, but he is a faithful servant."

"You have it all wrong. I met Amcheck by chance in a wine shop in the lower city years ago."

"Come now, Venustus darling. We all know how good you are with your throwing knives. My husband and I have been protecting you. No one else knows who you are except Saben and Amcheck. If anyone else knew, you would have been captured the day you came to be a guard at Jerusalem. My husband and I are not your enemies. We did not turn you over to that old

Praetorian of your father when he arrived last year with that horrible gladiator. Then you defeated that mental midget Marius in my throne room at Machaerus showing my husband your true talents. Antipas wanted Claudia Pulchra Varus killed for decades. Three years ago we received the news she was murdered by her step-son. Now, are you ready for a surprise?" asked Herodias looking around to see if we were still alone. I was wondering where the Greek physician or her husband was. After Herodias was satisfied, she moved closer and almost whispered her revelation. "What you do not know is Amcheck, Saben, Antipas, and I were all in Rome that stormy night you threw that dagger into Claudia Pulchara Varus. You see, the plan was for Amcheck to kill her that night. Amcheck and my husband did arrive at your father's villa as guests for a party just after you killed lady Varus. Isn't it ironic that you beat us all to the task and then came and joined us as a guard? My sweet darling, nothing happens by accident."

"What are you talking about, woman?"

"Now, now. I told you not to call me 'woman.' If we are going to be friends, then we must show some courtesy. I am your queen-mother, not woman. Never forget that. You may call me Herodias but only when we are alone. Otherwise, I am to be referred to as your queen. Understood?"

"My apologies. Still, my queen, what in the name of Hades are you talking about?"

"You should be careful when talking about the world you cannot see. Hades is a real place, and to call upon it could cause you some serious problems." She wagged her first finger in my direction before looking back toward the closed door. "Now, I will explain to help your concerns. Antipas was able to get an invitation to one of your father's well-known, coveted Frigg Night parties. The invitation was for my husband and me to attend. Amcheck went in my place with Antipas telling Senator Vetallus I was ill and not able to attend. It was a horrible windy and rainy night. Would you not agree? It was a night we all will never forget because, when Antipas arrived at your father's villa on Esquiline Hill, he learned Claudia was already dead. Amcheck did not have to knife her in the *vomitorium* as planned. We later learned it was the senator's assumed-dead son who threw a dagger across the atrium hitting Claudia in the chest. Forty feet I believe was the distance of the throw. Who could do that besides you? Now, do you see why my husband feels obligated to protect you?"

"That would make a great story if it were true," I said with a little amusement in my voice.

Chapter Five

"It is a true story. Actually, it is not a story; it is what happened. Honestly, you are alive because I had feelings for you the first time I laid my eyes on you at that 'bird-cage' at Machaerus with that desert beast screaming horrible things night and day about my husband and me. When I learned my husband was secretly visiting with John, well that was the twig that broke the camel's back. I knew he was visiting him because I could smell the stink on him every time he went to the pits in the basement of that palace. That had to stop, and that is why I had to arrange the desert creature's death. All of that happened after you arrived with Amcheck and beat that horrible gladiator. I have hated gladiator Marius since I watched him from Tiberius's box in Rome on the day he murdered everyone who came against him. That was the day I married the Old Fox," she tweeted with a little girl smile.

"I remember you. You were beautiful as you sat in the emperor's box."

"You are so sweet. But, you being there that day, must have meant you were just a child." She held up in her right hand holding my long, thick braid of hair with the red leather tie at the top. "This is all I will ever get from you, my love," she finally said moving back and forth checking to see if anyone had arrived through the door to this elegant room. I looked at the walls noticing for the first time several stunning murals painted on them. Herodias began singing some chant under her breath with closed eyes with my braid of hair to her nose. After her singing had stopped, she took a long sniff and a glow arose upon her face matched by a broad smile and a sparkle in her opened eyes. "Now do you understand why I want your hair? I can never have you as any man and woman have each other. I know I am a sinner like John the Baptist accused me, but that was not the reason I wanted him dead. It is true I left my husband Philip in Rome for the old fox. You see, I fell for Antipas the first time I saw him when I was just a girl. It was when Antipas arrived in Rome to petition Augustus just like the story that pseudo-prophet Jesus told. I wanted to marry my Uncle Antipas but made a mistake by marrying the wrong uncle and having Salome. What a man Antipas was, so young and with body and purpose. We make an unbreakable team, and I would never damage my unholy union with my Uncle Antipas."

For some mysterious reason, I could not take my eyes off Herodias. I believed she might be crazy, but now I knew she was totally gone in mind and soul. She moved up to whisper something to me; and I wanted to crawl away, but my head wound prevented any movement. "Here is the truth. You, darling, are my true love; and with the help of your hair, you will soon love me as well. I cannot leave Herod for you because he is going to be king of the Jews someday, and I will be his queen. But you, my dear Achilles, not

Venustus, is the person I genuinely love. I know that Antipas is my uncle just as my daughter is now married to her granduncle Philip, Tetrarch of Ituraea. But understand that I have deep feelings for you. These last few days taking care of you and keeping your body cool with wet rags have brought me more pleasure than I can remember. However, you are too young for me; and, if Antipas knew any of this, he would give you to Senator Vetallus in a heartbeat, not for the money but to destroy me. So what I have shared with you is your weapon against me. I have confessed my sins to you; and now, like it or not, you hold my life in your hands. But to hurt me, you will have to die; and that would, indeed, kill me."

I could not believe nor process all that I was hearing. Was this woman real, or was I dreaming? What do you say when someone like Herodias has just confessed such intimate things? I opened my mouth to speak, but it had to be quick because I could hear footsteps coming down the stone hallway toward this room.

"I am Venustus Vetallus, and you are a beautiful woman; but I see you only as I see my long-departed mother, who was avenged the night I put that dagger into Claudia's heart. If you wish, I will consider you as my mother if that will make any sense to you."

"Thank you, my love; it does, and I will be your mother," she said with tears falling onto the long strands of my long hair that was still in her hands. At that very moment, the door to the room flew open and in stepped Herod Antipas, Phoneinus the physician, Salome, and Amcheck, all in that order.

Herod looked at me and then bellowed out to Phoneinus demanding to know wheter I was going to live; and the doctor looked at me and said, "Of course, just look at him. He is awake and sane of mind. It will be perhaps another five to six weeks before he can assume any duties as before, but I predict a complete recovery. If it had not been for your wife and Salome keeping his fever at bay, there would be an adverse report crossing my lips at this very moment." Herodias hugged her husband with tears unashamedly pouring down her face. When she pulled away and used a towel to clean her face, she quickly asked Herod if she could keep my hair. She showed him the scalp, and he called her a silly woman but allowed her to keep my hair as a memento if she wished. I closed my eyes to all this insanity realizing I was going to be her prisoner for the next month and a half.

"Achilles lost his mother when he was just a boy. Could I adopt him as well?"

"No, but he can be your son just between you and me if you wish; that is until he recovers completely." She clapped her hands, and I wondered whether if I did eat that magical apple and this was all a fairy tale from a faraway land where everything was upside down.

Reality returned when Phoneinus began to push at the back of my head. When he finished his pushing, he carefully unwound the bandages and declared he had to clean the wound with some kind of oils mixed with tree moss. Everyone waited until my shaved head was rewrapped, and I ate some sweet bread mixed with goat's milk. After that meal, Herodias handed me a cup of sour wine mixed mostly with water. Before I was finished drinking, the physician Phoneinus was dismissed but not before he pleaded with Antipas that I needed to sleep and rest. Herod said I would have plenty of time to rest, but first he needed to talk to me. The moment Phoneinus left I again noticed the erratic chanting out the window. Now with the sun up it seemed to be growing louder. There was also the increased noise of Jerusalemites preparing for the Passover celebrations from all over the city.

Herod Antipas, his wife, and my so-called friend Amcheck stood next to my bed, and Herod began the interrogation. "I know this is hard to accept, but do not hold it against us for not revealing the truth about our knowledge of your being the son of Senator Vetallus. You are Achilles from now on, and no more will be discussed other than you being one of my guards. This Roman tribune, who crushed the back of your head, is still alive. I was not able to communicate to Amcheck before the flogging to do his best to kill him. That little act on my wife's part about whipping the tribune here in this palace was preplanned by me. Also, Amcheck declaring that you are a Jew and circumcised was also due to my orders."

I looked at Amcheck noticing his head down and realizing he would not look me in the eyes. Now I understood why he did the same during the proceedings between Pilate and Demos. Antipas looked over to Amcheck seeing I was staring at him. Herod dismissed whatever was happening between Amcheck and me and began talking again. "Pilate allowed only one strike to the head, which is why the young tribune still lives. Perhaps Amcheck could have laid the lead tips into his scalp instead of his face, and that would have finished him off; but it is what it is. The plan was to kill him with only the leather whip. Normally the best plans get skewed and stranger things have happened. When the Roman recovers, which will be much longer than your recovery, he will return to kill or capture you. I believe it was some scar on your right arm that convinced him. Up until then, with your being circumcised, we almost convinced all the Romans. I could have this tribune murdered at the Castle of Antonia; but if I assassinate him, it will bring the hammers of Hades down upon you and me. Yet, once this tribune reaches

Rome and is able to talk to your father, this country will be swimming with bounty hunters like fleas on a dog. In a few months' time, it will be difficult to hide you as one of my guards. As it stands, within the year a letter will eventually arrive from Rome telling Pilate who you are and to have him arrest you."

I closed my eyes as the pain in my head began to increase. I guessed the physician had mixed some kind of drug in my watered wine, for I was also becoming sleepy. I wanted Herod to stop talking, but he would not. The sound of his voice was hurting my head as well as all of these new revelations.

"My plan is simple, but it will serve all of us in many ways. First, I have problems with this Jesus. I do not know who he is. He could be John back from the dead. He could very well be the prophesied Messiah or some prophet from the past who has come back to do something. If I am correct, then my days of ruling are over. Things have never been the same since I went to Rome over that incident concerning my brother Archelaus. The final insult was bringing Herodias to this land as my queen." I looked over to Herodias and saw her husband gently touch her face with the back of his hand. For just a moment it was one of the sweetest gestures I had ever witnessed. Looking back at me he continued. "You see, my first wife, daughter of Aretas, king of Nabataeans, escaped to her father's capital at Petra once she learned about my marriage to Herodias. That was a dozen years ago, and things have only gotten worse. I will soon have a frontier war that I cannot win without Rome's help. If this Jesus is the Messiah, he will become the rightful king no matter what my father tried forty years ago to stop. Perhaps you never heard of the slaying of over twenty children two years and younger at the time this Jesus was of that age after being born in Bethlehem."

Herod stepped away giving me a few moments to close my eyes and rest before more of the story began. When I reopened them, I noticed Herod taking a quick sip from a silver cup. I thought to myself, "here comes a long story."

After the drink, he handed the silver vessel to Nina who had appeared from the direction of the door. "I still remember those Zoroastrian magi-priests arriving and starting all the problems. These magi came from the land of Amcheck's people, the Parthians. If the magi had only reported to my father after they had found this newborn king, I would not be having these Jesus or John the Baptist problems. But, I am the only person that is convinced the Zoroastrian magi found this child up in Galilee and not Bethlehem. I tried to tell my father as much but he did not believe me. You see after these stargazers saw his star in Parthia, it took almost a good year before they arrived looking for him. The year the star appeared was about three or four years before my father, Herod the Great died. I remember the star appearing three different times that year. The third time was when the magi arrived here in Jerusalem, and that time the star stood low in the northern sky, which would have guided them to Nazareth, the village where Jesus grew up. It is important to understand that the third star appeared almost a year after the first appearance that was high in the center of the sky. The first was in the spring and the third star appeared in the middle of winter. The Jewish Scriptures recorded the birth city of this child to be in Bethlehem, a few miles southeast of Jerusalem, and that is what fooled my father back in those days. I was a little younger than you, Achilles; but I remember everything clearly. We now know this Anointed One was born in Bethlehem as the prophet Micah predicted, but that is not where he grew up. This strange birth happened because the first Roman census demanded the different tribes of Israel return and be counted at their ancient ancestral homes. You see, the Messiah is to come from the tribe of Judah, specifically through King David, who was from Bethlehem. This census was order by Sentius Saturninus, a *consular* and imperial *augur* for Augustus, under the eye of the Syrian Roman *Legate* Quirinius. Killing the children in only Bethlehem was foolish. It is now apparent that this Jesus had gone back to Galilee many months before my father slaughtered the children of Bethlehem. By the time of my father's spies learned about the mistake, it was learned that Jesus's family had since fled to Egypt. It was some years later after my father died or sometime after my brother Archelaus was banished to Gaul when the family later returned to Nazareth. Precious treasures were given to the young king by these Parthian magi, and that is how the parents were able to relocate to Egypt and live there for some years. By the time of my father's death, all was forgotten concerning this Anointed One."

Herod stopped there and I looked at Amcheck. He was still looking at the floor like a little boy caught telling fibs. "Now Amcheck has told me you are angry with me for killing the Baptist. You have every right to be angry. I now believe that was a mistake, but we all make mistakes." Looking over toward Herodias, I noticed that she also lowered her eyes after this confession of her husband. Apparently Herod Antipas was clueless about the role his wife had in the death of the Baptist

"I will never be king of Jerusalem. My wife believes otherwise, but the people will never forgive me for killing the Baptist because most of the peasants see him as the first prophet to be sent by their God to this Promised Land in over four hundred years. Also, the Romans will not leave quietly being as entrenched in this land as they are, no thanks to my brother Archelaus. Oh, how I hate my brother. I will tell you a secret," whispered Herod looking like a little boy ready to show his pet snake to his friends. "It was on the 50th Anniversary of Actium when Angelus, my number one assassin took the life of my brother. That was when he was living in the province of Gaul. Unfortunately, that assassin was captured by the Romans and executed. But, he never revealed who gave him the orders to kill Archelaus. This was years before Amcheck replaced that gifted servant Angelus. The 50th Anniversary of Actium was also the day I wed the lovely Herodias on Palatine Hill with Tiberius in attendance and later we attended the great gladiatorial victory by Marius, the very same man you defeated at Machaerus last year."

Herod moved even closer to my ear; yet, everyone in the room could hear what he said next. "No one knows about the death of Archelaus and who was behind that deed. But today I am with friends. My only other friend is Saben, but I could not leave my brothers alone out in the streets protesting Pilate without someone guarding them." Stepping away from me, Herod Antipas smiled at his wife and Amcheck before continuing. "You see, Jesus's story as related by my brother Philip five days ago was correct in his assessment. The parable was about my brother and me, but I won in the end. Don't you all see?"

I could feel my eyes narrowing as I tried to understand the rantings of this madman who wanted to be the king of the Jews. "Now onto the shields. Achilles, did you see all those shields hanging on the walls when that Roman tribune was flogged?" I slightly nodded my head feeling even more sleepy than I could ever remember. I needed to speak to keep myself awake. "They looked impressive. I personally don't understand why you and your brothers would want them removed by Pilate."

Herod took my statement without malice and explained. "First of all, those shields are not solid gold but only gold coated over wood. Pilate wants me to think Rome has given me the title king of the Jews by receiving the shields but without the title. Only I and my brothers would know this, and what good is that to me?"

I wanted to point out that he should accept the shields because he might need Rome's help to fight the King of the Nabataeans. I would have voiced my thoughts, but my mind was almost ready to shut down. With all my power, I willed myself to stay awake to hear what else was going to be stated by this strange man. I now understood the bond that held him and Herodias together, and it was a dark *nexus*.

"You will be king of the Jews someday!" declared Herodias as if she were a prophetess.

"Perhaps the Fates will make it so, but Achilles and Amcheck are my sword and knife until I become king of the Jews. I know my mother was a Samaritan and my father was only half-Jewish, but the people would rather have my rule over a foreign Roman. You see, I have been given a star; and it is you, Venustus, son of Venus, the morning star." Herodias loved that analogy, but Amcheck was still looking at his feet.

"Son of Venus, I know this is a wagon full of history to unpack; but you did attend the Lyceum for many years, and perhaps you are smarter than all of us in this room put together. Your being one of my soldiers makes you more dangerous than you will ever know. Now here is my plan that will serve me and protect you. In five or perhaps six weeks, when you are able to travel by horse, you and Amcheck will accompany Nicodemus into the land of my mother."

I lifted my hand to stop his rapid talking and asked in a weak voice, "Who is Nicodemus?"

"You know him. He was the old man you were visiting when that Roman tribune ambushed you."

"Please stop. My head hurts too much to understand half of what you are saying."

"You don't know who Nicodemus is?"

"No! I just know an old half-blind man who seems to know the Scriptures and the history of this land more than anyone I have met."

"You are correct about both. Nicodemus is also one of the 70 members of the Sanhedrin. That is the highest court in all of the land of the sons of Herod the Great once ruled. The Sanhedrin even has pseudo-power over Rome."

Herodias interrupted by saying, "I disagree with that conclusion. Pontius Pilate controls Caiaphas's and Annas's priestly robes at the Castle of Antonia, and there rests the power of the Sanhedrin."

"Brilliant observation, my dear. However, no one will feel the absence of Nicodemus if he just happens to take a trip down the Ridge Road for the next year."

"The Ridge Road? For the next year? What are you talking about?"

"You cannot stay in Jerusalem without my protection. I am only here at Passover. The Romans have political control of Judaea, but the Sanhedrin and their Temple Guards control Jerusalem. Only when Pilate comes to this city during Passover week, everything changes until he leaves and spends the rest of his time on the coast at Caesarea; and Jerusalem goes back to Sanhedrin rule. Jerusalem is a strange, isolated city. It isn't even on any main highway including the Ridge Road."

"What is the Ridge Road you keep mentioning?"

"Three roads tie together what the Greeks call Mesopotamia and *Aigyptos* or Egypt. I am sure that, at your elite Lyceum, you learned *aigyptos* means the gift of the Nile. Anyway, Jerusalem is located between Mesopotamia and Egypt but not on any of the three highways cutting through this land. One road is called the International Highway that runs from Egypt through Gaza along the sea but then goes in toward the foothills of Judaea north through Megiddo passing from west to east of the Jezreel Valley until it reaches Capernaum at the top of the Sea of Tiberius. From Capernaum, the International Highway runs north and then east passing through Damascus and up to the Euphrates River. Another highway is called the Jordan Rift Road or Jordan Valley Road. It is the road from the Sea of Tiberius going down the Jordan River to Jericho and up through the Wadi Kelt, the narrow canyon between Jericho and Jerusalem. No Jews who live in my region of Galilee will travel the natural way through Samaria, which is to take the Ridge Road. They normally take the Jordan Rift Road, not the Ridge Road. There is great animosity between the Jews and the Samaritans that dates back before I was even born. After you are healed and can travel, you, Son of Venus, will travel to Samaria along with Amcheck and Nicodemus. While you are in Samaria, I want the three of you to find every place this Jesus has visited; but you must always stay on the Ridge Road."

I tried looking at this man hovering above me. I could now see why his wife and Jesus both called him "that *Old Fox*." The scenarios he was weaving seemed logical and calculating, to say the least.

"My queen and I are thankful to you for taking the life of Varus's wife. Even Amcheck is pleased since he most likely would not have survived her assassination."

Looking over at Amcheck to see his reaction, he was still looking at the floor in a portrait of shame. Herod smiled at his submissive looking assassin and turned back to me with the same smile still spread across his face. His teeth were not rotten, and I briefly wondered what his secret was.

"On that fateful night, you, Achilles, accomplished the impossible only because the deed was endorsed by the god Mars. I want you to know how grateful we in this room are to you for the demise of that evil wife of Varus."

"One last question before I pass out from the pain in my head. Why would Nicodemus leave Jerusalem for an entire year? I believe he is too old and frail for such a trip."

Everyone laughed at that, which to this day I never learned what was funny. Perhaps getting my head cracked open made me humorous. I didn't feel funny. What I felt was quite the opposite. There was the revelation of

Chapter Five

Herodias's love for me, the identity of Nicodemus, and the truth about Amcheck sharing all my information with the Old Fox and his wife since day one. I also was confused and shocked by the news that Herod had been preparing me to be an assassin. I couldn't even begin to process that Amcheck would have killed Claudia had I not shown up to rescue Eli. I decided to release all my thoughts knowing I would pass into deep sleep. However, my last thoughts were pleasing because, if I were looking for Jesus, I would find Messina and my dog. If that happened, then I would take Messina and Zoe and run to the land of the Panchatantra. At this juncture, what difference would it make what strange land I ran toward?

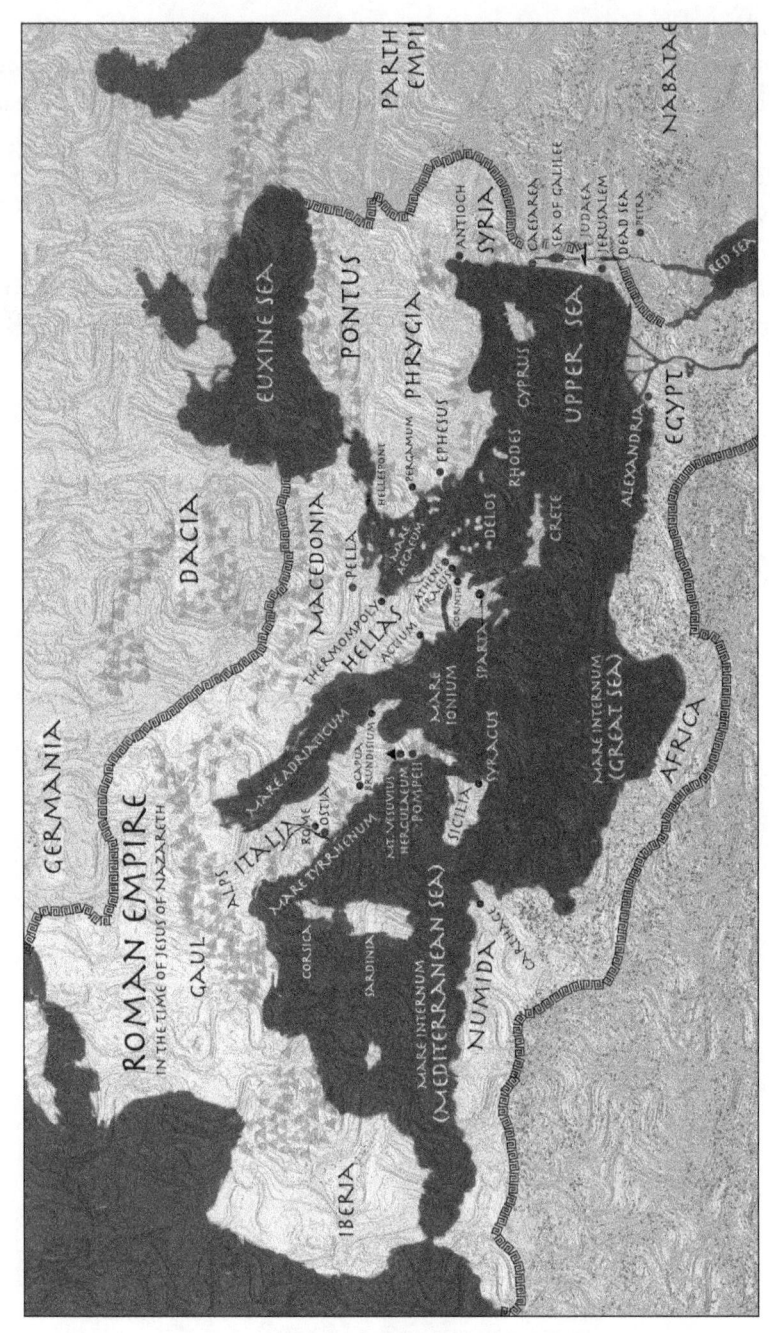

ROMAN EMPIRE
In The Times of Jesus of Nazaeth

CHAPTER SIX

Jerusalem – From Passover to a week before Pentecost in Tiberius's 18th year. Pontius Pilate's 6th year as Prefect of Judaea. The start of the 4th and last year of Jesus of Nazareth's public ministry. *(32 AD)*

A man that has friends must show himself friendly, and there is a friend that stickest closer than a brother.   King Solomon, Book of Psalms

W as Amcheck really my friend? I now believe with all my heart that Eli was a true friend. Eli began as my slave playmate; and, as a young man, he bravely sacrificed his life for mine. Yes, Eli had been my friend, even when I had doubts. There is no greater demonstration of love or friendship than for someone to give their life for another. Amcheck, however, had been pretending to be my friend since the day we met. He had being playacting his faithfulness to me because of his obedience to the orders of Herod Antipas. Now I felt like a fool. I desperately needed a friend, and I had no one to trust. Eli had become a real friend, but he was now dead because of my refusal to bow to the Jewish high priest. On that point, the man named Caiaphas was a man who needed to die; but I also understood it would be to my demise if I struck down a man who was anointed as Yahweh's high priest.

Spending hours in bed, I wondered about this old scholar named Nicodemus. What role was he to play in my future? Was he going to become my friend? I did find myself praying for a real friend, someone I knew without a doubt would not betray me down the road. I needed someone desperately whom I could trust to be a faithful and genuine friend. At times I found myself begging God for a friend in this world that I could trust with my life. The words of Amcheck spoken to me after the flogging of Demos, "no one hurts my friend and gets away with it - you remember that when you have to cover my back," sang like a dark enigma as I drifted in and out of sleep. Over and over it plagued me as to why Amcheck said what he said. Perhaps he knew I was going to soon learn the truth about him, and it was his way of telling me he was a faithful friend or another statement on a long list of lies. Then, again, maybe our relationship started out as a fallacious friendship; but it grew to one of acceptance much in the same way Eli, my childhood slave, became a loyal friend. At my lowest points, a dark, sinister voice screamed into my head that Amcheck could have collected the reward from my father, but he never did.

Over the next few weeks, my thoughts fanned out in a flight of ideas that had no order to them. Hundreds upon hundreds of opinions, views, and dreams came and went during those long hours of waiting for my head to heal. There were times, even in my sleep, where I found myself praying to the God of John the Baptist. When my mind turned to Jesus, I was utterly mystified and bewildered. I did not understand anything about why he was doing miracles and telling such strange stories. The biggest mystery was the statement Jesus made early in his ministry concerning the Temple and calling it his father's house. What was all this supposed to mean? Then there was the statement about Jesus building the destroyed Temple in three days. What was this all about?

During the days convalescing in the queen's bedroom, I reflected on many of my past decisions. I had placed a great deal of my young life in learning and training for revenge. All my young years as a teen living in Athens seemed consumed with the pursuit of death for Claudia and my father. After my vengeance, then came the two months in the tunnels underneath the synagogue in the 14th district of Rome. Once I reached Jerusalem as an Israeli, a depression came over me that never seemed to abate. I tried to cover it with alcohol and work. When Messina revealed she was going to marry Demos, all I wanted to do was drown myself in the waters of Bethesda. I concluded the wages of revenge had poisoned my well-being. That was precisely what both Zeno and Hector told me would happen.

Hector and Grillius were perhaps my only close friends. I never got very close to any of the Greek anglers out of Piraeus. They were old and simple men, and their only interest in life was fishing. I just could not find anything to discuss with any of them besides weather, nets, hooks, and the different water animals we hauled into our little boats. My only acquaintance with the opposite sex was Messina, and I barely knew her except for a few short encounters. And now I was having a hard time forgiving her because of her decision to marry that *thag* Demos Deva. I desperately wanted her in my group of people I knew I could trust with my life; yet, I still wondered if I would ever get over her decision to marry Demos. I found myself praying to Yahweh during the darkest times of night over and over about this matter. I must confess that, after begging God to heal my heart, I began to find rest over some issues and decided that maybe my prayers were being answered. I started to accept with a sweet sense I was going to soon find healing from this deadly heart and head wound that contentiously vexed me. I kept hearing a new voice telling me that patience was a virtue, but there was also a dark voice telling me to give up all hope. It soon became apparent that there was a spiritual war being waged for my soul, a struggle between choosing the light over darkness.

During the end of my fourth week of convalescing in the queen's bed, I was greeted with the most excellent antidote to my physical and inner strife. It happened in the middle of an afternoon when the city grew quiet for a short time during the hottest time of day. Herodias had hovered at my bedside regularly over the past four weeks and proved to be a proficient nurse and surrogate mother. However, I never felt I could trust her further than I could spit. I tried to be gentle and respectful of her since she rarely left my side. It was as if her new purpose in life was to live with me in her bedchamber located on the top floor of Herod's Palace. It would be during these quiet moments in the middle of the afternoons when she would sit in a strange overstuffed chair and nap. I would lie still and listen to her slow breathing, and it was then I would feel safe enough to once again start my dark musings over the lack of companionship. With the loss of Amcheck, there was a substantial need for a sincere and staunch friend to be faithful to my fragile inner needs. I believe all humans need just one person to fulfill this void at different times in our lives. If we could not share our experiences with someone real, palpable, and touchable, what was the purpose of living? On this particular afternoon, I decided I could not stand this loneliness much longer. If something did not give soon, I would not have the strength to continue fighting to live. The pain in the back of my head was not getting better, and this worried me. Just lifting my head caused a great deal of pain, and it had been almost a month since the injury.

Suddenly my thoughts were interrupted by a loud knock at the door announcing someone wished to enter. I moved my head the best I could toward the door. When the wooden door slowly creaked on iron hinges, there stood God's answer to my most immediate problem. At first, I did not entirely comprehend who was standing in the doorway. It was an older man with a purple-scarlet robe wrapped around him like a beautiful blanket. He stood frozen, not saying a word. I moved my head a little more and still did not understand who was standing at the open door of the queen's bedroom without any expression on his face. Behind the old man appeared Amcheck, also without expression and his eyes still looking down. Looking harder at the aged man in the red blanket, I noticed his military boots, boots that were identical to mine. I looked at my feet, which were still sporting my military boots. As strange as it might seem, I refused to allow even Herodias to remove my footwear. Every time she approached the subject, I just said, "If I die, I am going to die wearing my boots." Besides, with my Spartan shoes on my feet, I could push against the bronze bed frame when the pain in my head grew too much to handle. It just felt better to push against something hard over concentrating my thoughts on the agonizing throbbing in my head.

Turning my gaze back to the door, I now noticed the man in front of Amcheck had long hair tied in a ponytail falling to his waist. "Never tongue lash; only stare" came to mind. I was the first to smile at the recognition of my old *paidotribes* from the Lyceum. Just as the sun rises every morning, there abided Grillius as faithful and steady as a giant cedar growing in the mountainous land north of Galilee. I dismissed his somberness, for he was that kind of a man. No nonsense and boyish bilge for him. All I could think of was Yahweh had answered my feeble prayers. There in the doorway was my true friend standing in front of my fake friend. Here was someone I finally could trust to protect me and help me with my future uncertainties.

Herodias must have awakened at the change in the air made by an open door, for I heard her before I saw her. "You must be the Spartan we have heard about." She then scurried to grab his hand in a most unladylike manner. "I must say you taught our wounded warrior well, for I witnessed his fighting skills myself. It was an unbelievable victory over Rome's greatest champion of the arena. You did splendid work with your apprentice. Please enter my bedchambers. I am the wife of Herod Antipas, Tetrarch of Galilee and Perea. Please enter, and greet your long-lost pupil."

In walked a shy-looking Grillius followed by Amcheck. When Grillius reached my bedside, he did not say anything to me other than ask, "May I remove his bandages?"

Chapter Six

"No, you may not," retorted Herodias. "He is under the care of my personal physician."

I answered Grillius's request. "Yes, he can. Please rescind your mandate, Madam Queen. Grillius is more than a *paidotribes*. He is a skilled surgeon, equal to Phoneinus, if not preferable." I held up my right arm for her to inspect. "Had he not netted all the cut muscles and nerves together, I would have lost not only this arm but most probably my life. Look at how my fingers still open and close. It is short of a miracle. Grillius did all of this, plus he prevented any infection. My Queen, you first need to ask why he wishes to examine my head."

Herodias was apparently stunned by Grillius's strange request and my salient response. After some thought on her part, she said, "Spartan, why do you wish to inspect my physician's work?"

Grillius finally smiled at Herodias; and, in a voice of authority, he stated, "Even before I opened the door, I could smell the infection. Eunus will be dead by nightfall if I do not survey the wound."

Herodias turned to me; and, with an intense look in her eyes, she said, "Achilles, you are more than an adopted son to me. To prove it, I will allow this." Turning back to Grillius, she said, "Go ahead, Spartan."

Grillius went to work with hands that showed everyone he was an experienced man of medicine. After the wrappings had been removed, it was evident to all in the room that my wound, indeed, had infected. Even I could smell my own rot after the wrappings were removed. I noticed Herodias and Amcheck placing their hands to their noses. Grillius turned to Herodias and asked, "What did your physician use to set the bones together in his head?"

Herodias shook her head like she did not know.

"It looks like cement," commented Grillius. "This all has to be taken out, or he will be dead by morning. Look at his forehead. He is sweating from the infection, which means it is already in his blood."

"We must bleed him first. I will call my physician," cried Herodias, now visibly worried.

"You will not call him. I will fix this without his disturbing knowledge. I know his type. If he learns about me, he will bleed Eunus to death before the sun sets. Now I must hurry, and I will need several things. Are you willing to work with me, Queen? I will also need a young slave who can run and fetch whatever I need during my operation."

"Tell me; what is it you are proposing to do?" asked a worried but compliant Herodias.

"I will need several gold coins that I can melt down and form a plate to replace this disaster your physician has made. I will need to remove the fractured bones and clean the wound. The wound will then need to be irrigated with a special solution for several days. I will have you mix and administer a solution every two hours. It will take several nights and mornings before we are done. By then, I will have made the gold plate to replace the broken bones. If I have help, Eunus will survive and be just as normal as he was before this accident."

"What about the patient?" asked Herodias. "How will he withstand the pain while all this is happening?"

"Do not worry. I will have you mix a drink that will put Eunus under its influence. It will only last for about four hours, and then we will give him another drink and so on. Now we must hurry if you wish to save his life."

Herodias looked at me with genuine worry. "Achilles, what do you want? Do you trust this Spartan?"

"Do what he says, and I will live. All will be fine," I said with a weak smile. Grillius clapped his hands to get everything moving. Herodias twirled in a strange half circle and left the room leading Grillius and Amcheck with her. A few moments later Herodias returned alone and came up to me speaking in a voice that was close to being a whisper. "I gave you a gift today to show you how much I love you."

I was taken back when she used the Greek word *eros* for the word *love*. I began to worry about her true intentions but dismissed the thoughts when I realized I might not even survive the night. After thanking her for finding Grillius, she continued talking while moving back and forth in some kind of bee dance. "It took some time and money to find your old teacher. It was Amcheck who told me all about your Spartan *gymnos* scholar. But I knew nothing about his abilities as a surgeon. I will tell you the truth; I do not trust Spartans. I know that is silly of me, but it is the truth. Until today I have believed all Spartans to be laconic and brainless. This man defies all of those preconceived ideas."

"I think you will find him a little laconic, for that is the origin of that word. You see, Sparta is located in the district of Laconia."

"Perhaps so. I was able to persuade my husband to hunt the Spartan down in the hope that your old teacher could help us find the Carnalus Scroll."

Her words confirmed what was really at the heart of everything. Everyone wanted this elusive scroll.

Chapter Six

"My true intentions are to help you feel safe. The Spartan is a bit old but the fittest man of his age I have ever seen. But I know how much you love this man, for you talk in your sleep."

After her strange announcement, I felt naked in front of this woman who was older than my mother if my *mater* were still alive. The door opened again, and in stepped Amcheck and the slave girl Nina. Amcheck was carrying several palm lamps, and Nina had her arms full of white towels. Herodias turned to Amcheck and asked if Grillius was able to find all he needed in the kitchen. He reassured her all would begin soon, and Amcheck again left the room. I found myself praying to Yahweh for strength to endure whatever was to follow. I also asked for Grillius to have special skills beyond even what he understood.

Soon Amcheck returned with Grillius, both carrying arms full of bottles and clay vessels. Grillius began working with the contents of the clay jars and glass vials at a nearby side table. Two slaves brought in a brazier supported by three short legs making it about half the height of a man. Grillius ordered that it be placed near the open window. A third slave carried hot coals and put them in the brazier, and soon it was blazing away. Grillius then handed Herodias a cup and asked her to have me drink all of it. It tasted like wine mixed with almonds, but I drank all of it before Herodias and Nina set up a water clock near the corner of the room. It was at this time I closed my eyes and fell into a black void.

I did not return out of this dreamless state until two days later. It was early morning when I emerged, and I could hear Herodias breathing in her sleep from behind me in the overstuffed chair. When I called out, she came to me with a beautiful smile because I was still in the land of the living. She told me that Grillius was an excellent surgeon as I had stated. She said Nina and she irrigated my head wound for two days before Grillius placed a golden plate into the hole behind my head. She was excited to tell me I had 12 Roman *aureii* in my head. I made the calculation remembering an *aureus* was equal to 25 silver *denarii*. An *aureus* was about the same size of a *denarius* but much heavier. She told me she would keep this little secret from her husband. "The Old Fox is tight with money," but she contributed the Roman gold coins for Grillius to fashion into what he needed. When I asked why my thigh hurt, she told me Grillius had cut a piece of skin from there to graft over the golden plate at the back of my head. "Your teacher told me he learned a great deal of his medicine from the Guptas who lived on the Ganga River in the ancient land of King Asoka." She said Grillius had visited this land where there were many hospitals for the sick and each one was free of charge to the patients.

"Can you imagine any ruler using the people's taxes for such a thing? But it is a marvelous idea." Herodias appeared thrilled to tell me she learned something from Grillius, the Spartan. "Did you know that all the doctors of medicine in the land of India wash their hands before all operations, and they are careful to practice every form of cleanliness?"

"I am sure the Jews and men from this land would get along magnificently. The Jews you know also practice hand rituals of cleanliness."

Herodias laughed with me and went on to explain that the art of grafting was prevalent in India. "Your Spartan teacher even told me wealthy women had their lips enhanced by cutting the skin from their rectal area. Can you even imagine that?" she commented with an embarrassed laugh.

I waved my hand in the air as if shooing away a fly and then made a face to show her I had heard enough. She giggled and twirled a few times before calling Nina to run and alert Grillius that I was awake and with faculties.

Soon Grillius was at the door with a smile on his face. "Eunus, my lost student, we are now joined again in the land of the living." His smile showed more in his eyes than his mouth. I nodded the best I could and lifted my left hand waving for him to come forward. When he stood next to my bed, we grabbed each other's arm in the traditional elbow-to-elbow embrace but with the wrong forearm due to the position of my bed, which restricted my right arm's movement.

Herodias commented after our warrior greeting, "Your Spartan has agreed to travel with you and Amcheck for the next year. I will now leave you two alone so you two can reacquaint yourselves." Herodias closed the door so we could be alone.

There stood Grillius in his Spartan military uniform. The Spartans were the most excellent fighters, soldiers, and mercenaries the world had ever known. For centuries all Spartan males were separated from their mothers at age 7 to start a life of being a warrior. The naked little boys were given over to the city-state to train non-stop until age 20. From age 20 until 60, all males were members of the Spartan army. The only weakness became apparent after Sparta's defeats over three hundred years ago at the Battle of Leuctra and again at Mantinea, where together over 20 percent of what was the original *"status quo"* 9,000 soldiers were severely defeated by the Thebans. These two battles occurred within nine years of each other and over thirty years after the end of the two back-to-back wars between Athens and Sparta now known as the Peloponnesian Wars. Since it took 20 years to train one soldier, heavy losses in such a short time left Sparta too weakened to continue as it had before the

Peloponnesian Wars. The Thebans, who fought using the "oblique-phalanx" trick at Leuctra and at Mantinea, led to Sparta's deathblow as a world power.

After Sparta fell from it empire status, she still has trained warriors up to the present. Those who do not stay in Sparta hire themselves out as guards to foreign kings or as mercenaries in distant lands. Today Sparta maintains itself by offering wealthy Roman men trips to Sparta for twisted personal entertainment. The Romans come mostly in the summer to this unsophisticated city in Laconia, Greece, serenely surrounded by mountains, to witness Sparta females exercising in the nude, which had always been their custom. Another highlight is watching young boys being flogged in public without making a sound. This is considered a "status" vacation for any Roman nobleman. Throughout Sparta's history, there has always been a problem with a low birth rate because many Spartan men were encouraged to be lovers of each other. This, too, is another aspect of this ancient Greek city-state selling itself out as a tourist attraction to Roman men.

Once the room was empty, Grillius joked, "I always knew you would end up in a queen's bed somewhere but not quite like this."

After we had laughed together, I said, "I owe you my life, actually more so than what you did a few nights ago."

"I am no longer your trainer, but we are *Men of Equal Status*. This is what a Spartan calls his fellow Spartan. You may have started your training around age 11 or 12, but still that is a young age to begin. Now we will wear the same uniform and fight side by side with the same weapon: the falcata, if that is yours leaning up against the wall over there." I looked to where Grillius pointed and for the first time identified my sword was in this room. I tried to smile at his high compliment. "I understand I am to call you Achilles. I have accepted a job as your sitter and bodyguard for only one year, but consider me only as your equal. The money these Herods are offering is more than I have earned in a lifetime. They are generous with their money. As a teacher at the Lyceum, I earned only one *denarius* a day. The Herods are giving me seven *denarii* a day to just protect you. They have already paid me half a year's wages, which is plenty if they fail to pay the remaining at the end of a year." I watched as Grillius pulled out a bulging moneybag from inside his Spartan cloak. Holding the bag up for me to see, he said, "What they do not understand, at my age you can protect me more than I can keep you safe. You can see I am up in years and not as quick as I once had been. Once you are back on your feet, they will understand they made a mistake by hiring such an old man. Yet, I will not tell them if you do the same. Just having this bag of coins here should take me into a comfortable old age."

"Tell me how they found you, and what news do you have of my father?"

"Hector and his new Jewish friend are well and safe. They are hiding in the hills above the site of the pass of Thermopylae. The Persians under Xerxes knew of one goat trail when they used it to encircle King Leonidas and his 300 *hippies*. I know of at least three other hidden paths deep into the hills behind the Thermopylae Fire Gates. They are living in a secure stone hut more than a mile from the sea."

"What about Hector's home in Athens?"

"The Romans burned it. That was after they heard that you came to Rome from Athens. Hector and Anab the Jew came to me and told me the story of your plan to go to Rome and free Anab's nephew – a fool's plan if I ever heard of one – but revenge is a powerful force all of us have to experience to understand. Surviving as you have, you have now learned something about seeking revenge?"

"I have learned many things in the past three years. Perhaps I have gone soft, or I would not be lying in this queen's bed. Allowing a Roman to strike from behind with the flat of his sword is evidence that I did not learn everything I should have. Besides, the one who hit me was your snake student Deva, about whom you warned me."

Grillius was all ears now. With his head cocked to hear me better, he asked in amazement, "Deva, the student at the Lyceum who injured your arm?"

"It was Deva, the one who cheated and cut my arm; the arm you saved. I should have been more alert."

"Always be aware of your surroundings was your first lesson. Just remember it was the flat of the sword that struck your skull and not the edge. You can learn the easy way or the hard way. I do not think you will repeat that error. You will always be more than cautious when exiting doors from now on, or perhaps you will never use the same door you enter in the first place."

We both laughed, which led me to a coughing fit. My loud expulsion of air brought in Herodias and Amcheck along with Herod Antipas. They must have been at the door listening to our every word; yet, I do not think they discovered the location of Hector or the Carnalus Scroll. Grillius usually spoke in a low guttural tone for our protection.

"Are you all right?" asked Herodias.

"It is my fault; I should not have caused him to laugh," apologized Grillius.

Everyone was relieved, which made me feel somewhat of a celebrity. Herod Antipas put his arms around the shoulders of Amcheck and Grillius and announced his well-thought-out plan. "These two men are going to protect you from the Romans, including those two senators, Treverorum and

Vetallus. As you know, a small fortune rides on your capture; but I will give both of these friends of yours a gift above their wages if you are still alive this time next Passover. Should I say I will give each of you 200,000 *sestertii* by next Passover?"

"Isn't Passover less than a year from now?" I asked not believing Antipas would ever pay Amcheck or Grillius such a fortune. "What is going to happen by next Passover?"

"The next Passover is falling on a Jubilee year, which happens only every 50 years. It will start on the next Feast of Trumpets this coming fall. Since next Passover will be in a Jubilee year, there will be an added 100,000 pilgrims here in Jerusalem. I am sure Pontius Pilate will still be Judaea's *prefect* serving under the eye of the imperial *legate* in Syria. Pilate will bring at least half of his legion from Caesarea into Jerusalem believing there will be trouble, which there will be. Altogether there could easily be over a million Jews in this city next Passover. This will swell this small city here in the Judaean hills to a size equivalent to Rome's population living around her seven hills. However, I am counting on riots from the Zealots and adding to the likelihood of this pseudo-prophet Jesus declaring he is the Jew's long-awaited Messiah. I think Pilate would if he could bring all the legions in Syria to Jerusalem."

"Do you believe he is the Messiah, this Jesus, I mean?" I asked looking at Antipas standing between Amcheck and Grillius with his arms still around their shoulders. Oddly, both soldiers had their heads lowered looking somewhat embarrassed to find themselves in such an intimate position.

After my question, Antipas released the two men and seemed confused as he contemplated. "There are many now calling him the Messiah, whom the Jewish Scriptures predicted from the very beginning of time. I have talked to Nicodemus, and he tells me all of this is written in the Scriptures. He tells me that, whoever is the Messiah, he is predicted to become the King of Kings who will rule from Jerusalem. I believe Pilate will repeat most of what he did one week before Passover this year. He will send his Roman soldiers into the Court of Gentiles and kill a dozen or so waiting quietly to offer their sacrifices. It worked once; why not again? It will be a Pontius Pilate message to behave or else. If I might add, the Galileans he killed this year are my subjects, not his; and he will pay a high price for his arrogance if it happens again. Also, do not forget this Jesus is from Galilee, a citizen of my realm. If any more Galileans are killed on holy ground, then Pilate will end up just like the Jewish captain did on the day you and Amcheck assassinated him in front of the Temple near Solomon's porch." I looked at Grillius who was now looking at me with bafflement in his eyes. When he saw the shame in my eyes, Grillius lowered his head again and stepped away from Antipas.

Antipas pursed his lips before he continued his diatribe. "After Pilate killed the Galileans in the Temple last Passover… well, you see… there were no more uprisings. The Romans, who are master diplomats, have no imagination except brute force. But this coming Passover will be different. My spies tell me the Zealots are planning an armed uprising during the week before Passover. That is why you three must be back here in this city one week before Passover begins. I should also say there is a plan taking shape in Rome that might entirely change who sits on Palatine Hill before next spring if not sooner."

"Tell me; is my father Senator Vitallus involved?" I asked.

"Yes, your father, Achilles, is possibly involved in what is already happening in Rome. The good news for me is Pilate is not aware that these changes could be bad for him. I have some sources coming out of Rome indicating that Senator Vitallus is planning to either poison or assassinate Tiberius within the year and place your half-brother, Julius Vetallus, in his place. This could be a reality since Sejanus's plan to murder Tiberius and take the throne for himself has finally failed. The only obstacle to your father's plans is a scroll you know about that reveals some evidence who the real father is of Julius Vetallus. No one is disputing that Claudia Pulchra Vetallus Varus is the grandniece of Augustus and the mother of Julius but then who murdered the real father of little Julius. Everything in this world revolves around bloodlines. Before Sejanus's failed stratagem, he believed that being married to Tiberius's dead son's wife, he had the bloodline claim of divinity. The problem was most Roman noblemen suspected Sejanus had a hand in the murder of Tiberius's son. Therefore, it seems more probable that your father, Achilles, will maneuver your half-brother onto the throne now that Sejanus is no longer a problem for anyone. Still, to stop him will require a certain scroll."

I wondered why Antipas kept referring to Sejanus in the past tense. I wanted to ask about this, but how does anyone stop the Old Fox when he is busy scheming in such a tangential way? "Now, if the latter happens, it would be helpful if I could expose your father by showing Tiberius the Carnalus Scroll. There is a powerful rumor that a particular Greek *didace* named Zeno gave Senator Vetallus's elder son this incriminating scroll before he left Rome at age ten. You see, I would rather have Sejanus or Tiberius on the throne, not your father. Besides, if your father is on the throne via your brother, I will no longer be able to protect you. Your father is allied with Senator Treverorum; and he is the father of Demos Treverorum, the boy Pilate had whipped in my throne room, more than a month ago. There will be a terrible price to pay for both Pilate and me if your father gains the throne of power with your half-brother as the puppet emperor. Therefore, you can see how important it is to expose your father to Tiberius and the sooner the better. My plan is simple: you, Achilles, produce the scroll; give it to me; and be done with your father. All bounty hunters will stop looking for you, and I will gain the favor of Tiberius. You see, I have worked hard finding the heart of Tiberius. That is why I built a city on the Sea of Galilee and called it Tiberias. Today all Roman maps show the lake in Galilee as the Sea of Tiberius, not Galilee. I have nothing to gain by having a Vetallus on the throne as emperor, even though I have his son who murdered the future emperor's mother. Your father has vowed to kill you himself if anyone brings you alive to him. He hates you, Venustus."

I decided to use the old stare tactic. I looked at Herod and acted stupidly as if I wasn't sure what he was talking about. After my stare, the Old Fox threw up his hands and walked toward the door. There was a tense moment until he returned to my bedside. "I know people think we Herods are stupid; but trust me, I know stupid; and you, Achilles, are not stupid – so don't play that game. I have many contacts in Rome, who regularly keep me informed on imperial matters. I even have a spy at Capri and another at the Imperial Palace on the Palatine. My number one spy is Herod Agrippa, son of Aristobulus and grandson of Herod the Great, my father. He attained this name from Tiberius's stepfather's late friend and best general known simply as Agrippa. Caesar Augustus's Agrippa is the one who built the *Pantheon* and has his name carved in stone over the entrance to this temple if anyone doubts my words. I am now going to play a dangerous game that you will understand. And yes, it has to do with that Carnalus Scroll."

Turning to Amcheck, Herod told him to bring in "our guest." I seemed confused as I watched Amcheck move slowly toward the door. His head was down with a look of shame but was being obedient to his master. After opening the door, he said something to someone out in the hall; and then in stepped a Jewish-looking man. Behind the man was an older Jewish woman who did not enter the room but stayed at the open door. I recognized her as being the wife of one of Herod's stewards. Behind her appeared another woman, much younger. The older woman stepped aside allowing the most beautiful woman in the world to enter the room. It was none other than Messina.

Herod Antipas with excessive glee waved his hand toward the doorway. "May I introduce Messina Flavius, ward of Senator Vetallus. When she marries, she will perhaps be the wealthiest woman in the world. She is the heir to the fortune left by her late father, Flavius of Ephesus. Her companion standing over there is Judas or Y'hudah from *K'riot*, a town some twenty miles south of Jerusalem. This Judaean is one of the closest disciples of Jesus, and the only disciple who is not from Galilee. When Messina heard about the trial of our Achilles and the flogging of Demos, she made a request through my steward's wife, who is a secret follower of this Galilean holy man Jesus. Messina asked to come to Jerusalem under the protection of Judas, the only Judaean disciple of Jesus. She has been following Jesus of Nazareth for some time along with some other women. One of those women happens to be Joanna, the wife of Chuza, the woman out in the hallway, the woman who made the request for Messina." While Herod was introducing Joanna, a middle-aged man stepped into the doorway; and Herod introduced her husband Chuza. "I should add Chuza is my trusted chief steward here in Jerusalem, and I do not hold any animosity toward him because his wife Joanna follows Jesus. If Chuza says Jesus and his disciples are connected to the violent Zealots, then I believe him. If he says otherwise, I would believe that. However, one of Jesus's disciples did come out of the Zealots but I am told he has changed his ways."

While Herod was speaking, I was staring at Messina. She was wearing a simple white Judaean robe looking very much like the last time I saw her. I could see those unusual flecks of gold and red in her dark auburn hair because the hood from her cotton cloak was hanging back behind her head. Her cloak was the same color of her robe and looked very comfortable. What made my heart ache was looking at her translucent azure eyes and flawless skin, which seemed to glow from the light coming in through the open window. When our eyes met, she smiled showing her deep dimples on both sides of her mouth. I nodded to her with evident affection, a fondness I was sure Herodias even noticed.

On the unserious side of things, this Judas disciple of Jesus did not impress me at all. He did not look Galilean, besides the fact he wore the robe of a Judaean and not what the people wore up north in the Galilee. Besides his expensive clothes, this Judas character appeared to be somewhat shady with his eyes moving from each individual in the room as if he were trying to memorize each face and later could make a report for some coins. I remember Felix, the Praetorian Guard, with the same kind of darting eyes but not as obvious as the eyes of this disciple of Jesus. Felix had confessed to me that night at the tavern he was a seller of information, which undoubtedly paid a reasonable price if someone knew where to sell it; but here was a different kind of operator, who was not good at what he did.

"Thank you, Y'hudah," said Herod. "Please wait outside the door." Chuza moved back into the hall to allow Judas to exit the room. I watched Chuza

Chapter Six

take Judas by the arm and direct him away leaving only Chuza's wife in the doorway. Once Judas and Chuza were gone, Herod waved for Joanna to close the door. That she did placing herself outside the room.

With the sound of the door closing, Herod turned to Messina and said, "I am sorry to have you join us, daughter of Flavius, under such circumstances." His words sounded sycophantic and obsequious. "Now, would you please repeat the story you told me earlier when you witnessed in Rome the torture of the slave of Senator Carnalus a dozen or so years ago in Senator Vetallus's villa?"

"I do not mind. It was horrible. I was just a little girl but had to watch by orders of Senator Vetallus. The slave's name was Zeno; and he said before he died that he gave a scroll to Venu… I mean Venustus, the one lying before us in bed," she said pointing at me. "The slave Zeno apparently had proof along with a scroll that the murder of Senator Carnalus was orchestrated by Senator Vetallus along with his wife, Claudia Vetallus. This happened many years ago shortly after Senator Vetallus also killed my father in Ostia. The same day my father died was the same day Venustus's mother was murdered by Claudia Vetallus, and the same day as Senator Carnalus."

"Is this all true, Achilles; or shall I call you Venu?" asked Herod with a strange look on his face and then a wink.

I did not know what kind of trick was being played on me. I decided to be as truthful as I could and die if that was the outcome of telling the truth. "It is all true except the scroll is gone," I flatly confessed. "I left the scroll in Athens years ago before I returned to Rome. I left it in the house of a priest of Nike named Hector without his knowledge. The home, according to Grillius, was burned to the ground by my father's agents a few years back. The very same man who had the house burned also killed the slave Zeno. This man was the one with Marius the gladiator near your birthday last year. He was present on the day I beat Marius in your throne room when he charged me with a sword. I should add, if it makes any difference, Zeno was a freedman at his death in my father's villa. Senator Carnalus had freed him on his death with a written document. So Zeno died a free man but not as a citizen of Rome. He gave that up to save me. I actually owe that man my life, just as much as I owe you and your wife my life."

"This is not a problem; you do not owe me anything," stated Herod Antipas with a theatrical wave of his hand. "Now I know what you are thinking, but I do not want nor really need the Carnalus Scroll. I will only have to leak out the information that I have the elder son of Senator Vetallus and the scroll. I can produce my own manuscript, and I still have your father in a trap. All

I need is for you to remember its contents, which I can falsely reproduce as the real Carnalus Scroll."

"I am sorry to interrupt, but why is the scroll important to you if the bloodline of my brother is not in dispute?"

"You must understand one thing. I desire the title that my father had before me. Actually, I deserve the title 'king of the Jews.' When I become king, then Herodias will be the queen she was born to be; and all this will be accomplished before the next Passover, a year from now. However, Venu-Achilles must be alive as evidence of the scroll's existence before Tiberius and Achilles' father, Senator Vetallus. If you are dead, who will believe me? You see, Tiberius will reward me with that title once he understands I have protected him from death by Senator Vetallus. It is only fair. I will only ask that my title as king be the just reward for saving the emperor's life. It is all really straightforward and truthful, even if the scroll no longer exists."

"For now, we must leave our sick patient to his rest," stated Herodias in a sweet and soft voice.

Everyone agreed and turned to go including Messina. She smiled at me trying to tell me something with her eyes before she turned to leave.

I needed more time to understand what she wanted to tell me. "Oh, Messina, if you see Jesus again, ask him to say the word so I will get better. And please tell me about my dog."

Messina stopped near the closed door and said, "I will ask the Master. He will be pleased to hear your request, this I know. Now, in regards to your dog, he is outside this door waiting to see you." With that being said, Chuza opened the door; and Messina made a low whistle sound. To my surprise and delight inbounded Zoe. He ran and placed his front paws on the edge of the bronze-framed bed and licked my face until I hurt with joy. Messina again gave a low whistle, which Zoe obeyed as I had never seen before. Someone had trained this wild dog of mine, and I wondered to whom the dog now belonged. Zoe walked with his feet almost prancing like a happy horse as he followed Messina out of the room. Only Herodias stayed and closed the door leaving me alone with her.

"You know this girl Messina?" asked Herodias without any emotion. I wanted to be angry at Messina for revealing the Carnalus Scroll, but I discovered she was just trying to protect me. Maybe she was in a way, but I could not understand everything that had just happened. However, it could have been Amcheck who was the one who told Herod of the scroll; or did I not tell him? Either way, the scroll had to be nothing but ash from the house fire. There was the off-side chance it was still safe in the rubble in Athens, but

Chapter Six

most likely it cooked inside the stone hole from the heat. My best plan was to deny it survived and maintain its destruction. I nodded yes to Herodias, also without any emotion. Herodias smiled showing me she feared no threats from any competition.

"I would say that girl is in love with you. I cannot read minds, nor can any man; but sometimes people's actions speak so loudly we do not need to hear a word the person is saying."

"That is an incongruous thing to say," I said trying to hide my inner feelings to protect my beautiful butterfly from this lunatic woman. One thing for sure – I understood at this young age what a power jealousy was. I would place it up on the top shelf as a potent and unpredictable force.

"You have shown me that you did attend the famous Lyceum because you use such words as *incongruous*. I believe you when you say it is not correct for me to surmise something that I cannot support other than a woman's intuition."

I tried to give her the sweetest little-boy smile I could conquer. No more was said about Messina, and Herodias went back to being the dutiful nurse she had become to me over the past month. Within three days I felt almost normal. I wondered if Jesus had healed me from long distance after Messina spoke with him. I concluded that something supernatural had happened on the third day after she left with Zoe and the Judaean disciple. Whatever it was, I did not tell anyone and decided to wait out the time Grillius said it would take for my head to heal, which extended my stay in this room for another four weeks.

During that time I became what I call a flatlander. Few people came to visit, but I learned the art of rest. I acted as if I were bedridden but rolled over every few hours to find a new position of rest. Now that the throbbing in my head had ceased, I learned to listen to the sounds of the busy city during the day. I could tell when it was the Sabbath by the quietness. I learned to enjoy the sounds of the night over day. Actually, I enjoyed the lack of visitors; but my questions concerning Herod Antipas's plans for me in the next months did occupy a great deal of my time when I was not just listening. I realized my mental capacities were not harmed by the fractured blow upon my skull. One important observation made during the long days of listening to the sounds outside the window of Herodias's bedroom was how humans wasted much of their time doing whatever it is they do. I concluded that a person required leisure time to contemplate what life was all about. I found myself thinking a great deal concerning the Creator.

Thinking about the Creator is not utmost in most people's daily thinking. When I eventually left this room, I wanted to change. I wanted to know God personally. By the time the four weeks had passed, I foolishly accepted that this was not possible; and it saddened me. However, for the first time in my short life, I found myself talking for hours to Yahweh as if He were sitting at my bedside. I now understood what John the Baptist meant when he told me he was closer to his God in the pit than when he was free out in the desert. I realized, when one's time is almost over, nothing can protect from the evil that will come to visit. The evil day John the Baptist died was the most excellent day of his life. In the larger scheme of things, it really didn't matter who was behind his death. This I tried to tell myself, but I was not sure I really trusted what I wanted to believe. I also realized most humans wished to live righteously; but the old philosopher Plato said in one of his dialogues that four things robbed us humans of that freedom to do good: the desire for wealth, fame, power over others, and selfishness. Most humans wanted only one of these four vices, but Herod and Herodias along with my father in Rome desired all four at the same time. Herod, Herodias, and my father were slaves to their choices; yet, they did not even know why. With the cessation of these four things, men or women are truly free; and only then can any of us have a chance to make the right ethical decisions for our lives.

I considered that my mother and perhaps Messina were the only two creatures who knew this truth besides John the Baptist and his cousin Jesus. The irony is my mother, a slave, and Messina, perhaps the wealthiest woman in the world, were the only free females I had known. I truthfully could not say I knew John and Jesus very well, but I wanted to believe I did. My mother and Messina both put their hope in the Jewish Messiah and the kingdom of God. I believe they both understood more than I on these two subjects. They both realized the way to eternal freedom was coming via the Messiah. With the Messiah would follow the kingdom of God. John the Baptist was convinced that Jesus of Nazareth was the Messiah, the long-awaited Redeemer whom Job in the Jewish Scriptures talked about in the middle of his extreme suffering. Jesus himself believed he was the Messiah because he said as much during my first time with him at the Temple after my first encounter with the captain of the priestly guards.

Unfortunately, I was still on my quest concerning Jesus; but I was now sure that becoming a Jew as Rabbi Issachar had instructed me in the 14th District of Rome would assure me eternal life. Becoming a proselyte Jew was not some magical formula to understand the Jewish Scriptures and the Law. What I had at this point in my young life was just a little faith but not

Chapter Six

fully developed. I felt like I was spiritually still in the womb. I was growing much like my skull was knitting around the golden plate in my head; but I still needed to be birthed, and it was going to be painful. It was true that I renounced the polluted Jewish system and all its sects; and yet, being circumcised did save my life the day Demos was flogged.

I would like to digress at this point and make an observation about becoming a proselyte Jew or a *Yisrael*, the word I refused to use. I had become more or less an orphan in an ethnic family who accepted me only because of forced tolerance. As a *Yisrael* one is never allowed to think for a moment that he is genuinely a son, even though he bears the covenant mark of circumcision. To be a proselyte Jew, even in this land of the Jews, meant one was still considered an outsider by those who were born into Judaism. A *Yisrael* was perceived as a pretender since he never had a physical bloodline connection from the common progenitor, that being Abraham, Isaac, and Jacob. One could only be a *Yisrael* by spiritual parturition, not by physical birth; therefore, as a *Yisrael* I experienced a form of spiritual discrimination.

My final quandary was what God thought of me. I was being asked to help the two people who killed His greatest prophet. Was I to obey Herod and Herodias and forgive them? What a strange position to find oneself. They wanted me safe and well only because I had something they wanted: the Carnalus Scroll and the ability to kill people. Yet, Herod had said it did not matter when I told him the Carnalus Scroll was burned in Hector's house; but was he telling the truth? My thoughts also began to haunt me regarding Eli and Messina. There were times I concluded that three years ago I should have taken Messina over the wall in Rome and out of that evil house. I would have had to sacrifice Eli, but he did die anyway a few months later in the Temple at the hands of the pseudo-holy military police and the soiled captain of the Jewish guards. If I had selfishly escaped over the wall with Messina, I wouldn't be in this bed because I never would have killed Claudia, the ex-wife of Varus. Instead, I made the choices I did and almost died. Was I now alive because no matter what messes we humans make are overseen by a powerful and sovereign God? I had no answers other than I needed to find the truth concerning Jesus, just as John the Baptist had. I wanted to be free as John was in that pit. What I am really trying to say is those final four weeks living in the Queen's bedchambers were a time of coming closer than ever before to that liberated state.

Three days after Messina had visited with Zoe, I was able to stand and walk without the pain in my head. I kept this knowledge from everyone. I knew in some strange way I needed the coming four weeks to slowly strengthen my body. Herodias must have sensed my improvement for she had stopped spending the nights in the overstuffed chair, and this freed me to spend these dark hours walking the floor of my cage. Herodias came only at each meal time. I would eat as she watched, and I pretended to be tired and in need of sleep. It wasn't a hard act since I was exhausted from walking all night. She would stay until she thought I was asleep and tiptoe out of the bedroom. Sometimes at my evening meals, she came in drunk and would stay longer. On these evenings she would typically reveal some secret of her life. I actually enjoyed these visits and would just listen to her babble on. At times it was hard hiding my shock at some of her revelations. I did not doubt these tales were true; but, of course, people at times perceive the truth in many different shades to make reality acceptable to their own view of what actually happened. We all are guilty of justifying many sins by weaving a maze of imagination, which really is only a form of rationalization. I was sure she loved the monster who wanted to be king of the Jews. Had she been born in a humbler situation and never married Herod Antipas, I was sure she would have been entirely different, but then, maybe not.

Herodias told me two phenomenal stories one night after I ate my evening meal, and both had something to do with my own life experiences. The first story was the day she wed Herod Antipas. She was about thirty-five years old when she married her second uncle after he stole her away from his brother, Herod Philip of Rome. Herod and Herodias conducted their marriage vows in a small room at the Imperial Palace on Palatine Hill in the presence of Tiberius. She told me how both signed the legal document on the morning of the 50th Anniversary of the Actium Games about the same time my mother was being murdered by Claudia. The wedding party retired after a small, late breakfast of exotic peacock tongues and chameleon brains, both dipped in a sweet-and-sour sauce. After the meal the party attended the famous 120-men *munera* match-off as Tiberius's guests of honor. Perhaps Herodias had forgotten Herod had already mentioned their wedding in this very room concerning that aberrant day when they both watched Marius defeat all his competitors winning the wooden sword and his freedom. Throwing this thought aside, I vividly remembered seeing both of them with Tiberius in the middle of that scorcher of a day. While I was listening to her wedding-day story, I could not believe I had been shivering in the bushes naked while she was enjoying the killing of other humans for sport. She told me she remembered the commotion in the above senatorial section when Senator Vetallus learned of his son's suicide off some bridge into the Tiber. "Isn't this a small world" was all she said concerning that event.

Chapter Six

The second story Herodias told was so shocking, I am afraid I will have to reveal the details at a later time. All I wish to say now is the time frame of this story happen on the night I killed Claudia. I since learned Amcheck and Herod Antipas had arrived at my father's villa shortly after I had done my damage and escaped over the wall with Eli. However, now I learned about the whereabouts of Saben and Herodias on that stormy night. I almost vomited the meal I had just finished when she told me what she was doing. After she finished her second story, Herodias must have sensed my discomfort and told me it was time for me to rest.

I can confidently say that one side of Herodias was mentally sound, but there was also something seriously wrong with this woman; and it was mostly spiritual, not mental. The day she told me her wedding story I almost felt sorry for her. After her second tale about a decade later during the storm when Claudia was killed by my hands, I began to believe that perhaps demons were living in this woman. From this day forward, I started looking at her differently. At times I almost could see something sinister when I looked deep into her eyes. Her behavior always changed drastically whenever the subject of Jesus came up. Her voice would change a few octaves higher, and spittle sometimes flew out of her mouth when she spoke. My observation of Herodias was she at times seemed in control of herself but never when she was drinking alcohol. It was at those times that it was apparent something else lived inside her, and it wasn't very nice.

After Herodias had left that night, I began thinking about the rumors that I had heard about the man from Nazareth casting demons out of people. I knew of at least four different people who had been delivered by Jesus. I began to speculate, if I could get Messina or maybe Chuza to bring Jesus to Herodias, well, perhaps Jesus would free her from these demon guests. From what I had witnessed, Herodias had to be infested with more than one of these spiritual beings, which were evil and dangerous when provoked. I was comforted by the fact these evil beings living inside Herodias could not read minds, or she would be instructed to poison me at my next meal. I am not making her guiltless in the beheading of the Baptist, but I am confident these evil things suggested to her a year earlier how to arrange his beheading. Hopefully, she would not turn on me.

I then began contemplating the thought that perhaps her husband and her daughter also had evil beings living within them, may they be fallen angels or the wandering spirits called the *Nephilim*. Maybe the *Nephilim* could not enter inside people, but perhaps the *Rephaim* or offspring of the *Nephilim* could. That would be these spirits of the dead giants produced by the *Nephilim* and human women in days of old, especially in the pre-flood days. Yet, the Scriptures also speak of post-flood giants or titans. Most Jewish scholars at the Temple would deny any of what I just said; but the more I stared at the pinkish, fluted ceiling, the more I thought there had to be some invisible world we humans could not see except with the eyes of faith. I concluded that the demon explanation was a logical answer for some of Herodias's strange behavior and actions. Her twirling her hair with her fingers while she told her stories and her jerky body movements, more pronounced when liquor was flowing through her veins, only told me she was being visited by some strange, powerful, evil forces. I remember praying that night to the Creator of the Universe to protect me from her demons; but I must confess I made some poor choices of my own after that night, which perhaps opened my doors to these demonic creatures that tried to possess me. It could have also been the power Herodias held over me by possessing my length of hair as a familiar object, giving her demons a doorway to influence me.

Salome never visited during my convalescence since the day I regained consciousness, long before Grillius arrived. I assumed she had left with her new husband. The next time Herodias brought me my supper I asked about Salome, and about the events on the night John the Baptist died. She showed no shame on her part of this ugly story. She even bragged about getting her own daughter to perform a lewd dance for Herod and his guests on Herod's birthday at Machaerus, which led to the beheading of John the Baptist. It was also on this occasion when Salome became infatuated with her Uncle Philip. Herodias told me that, about a week after the flogging of the Roman tribune, Salome left with her grand-uncle-husband to Ituraea, his region of rule. Listening to Herodias, I realized that the Herodians were a tangle of incestuous marriages that were hard to keep straight for even the members of the family.

However, this was quite common with many royal dynasties, especially Egypt's ruling families for over three thousand years. The last ruler of Egypt was the woman Cleopatra, first married to her younger brother before Caesar came to Alexandria when she was 18 years old. The Ptolemys (starting with the former general of Alexander the Great) practiced brother-and-sister marriages mirroring all the other Egyptian rulers for the previous 3,000 years. Cleopatra VII was the product of 11 previous brother-sister marriages in the Ptolemy dynasty making her the 12th incestuous product of the Ptolemy clan. The Ptolemy family would say this was the same as breeding a good chariot horse since staunch runners generally produced other swift horses. Rarely spoken about are the strange weaklings or crazy-minded horses created by inner breeding. Either you get a disaster, or you get qualities that are spectacular. This practice, undoubtedly condemned by the Mosaic Law, works with humans such as Queen Cleopatra and Queen Herodias as well as horses. Two of the most stunning women I have ever seen would include Herodias and her daughter Salome. Queen Cleopatra was gifted in almost a dozen languages and evidently charmed two of Rome's greatest generals, Caius Julius Caesar and Marcus Antonius. I should add one variance to my observations; Salome and Herodias both were much further down the road that excelled in the realm of evil than any woman I have ever come across, notwithstanding Claudia Vetallus Varus. This duo's complicity in procuring the beheading of God's greatest prophet says volumes. Without doubt Salome, Herodias, Claudia, and Cleopatra all violated Plato's formula for freedom of choice. All four gave away their freedom to become slaves to not one but all four of Plato's debilitating vices. I am sure all four women would disagree with my assessment and would argue against my conclusions with their twisted logic until the sun burned out. Nevertheless, make one wrong choice; and blindness and bitterness replace love causing all future decisions to be skewed inside this mystery called life. Cleopatra proved Plato's theory correct when she committed suicide rather than repenting.

From some scrolls I read as a youth at the Lyceum, I learned Cleopatra tried to seduce General Octavius after Antony fell on his sword, which in the end failed. Some legends say she died of snake venom, but I know of no woman who would place her hand into a basket of snakes thinking this will ensure a quick and painless death. But the truth is buried with the fact Cleopatra believed she was really Issus or Venus. Regardless, she left this world on a quick trip to Hades. "Poor choice, dear queen" – Cleopatra took all her ambition and bitterness to the grave, just like Claudia. Salome and Herodias were following Cleopatra's and Claudia's examples of evil and treachery; both women would soon end up on the same path to the underworld. And as Job said, *"Now my days are swifter than a runner; they flee away, they see no good. They slip by like reed boats, like an eagle that swoops on its prey."* I can personally declare as an old man, this is a true statement. As I have alluded, only Jesus of Nazareth was their only hope of escape; but he might as well have been on the moon because both females did not want to have faith in him but, instead, wanted his head also on a silver platter.

In the middle of the night, a hard knock came to the queen's door. I was walking the floor but jumped into bed to act like I was asleep. It was now the end of the eighth week of living in Herodias's bedroom on the top floor of Herod's palace, a good two to four weeks longer than predicted by Herod's medical man Phoneinus. Spring had now slipped into summer, and the room was still hot from the day's heat. From my bed, I called out for whomever to enter. When the door opened, there stood a new visitor. It was none other than the old scholar I had been visiting before Demos and his hidden soldiers "brained" me outside his *domus* door. He was dressed fashionably in a gorgeous, foreign robe that I did not recognize. He looked excited and not as old and decrepit as last time. He walked in by himself holding a simple clay palm lamp, took my hand after placing the light on a small table next to my bed, and gave me a warm expression of friendship. His gesture and presence were health to both my bones and spirit.

"My young friend, I just heard yesterday of your plight. Agents of Herod Antipas came to my home and told me what had happened to you. I was shocked to learn you were alive and well. You see, the very same men told me two months ago that you were found dead at my doorstep. Today I was told to visit the tetrarch here in the palace. It was then I learned you were alive and well. This is the first time I heard what happened to you after that morning we took our walk to the Kidron Valley and met the Messiah on the Mount of Olives. It was also the same day Pontius Pilate killed the Galileans. All I knew until today was a young man was carried away dead from my doorstep months ago. I searched for your body to place it in a nice tomb, but no one knew anything. Now I am overjoyed that you are alive. You will become even stronger than before, for I can see this in your eyes." There seemed to be a genuine delight in this old man that matched his words as he never took his eyes off mine.

"Are you my friend?" I asked.

"Certainly I am your friend. I would consider you more than a friend. I would call you a student of mine as well as a faithful friend. I did not know how much I *philos* you until I believed you were dead. Now that you are alive, well, I could not be happier. This is as if you have come back from the dead. What a blessing from Yahweh."

"Then why did you never tell me your name? Is it not Nicodemus?"

"You never asked. Besides, I always assumed you knew who I was or you never would have come to my home. Yes, my name is Nicodemus. It was my Hellenistic father who gave me this pagan name, which I do not like. I would rather have a proper Hebrew name."

"Fair answer. You, too, are my friend; but why not change your Latin name to a Hebrew one?"

"This would show disrespect to my departed father. Remember the fifth commandment tells us not to disrespect our parents. My father was a

Herodian and close friend of Herod the Great here in Jerusalem many years ago. He loved all that was Hellenistic. My father even had his circumcision reversed surgically so he would not be rejected in the Roman bathhouses here or in Rome. Now, like you, I submitted to circumcision late in life because my father did not have me circumcised on the eighth day. I waited until the day of his death; and then, after he was buried, I was circumcised. Herod Antipas told me just today about your humiliation of having to disrobe in front of everyone, including the queen, just to show your circumcision. This must have been awful for you."

"Thank you for your concern. I believe it is genuine. I was mortified; but due to the pain from my fractured skull, it really was not as bad as it could have been."

"It is strange how pain changes our view of things."

Changing the subject, I asked, "How old were you went you began to study the Scriptures?"

"I fell in love with the Scriptures when I was just in my early twenties. I was about your age. When you get to my age, you, too, will know the Scriptures as a master scholar. But I must tell you it was the book of Job that changed me the most. The debate in that book spans the ages with questions from both God and man in everything anyone would ever ask. I realized God is standing with us in this room right now after reading Job; yet, He is outside of our time at the same time. But today He is in our time. I came to this conclusion when I read about Moses talking to the burning bush. If God could step into a human moment and speak to Moses at the same time He is outside of time, all at the same time, then He is the God of the Universe, the one I will follow. According to many scholars who study the genealogies in the Scriptures, 'time' or 'creation' has reached its fourth day or 4,000 years since the counting of time began. To God, as stated in the Scriptures, a day is 1,000 years and 1,000 years is a day. You see, on the fourth day of creation according to Genesis, Yahweh created light. Now it is 4,000 years later or at the end of the fourth day. You see, we are living in the time of light. In less than a year, the Messiah, the light of the world, will come to Jerusalem and present himself."

I looked at the lamp because this old scholar had waved his hand over it like a good teacher uses everything to drill down his ideas. I felt a smile come over me before I asked, "And you believe the Messiah is Jesus of Nazareth?"

Nicodemus nodded his head with a twinkle in his blue eyes. "The Scriptures explained this thing we call time when the wise ruler, King Solomon, said, '*That which has been is now; and whatever things are appointed to be, have already been; and God will seek out that which is past.*' Isn't 'time' something we humans have constructed? With God, there is only now, which includes the past and future – all as one."

"Your words are profound. Have you ever been wrong in your interpretations of the Scriptures? Who taught you all this that tumbles out of your mouth like cold, refreshing water?"

"Only one man has scolded me for my lack of spiritual and Scriptural understanding. That was Yeshua or the one you call Jesus of Nazareth. About three years ago, I went to talk to him at night shortly after the Temple cleansing; and he asked me why a master of Israel did not know the things he was telling me."

"What things?" I asked.

"Back then I only went to Jesus because I believed he was just a prophet sent by God. I wanted to know what he had to say to this generation of Jews. I never was able to ask because he answered my unspoken question: '*A man must be born of water and of the Spirit, or he cannot enter into the Kingdom of God. That which is born of the flesh is flesh, and that which is born of the Spirit is spirit.*' He used the wind as an analogy of the spirit blowing here and there, and we hear the sound; yet, it is invisible. Before his rebuke, he said everyone who is born of the Spirit is like that."

"Like what? How can these things be?" I asked.

"Yes, that is what I said; and he replied, '*You are a master of Israel, and you do not know these things?*' You see, I went to him at night because I was a coward and afraid I would be thrown out of the Sanhedrin. He read my mind before I even spoke, and only God can do that."

"Well, it is true; no man can know another man's thoughts except God."

"You are the only person I have ever talked to who understands what you just said. In all my years, no one has ever said what you just spoke." I cringed a little inside myself because I had learned this from a demon-possessed woman, not long ago. "God has great plans for you; this I can see in your spirit, not with my weak eyes. You see, this Jesus is the 'burning bush'; and he is much more. This time God came into the world as the prophets said He would by being born of a virgin maiden. The prophets said that God would walk with us but that we Jews would collectively reject this mighty work of God and kill him. The prophet Isaiah called him *'Immanuel'* in Hebrew, which means 'God with us.'"

"You actually believe Jesus is God?" I asked as I physically pulled back in my bed but tried to hide my fear by sitting up with my legs hanging over the edge of the bed.

Chapter Six

"Yes, with all my heart. How else could you explain the miracles and the fulfillment of the prophecies? God has not only stepped into time but was born into time; yet, He is still outside of time. God is one but plural. Does not the *Shema* say, '*Hear, O Israel! Yahweh is our Gods; yet, Yahweh is one.*' The Greek Septuagint translates the Hebrew into Greek and says it much better. '*Hear, O Israel, the Lords our Gods is one Lords.*' It is correctly translated into the plural; yet, God is one. Does it not also say in the Scriptures that '*beyond is God; and in the past is God, and God is in the present*'?"

I nodded to his logic as he quoted Scripture almost afraid of what I was hearing.

Nicodemus continued. "Does not the Scriptures start by God saying, '*Let Us make man in Our image?*' *Then God created man in His own image.* Yahweh is telling us that He is plural or able to be in all places at the same time or even enter into what we humans perceive as the present while He is still outside of time."

"I do not know what to say."

Nicodemus smiled a broad smile and then said, "God knows what is going to happen tomorrow because it has already happened from His realm of being outside time in the third heaven. For this reason He could send an angel to tell a prophet what will occur in the future, and it will be true because it has already happened but not that we can understand. Think of a four-horse chariot that could move at such a speed around a racetrack that your eyes cannot see it, but that does not mean it is not there."

"Or a stone that is thrown from a sling," I added, to show I was listening.

The old man just nodded and continued, "Now the prophet hearing a message from the angel about his future has to believe by faith it will happen because it already happened from God's perspective. God is not a human; many of us make the mistake of projecting our perspective onto the Creator. It is also important to remember that God does not take away one's free choice, even if one knows what is going to happen in the future. God already knows what choice one will make tomorrow, even though one has not made that choice because it is today. However, the mystery of all that I am saying that it appears as if God at times is intervening in history. For an instant, take the time Moses was dealing with Pharaoh. Did not the Scriptures say God hardened Pharaoh's heart? Yet, the Scriptures also explicitly state Pharaoh hardened his own heart first before God hardened it. Do you see how blessed we are? Today, we leave Jerusalem, and we will spend many months following God Himself in the flesh."

"You mean following Jesus? That is not what I was told."

"Why else would I leave my beloved Scriptures in my home unless I could follow the living Scriptures?"

"This is news to me."

As if someone were listening at the door to our discussion, the door opened. In came Herodias, Herod Antipas, Amcheck, and Grillius. All were wearing clothes someone would wear if he or she were going on a long journey. "Are you ready to go, Achilles?" asked Herod Antipas in a jovial manner.

"Since you see I can sit up without any pain, bring me my clothes; and I will be." The bandages had been off my head now for several weeks, and I could feel the long stubble of my hair as it had already started to grow back after Grillius had shaved it off for a second time. Just as if Herodias were reading my mind, she secretly showed me my long hair from her inner *chiton*. In the lamplight I saw it and the red leather tie that went around her neck. She replaced it and winked almost as quickly as she produced it, only for me to see. I still could not understand what this woman was scheming. The slave girl I came to know as Nina entered with her arms full of my uniform – a new black tunic with red trim. Amcheck was also in his new uniform. Looking at Grillius, I was surprised to see him dressed like Nicodemus. He appeared as a wealthy merchant from somewhere other than Judaea. The only giveaway was his Spartan boots.

"We will all first travel to Herodium," announced Herod as if he were talking only to me. "We leave in a few hours and will spend tomorrow night there. From there my soldiers will escort my wife and me toward Masada while Amcheck, Grillius, Nicodemus, and you, Achilles, will follow the Ridge Road. You are never to leave the Ridge Road unless you are instructed by a written order from me. If you do not hear from me, you are to be back here at this palace no later than one week before the next Passover if not sooner. I am serious when I say, 'one full week before Passover.' Any failure to this will result in a flogging. That includes even your Spartan surgeon."

"I am sorry, but what exactly are we to do on the Ridge Road?" I asked not wanting to look at Grillius's expression to the last statement made by Herod.

"Grillius and Nicodemus are to act as wealthy merchants with two Parthian bodyguards. The guards are Amcheck and you. All four of you are going to stay together as you travel slowly spending weeks in each town along the Ridge Road. Amcheck has the itinerary of where you are to be. He is in charge, and all will obey his orders. I will flog any disobedience when you return if not before. If Amcheck deems it necessary for the mission, he will kill even his friends. However, Nicodemus will not be flogged or killed since he is a member of the Sanhedrin. But understand as well as know you are to obey as Amcheck instructs."

Amcheck had his head bowed just as he did when Demos was accusing me in the throne room. This was becoming a standard look for Amcheck. I now knew the answer to my *friend question* concerning him. He lived for money, and Herod Antipas was the source of that money. He was a slave to that idol. I also knew I had to be careful with Grillius, for his own safety. I suspected Grillius's loyalty to me as my protector was above Amcheck's love of money. Grillius would kill Amcheck in the blink of an eye; and at the first chance I had, I needed to warn Grillius that Amcheck cheated in a fight and would stab his mother in the back, literally. I decided I would play my role and spend as much time with Nicodemus as possible learning the Scriptures. Maybe this trip was from the hand of God. If I came upon Messina, perhaps Messina, Grillius, and I could escape this land.

"That is not what I was told!" protested Nicodemus. "I was told by you, Tetrarch of the Jews, to find Jesus and follow him."

"True," said Herod. "I said to follow him, not live with him. Maybe you were not listening. Jesus has traveled up and down the Ridge Road in the past several years. I am sure you will run into him. If not, you will interview anyone who has talked or listened to him. Achilles will write a report every night, and I will send a rider who will arrive each Sabbath to pick up the reports."

Nicodemus still visibly upset blurted out, "What is this all about? Why am I going on this strange trip for almost a year if I cannot hear Jesus speak himself?"

"I already have a 'someone' doing that. A disciple of Jesus works for my brother Philip, and my brother is now sending me weekly reports. I know just about everything Jesus is saying and doing. That spy's name is Y'hudah from *K'riot*. His father's name is Simon. He handles all the money for the small group that follows Jesus. He is the only one from Judaea and not Galilee. He is one of twelve of Jesus's inner circle of disciples. Achilles remembers him, for it was Y'hudah who was escorting the girl with the blue eyes, daughter of Flavius, who came to visit him four weeks back. Achilles also remembers the day Amcheck whipped that Roman tribune here at this palace. My brother talked about this spy. Well, it is this Y'hudah, Simon of *K'roit* character. What I want from you, Nicodemus, is to discover who Jesus is. That is something I believe only an educated man of the Sanhedrin such as yourself could ascertain."

"Who do you think he is?" asked Nicodemus looking sternly at Herod.

"I do not know. He could be John the Baptist back from the grave to torment me. Alternatively, he could be one of the prophets who never died, like Elijah or Enoch. He could even be Moses back from the dead. No one knows where Moses's grave is; does he? You are going to find out for me who Jesus really is."

I almost spoke up to save Nicodemus from this long trip, but Nicodemus's hand secretly informed me to not talk and leave it alone. I obeyed, and Nicodemus submissively lowered his head and said he would surely do as he was told.

"Superb! Then we all leave in two hours," as Herod pointed at the water clock that Nina had filled with fresh water and it dripped away in the corner of the room near the window.

Everyone exited the room. Now all alone I got out of bed and slipped on my new black tunic. Looking at my feet, I still wondered why I had on my boots now for over two months. I contemplated removing them and washing my feet when Nicodemus returned. He was holding his little palm lamp. Before the door closed, in came Amcheck. I started to unlace my boots when Nicodemus asked Amcheck why he had to go under these false pretenses. Amcheck was clearly angry but spoke in a patient manner to the old scholar. "If you stay here in Jerusalem, Lord Nicodemus, you will be killed. First, the Romans know you were seeing our friend Achilles when he was arrested and brought to Pilate. Before the summer is over, you will receive a visit from these bad men once they figure all this out. They will then torture you in their quest to find Achilles, who they know is someone else. Then they will kill you and dump your body in the city dump south of the city to hide their crime."

I was astonished to hear for the first time Amcheck using precise diction. No longer was he speaking in the third person or slurring his words. "Second, the Jewish leaders of the Sadducees want you dead because you went to meet Jesus one late night, a few years ago. This is now common knowledge of most of your enemies in the Sanhedrin. Jesus is now being branded as a false, demon-infested prophet, not a true prophet of your God. Anyone believing otherwise is in danger. You were also seen with Achilles talking to Jesus on the Mount of Olives, the day Achilles was captured outside your door here in Jerusalem. The Roman tribune I flogged two months ago here in this palace, whom you have no knowledge about, will return to this land in the not-far distance. He knows who Achilles really is because he recognized a scar he gave Achilles when they were boys. The real problem is this tribune did not die from my flogging because Pilate allowed me only one strike to his head.

Chapter Six

Had Pilate given me two strikes, I would have surely killed him. Since he still lives, old man, he will want revenge against Pilate, Herod Antipas, Achilles, me and you. This powerful Roman or his confederates will come to you first to locate Achilles. I would not be surprised if over a thousand bounty hunters are swarming all of *Palestina* looking for Achilles as we speak. You both will definitely be found if you remain in Jerusalem. That goes for me as well."

I could not see any weakness in his logic as he continued. "When we all go to Samaria, the most beautiful territory of *Palestina*, there will not be any Sadducee, Pharisee, Essene, Jewish lawyer, or religious scribe who will recognize you. Even bounty hunters, Sicarii, or even the Boethusians would not waste time looking in a region Antipas does not control; for the bounty hunters and Romans will soon conclude that Herod Antipas is hiding Achilles from them. As you know, all Hebrews consider Samaria polluted by what they call the Samaritans; and it is well known that Jews and Samaritans hate each other. Samaria is where we will stay until Herod has worked out his final plan, which is beyond us. We will play along for at least ten months; and then we all return to this city one week before Passover. After Passover has passed, Herod has promised me he will give each one of us enough money to run and hide as far from the Romans and the Jews as we wish. This plan is sound; and you can interview everyone who has had any contact with Jesus, which is what you want. Do you understand, Lord Nicodemus?"

Nicodemus looked at me, and I just shrugged my shoulders to show him not to worry so much about Amcheck. Yet, Amcheck made many excellent points about getting away from Jerusalem for a few months. Once again, I was amazed by Amcheck's speech and proper dictum of Aramaic. It was completely different from that day I met him in the wine shop; but still, at times, he did lapse into his old ways using plural forms when they should be singular. Perhaps living with me the past couple of years had made a difference, or he was a better spy than Felix. But the truth was I had been played the fool all along by Amcheck. I was away from him only these past eight weeks, but that absence made it easy for me to now notice this remarkable change. I had never heard more than a sentence of logic come out of him, but here he was showing a bright mind with facts organized in a resplendent fashion. I guess the maxim that bad company corrupts good manners is somewhat accurate if it is used in reverse. "Proper speech influences correct verbiage" could be a new proverb. But that was not the case. For the first time in my life, I realized how foolish I had been these past few years. I had deceived myself into thinking I was smarter than anyone else when I realized in this queen's bedroom that I was nothing but an arrogant youth thinking better of myself than

I should. I needed to grow up and quickly. It is not amusing to discover the truth about oneself, especially when it involves your own pride. I had been a fool for almost three years thinking I was safe by my own schemes.

For some odd reason, I remembered my mother's words: "Think of others as more important than yourself." If I had only done that, I would have figured out Amcheck long ago. Looking at Nicodemus, I tried to feel his pain; but it was difficult. Nicodemus looked over toward Amcheck and said, "Oh!"; he then turned to me saying, "If we are back a week before Passover, we will be able to witness Jesus returning to Jerusalem. That will be when the true king of the Jews presents himself at the Temple."

With a stern gaze directed toward Nicodemus, Amcheck said, "If you believe what you just said, you better keep it to yourself."

I needed to interject into this conversation because I didn't like the way Amcheck was treating my old friend. "Is that because Herod Antipas covets the title king of the Jews?"

"I will pretend I did not hear what you both just said," said a serious Amcheck. "I don't want to hear any more talk about the king of the Jews. Is that understood? Starting right now, I am giving the orders; and they better be obeyed!" He thrust a finger into Nicodemus's chest with some force to make his point. Nicodemus looked like a little boy who had been bullied by an older boy. The light in Nicodemus just a moment ago left; and with his head down in shame, he exited the room. After Nicodemus was gone, I looked at Amcheck with narrowing eyes.

"What?" sneered Amcheck sensing more than seeing my stare.

"He is an old man! Do not abuse him again in my presence! You show him respect; or we will have words, if not more than words! I will obey your orders, but you will not abuse that old man again."

I was angry, and Amcheck had a decision to make. We both stood our ground until Amcheck decided to back down. "I will apologize to Nicodemus, but did I not refer to him as Lord Nicodemus? Yet, you are always right, Schoolboy!"

"There is another thing. Stop calling him 'Lord Nicodemus' and me 'Schoolboy.' Your words are condescending."

"I know you are right," stated Amcheck with his eyes lowering. "What should I call him?"

"Do you respect your Parthian father?" When he nodded, I said, "We will all need new names since we can't use our own for the rest of the year; so call him by your father's name."

"Splendid idea! My father would have liked that; and, yes, he is one man I respected. He was called Batana, so we call Nicodemus 'Batana.'"

I smiled and began unlacing my boots. The smell coming up from the floor was overwhelming. I found a foot basin filled with water and put my feet into the cold liquid. While I sat soaking my feet, I asked, "When did Demos, the Roman tribune you flogged, leave for Rome?"

"The tribune, the one you call Demos, was carried by stretcher to Azotus Paralius, a small Roman port south of Joppa, two days ago. He was placed on an imperial bireme, one of those fast Roman vessels that travel day and night until they reach the wharves of Rome."

"Those are fast ships. I traveled on one of those imperial biremes. They travel by human power at a constant speed that is faster than a good horse in a dead run. Still, how did Demos survive the whipping you gave him? The infection in this climate should have killed him."

"Herod Antipas in a 'gesture of peace' sent our dear Greek physician Phoneinus to help that 'sassy boy.' Pilate foolishly allowed Phoneinus to care for him after he was racked with infection. Phoneinus went to the Castle of Antonia with a clay pot filled with over one hundred blowflies, which he released after he had Demos covered with a thin layer of Egyptian linen, the kind made from flax. The flies went to work under the cloth eating the infection and laying millions of eggs. Within a few days, Demos was crawling from head to toe with fat white maggots. After the worms had developed into flies, the cloth was removed; and Demos was moved under the direction of Phoneinus to a more decent room. Believe it or not, it was Herod Antipas who saved the very person who will probably have us all taken to Rome and crucified publicly in some amphitheater."

"That is, if Demos returns. Moreover, if he does return, I will kill him even if I have to sacrifice myself in the process."

"Maybe you will not have to worry about Demos, but what you will have to worry about are all the bounty hunters who will be looking for you before the next Passover, especially Marius and that pompous Roman named..."

"Mayus Lentulus?"

"Yes, that's him. We will keep a clear eye for those two. Now, what do you think about your Spartan friend?"

"If you are talking about fighting, remember he is the one who taught me all that I know. He might be old, but old men are the ones young men should stay away from. For starters, old men cheat; but that will be no surprise to you."

Amcheck patted me on the back with a smile saying, "I understand what you mean, and I will not take offense. Maybe I should consider it a compliment."

I wanted to say we will have words later about the past two and half years starting with day one in the wine seller's shop in the City of David, but I kept my mouth shut. I dried my feet with a small towel and began to lace up my boots. When I stood, I was surprised that I could walk with no pain or dizziness. My night walks had helped more than I realized. I carried the rest of my belongings to the torch-lit inner courtyard where 1,000 soldiers stood at parade rest. I had never seen that many soldiers all at one time and place. Perhaps Herod really did expect a war with the king of Nabataea. There were probably two hundred horses with riders and three enclosed litter-couches in which Antipas, Herodias, and Nicodemus would travel.

I was looking over to the spot where I had defeated Marius with wooden swords when a young stableboy brought me a horse to mount. The horse was a handsome, silky-black gelding named Zeus. I thought a name like Fly by Night would have been better than the pagan god Zeus. I'm sure the horse did not care about the origin of his name, and so I used Zeus considering the horse would not answer to the name Fly. I was the last to mount up in the courtyard, and Amcheck and Grillius reined in next to me. It looked like Herod's small army was ready to leave the city by the cover of darkness. Nicodemus waved to me from a litter before he pulled the curtains closed. I wondered why he was hiding behind a curtain since most of Jerusalem was now settled down in sleep. Those who were awake had to know Herod Antipas was leaving their city. It is hard to hide the presence of 1,000 soldiers, 200 horsemen, and many wagons of supplies, all making noise as we all tried to slither out of this ancient city. Besides, how do you keep armor, iron weapons, animals, and wagons from making noise?

Herod Antipas was correct, Jerusalem is all by itself on no significant highway or relevant road. To connect to either Egypt or Mesopotamia, a cutoff must be taken over the Judaean hills to get to a paved road to go either north or south. This secluded location was first chosen by King David over a thousand years ago to be his eternal capital. Its location and history made it the perfect choice. It was considered the spot where the patriarch Abraham was told by God to sacrifice his son Isaac; and since it was surrounded by cliffs, deserts, wilderness, the Dead Sea, rugged hills, and rocky valleys, the location is easy to protect. To defeat this city militarily would be a problematic endeavor. The city in the time of King David sat atop two hills, Mount Zion and Mount Moriah. Both butted up next to each other with craggy ground and steep cliffs on every side. Today, exactly one thousand years after King David, the city has expanded to seven hilltops, leaving the northwestern region as the weak point. Besides this only weak point, this isolated *polis* was otherwise a challenging proposition for any army trying to conquer it. In the past, armies coming to attack Jerusalem had used the Ridge Road as their principal avenue of travel before using several narrow byways that were easily defended. The preferred way for an army to capture Jerusalem was to make a long circling trek where there were no roads, going over land, and arrive in the north.

Since Jerusalem was selected for its defensive qualities, there were no fertile agricultural regions near the city; nor was the city known as an important manufacturing center. It was merely a city perched in a high desert many miles away from any real fertile land. However, rains in winter did provide ample water for fruit trees and grape vines that grew well in the rocky ground surrounding the city. The only primary spring of water outside the walls was covered and hidden years ago as Nicodemus explained to me the day we met Jesus on the Mount of Olives, the day I lost Messina and my dog. The pools of Bethesda were outside the northern walls but close enough for the Jerusalem inhabitants to shoot arrows and lob rocks from war machinery if any army tried to capture these water sources. The Castle of Antonia was in the perfect spot to protect these pools, and this was perhaps the reason Herod the Great had first constructed this citadel at its location.

The Mount of Olives is higher in elevation than Mount Zion as well as Mount Moriah. Going east beyond the crest of the Mount of Olives begins a barren desert. When the wind blows from that direction, Jerusalem becomes nothing but a hot furnace. However, when the wind blows from the west out over the sea, Jerusalem, in my opinion, becomes the most pleasant spot on earth. The hills around Jerusalem are usually cooler than the city itself. I feel this is due to the dense forest of huge trees on every side of Jerusalem that provide shade and trap any brisk air.

Unfortunately, all those trees vanished 40 years after this story, when Rome invaded from the north and destroyed Jerusalem and the Temple. Hundreds of thousands of crosses were made from the surrounding forests, which were used to crucify over half a million Jews, along with the construction of hundreds of siege equipment; and the thousands of campfires the Romans made each night to keep warm decimated these beautiful forests. As I am dictating this story, Jerusalem today is quite ugly due to the denuding of all the trees by Rome minus a few olive groves that the Romans left on the west side of the Mount of Olives. Today as I dictate this story, there is no

Temple in Jerusalem; and all of Jesus's prophetic words that he spoke against Jerusalem have now been fulfilled all within 40 years after he made them. Nevertheless, in the days of Jesus, Jerusalem was perhaps the most beautiful city in the world. A unique city because of its location and the abundance of ancient trees surrounding the hills outside the white, reddish, and yellow-tinted stones used to build all the grand buildings. The Temple itself was the centerpiece with its lofty but straightforward snow-white marble and its golden roof.

The coastal plain of Palestina was flat such as the Valley of Rephaim to the southwest of Jerusalem. The land by the sea had long ago been stripped of its forests to grow grain crops. This occurred many centuries ago by the Canaanites who occupied this low land long before Abraham even entered the Promised Land two millenniums ago. After the Canaanites had been driven from the land, Yahweh sent a new thorn into the side of Israel. These were the Sea People, who destroyed more of the forests. These light-skinned people were prolific shipbuilders; they also cleared more land to farm and used the wood to build their fleets of merchants' vessels. These people's descendants became the Philistines, who made five great cities along the coast. Some of these same people also became the Carthaginians, whose city called New Town west of Egypt was destroyed in the final Punic War. Living to the north of the Philistines, present-day Syria, these Sea People became the Purple People or Phoenicians.

Chapter Six

A READING AT THE GREAT LIBRARY OF ALEXANDRIA GIVEN BY EPAPHRODITUS

The year of the four emperors. During this year of civil war, the great fire broke out on Capitoline Hill destroying much of Rome's archives. Due to this loss, the scholars of Alexandria's Great Library requisitioned anyone with past knowledge to recreate the history of Rome. These short lectures were delivered on the afternoons of the seventh day of the week for a fee of 25 denarii. I have incorporated several lecture readings that I personally gave during this pivotal year.   **69 AD**

THE ROMANS ARE THE WORLD'S GREATEST DESTROYERS OF CULTURE AND DECEIVERS OF RELIGION

Other than the Great Pyramid of Egypt, Herod's Temple is the most magnificent religious structure to have ever been built. I know what you are thinking, but this is my opinion. But remember the Romans have defaced all of Egypt's four corner structures on the west side of the Nile, the side of death since that is the side the sun sets every evening. Religion is central to any society's beliefs, and Egypt is fashioned by the worship of the sun, Ra. Egypt's thinking is death is in the west and life is to the east of the Nile. The sides of the Egyptian pyramids were initially smooth being encased in white granite-marble before Julius Caesar's engineers tore off the stone facings and shipped most of it back to Rome. Augustus, who came after Julius Caesar, continued the practice and boasted he took a red brick Rome and turned it into marble – stolen marble, I might add – mostly from the pyramids and temples from the Karnak and Luxor complexes. All living in Egypt know that Karnak is only one mile east of Luxor, and the roadway is flanked by crouching stone sphinxes, which sit on both sides of the one-mile road connecting these two temple cities deep in the interior of Egypt. Both cities are on the side of the Nile where life is, the side of the river where the sun hits first when it comes up each morning. Approximately ninety pyramids in Egypt were plundered of their limestone and marble casements, and Rome defaced each one in one way or another.

The Romans are the world's greatest destroyers of culture and deceivers of religion. All the Greek myths have been changed by Rome's writers and the gods renamed, except Apollo, the god of light. If you cannot see what I am driving toward, it does not matter; you are where the Romans, as well as the god of this world, want you. We do perish without knowledge – correct understanding is most vital for our journey in this life. Correct knowledge does not give us eternal life; only God can do that through our faith in what He did on that dark Passover on the 80th Jubilee that occurred in Tiberius's 19th year.

King Solomon stated in the Scriptures that true wisdom begins with the fear of Yahweh. This collective lack of fear is precisely why there never has been, to my knowledge, any universal practice of a Jubilee Rest or even a seven-year Sabbatical Rest. A one year rest would not benefit any kingdom on earth, but would benefit the average person, slave or free. If rulers reject a year of rest as ordained by the Creator, what things do kings celebrate? I would suggest all human authorities focus on the very things that keep the empires alive, even after they are dead. That would be its monstrosities made out of concrete and stone: theaters, arches, aqueducts, amphitheaters, hippodromes, and bathhouses. Look at all the structures listed as the Wonders of the World by Antipater of Sidon, even though most have disappeared. Besides those, I can not think of anyone alive who remembers Solomon's Temple, and no one I have talked to has discovered Noah's Ark. There is no evidence other than piles of dust and dirt in Babylon where the Hanging Gardens stood; yet, people have faith that they all existed at one time.

The Hanging Gardens of Babylon are believed to have been built during the time of the ruler Nebuchadnezzar. He had ordered the construction of a massive mudbrick stepped pyramid, which stood on the plains of the Euphrates River located in the center of the city. The story goes that Nebuchadnezzar had the brick mountain erected because of one of his homesick wives from some mountainous region where she had lived as a little girl. The massive number of trees and garden plants burdened the manufactured mountain with a need for water never seen before. A complicated pumping system had to be invented. Once the pumping system was operational, there was much water taken out of the Euphrates River to water the forest of trees and plants that grew toward the heavens resulting in a massive waterfall from the top of the structure. A canal had to be built to drain the runoff back to the river. The Hanging Gardens were described as a mountain that was higher than any hill in the Judaean chain of mountains, and it was *constructed just for one lonely girl. The power of the female will always entangle the minds of men. Time, war, and neglect have also reduced this wonder into a pile of dirt. And does anyone alive today know who carved the giant sphinx out of a solid piece of stone on the Giza Plateau? As King Solomon said long ago, all is vanity.*

CHAPTER SEVEN

Jerusalem to Herodium - Early summer in Tiberius's 18th year. Pontius Pilate's 6th year as Prefect of Judaea. Jesus of Nazareth's 4th and last year of public ministry. (32 AD)

Concerning Herod the Great: Having immortalized his family and friends, he did not neglect to make his own memory secure. He built a fortress in the hills facing Arabia and called it Herodium after himself.

Josephus, War Book

Moving quickly in the dark, Herod's troops moved in precise order through the narrow streets of Jerusalem. More than one thousand soldiers marched or rode horses toward the Water Gate on the southeastern side of the city. In the middle of this impressive entourage were three litters. Comments yelled from the few people up at this dark hour, pedestrians who had been pushed to the sides of the narrow streets, revealed correctly two of the three occupants in the curtained couches. No one mentioned the name Nicodemus; but I heard the name of Herod Antipas called out several times along with the name Semiramis as his sorceress wife and waving with their sandals in their hands, a sign of disrespect. I smiled inwardly hearing Herodias being compared with the legendary founder of ancient Babylon. Semiramis, the ancient and evil Babylonian Queen was not a nice person in any of the legends I have read. People in the darkness of deep alleys also yelled out in clear Aramaic that she was the killer of the Baptist and was pulling the strings of the "Old Fox." Another voice called her an immoral, incestuous, adulterous snake from the loins of "Herod the *Luna*." I even heard someone call her the "Necromancer Queen of Hades." I was happy Nicodemus was not associated in any way with Herod Antipas and his enchantress wife-niece. The bulk of the people yelling, especially from rooftops were delighted that Herod Antipas was leaving Jerusalem. The ones on the roofs became dangerous because from there came occasional rotten fruit, which pelted all three litters. The curtains on each one had been drawn, and mercenary shields took the brunt of the venomous actions of the Jerusalemites who hated this man, his niece-wife, and his father before him. It is true that the father gave them their magnificent Temple made of white marble and its golden roof, but the son's killing of John out in Peraea had been the breaking point. Herod's Temple was undoubtedly one of the great wonders of the world that had been standing in its glory now for 49 years, but that could not sponge their deep hatred away.

The next Passover was not only going to be the 50th year of the rebuilding of the Temple, but the next Passover would also be a double land rest. This is because the 80th Jubilee since creation will occur at the end of the seventh year since the last Sabbatical Year. The Law of God demands the taking off of two years in a row. But, this was a burden to most Jews, who had decided that making money was more important than resting from any activity. Besides, both the Jubilee Year and Seventh Year events were argued as being archaic and outdated. Wasting two productive years doing nothing was considered a massive waste and besides this was a different world from when these rules were first given. But, if these two events were to be implemented this is how it would work: the Sabbatical Year would end at the next Feast of Trumpets, which would mark the start of a second rest year with the Year of Jubilee, the 50th year since the last Jubilee. All of this would end and start in the fall or approximately four months from the time we left Jerusalem. Thus, the next Feast of Trumpets ended the Sabbatical Year meaning a land rest of one year where no work for anyone was over. Then the Jubilee Year of rest would begin. That means a second, back-to-back rest-year of no working the land by anyone. What a fantastical event it would be if everyone took two years off and did nothing but rest. If that were to happen, I am guessing that most would want to get back to work once the two years ended. I am not promoting laziness, but there is a need for people to shift their lives and seek intellectual and spiritual activities that are almost impossible when forced to work all the time.

I admit it takes a great deal of faith for a large family to survive almost three entire years without farming two of the three years and believing Yahweh will meet all their needs until the new crops could be harvested. In the Year of Jubilee, liberty was also proclaimed to all Israelites who were slaves if they wished to be released meaning they went free. All ancestral possessions also had to be given back to their original owners. This included lands and houses outside of walled cities that somehow were lost and had to be restored to the original owners or clans. Finally, there was to be no working of the land for one year making it the second year in a row. During this time of rest and no working, the people were to spend the time learning and reading the Holy Scriptures while their fields were left fallow. This seemed to me to be a brilliant plan by the Creator, for a double year off happening only once in a person's life. I suppose, if someone lived long enough, he or she could experience this event twice in his or her lifetime, but not likely. The two years were to be spent in study and discussion of the Scriptures; how would that harm anyone? Knowledge of God's truths was paramount in producing moral and righteous living, which would benefit everyone, including God who observed all that man did.

For this year and the next, the people were to live only on what the fields produced in the sixth year. It actually would take the third year after the two rest years to bring in the next harvest. The idea was Yahweh would provide three years of food in one year for the Children of Jacob if they obeyed Yahweh. During the three years, anyone could also live off whatever grew spontaneously. That alone would be enough for all the families in the Holy Land. There just would not be any excess for taxes and profit, something the Romans would not tolerate. That sounded perfect for me, but not for Herod or Tiberius. Many Jews did not adhere to this law, thinking it was unreasonable to allow people not to work every seventh year and then two years in a row when there was a Jubilee. Once again, I personally think it is a marvelous tenet to follow. It was to be a time of coming closer to the Creator of the land at least once in anyone's lifetime. The wording is unambiguous in the Torah about leaving the fields and orchards unworked. The Hebrew people in the past were severely punished by Yahweh for not following this statute. This was the stated reason in the books of history and the prophets found in the Scriptures for the 70 years of captivity in Babylon. The prophets Jeremiah and Daniel both state that the reason for the 70 years of captivity was God's way of providing the land a rest it did not get by Yahweh's people. The math seems correct for a catch up of the Jews missing the years of not following the practice of giving the land a rest before the coming of Nebuchadnezzar the

Chapter Seven

Babylonian. After the 70 years were up, Cyrus the Great came and liberated Babylon allowing the Children of God to return to the Promise Land and pick up where they left off before they were removed.

To me, it makes sense; since man is originally made of dirt, why not give all dirt a rest? What is the harm? People could spend a year or two just studying the Scriptures. The prophet Hosea says in the Scriptures, "*My people are destroyed for lack of knowledge.*" If they followed this rule, there would be less ignorance; people would have the needed time to study and learn. I still remember that peaceful summer just reading in Athens after I was allowing my wounded arm to heal. This was the blessing I received after Demos had cowardly cut my arm at the Lyceum *munera*.

In Rome, sitting in my darkened, underground stone cell dictating this story, I just heard the city crier yell out "two hours after midnight." I must hurry and return back to the night we all were leaving Jerusalem. That night's march through the streets of Jerusalem also was occurring at about two hours after midnight. Why the dark hour? It seemed to me Herod Antipas was trying to escape while most of the city was asleep. Riding Zeus next to Grillius wearing Parthian robes, we passed Nicodemus's home; and I nodded toward the front door patting the back of my helmet. He understood my meaning with a nod. Seeing a lone pillar near the entrance of Nicodemus's home, I now realized where Demos must have been hiding before he struck me from behind.

Once we reached the Water Gate, I thought back to that day Demos was also sitting on his horse at this very gate. That day, which was several months in the past, all happened on that extraordinary day when Jesus asked for an extra year. I now realized, if I had spotted Demos at the Water Gate, he, too, had seen me and placed me with Nicodemus returning from the Mount of Olives. Like the snake he was, Demos waited to strike when I was unaware, a classic move by the cowardly *thag* he was.

Herod's army soon left the city and now appeared like a long snake slithering in the night slowly crawling south. It was about this time in the cool of night when Grillius leaned over and asked, "Why do the people hate Herod? I do not think I would want to rule a people who hated me as these Jerusalemites hate Herod."

"Herod Antipas," I quickly replied, "along with his wife had a famous Jewish prophet beheaded a little over a year ago. The people of this land have had many prophets sent to them by their God; still, there have been more false prophets than true prophets. In their holy book, the Jews were warned about false prophets and were instructed to kill them. Unfortunately, many true prophets have been murdered along with the false ones. Yet, after people realized they had killed a real prophet, someone had to be blamed. Herod Antipas is now being blamed by the average Jew for killing a holy and righteous man. The ruling majority of elders are happy he killed this man, but they are grossly outnumbered by the lower-class Jews. To make things worse for Herod Antipas, Israel has not had a true prophet in over four hundred years until this John the Baptist came to them from out in the desert. He never came to the Temple, even though he was a Levite, which means he was a priest like his father, but wanted nothing to do with the Temple and its system."

"Do you think he was a true prophet?"

"I was one of the last humans to talk to him face to face. I believe he was a true prophet who condemned the wickedness of the evil priesthood in Jerusalem. He preached that the people should repent and be baptized as a symbol of coming out of the wicked system. In my opinion, he was the real product, a true prophet to which I can attest. He is the first to appear after a long absence; and, with the help of Herod's wife and her daughter, Herod beheaded John. It happened at Herod Antipas's birthday *orgia*, and the prophet's head was presented to Herod on a silver platter."

"I am afraid you will have to teach me about this land, its people, and their ways. Maybe you can do it when it is not so dark and I can absorb what you say." I noticed Grillius was having trouble seeing from his horse. However, I knew him to be an expert rider from what I remembered at the Lyceum; and, actually, he taught me how to ride by using my thighs to stay aboard even in a full run. It was hard to believe that I was riding next to the man who taught me to ride. He had instructed the other boys and me at the Lyceum to think like your horse in order to stay aboard even in a full run. I smiled to myself and was filled with joy because I had been reunited with a real friend.

Looking over to Grillius, I said, "I would enjoy teaching you, and I will also give you all the details since I left Athens."

"And I will do likewise," smiled the old, long-haired, bearded Spartan, who still scared me a little, especially when I looked at him in his foreign robes with his hair flowing down to his waist. The moon was about a week from being full allowing all to see clearly, primarily when there was an opening in the cloud cover. After my words Grillius gave me a crooked grin, perhaps due to a broken jaw at one time. His right upper eyelid drooped to almost a slit making it appear like the eye of a snake. His left eye must have been his dominant eye because he was now squinting through it, even though he had a long white scar running from his left eyebrow cutting across to his nose and on over to the right side of his face. He was always watching and sizing up people, events, animals – you name it. He was the most aware person I had ever known, and he put me to shame in this area. If I had learned that skill, I would not have spent eight weeks in bed with a fractured skull and lost my hair to that witch Herodias.

Thinking about my fractured skull, I began to wonder why I did not suffer any pain from it until I remembered it had to do with Jesus three days after Messina left my room. If I were having pain, I would keep it to myself. I learned when I was a fisherman that humans do not really care if you are in pain even if they say they care. The old fishermen taught me people think only of themselves. "Humans are selfish to the core and only talk about themselves whenever they have a chance," was the comment made by one old angler while we were pulling in an empty net. Now after many years, I learned to accept pain as a friend, which sometimes saddened me when my friend was not present. As strange as this might sound, for me, suffering pain in silence became an art form. Over time I developed the ability to talk while someone else was sticking a hot branding iron into my hip. It did take years to hone this hardness, but there is a danger in developing this kind of a hardened heart.

Little boys of Sparta were trained to start at age seven to withstand great pain. I noticed Grillius never complained or showed signs when he was injured, even when I could spot his back was out of line or he was limping when he thought no one was watching. Grillius commonly spouted a maxim: "A man will die on schedule, not a moment before it is ordained, and not a moment after." I concluded that, while we live, it is important not to burden others with our own troubles unless it cannot be helped. If you know the day of your death and it is not today, why complain about all the pain you are in? No one really cares. Maybe my thinking is faulty on this subject, but I know of no one who wishes to be around someone who complains about how he or she is suffering.

Yet, I did learn that when it comes to God, it is fine to tell Him how you hurt; and talking to Him also seems to help. It took many years in my future to learn just how much the Creator cares. He knows what you are actually suffering, and He is that friend who is closer than a brother. I used to think this aphorism was about a close human friend but later learned this was false. Based on a long life filled with many experiences, I have determined that every person you will call a friend will become a disappointment in time. Therefore, God is that friend who never disappoints. We will disappoint Him without a doubt, but we receive complete forgiveness when we repent. This is one of those little miracles each one must learn and experience to appreciate. This subject always reminds me of the words of the prophet Isaiah. He talks about an eagle tearing up her nest on a high, craggy cliff when it was time for her babies to learn to fly and fend for themselves. The mother will push her young out into nothingness; and, if the falling chicks fail to fly, she will catch them on her wings and bring them back for a second try. This will continue until they have learned to fly. Life is precisely what our Creator has created for it to be. To understand Job, as told in the Scriptures by the Creator Himself, is to observe the birds of the air, the creatures on the land, and those below in the waters. Sometimes God will allow what is safe and comfortable to be pushed into something that is terrible, terrifying, and tremendously unbelievable. Before you crash into oblivion, God Himself will catch you and start the process over until you learn to become whatever it is you are to be.

Less than two hours outside of Jerusalem, we passed a small structure made of stones with a small dome-type roof. I rode around it and a sign written in Hebrew said this was *Rachel's Tomb*. I knew nothing about this woman and made a point to later ask Nicodemus. When I did, I learned Rachel was the patriarch Jacob's favorite wife; and here she died while giving birth to Benjamin. This happened before Jacob reached the ancient town we were going to soon pass through, Bethlehem. Her tomb was lonely looking sitting by itself for the past 1900 years. I sat on my horse as Herod's footsoldiers marched by and I wondered what this had to do with Jesus, considering he was born in the town not far from here.

When I loped my horse back in line with Grillius, I found myself in a flat area of open fields surrounded by sloping hills. I later learned this area was called Shepherds' Field. After we crossed this wide space nestled in the Judaean hills, the moon went down over the horizon; and we entered the darkest time of night. Still, there was enough light to see several flocks of sheep that had moved out from their protective pens coming forth to eat the lush grass. As far as the eye could see, there were sheep quietly walking in shadowy groups. The sheep that were closer were standing around eating or looking with uncaring eyes at the long line of soldiers moving toward the southwest. Nicodemus later told me these were the temple flocks that were pastured by Levite shepherds. These sheep were being cared for until each one was sacrificed at the morning and evening offerings in front of the Great Altar in Jerusalem. As we passed by the thousands of white and spotted sheep, I told Grillius about the village ahead of us being the town where Jesus of Nazareth was born. He made a sign indicating he did not understand what I was talking about. I realized he was perhaps the only person in *Palestina* who did not know about Jesus.

Chapter Seven

Once we reached the village of Bethlehem, a line of light blue appeared on the eastern horizon. Herod's mercenaries moved through the narrow streets with great caution. Several dozen missiles of rotten fruit came flying from dark alleys and rooftops. Someone threw a rock instead of rotten fruit and struck a soldier in the arm. He had to be doctored but not until we were several miles outside of Bethlehem. Herod Antipas had called upon Grillius to manage to the wounded soldier, who required some stitches. I wondered how many hamlets of Jews hated Herod. I later learned that Bethlehem had a particular hatred for Herod and his soldiers, going back 40 years. I learned that memories of people die only after many generations have passed. To think that memory of revenge passed from generation to generation, in particular among these Semitic people, may they be Jews, Samaritans, or Arabs, is a sobering thought. I am guessing that this hostility was not necessarily because of Jesus being born in this town, but more so for the victims killed by Herod Antipas's father decades ago. Most of Herod Antipas's mercenaries were not even alive when Herod the Great's soldiers carried out his evil orders, but that did not matter to these people.

After Grillius had finished with the wounded soldier, he came up to me asking about Jesus, who was born in the town we just passed through. He explained to me the soldier he tended to was talking about Jesus and the reason he was hit by a rock from some Bethlehemite. I told Grillius about this prophet of God being born in Bethlehem about 40 years ago and how Herod the Great tried to kill him but instead butchered the children aged two years and younger in this region.

"These people have memories that go back 40 years? They sound like a bunch of Greeks who remembered the Persians burned Athens down 150 years before they returned the favor by burning down Persepolis," recited Grillius. I asked if he was talking about the soldiers of Alexander the Great and he said yes. Changing the subject, I told Grillius that this was the same Jesus Nicodemus wished to find, and that I was to interview people who knew him. Grillius seemed to be somewhat obtuse concerning the significance of Jesus, so I said, "Jesus is an interesting Jew. I will explain more about him when we have more time."

Word came to us that the small army was going to rest for about an hour and eat our first meal of the day. The sun was soon breaking over the eastern hills as each soldier was handed a piece of meat rolled in bread. These breaded meats had been prepared in Herod's palace kitchen before we left Jerusalem. After consuming my meal, I found a flat grassy area and fell asleep for what was left of the hour. Soon it was time to resume our march.

Out in front of us was a massive forest of thick oaks, sycamores, and cypress trees looming up in the direction of our march. The soldiers were on full alert, for this would be a perfect place for a Zealot attack. Riding through this green paradise, the temperature was cool and most pleasant. I would rather pass through this quiet realm of green than pass through a village of unfriendly people. Had Bethlehem not been under the protection of Rome and Pilate, Herod may have been somewhat brutal toward the rock throwers. I was surprised but glad he let the Bethlehemites alone. I was beginning to feel winded from the months in the queen's bedroom and decided that I might have embarrassed myself in a fight.

Thinking about my profession, I thought of a quote of Jesus: "Love your enemies; pray for those who mistreat you." A man at my wine shop told me that he heard Jesus say this controversial statement. He said he was unhappy with these words of Jesus because most Jews live for revenge and to do otherwise is a great evil. "Turn the other cheek when struck, and surrender your cloak if someone steals it from you. Forgive those who mistreat you" were other quotes from Jesus that also made this man upset about the religious man from Galilee. I did not disagree with the man when he told me these statements, but it would be many years for me to understand these challenging teachings as the true words of God. *Mercy triumphs over judgment* works even when it does not feel right. To show mercy is to practice what my mother taught me about thinking of others.

After leaving the dark forest, everyone started to breathe a little easier. Amcheck rode up to Grillius and me and told us we had now covered about twelve miles since leaving Jerusalem. I nodded to his news but wondered why it took this long to cover only a short distance. Since this was the first time I had marched with other soldiers, I began to understand the logistic problems of armies on the march. Men and animals walking in a long line is not an easy task. If one person stops or falls accidentally, the rippling effect runs along the line of men stopping everyone behind them. It was like this for the entire journey. Move, stop, wait, move, stay, wait. I foolishly thought a better-trained army could move much faster, but years later I learned that this was a foolish idea. All armies, well trained or not, march with the same difficulties. They can only move at the speed of its slowest soldier. If I were not on a horse, I would have been that slowest soldier.

It was not long before we entered a second forest, but this one had mostly sycamore trees. When we exited, we found ourselves at the ancient ruins of Tekoa. It was here at Tekoa where the prophet Amos had been born and lived before Yahweh called him. Tekoa was also the village where Joab, the oxymoron general of King David, was from and where he recruited a wise woman to go and persuade the king to bring back David's banished son Absalom. That incident, recorded in the Scriptures, shows that a decision to receive back a sinner without that person's repentance is a disaster, a lesson I am sure King David learned the hard way. Today only a small handful of people lived in what remained of ancient Tekoa. The decaying buildings and homes showed this must have once been a famous town. My guess was that in about a hundred years the remains of Tekoa will be eaten up by the forest of sycamore trees that surround the ruins on all sides. We rested here a good two hours and ate our middle-of-the-day meal of bread and watered wine before our final push to Herodium, the final destination for this day's march. While most soldiers took long naps on the grass and under the shade of trees or old walls, I had an amazing talk with Nicodemus.

While I was eating with Grillius, the old scholar of the Sanhedrin signaled for me to join him behind a wall near the edge of what was left of what was once a considerable building. He was not as tired as I was since he had been traveling in a litter. I remembered as a little boy riding in a litter and recalled that it was much more comfortable than walking or riding a horse. As he waved me over to him, I noticed he had a look that reminded me of a wild animal in danger. His head was moving to the right and left as he looked for apparent danger. When I reached his side, Nicodemus said, "I must tell you something, for it has bothered me ever since I found you in that enchantress's bed."

"You mean Herodias?" For some reason I took offense. "She saved my life after I was 'skulled' by the Romans at your front door."

"You are right. It is my entire fault. And now you are in grave danger."

"What are you talking about?"

"That day, the one on which you were injured, you remember when we were at the entrance to the Garden of Gethsemane and you were talking to that group of women who preceded Jesus?"

"Yes, I remember talking with a woman along with Jesus's mother."

"Well, when you were talking to the women, Jesus came over to me and put his hand on my shoulder. He had a sad but serious look. He wanted to talk to me. Do you remember him doing that?"

"I believe I noticed Jesus's hand on your shoulder, but I did not know he had talked to you. What did he tell you?"

Nicodemus froze in deep thought trying to remember every word that was spoken to him by Jesus. When he was ready to answer my question, he began looking around like a hungry dog that was afraid some other dog was going to take his food. "Jesus kept his hand on my shoulder and looked almost through my eyes and asked about you. He said, 'That young man talking to the women, do you see him?' I said, 'Of course.' He said, 'Now, when the Son of Man comes in His glory and with Him all the holy angels, then will the Son of Man sit upon the throne of His glory; and before Him shall be gathered all the nations to be separated. Before then the Son of Man is to be betrayed and crucified just as I told you the time you came to me in the dark, the first time we spoke. I told you that the Son of Man must be lifted up as Moses lifted up the bronze serpent in the wilderness. Whoever looks upon the Son of Man as those looked at the bronze serpent in the wilderness with Moses, only those will have eternal life. Do you understand what I am saying?'"

"Was he speaking figuratively or literally?" I asked.

Nicodemus looked around again to see if we were still alone. "He was speaking literally. He said he had two tasks for me. One was to help bury his body, but it was to be for only a few days."

I looked at him in shock but asked why only a few days. Nicodemus quoted the psalm that stated that the Son of Man would not suffer decay. Then Nicodemus said, "Jesus whispered he was going to be crucified by the Romans after the Sanhedrin turned him over to them to be killed. I argued that I was part of the Sanhedrin, and I would never let it happen. He did not answer me but instead said that until that day my second task was to answer all the questions that the one over there will ask. Jesus again looked over at you talking to his mother. He was talking about you, and he told me to answer all your questions. Jesus looked over at you a third time to ascertain if I understood. I solemnly nodded; and then Jesus took his hand away from my shoulder and said, 'Remember the religious leaders search the Scriptures for eternal life, but the Scriptures are only about me.' He did not ask if I knew what he meant by that statement or not but only turned and went back to his disciples. You finished your conversation with the women, and shortly after that we learned about the blood of the Galileans being mingled with the sacrifices by the Romans. Do you remember?"

"How can I forget?"

"Now you see why I am here with you following the orders of that man who killed the Baptist, the son of the evil one who killed the children of Bethlehem. This is an arduous task for me. And that witch of a wife traveling with us, I can feel that she has a great hold on you. This is what is tormenting me beyond endurance."

"What kind of hold?"

"She secretly worships the goddesses Isis and Hora. They are the same but with different names. I know that she learned the dark arts of Hora and Janus during the years she lived in Rome. Do you know anything about Janus and his goddess-cohort Hora?"

"One night a few years back when I was running from danger in Rome, I hid in Janus's ugly temple that stands across the Tiber. I know Janus's wife is named Hora, and I believe she is the origin of the slang word *whore* or *harlot*."

"I have never heard of such a slang word, but it makes sense. But Herodias is evil and has power over you. Does she have something that belongs to you?"

"Like what?"

"Anything that belongs to you. Did you give her anything while she was taking care of you in her bedroom?" Then Nicodemus looked pale and embarrassed. "You did not do anything sexually with that woman during that time? You must tell me the truth."

"Nothing happened. She said she loved me; but I told her to think of me as her son, and I would look at her as my mother. Now why ask such a question?"

"Evil spirits can be transferred during the intimate act of sex when people become one. It says as much in the Scriptures in the opening chapters of Proverbs."

"I will be honest with you. I agree with you, and I do think she has evil spirits living in her. That very thought crossed my mind while I was recovering in her bed. I thought that maybe Jesus could order them out of her."

"Still, it is important to know whether she has anything of importance to you. Does she hold anything that belongs to you?"

"When I was unconscious, her Greek surgeon shaved all my head; and she now keeps a long lock of my hair tied by a red leather band. She hangs it around her neck, and my hair hangs between her breasts."

"That has to be the familiar object. You must get that away from her and burn it."

"Are you serious?"

Nicodemus did not look like he was joking but quite the opposite. "You must burn it, for she has taken it and made a 'familiar object' out of your hair. With your hair in her possession, she has power over you through the Prince of Darkness. This is all dark magic, divination, and sorcery, which are all forbidden to be practiced according to Moses in the Torah."

"I do not understand, but I will do my best to get it from her."

Nicodemus muttered that I had better do more than my best. After he was quiet, I asked, "What are you now thinking about?"

"Your name. What do I call you, now that you are a fugitive and in hiding?"

"I don't know."

"When you became a Jew and were baptized, did the rabbi in Rome give you a Hebrew name?"

"He was afraid of the Romans after I was baptized in the Tiber, and it was dark. There was no time to come up with a new name. He just said something about the morning star."

Nicodemus wagged his head in frustration. "I am too old for this, but I will do what Jesus asked of me. You must understand this is the only reason I agreed to leave my home, my scrolls, and my books. It is true I foolishly did believe Herod when he said I would be able to follow Jesus, but now I am committed."

"Unfortunately, your life could be in danger because of me."

"Being here with you and your Spartan friend does give me some comfort, but I miss my books and scrolls."

"How old are you?" I asked.

"I have been around the sun over seventy times."

"Around the sun? Oh, now I understand. It takes one year to circuit the sun, and you are 70 years old."

"Correct. I have been around the sun exactly 70 times, but that only makes sense if one does not believe in Ptolemy's geocentric theory."

"Then you are one of the few who follows the teaching of Aristarchus's heliocentric theory?" I asked trying to hide my joy and the smile I felt crashing over my face. I could not believe Nicodemus believed the same as I on this subject.

"Yes, it makes greater sense to me. If you observe the shadows on a basilica ceiling that has a perfect circle in its roof, what do you see?"

I was thunderstruck and realized it was a rhetorical question, so I did not answer. I could see Nicodemus wanted to answer his own question thinking perhaps I did not have the correct answer he wanted to share. Humans are funny sometimes; but that is partly because we cannot read other men's minds, nor can we communicate without speech even though we actually express a great deal without words. "You will always see an elliptical shadow at sunset or sunrise along the edge of the circle, which I think confirms Aristarchus's theory."

"You are a brilliant thinker," I exclaimed. "I never thought of that, and I think you are right," I said showing my amazement.

"I tell you what; since you were perhaps the last friend to speak with John and you believe in the heliocentric theory, I will call you Iob Aristarchus."

"What does Iob mean?"

"From the book of Job, Iob is Hebrew for Job. It is pronounced more with an 'e' sound along with a long 'o,' *E-Ob*. If anyone had a life of trouble, it would be you and Iob."

For the next few months, Grillius and Amcheck began calling me "E-Ob Air-is-STAR-cuss" with an emphasis on STAR. I did not care for my birth name Venustus thinking I was named after a pagan goddess. When I learned Venus was also a whimsical star also known as the morning star that changed my thinking; and I eventually accepted Venustus over all other names. The reason was because I believed that Venus was the most beautiful star in the heavens and not a goddess. During the remainder of this trip, I insisted that they drop Iob and just call me STAR.

A trumpet sounded signaling to mount up and finish our march. Nicodemus left to find his litter; and, in less than an hour, we were at our final destination for that day. Why we spent two hours on a break when we only had an hour more to march was a mystery to me. What wasn't a mystery was realizing how close Tekoa was to Herodium, which explained why Tekoa was now an abandoned town. Herodium was a new-looking Hellenistic town in the middle of nowhere. Tall and towering cypress trees had been transplanted decades earlier along with now-huge cedars that came from the north of Ituraea. All the plantings were quite beautiful but could not compare to the massive structure in the center of this town, which I later learned was the final resting place and mausoleum for Herod the Great. It was a structure of two circular walls of curved ashlar blocks forming an *opus reticulatum* construction. The stones had been cut not far from Jerusalem; and all had been transported here as a burial site and now stood as a monument to the now-dead Herod the Great, king of the Jews. Perhaps Herod the Great chose this place as his final resting place because it was the location of a great victory he had over the Jews who were trying to flee to Egypt or perhaps to Masada after the Romans had taken this land as theirs. This place was also the location of a great battle between Herod and the Parthians about fifty years ago. Herod the Great had defeated the Parthians, who were moving south after their many victories in Syria. This magnificent artificial mountain was first built on this site to mark that battle. Now situated as Herod's mausoleum, it was one of the most splendid of all burial mounds I had ever seen. Besides being a monument to Herod and his battles, it also served as a formidable fortress in this wilderness of Judaea. Just looking at the massive cone-looking mountain, I realized it must have taken many years to build a mountain atop a mountain. Hundreds of slaves had worked many years under Herod the Great's instructions. This artificial hill was shaped something between a volcano cone and a woman's breast. At the apex of the hill was a double-walled citadel with four towers. As a guard of Herod Antipas, I would have preferred to serve here over Jerusalem because it seemed safe and peaceful.

Shortly before sunset, Grillius and I walked up the 200-plus white marble steps to the top of the hill fortress and found a quiet spot on the wall looking north.

"What is that in the distance that is reflecting the light?" asked my old Spartan teacher and friend.

After looking at where he pointed, I realized what it was. "That must be the golden roof of the Temple from where we marched this morning."

"You mean we traveled the good part of a night and day and we can still see Jerusalem?"

I knew what he meant, but the route was not a direct one to this location. We had to travel around valleys and hills to get here. I began explaining my views to my old friend. "Herod the Great probably chose this spot to be laid to rest knowing this location would be safe from looters. Had he built his monument-tomb in the Valley of Kidron outside the walls of Jerusalem, where most of the dead kings of ancient Judah are buried, the people would have desecrated it by now. Only a paranoid fool afraid someone would steal his dead corpse would instruct that he be buried in a fortress mausoleum out here in the middle of nowhere."

We spoke until it was long past dark. Grillius first told me he had no idea I had traveled to Rome to rescue Eli. When the news arrived in Athens that a student of the Lyceum had killed the wife of old Varus, no one seemed interested. However, Grillius worried when he learned of the details of her death and the fight that ensued with guards at the Roman villa. After discovering the details of the fight, Grillius rightly speculated the young warrior had to be me and that the dead woman was the wife of the wealthiest man in Rome, Senator Vetallus Crassus.

"The news came on one of Rome's fast ships along with men hunting for a priest of Nike. I found your father Hector and an old Jew who was living with him, and we left Athens dressed as foreign merchants pulling a handcart." Grillius went on to explain how the three of them traveled to Thermopylae, the site of the famed Spartan defeat against Xerxes, the Persian king. "After I had Hector and the Jew settled at Thermopylae, I returned to Athens. Sure enough, it was only hours after I returned to the Lyceum when a half-blind, limping ruffian named Lentulus visited the school along with a few of his *thags.*" I smiled to myself realizing Grillius must have learned the word "*thag*" from us boys at the Lyceum. Grillius told me he was questioned at sword point until he freely confessed all that Lentulus wanted to know. Grillius gave enough of the truth to spare himself but not enough to get Hector killed. A few days later Grillius learned Hector's home in Athens had been torched, and then the Lyceum also suffered a mysterious fire. The fire at the Lyceum was put out very quickly because Grillius was expecting it and had organized the slaves and a few teachers for such an event. Grillius caught one of the arsonists, and the firebug revealed that Lentulus was the one who had paid to have the Lyceum burned to the ground. "I asked the firebug if he wanted justice or death. The Torch Man said 'justice,' and I cut off only his right hand and allowed him to live."

Having Grillius in a talkative state, I asked him if he would tell me his life story before he came to the Lyceum. He looked at me with a funny look and then told a most adventurous and captivating story. Grillius was born in Sparta and had become a *hippie* at age 21, a *hippie* being one of the 300 guards of the warrior king until the age of 30. He later left Sparta and was hired at the Lyceum to teach young boys of the Empire to become men. After only one year, Grillius returned to Sparta to claim the woman he loved. The leaders of Sparta accused him of treason because he had sold himself to Athens, the ancient archenemy of Sparta. He tried to explain he was only a teacher, not a mercenary for Athens. The Spartan leaders proceeded to give him the *ostrakon*. The *ostrakon* was adopted from ancient Athens when the Athenians developed democracy. To be an Athenian citizen, both parents had to have been born in Athens, which allowed them to vote in the *Agora* with a broken piece of pottery thrown into a yes or no basket. All male citizens over the age of 21 were required to vote each morning on all the rules and laws that came before them. The voting token was an *ostrakon*, a broken piece of pottery, which could be found everywhere on the ground in the *Agora* due to the many broken pots and vases. Soon the idea of voting with an *ostrakon* to remove someone who had become undesirable became a straightforward affair. If anyone received a larger-than-fifty percent *ostrakon* vote, he was banished from Athens for the next ten years. Thus, this Athenian custom became known as receiving the *ostrakon*. From that word came the words *ostracism* and *to ostracize*. Sparta many years later liked this idea and adopted the same villainous technique, except the council of men over 60 were the only ones allowed to vote. Therefore, Grillius was voted out of Sparta for ten years; but all he wanted was the woman he loved. Grillius's love was not allowed to leave Sparta when Grillius was banished, but she said she would wait the ten years. Grillius left Sparta and returned to Athens to work at the Lyceum.

During the summer breaks over the next ten years, Grillius wandered to Thermopylae and discovered the famous "*Effeactus*" goat trail named after the cowardly Greek goat herder, who for gold sold out the Spartans and their allies to the Persians many centuries earlier at the time of the Persian Wars. Today in Greek, if someone has a nightmare, he is said to have had an *"effeactus"* in the night. Grillius followed this trail around the hills above the pass and the sea. He also found other paths and eventually found an old goat herder and his wife living in a stone hut several miles west of Thermopylae. They adopted him as a summer helper; and, for the remaining years of exile, Grillius worked and lived in their stone hut becoming a son to the old man and his wife. When the ten years were up, both the old man and his wife had since died; and Grillius returned to Sparta to claim his love. Sometime in those ten years, the woman stopped waiting for Grillius and had married the son of one of the kings of Sparta. This broke Grillius's heart. Grillius became bitter and left Sparta, never to return.

He spent the next 25 years fighting for one ruler or another until he was no longer able due to age and wounds. He first traveled past the Khyber Pass and found work as a mercenary around the Ganga River fighting for one Gupta Raja or another. He then went northward by ship to the Han Dynasty, which included the area from the Pearl River up to and beyond the Yellow River. Once again, he worked as a mercenary. Later he traveled north again by ship to a land known as the Four Islands. Grillius discovered these people would not allow foreigners to serve in their armies. He stayed long enough to learn their arts of medicine and iron works. Grillius found these island people only superficially friendly. Their behavior made some sense after he learned about their religious beliefs. The critical point was their teaching concerning their origins. They believed they were part human and part *kami*. *Kami* was their word for the divine or the name for an invisible angelic being. Grillius felt they projected a spirit of superiority and they also felt the same about the Four Islands. Their principal deity was the sun goddess *Amaterasu*, who first created their island homeland making the Four Islands the holy land. Grillius said they were not unkind toward him as a Greek but never accepted him as an equal.

After a few months, he retraced his path and returned to Athens. The Lyceum hired him once again to teach their young students the arts of war. He had only been there a few years before I arrived as a young student. I tried to do the math and was shocked to discover Grillius was just a few years younger than Nicodemus. The difference in their strength and fighting ability was unbelievable. Grillius looked and acted as if he were maybe fifty years old but in reality was perhaps fifteen years beyond that.

"How did you know I was here in *Palestina*?"

"A Herodian soldier found me at the Lyceum. I was out in the exercise yard when this soldier introduced himself as Saben of the Jerusalem Guards and offered me a very lucrative arrangement. When I learned you were in Jerusalem and at the edge of death, three concerns prompted me to come to your aid. First, I concluded you might need my medical skills. Second, you were going to need some protection from anyone working for your father trying to kill or kidnap you. Third, Herod Antipas offered enough money for me to retire comfortably to that old stone house where Hector and the Jew named Anab are now living."

I touched Grillius on the shoulder showing him I considered him a good friend. After I removed my hand, Grillius told me he accepted Saben's offer; but it would be about a week before he could leave in order to settle his affairs in Athens. I believed this was a lie since Grillius owned only his clothes on his back and his sword. I wondered what affairs he was talking about. Grillius dispelled my suspicion when he told me he needed time to go see Hector. I paid a slave to follow Saben to the docks and guarantee me he had left before I went to Thermopylae.

"This Saben along with Amcheck are two men I do not trust."

"I strongly agree with you."

"I hired a horse and made a quick trip to Thermopylae. Hector was delighted to hear you were alive and living in the land of the Jews. Anab the Jew was also happy thinking his nephew was alive and with you."

"I am sorry to report, but his nephew is dead. I will explain later. Please continue," I implored.

Grillius told me his days teaching at the Lyceum were almost over because of his age, and some teachers suspected the fire at the Lyceum might have had something to do with him. "They all understood I knew it was going to happen before it did, so in a way they were right. I returned to Athens, quit my job at the Lyceum, and traveled here by ship."

When Grillius asked for my narrative, it was short and to the point. I began at age 10 with my mother's death and escape from Rome with the help of Zeno. When I reached my narrative at Athena Nike with the old Jew named Anab, I could see Grillius stand up straight and listen intently. When I spoke about Demos on the bireme and the dagger being thrown into the sea, Grillius laughed, something very rare for him. Grillius loved the part about how I disarmed Demos on the ship since he had spent many hours teaching me that hand move. I also told Grillius of my encounter with Felix at the *popina* and how I obtained a bag of money and the red-scabbard falcata along with Felix saving my life after killing my first man. Grillius with all seriousness told me Felix did not save me. "Felix only saved Demos and his other *thag* friends." Grillius was confident that I would have killed all of them had the Praetorian not shown up. I never thought of that until he mentioned it and began to believe he might be right in his assessment.

Grillius made a good argument when he asked, "Why else would this Felix character hold you up at the *popina* unless this was all a tactic to give Demos time to gather his little *thag* army to intercept you on the way to your *patra's* villa?" Hearing Grillius's conclusions concerning Felix, I still was not sure that Felix was my enemy. He may have been at first, but something changed him by the time he did arrive stopping the fight that did save Demos's life. I purposely left two details out of my story. The first was the meeting of a homeless Felix in Athens, and the second was the Spartan cloak I had hidden at the Painted Stoa and now it was hidden at the barracks in Jerusalem. I guess I was ashamed about both stories; but, looking back, I am sure Grillius would have been proud of the fact I wanted to emulate him with the cloak, and it was only my pride that was hurt regarding not being aware of my surroundings. However, there was something I would later learn from what Jesus said: "What we do in secret will someday be yelled from the rooftops." This is profoundly true, for whatever we hide will be revealed in time. Grillius later found out about my Spartan cloak and the surprise meeting with Felix as a homeless man. I had to apologize for leaving those details out of my tale of my life that night at Herod's mausoleum. Grillius was gracious and forgave me in an instant when I later repented to him.

Grillius rarely smiled, but he showed a great grin when I told the details of my fight that stormy night against Lentulus and Marius at my father's villa. Grillius also seemed to enjoy my story of meeting Messina at the dockyards of Ostia but was saddened when I had to watch my father murder her *patra*. When I told of finding Messina at my father's villa the night I killed Claudia and cut Marius's hand on the wall during my escape was a surprise to Grillius. I also spoke of how I saw Messina again in Jerusalem with Lentulus and Marius, the gladiator but I left out the bump and spin trick I used on Marius. About a month later sitting around a campfire, Grillius learned about the details of that event from Amcheck, and he just gave me a look of disapproval.

Sitting under the stars at Herodium, Grillius only said, "Three times you have accidentally run into this girl. I must meet her because she sounds like an unbelievable story."

Chapter Seven

"Actually, I have run into her four more times since then. I spoke to her at a pool in Jerusalem, again at Machaerus, on the Mount of Olives, and when she came to my bedside with a strange disciple of Jesus of Nazareth."

"God must have plans for you and this girl. I will meet her and give my approval or not," commented Grillius. He silently nodded his delight when he learned that I bested Marius the gladiator, twice. When he asked what trick I had used, I only told of the second encounter of stepping to the side of his swollen eye to grab the top of his outlandish ponytail. I knew he would rebuke me if I told of my bump-and-twirl technique used during the wooden swords contest the first time Marius and I fought. If Grillius had explicitly asked about the way I had hit Marius in the face with the wooden sword, I would have told him the truth because friends do not lie to one another. At the time, I was hoping Grillius thought I was able to get off a lucky hit into Marius's face. Shame and embarrassment are funny things, and it is best to be open about all our failings if at all possible.

I next conveyed the events around Rabbi Issachar and my conversion to Judaism. Grillius's reaction was predictable. I knew he would have a hard time accepting my embracing this religion, especially the "legalistic system of Judaism" as he called it. He appeared saddened when I divulged that the highest religious military person of the Temple Guard had murdered Eli. I then quickly explained my rejection of Judaism and how Amcheck and I settled that score. Grillius crossed his arms and nodded several times after I told him what I did to this quasi-religious man. He then said, "Life is like the board game Foxes and Hounds. When the game is over, you must sweep the board of pins. Besides, the man deserved a broken jaw along with his leg swept before he got a knife in the back."

After explaining my rejection of Judaism, I again warned Grillius concerning Amcheck as a false friend. Grillius grunted and said, "During the next ten months, we both must keep a clear eye on the Parthian as well as that Herodian captain."

I finished my story about Demos cracking my skull at Nicodemus's front door. I included Amcheck's brutal lashing of Demos, but I also told him Demos still lives. It was very late when we went to sleep in the soldiers' barracks at the base of the fortress hill.

In the middle of the night, only a few hours after Grillius and I had fallen asleep, soldiers began moving around in the dark, which woke both of us. Not long after the soldiers started dressing, a summons from Herod Antipas came to Amcheck, who ordered Grillius, Nicodemus, and me to appear before the tetrarch. The palace at Herodium was located at the foot of the high, volcanic-looking fortress. Over a thousand men were lining up to move out in ranks of four abreast. The long line of soldiers had every fourth man holding a torch.

All four of us met Herod next to his litter, and the tetrarch looked happy when he told us to begin our journey on the Ridge Road as soon as the sun came up. Herod then pointed to an enormous wagon. "That is your refuge and your ruse. Amcheck will instruct everyone before you leave. Remember to leave at first light, and Hebron will be your first stop. Amcheck knows where I want you; and, once again, he is in charge."

The Old Fox waved us away and then he called out to some officer, instructing him to have his spearmen line up by twos and not fours. Great confusion erupted as men began changing their marching order. Herod's happy mood was now gone, and he seemed agitated while the soldiers rearranged themselves; perhaps his irritability was due to his being up at this early hour two nights in a row. Returning his gaze to us, standing not far from him, he confessed he was a little cantankerous at this hour. "I want to reach Masada before the middle of the day because of the heat down near the Dead Sea." I understood entirely what he wanted and kept my mouth shut. I did look over at Herodias's litter but did not see her.

"Achilles!" barked Herod while I was looking at her litter. "My wife wants to speak to you before she leaves, and she is not in her litter. She is over in the pool area," he said pointing at a large wooden door where a guard stood holding a torch.

Grillius quizzically looked at me, and Nicodemus pointed to his head to remind me to get my hair from her. I nodded that I understood as Nicodemus stood pulling at his scraggly gray hair. I turned and walked with a slave who led me to the large door with the guard holding the stick with fire leaping from its end. The slave opened the door and motioned for me to enter. I found myself looking at a large pool on the other side of the door. I thanked the slave, which surprised him, and I passed alone through the thick opened door. Inside were several women slaves holding cotton towels in the room that smelled of rose-scented water. There were torches on the walls along with several braziers burning wood chips that illuminated the water that was moving as if someone were swimming.

"I am over here, Achilles! Come to me!" I circled around the pool until I saw Herodias in the pool swimming with nothing on but my long, braided hair that was around her neck. I wondered how I was going to get my strand of hair from her. It would not look good if I attacked the naked queen. I did not have any weapons on me since we were summoned to come as we were in our tunics. I was confused by the fact everyone was ready to leave and here was Herodias taking a middle-of-the-night swim. When she started to swim toward me, I turned around. I kept my back to her while I listened to her step out of the pool. A slave girl ran past me holding a white cotton towel. "Do not tell me you have never seen a naked woman before?"

I did not answer and stayed put with my back to her. "Did not my husband tell you to come say your farewell to me?"

"Yes, but I did not know you were swimming."

"You mean naked?"

I still kept my back to her. I could hear her laugh as the towel fell to the stone floor. I was petrified until I heard what sounded like clothes being arrayed upon her by her slave girls. "You can come now, my young soldier. I am decent for your virgin eyes."

I turned; and, true to her word, she was now clothed in an elegant, blue silk *stola* with a matching *palla* covering her gown. She had her hair already done up and had not gotten it wet in her swim. "By the goddess Isis, you are a virgin, are you not?" she said with mixed shock and mockery in her tone.

"I follow the Mosaic Law, and fornication before marriage is strictly forbidden."

"In the names of Osiris, Isis, and Horus along with Janus and Hora, you sound just like John the Baptist. Do not tell me you follow him?"

"What is your religion, my lady?" I asked, trying to turn the tables away from me and onto her.

"I am a liberated Hellenistic woman who embraces Epicureanism. I embrace all the sex goddesses and participate as a priestess at certain temples to help men have their sins forgiven," she said with pride and indignation.

I stepped back in shock because those words were almost exactly like my father's the morning we were going to the amphitheater in a litter. Just the word Epicureanism was enough to cause a strange anxiousness to pass over me. Nicodemus was right; this woman was diseased with sin and depravity.

"What is wrong? Have Griffins gotten your tongue?"

"What are you talking about?"

"You asked me about my religious beliefs. I do not have a religion, but I do have *ethos*. I am only answering your question because I love you. I have been Diana in the Great Temple of Ephesus. I have been Ishtar in Babylon and I have played Isis in Alexandria."

"I do not understand. How do you forgive men of their sins?"

"Oh, Achilles, you are so unsullied. Maybe that is why I love you. You are a child in a man's body – and what a body you have, indeed – the body of a god. It was I who told my husband to call you by the name Achilles. He wanted to call you Hercules, but Achilles is more fitting since you are not 8 feet tall. Well now, since you asked, I allow men to deposit their sins inside me; and, when my *lunar* cycle comes, I shed blood; and all these men's sins are forgiven. Do not your Scriptures say, '*Without the shedding of blood, there can be no forgiveness of sin?*' You see, there is no need to be barbaric and kill a poor, innocent animal to have one's sins forgiven. A priestess can do it without all the death and carnage along with that smelly, greasy smoke like in Jerusalem. Did you not smell that awful smell when the wind shifted from the desert and blew into my bedroom? The stench from the 'Jew altar' is something I will not miss. How barbaric is that?"

"When you are in Rome, what goddess do you become?"

"There is only one sex goddess worthy of me in Rome; and that is Hora, the wife of Janus, the god of gates and confusion."

"Where is that temple? I know of no temple to Hora in Rome."

"There is a very small one but you are right. The temple I use is across the Tiber outside the walls of the Seven Hills. It is on Vaticanus Hill."

"And you have sexual relations in the temple that is on Vaticanus Hill?"

"Only when I am in Rome. Nonetheless, I do not like Hora," Herodias said with a forlorn look on her face.

"Why do you not like Hora?"

"She, unlike Isis, Diana, Ishtar, and the others, demands the blood of a maiden girl to be sacrificed at the foot of her two-headed husband's feet before any sins can be forgiven by her." She then stopped talking while her mind wandered somewhere. I stood waiting and was chilled to my bones when she smiled and said, "I do not think I will go see Janus anymore. The last time I was in Rome visiting Janus all I remember was a risky, dangerous, but an exciting thrill. Then an awful, morbid cloud comes over me for days afterward."

"When was the last time you were in Rome?"

"You remember – when you were in my bed – I told you already. It was the night Amcheck and my husband went to your senatorial father's villa to sacrifice his wife. That would have been about three years ago. It was a most wicked night of wind and rain, which I know you remember. It really was a horrible, stormy night. I thought Janus was going to destroy the world. I had purchased the most beautiful virgin in the slave market that afternoon before the storm struck the city with a force I had never seen before."

"You were in Janus's Temple on the night I killed Claudia?"

"The night you killed Claudia Varus – yes, it was that very evening. I am impressed that you now remember. It was a stormy night, was it not? Yes, we both shed blood that night. You, Claudia; and I, a maiden for Janus. I knew there had to be a connection. You and I are bonded by the shedding of human blood, the blood of women. I now remember hearing the news the next day in the Imperial Palace when I awoke. Soldiers were everywhere looking for the killer of old Varus's wife. At first, I thought they were looking for Amcheck."

"Was your husband with you in the temple that night?"

"Never! Besides, I told you he was with Amcheck on his way to some *orgy* of his own; and he was on his own mission to kill the second of the last enemy." She then gave out a hideous little laugh. "I guess you killed the last two enemies of my husband when the captain of the Temple died, and maybe that is why we both adore you. Nevertheless, I love you; he only likes you. He knows not a thing about my priestess work; and you are never to tell him, or I will have your throat cut – just like that blond slave I killed three years ago."

"Your secret is safe with me. But I do want my braid of hair to wear around my own neck," I lied.

Herodias's face lit up with a broad smile that I could clearly see from the light of a torch. It looked like she was reading my mind and knew I was lying. After her look vanished, her head went to the right; and she started talking as if there was someone else standing there. "When we meet in Jerusalem next spring, you will be invited to attend a special *orgia* dinner." Turning to look directly into my eyes she finished by saying, "my virgin Achilles. If you come and deposit your sins with me, I will give your hair back." She pulled the wet scalp out of her *stola* and touched it to her lips in a sensuous fashion that made me shiver at the thought of what she had just revealed. "Well, what do you say to that?"

"What about your husband?"

"He will not be there. He thinks he is part Jew because of his mother; but she was only a Samaritan, who is only a half-breed Jew. His father was more Edomite than Jew. At times, the Old Fox tries to follow the dusty laws of Moses just like you. Nevertheless, he has been a bad boy at times; and, if the people knew what I know, he would never become the king of the Jews. You, on the other hand, will come see me; and I will show you the things that the horrible desert prophet and the other legalistic Jews call evil. I will even forgive your sins," she said with a wicked smile and a quick wink.

"I think I will pass on your invite."

"You will come because I will order it!" she said with the strike of a cobra. "I have special powers that will make you come. Besides, you owe me your life for those eight weeks in my bed. If it had not been for me, you would be rotting in a grave at Potter's Field. Now we will part, but I will not stop thinking about you. Will you be thinking of me?"

"I want my hair back, and I do not want to wait until Passover," I said in a gentle voice since the Scriptures teaches a soft answer turns away wrath.

"What? My treasure above all treasures! Never will you get your beautiful whip of hair, my love, unless in the spring when you receive my invitation. Please do not disappoint me. Only then will I return your treasure since you want me as much as I do you. You see, I am like Delilah; and you are my Samson. As long as I have your hair, I have power over you. That is why you want your hair back, is it not? You think you are falling to my powers? Well, the truth is you are, my love. However, do not worry; I will keep your power, and our secret will be safe until the spring."

She put my hair back inside her silk *stola;* and, in the flickering torchlight, I noticed that she was not joking but was quite serious. I could also see that she was spiritually dangerous. She made an "O" with her lips and then made a sound like someone kissing. I stood frozen as she walked around me without touching me but close enough for me to smell the wetness of her hair. After circling me once, she sauntered in the direction of the door I had first entered. Turning to watch her, I now spotted two slave girls obsequiously following seven steps behind. Long after she was gone, I stood alone thinking of all her disturbing words. Everything Herodias said to me I have never spoken about until now, not to Grillius nor Nicodemus. Years later I found several scrolls about sex worship in the Great Library of Alexandria, and after reading each one, I discovered Herodias was correct about blood and sex rituals. I am not sure how long I was standing in the pool room, but Grillius came looking for me after the entire military entourage had left for Masada.

"Eunus, why are you standing all alone in this bathhouse?"

I lied to Grillius and said I was just mesmerized by the design of the room. The truth was beyond my understanding. It was like I was frozen solid by a massive cold front of weather, which had placed me in peril.

"What is so special about this pool?" asked Grillius looking around at the shadowy room.

"I have never seen a pool with such huge columns, especially with one in the middle of the pool," I said compounding my lie.

"What are the pools like in Rome?"

"The ones in Rome are vaulted and do not require pillars amid the water such as this one that supports the ceiling."

"Well, I have never been to Rome; but maybe you can escort me there and show me a pool without columns in the water. Now let's go back to sleep; we are to leave in a few hours."

I returned to the barracks with my old *paidotribes* but could not fall back to sleep until it was time to wake up. When Amcheck kicked me awake, I discovered I was in a surly mood. I threatened Amcheck telling him, if he kicked me again when I was asleep, I would put a dagger into his left eye. He was surprised by my response and shook his head in befuddlement as he left the barracks. After he was gone, I discovered I was all alone. The only other time I felt this isolated was when I was huddled in the bushes naked listening to chants coming across the river from the Roman amphitheater, saying, "Strike him! Burn him! Marius!" It was as if I had been cursed by Herodias and she had ordered a demon to oppress me. From that day forward, I started to have tormenting dreams and horrible mood swings. One recurring dream was Herodias swimming with my lock of hair hanging between her breasts. A second dream was being pushed off a high cliff where I would fall and fall but always woke up covered in sweat before I reached the bottom. I knew I had to get my hair back from her and burn it, even if it cost me my life. If I failed, I felt I would be lost for eternity.

A READING GIVEN BY EPAPHRODITUS AT THE GREAT LIBRARY OF ALEXANDRIA

Given in the year of the four emperors. 69 AD

THE CULT OF SEX AND BLOOD

Throughout time, most would agree women are the life-givers and men the life-takers. Here at Alexandria, what is left of the most magnificent library are ancient scrolls concerning blood and sex rituals. I first read these years ago because a famous queen told me about temple prostitutes. This queen who revealed to me about temple prostitution was Herodias, the wife of Herod Antipas, the tetrarch of Parea and Galilee. When I first learned of such tales, I was just a young man and perhaps somewhat naive for my age. Actually, it was three years before learning of these things from Queen Herodias that I came upon such activities by chance. I had taken refuge in the famous Janus temple located in Rome on Vaticanus Hill. What I witnessed was the aftermath of a blood and sex ritual that still today gives me chills. Inside the temple, I found a young beautiful blond slave girl with her throat opened and a dagger in her chest. Blood and sex was not a new way to appease the gods for forgiveness of sin but has been practiced for thousands of years. Every culture in the known world believes that without the shedding of blood, there is no forgiveness of sin. Adding sex to this practice makes it even more addictive to those participating.

This ancient activity was even practiced by patriarch Judah in the Jewish Scriptures when he had relations with his daughter-in-law Tamar, who played the temple prostitute without his knowledge that she was his daughter-in-law. This woman named Tamar ended up giving birth to what had been promised her, but by Judah. Tamar gave birth to twins, Pharez and Zarah. Zarah had a scarlet thread tied on his hand when he made the first breach with only his hand but was forced back by Pharez. I could give my understanding of the 'scarlet thread' but will share with anyone privately if asked after this lecture. For now, let it suffice that the kings of Judah, starting with King David, came through the line of Pharez, which would include today Jesus of Nazareth, based on his line through his adoptive father, Joseph ben Jacob or just Joseph the stonemason. The biological lineage of Jesus through his mother Mariam was through Heli or also called Eli. I once met this kind man and had a pleasant conversation with him one afternoon in Nazareth, during the time Jesus was off preaching. The bloodline of Jesus through Mariam split with the woman Bathsheba or daughter of Sheba the Hittite. Bathsheba's son Nathan by King David was in the lineage of Mariam. Joseph the stonemason's genealogy was the same line as Miriam, except it split with Bathsheba's son Solomon. The famous King David was the father of both boys. After Solomon came Rehoboam, son of Solomon, and all the other kings of Judah up to Joseph, the stonemason. Obviously, there have not been any kings for hundreds of years; but the lineage would have made Joseph of Nazareth the rightful king had there been a Jewish monarchy in Israel. After the death of Joseph the stonemason, the kingship would have moved to his eldest son; and that would have been the adoptive child Jesus.

For this reason, Jesus was the rightful king of the Jews when he stood before both Herod Antipas and Pontius Pilate, the Roman governor of Judah at the time of his trial. Had Israel been independent of the Romans and the Herods, Jesus of Nazareth was the rightful king through the line of Joseph of Nazareth. This was all recorded in the Temple records in Jerusalem, which may be in jeopardy because General Titus now has three legions surrounding Jerusalem. If the Temple and the High Priestly Palace ends up burning because of the Romans, then all the birth records and other ancient documents will perish. Just like the fire this year in Rome that destroyed many of Rome's histories and other valuable records. Fire is also the culprit of a massive amount of loss of manuscripts here at this great library.

Returning to the act of temple prostitution, I should add that this practice was strictly forbidden in the Jewish Scriptures. However, it was the power of sex, lust, and pleasure that pulled the people of Yahweh back into this sin time and again. Strangely enough, the Israelites were guilty of this activity because of their Gentile neighbors. The history of the Jews shows many times God's people committing the error of doing whatever their hearts desire, especially when it came to Yahweh's proper context of marriage. It was the sex goddess Astarte, a Semitic goddess of fertility, introduced by the Phoenicians and perhaps a copy of the Babylonian sex goddess Ishtar that reigned in the land of Palestina even before the days of the Canaanites. The Greeks' Aphrodite and Rome's Venus and Hora, technically the same goddess, presently rules supreme in the Roman Empire. Even my name Venustus, or its Greek equivalent Epaphroditus, is tied to all these pagan sexual rituals. The Egyptians have Isis, and the list goes on.

Satan, the fallen angel Lucifer, just uses the same old practice but changes up the names slightly to cause confusion. Thus, Janus and Hora are the most honest of all because they are called exactly what they are, gods of confusion.

In the land of Palestina centuries ago, having sex around Asherah poles or altars in groves of trees served the pagan gods Baal, Dagon, Marduk, and Enlil. God instructed the Israelite Joshua to destroy all the Canaanite people in the Promised Land, not because the Hebrews were more righteous; but these Canaanites were far more debauched and morally corrupt to the point they would never repent. The Hebrew deity named Yahweh gave the Canaanites four hundred years to repent, but they had only grown worse in their evil ways. Since Yahweh is long-suffering, people believe they will never be punished for their collective sins. Yet, a day will come and surprise everyone like it did the cities of Sodom and Gomorrah. It has been almost forty years since the murder of Jesus of Nazareth in Jerusalem, and perhaps the Roman legions that have Jerusalem hemmed in will end up being that judgment upon the House of Israel for rejecting their Messiah.

Now I will speak concerning the results of this practice of sex and blood. Millions of unwanted children, over the years, have been produced and are why so many societies practiced sacrificing children. Many nations have chosen to offer up these unwanted children on the eighth day after birth. Some of you look at me as if I am out of my mind. Tell me; are there not fields upon fields of murdered children outside ancient Carthage? When Rome finally made the accusation in the Roman Senate that Carthage breached its treaty with Rome, Carthage was blockaded and eventually razed to the ground to never rise again. This date, over four hundred years ago, will never be forgotten in the halls of Rome because it ended the extended period of what the Romans called the Punic Wars. I once read a book at the Lyceum that described those three bloody wars, which ended with the Romans plowing the fields outside of Cartage with salt to make the soil useless. In the process of this plowing, the Romans discovered thousands upon thousands of baby skeletons buried outside this ancient city. The book I read speculated on why there were so many baby skeletons, but the writer had no appropriate reason from what I could comprehend from his words. Today I would propose the idea that all the baby skeletons were a result of the unwanted children produced due to sex-fertility worship. Years later I researched my theory at what remains here at the Great Library of Alexandria; and I believe my conclusions to be correct, which are based on other ancient writers. These children were either first-born males all sacrificed to Baal eight days after birth or unwanted children produced by the *sex and blood rituals. And let us not forget what is done in Rome. Do not the women drink silphium every two weeks to prevent unwanted children. This drink comes from the plant that grows on the coastline of Africa, and the leaves resemble the carrot plant. Silphium also provides a way to abort after a woman discovers that she is with child?*

Oddly enough, there was another temple prostitute in the lineage of Jesus; and she was the Canaanite woman from Jericho named Rahab, the great-grandmother of King David. I was also horrified when I read in a synagogue scriptorium about King Solomon, who was considered the wisest man in the world; nevertheless, he introduced the sex worship of Ashtoreth into his kingdom of Jews. I guess being wise and smart are two different things. Solomon asked for wisdom to rule God's people when he should have also asked for wisdom to rule his own life. Disobedience has its consequences. Solomon was instructed by Yahweh not to marry all the women he did for political reasons; and that, too, cost him his wisdom. In my opinion, having hundreds of non-Jewish women as wives would destroy any Jewish man. After the death of King Solomon, 10 of the 12 tribes broke away from Solomon's son Rehoboam; forsook Yahweh; and worshipped Ashtoreth, the goddess of the Sidonians as did Solomon in his last years along with worshipping other foreign gods and goddesses, including bull calf worship.

Ashtoreth was the counterpart of Baal, the supreme male god of the Phoenicians and Canaanites, whom they revered with self-torture and human offerings, besides sex, but always with blood. Astarte poles were in every city and village in those days. These were wooden poles of the naked goddess Astarte standing in the center square of the ten tribes' towns and villages. In the springtime, men would have mass sex parties around the Astarte poles with sex priestesses. King Jeroboam of the ten tribes of Israel also promoted the corrupt practice of golden-calf worship by erecting a gold calf statue in Bethel and another in Dan. All of this is reminiscent of the time Moses was on the mountain receiving the two stone tablets and his brother Aaron was fashioning a golden-calf for the children of Israel. When Moses came down from the mountain in late spring, the people were dancing around Aaron's golden-calf. In Egypt at this same time, Isis was a mother goddess, primarily as the mother of Horus. One significant manifestation of Isis was the Great White Sow of Heliopolis and the Isis-cow giving birth to the Apis Bull of Memphis. It should be noted that Apis worship, since the days of Moses, has spread to Syria and Greece and is presently well established throughout the Roman Empire. Do not the Roman legions that worship Mithra submit to a bull-blood-baptism at their initiation to their religion?

Even today, dancing around a golden-calf in the springtime seems to have become a common practice in the Roman Empire. Even before the worship of the goddess Ashtoreth, the Canaanites and others practiced sexual worship in the springtime under any large tree. The Babylonians called this festival "Easter" after Ishtar, their sex goddess. Bird eggs, which are symbols of fertility, were colored and hidden for children to find. White lily flowers, another sex symbol of the female, were also handed out to each man who had sex with a prostitute priestess on Ishtar or Easter Day in Babylon. Due to this massive sex business in Babylon, a law was written that required every female of the city to participate as a prostitute for at least one full day in her lifetime. Many women waited until they were married before picking a day to fulfill this appalling law. Even all the queens and kings' concubines had to participate at the sex temples in this capital city that straddled the Euphrates River. Males would walk up to any woman sitting next to a small rug or mat in the open and interior halls of all sex temples. Money was thrown onto the mat, which a male priest would collect; and the man's sins were then quickly deposited in the act of spiritual fornication. Sometime in the next month, the female priestess would have her normal monthly issue of blood; and the washing away of the man's sins was completed. For thousands of years, from the Tigris River to the pillars of Hercules, this twisted idea of lovemaking was rampant but lucrative.

Yahweh of the Jews destroyed the ten tribes by sending the Assyrian, Sargon the II, most likely for this and other sins. At that time in history, at least 10 percent or close to 30,000 of the wealthiest people were taken from Israel to the land of Assyria as slaves due in part because of this spiritual transgression. Those Hebrews who remained began to intermix with the Assyrian population that had been transplanted into the land of Israel. For the next two hundred years, the Assyrian government moved Persians, Medes, and other conquered people into this fertile and beautiful land of Ephraim and Manasseh. The thinking by many kingdoms was to intermix populations so everyone lost a sense of nationalism along with their religious identity. Sometimes it worked, and sometimes it did not. Eventually these people living in the area between Galilee and Judah became the hated Samaritans because they were only part Hebrew and part something else. This is the reason why Galilean Jews still today will not travel to Jerusalem by passing through Samaria. This highway that passes through the center of Samaria is called the Patriarch's Way or the Ridge Road.

Chapter Seven

Many tales of the lost ten tribes of Israel have spread, but they were never lost. For instance, after the Assyrian invasion of the ten northern tribes of Israel, King Hezekiah of Judah put an end to Astarte sex worship in this area as well as his kingdom of Judah. It was Hezekiah, King of Judah, who invited the ten tribes to come to Jerusalem to celebrate Passover after they were supposedly lost. The Scriptures record the men of Asher, Manasseh, and Zebulun humbling themselves and traveling to Jerusalem to celebrate with the other tribes the long-neglected feast of Passover. These Israelites also celebrated the Feast of Unleavened Bread for seven days that followed Passover. From this time in history, the term Israelites and Jews became an interchangeable term, even in the Scriptures when referring to the 12 tribes of Jacob-Israel. For many centuries all members of the 12 tribes are registered in the Temple birth records and tax rolls located at the Temple in Jerusalem. Therefore, there are no lost tribes in occupied Palestina. It is true some of the people from the tribe of Dan may have migrated into the lands of the Barbarians past the Caucasus Mountains and went west naming several rivers after their tribe such as the Danube River. Still, I met many men from the tribe of Dan in the Promised Land when Tiberius was the Emperor of the Roman Empire. I should also note that many men from the dispersed ones by the Assyrians did become feared and skilled mercenaries. Just like the Spartans who are now all over the Roman world, so are many Jews, all for the same reason – hired soldiers.

One final observation: do not men, generally speaking, worship the naked body of the female? And, when a woman discovers this great weakness of men, she uses her power to gain what she desires, which is to be needed and protected by the male? If you do not believe me, why are there so many statues around the Roman Empire made from marble and bronze depicting naked women? In a marriage, this bond between a man and woman works; but a violation of it leads to the fall of any civilization, no matter how powerful. My opinion is some men try to escape the power of women by giving their passion to fellow men, perhaps because men do not require all the fuss when it comes to the eros game. Once again, this is my own bias; but it might be a good bias. Even the ancient Spartans in their glory days as a dominant city-state in the Peloponnesian portion of Greece promoted this practice of men taking care of each man's sexual needs; yet, Sparta today controls nothing. The 150 companion couples of the Greek city-state Thebes were the most celebrated warriors ever encountered by Alexander the Great. However, today Thebes is nothing. The ancient stories of the Scriptures tell of the Benjamites of Gibeon and their sinful, out-of-order lust, which led to the perishing of almost all the people in the tribe of Benjamin. King Saul, the first king of the new nation of Israel one thousand years ago, was a Benjamite; he proved that repentance could restore an old spiritual injury. Nevertheless, no one survived the same-sex practice, along with unkindness to strangers like the ancient cities of Sodom, Gomorrah, and the other cities that use to make up the southern end of the Dead Sea. They all had one thing in common: men lusted after men; and they were not kind to the poor and strangers, especially the two angels who came to visit Lot.

CHAPTER EIGHT

Herodium to the Ridge Road – Early summer in Tiberius's 18th year. Pontius Pilate's 6th year as Prefect of Judaea. Jesus of Nazareth's 4th and last year of public ministry. (32AD)

Our study as philosophers requires us to honor truth above our friends.
                                 Aristotle

I grabbed some bread and figs at the palace kitchen before I met up with my three traveling companions. They were all standing next to a colossal wagon that had one axle and two wheels that were as tall as a grown man. A dome-shaped canvas covering stretched over wooden stays on the back of the wagon providing a private interior. There were four horses hitched in the fashion of a four-horse chariot, all four abreast. Looking at this cart, I realized it would take up the entire road making it difficult in my estimation to maneuver through small villages. I had never seen such a monster, even in Rome. Walking around this giant beast of a vehicle, I saw two saddled horses pawing at the earth from their tie ropes. One of the horses was Zeus, and the other was Grillius's mount.

 Amcheck smiled and said, "This wagon was purchased in my home country of Parthia and secretly delivered here a few weeks ago. This will be our home for the next nine to ten months as we travel the Ridge Road."

After Amcheck had introduced the wagon, I apologized to him; for I felt guilty for treating him the way I did this morning when he woke me. He smiled and told me to forget it and that there was nothing between us. I wondered if he was telling the truth. Words are cheap, and actions are more expensive. Only time would say if he really forgave me. To me, forgiveness means to forget; and, if someone does not forget after telling you that he or she has forgiven you – well, apparently he or she never forgave you in the first place. Yet, over the years I have always wondered if it is possible to honestly forget everything done to us. Perhaps asking God to heal our memories is the only solution.

I then said, "How are we going to look inconspicuous in a wagon that everyone will be talking about on the Ridge Road and beyond?"

Amcheck smiled again. "That is the beauty of the obvious. Someone who wants to remain inconspicuous would hide somewhere most people would not think to look. If you were looking for a viper, would you look at a pile of rocks or a beautiful palace full of wealthy patricians and impressive pools? This is the greatest illusion of disguise that Herod the Fox devised along with my own suggestions, of course."

"Herod the Fox? Is that what he is?" I asked. I thought to myself that Herodias believes she was the origin of that title but, I also remembered it was Jesus of Nazareth who branded Herod with it. All three looked at me wondering what I meant. I shrugged and said, "Never mind; now tell me the plan."

Amcheck began to explain. "First of all, we all need new names. I have given Nicodemus a Parthian name, Batana. Nicodemus says that Achilles will go by Iob Aristarchus. I think it would be much easier to call you Star for short, for no one wants to be called Iob. I have decided to call Grillius Leonidas, the name of the great king-general of Sparta who died at Thermopylae back in ancient times. I will be called Belkin, an old Parthian name from my own family. I was actually called Belkin when I was a child. Any problems with our names?" We all agreed to our new identities. "I have also made some changes in our roles. Herod wanted Leonidas to be a merchant, but I do not think that will work. Since I am in charge, I have changed a few things. Leonidas will be a Spartan and will dress as a Spartan mercenary. There will be no need to act, and he can just be himself. Star will be disguised as a Persian mercenary; and, if anyone asks, you, Star, are from Sardis. Batana is also from Sardis, and I will tell both Star and Batana all they need to know about Sardis in the event anyone questions them. Leonidas has it easy since he is a Spartan. I, too, will also be from Sardis; and, therefore, I will do all of the talking to convince anyone Batana and Star are Parthians. Any questions so far?"

"I have one," I said. "How do we treat each other in public?"

"Very observant, young warrior," answered Amcheck still relishing his new-found position. I did not think I was observant at all because I was having a hard time remembering Amcheck was to be called Belkin and Nicodemus was Batana. "Star will be a mercenary guard of the wagon along with Leonidas. The two saddled horses are for both of you to ride. Batana, being the eldest, is along for the ride as the senior salesperson of this small caravan." I looked at both Nicodemus and Grillius and still wondered who the eldest really was. "I will be the master merchant and, once again, will do all the talking. I will have to change clothes with Leonidas, who, I am sure, is more than pleased to get out of those foreign robes and to dress like a Spartan. This is not what Herod wanted, but he is not here. Along the Ridge Road, Star, you can do your investigations on this Jesus of Nazareth along with Batana but only when we are not selling the 'gimbals.'"

"What in the name of Olympus is a gimbal?" blurted out Grillius-Leonidas.

Our leader, Amcheck-Belkin, went to the rear of the wagon and threw open the back-canvas flaps that looked like the material used for sails on a large sailing ship. Inside were two cots with many little wooden boxes up front. Amcheck-Belkin used a wooden step attached to the rear of the wagon and climbed inside. We all watched as he picked up one wooden crate and came out with a crazy grin spread on his ugly bearded face. When he handed me the box, I was trying to envision him as a prosperous merchant with a long scar running straight down his left side of his face from his forehead to his chin. He was not going to be able to sell a lot of gimbals looking like some kind of road bandit. I thought he was going to scare most buyers away. His old face injury cut precisely across his left eye, but the thick bone of his eyebrow saved him from what looked like a sword strike at some time in his life. He was not blind in that eye but certainly did not look like a friendly gimbal salesman. As time went on, I was right since we sold very few gimbals. "Open it, Star; and tell everyone what a gimbal is."

I used one of my heavy, iron throwing knives to pry open the small nails that held the box shut. Inside, surrounded by straw, was an eight-sided, cube-looking object with a little hole on each flat side. There was a bronze ring device with a metallic base for the cube-looking object of eight suspended sides once it was erected. With the slightest touch, the eight-sided part could spin always stopping with a flat surface facing up and a corner pointing down. Belkin-Amcheck produced a small alabaster vial that had also been buried in straw. He held up the alabaster container and declared that this object was filled with the finest black ink in the world, ink from the Chola region of the land of the Indus people. "This ink," he said, "is poured into the gimbal." The three of us were looking at the somewhat cube-looking device on the back floor of the wagon where Belkin-Amcheck was pointing. "Now that you have seen everything, does anyone know what this is?"

No one answered, and Amcheck continued in Greek since Grillius did not know Aramaic. "I am surprised that neither Nicodemus nor Achilles have never seen a gimbal," commented Amcheck. "And you, Grillius, you worked at the Lyceum for years; are you sure you have never seen one of these?"

"It is new to me," he said.

"I will give you all a hint," baited Amcheck. "Philo of Byzantium invented it several hundred years ago. He was also called Philo Mechanicus, who actually lived most of his life in Alexandria."

Nicodemus-Batana blurted out, "Now I know! It is the famous eight-sided inkpot with an opening on each side and can be turned so that any face is always pointing up. Dip a pen into the top hole and ink your pen with fresh ink. The device will never drip ink from the other openings, no matter what way you turn it; and you can spin it at any time to keep the ink from getting too thick."

"What is the selling point?" I asked.

"What do you mean?" retorted Amcheck-Belkin a little perturbed at me maybe because he was still angry from this morning's wake up and his forgiveness was not yet complete.

"How do we sell it as something unique if it has been around for hundreds of years? And why would anyone want this expensive inkpot over an ordinary, cheap, clay pot?"

"We say spinning the gimbal mixes the ink and the ink never congeals. It is a mixing device for scribes. The spinning will prevent unused ink from drying and being wasted. We also sell special ink from the land of the Indus. This ink is the finest and blackest in the world. In addition, we sell them pens, which come from Cathay, the land of Chin. That would be the people who built a Great Wall north of the Yellow River that runs over a thousand miles."

Nicodemus added, "I believe the pens are made from this faraway land from a tree called bamboo. This land is also where Rome gets all its silk, jade, and *kaolin* pottery."

"Is that why the pottery from Chin is called *china*?" asked Grillius-Leonidas figuring this little word usage was in connection to Chin. The only problem is I already knew that Grillius had lived in this land and knew much more than he was letting on.

Nicodemus-Batana said, "I never thought of that myself, but it must be the reason. I have seen *kaolin* pottery; and, when it breaks, the broken insides do look like the color of human bones."

"Maybe that is why people also call it 'bone *china*,'" commented Grillius.

Amcheck-Belkin started looking miserable with all our questions and observations. He just wanted to tell us what he and Herod had arranged for us to do while we tried to disappear into Samaria. To add to his frustration, I made what sounded like an innocent comment. "I do not think the ink is mixed when this thing turns. I think it is all an illusion to make people believe that it is being mixed."

Amcheck-Belkin took his finger and spun the eight-sided, cube-looking device. There was no ink in it, but it did turn with the slightest touch and always stopped with a flat side up with an ink hole ready to dip a pen. "I do not know how it works. But, why would you say the ink does not mix?"

"Let's tear it apart and have a look," I suggested.

"No! We are not going to tear one apart to discover the truth, for they are too expensive. These gimbals, the ink, and the pens are going to be our only financial support for the next ten months. We tell the customers whatever to sell these items. Besides, Star, you will not be doing the selling; you are just a guard. With two guards and this unusual wagon, people will think we have something of great value. Don't the Samaritans love to write stories, poetry, commentaries of the Torah, and other books? Herod thinks the gimbal is something they must have; and this whole thing is his idea, not mine."

"I understand," I said submissively. "I am just a guard, and you will sell the gimbals."

"That is the plan. Now here are your disguises." Amcheck-Belkin stepped back into the wagon and came out with his arms full of clothing and other objects. He threw them on the ground in piles of purple, blue, and red cotton. When I dressed, according to Belkin's instructions, I looked like a Persian warrior mixed with the armament of a Greek mercenary. I had on long cotton pants, which I had never worn in my life. They reached my ankles and tied there causing them to balloon out at the bottoms. They were of a dark purple color with scarlet and black designs, very foreign-looking here in Judaea. I left my black leather cuirass on because it had the special holders on the sides for my two throwing knives. Over the cuirass, I put on a long red coat that ended at my knees and tied at the waist. I said I probably looked like a *lictor* since *lictors* always wore a shorter red coat when they were not in Rome. When in Rome, the *lictors* always wore a simple short white toga; but, because of some tradition, *lictors* always wore these little red coats when outside the imperial capital. Even Pontius Pilate's *lictors* were wearing red coats the day Demos was flogged. "All that is missing is an ax wrapped with birch rods," I added with a laugh.

Amcheck tilted his head and gave me the snake eyes. "You do not look like a *lictor*," he said in a stern voice. "A *lictor's* coat ends at the waist, and your coat ends at your knees. This is how a Parthian soldier dresses."

I knew when to keep my mouth shut, or did I? My only problem was my Spartan military boots would be hidden by the blooming purple pants. This I did not like at all.

Grillius-Leonidas was able to show his boots with his red Spartan tunic that ended above the knees. I did notice that Grillius did not have nail-headed soles like mine. This new pair I now was wearing was made like a Roman legionary's sandals. When I walked, if I dragged my feet, especially at night, sparks would fly in every direction when the iron hit a hard stone surface. I did this at times to amuse myself and to also sharpen the nail heads, which could be used as a deadly weapon when one kicked someone or stepped on his toes during a fight. Grillius-Leonidas was given a new bronze Corinthian-style helmet that covered his face and cheeks with a nose guard extending from the middlebrow. The eyeholes looked menacing when the helmet was not cocked up on his head allowing his face to show. I am sure this helmet brought back old memories for him as he knew exactly how to wear it in its two positions. One was for combat, and the other was the non-fighting position. The latter required the helmet to rest on top of the head at a specific angle, which at one time must have taken a great deal of practice to get it just right. Grillius's new helmet also had a red horsehair plume starting at the top, flowing down, and mixing with his own long hair. To protect his chest area, Grillius wore a dark brown, molded leather cuirass with bronze studs interspersed for protection. It looked like it was just recently made and was very masculine looking, rippling with what looked like stomach muscles. I, on the other hand, felt like a fairy-nymph from some strange story in the Panchatantra jumping around from flower to flower in some incanted forest wearing long, decorated purple pants. I discovered pockets and wondered if one of them contained some fairy dust.

My helmet was made of light copper, which shimmered and gleamed in the sun. It was a conical-type helmet, but it did not protect or hide my face. Grillius-Leonidas said that was not going to work if the idea was to protect my identity. Amcheck-Belkin agreed and went back into the wagon rummaging until he found what he was looking for. He came out with something entirely different but perfect for my situation. For starters, it was going to hide the scar under my eye since that was a distinguishing feature my hunters would be looking for; and, second, it looked more menacing that Grillius-Leonidas's helmet.

Amcheck said, after he had tossed me the distinctive helmet, "Herod thought this would be more to Achilles' liking. Antipas went through his armory at Herodium for a long time until he found this one. I argued with him, but I guess he was right. Herod felt it would work better than that copper-top cover. I explained to Herod that a Parthian would never wear such a helmet, but Achilles might just make this one work."

Looking at the helmet in my hands, I recognized it from the mosaic in the atrium of my father's villa in Rome. It was in the war scene under which Claudia died, which showed Alexander of Macedonia; and he was wearing the exact helmet.

Amcheck explained, "I told Herod that it might make you stand out."

"Not any more than this wagon does," I shot back with my eyes still on the helmet in my hands. I then placed the fancy headgear over my head, and it fit perfectly. It was surprisingly comfortable and well balanced. Even though it was ornate beyond description, it was not heavy like the Roman iron pots that all Romans footmen wore. It was made of thin bronze and looked more Greek; it had a red-and-purple horsehair brush at the top with a long, red horsehair tail behind it similar to Grillius-Leonidas's helmet. It also had hinges on the sides with two face shields that could close and snap together at my nose area leaving a narrow slit for the eyes that looked considerably ominous when the face shield was locked. When open, the face shields still looked somewhat sinister making the open doors to appear like bird wings stretching out from each side of my face. With them open, I felt like Hermes, the messenger god with his winged helmet. The face shield, when closed, definitely hid my face. With my long hair gone, which I am sure Demos also described to those hunting me as another possible distinguishing mark, and having this helmet on my head would help hide those features. A closed helmet in combination with purple pants and a red coat all added to my audacious disguise. My only consolation was my red falcata scabbard hanging from its shoulder strap matched the red jacket.

Both Amcheck-Belkin and Nicodemus-Batana put on silk robes of Persian design. Their clothes looked bulky but covered their bodies from shoulder to foot. There was an upward angle on the front fold starting at the left bottom edge and ending at the right shoulder. Four other hems came crisscrossing the men's bodies at different upward angles. All edges of their silk robes had strange, fringe-like tassels running along from top to bottom. Their slipper-like footwear was made of thick leather dyed purple and blue to match each of their robes. The shoes seemed comfortable to wear. Both men also wore tall, tower-like headgear made of a thick cotton material that peaked at the top. The hats or turbans matched their silk robes. With their beards and age, both men convinced me immediately, especially after I saw them in costume. Perhaps this deception ploy was going to work, except Amcheck still looked scary with his facial scar running through his eye. Apparently this was the clothing of a wealthy Persian or Parthian merchant. I began to think that, instead of bounty hunters, we were in more danger from thieves trying to rob us of our clothes. Yet, this bold ruse of an immense wagon and strange-colored, king-like robes just might work.

After our clothing inspection had been completed, Grillius-Leonidas and I mounted our horses. Belkin and Batana got up together on the cushioned wagon seat. Belkin grabbed the reins of the four horses, and Grillius-Leonidas led the way on his horse down the road. I followed behind the wagon and felt comfortable on my padded Persian saddle until I started eating all the dust coming from the horses and the two massive wheels. Unfortunately, this was the order of travel given by our leader, Amcheck-Belkin; and it was never going to change. At first, I thought he was putting me in back to punish me for the way I treated him this morning but later concluded he was trying to protect me by being last and out of sight.

We left Herodium late morning and traveled most of the day. When we reached a desert region it became sweltering hot, and I wanted to take off my helmet; but I opened the face doors to get some air. The dust thrown up by the horses and wagon became insufferable. Later that night after we reached our first destination, I was constantly coughing up dirt from my lungs and blowing dark-black mucus from my nose. This was going to be a standard practice each time we moved along the Ridge Road. Dirt and dust regularly covered the road even when we traveled along flat paving stones. What was needed was a good rain to wash off all the dirt. Grillius later suggested I wear a cloth over my nose and mouth. His suggestion helped a great deal, but I must have looked somewhat dangerous with a purple cloth covering my face tucked tightly under my unique helmet.

We reached Hebron before nightfall, and I was not impressed with this Jewish village at the edge of the old kingdom. The only structure that was worthy of notice was the Mausoleum of the Patriarchs built by Herod the Great. The tall, stone, fort-looking structure had high straight walls designed with evenly spaced lines that jutted out artistically. This unique structure was built over the most famous cave in the world, the cave of Machpelah. It was first purchased about two thousand years earlier by Abraham to bury his wife Sarah; inside this encased grotto also contained the bones of Abraham, Isaac, and Jacob along with their wives. The only wife not resting in the cave was Jacob's favorite wife Rachel, who died outside of Bethlehem, which I had discovered two nights earlier.

Nicodemus-Batana said Hebron was one of the oldest cities in the world besides Jericho, and it looked like it. This ancient-looking town stood on a sloping hill of a shallow valley that looked out into a barren desert that seemed to stretch out forever. The only vegetation was what looked like fields of grape vineyards. I was hoping the city had good wine, which turned out to be true. Hebron's wine is considered some of the best wines in the Roman Empire. That night I tasted my first cup of Hebron wine, and I have never drunk anything better.

When I asked how far we were from Jerusalem, I was told we were only about nineteen miles southwest of the capital city. Batana-Nicodemus said the oaks of Mamre were not far from here, which is where Abraham camped in a tent for many years. Mamre was also where Abraham encountered two angels and God Himself in human form. Nicodemus explained all the detail of that long-ago event. "After eating with Abraham, the two angels traveled by foot to the Dead Sea region before it was the Dead Sea. Their orders were to rescue Lot and his family. Their mission was successful the morning after their arrival when Lot, his two daughters, and wife were all escorted out of the city by the two angels. Once they were safely away, the destruction of Sodom and the other cities of that region began. This destruction was due to the inhabitants' sins that had reached up to the Halls of Heaven." I remembered hearing this story from Amcheck on my way to see John the Baptist; and now I wanted to read the story myself, especially since it did not pay to get Yahweh angry.

Nicodemus went on to say, "Hebron was the capital of David's kingdom for seven years before David captured Jerusalem from the Jebusites and transferred his capital. Hebron was also where Absalom started his defiant resistance against his father David. This old town was Absalom's temporary capital before he captured Jerusalem and drove his father east over the Mount of Olives and down across the Jordan River. This ancient city may not look important, but it is pregnant with history."

With the history lesson over, I noticed the sky was turning a deep purple-red. Leonidas-Grillius said something about the color of the sky and commented about a lovely day tomorrow. I agreed with him, and we pitched our first camp of our Ridge Road journey. Amcheck-Belkin had selected this site outside the ancient city near the stream of Eshcol. I was looking for oak trees but did not see any, just scrubby, bushy-type trees, the kind that habitually springs up along any river or creek. The two pseudo-wealthy merchants slept inside the wagon as the two guards took turns watching over our precious cargo of gimbals. Amcheck-Belkin told us to use the Jewish system of two-night watches. The Romans typically had a three-night watch system because sleeping on watch was a death penalty in the Roman legions.

During the night as I sat near the fire, Leonidas-Grillius walked up and informed me it was my turn to stay awake and guard. I was not tired at all, and this was when I actually studied a gimbal. In the light of the fire, I stared at the bottom of the base where there was stamped the word Pergamum. I concluded that the gimbals were the product of this city, the Roman capital in Asia where the city leaders had made an enormous altar to Zeus. I would later learn that this Hellenistic city Pergamum had lots of manufacturing. A cultural center in Asia Minor, Pergamum was located about fifteen miles inland from the Aegean Sea. This capital town had been constructed in a royal situation atop several acropolises that formed one giant hill. Pergamum was also the first foreign city to erect a temple to Augustus as a god, which established the first Caesar cult outside of Rome. These days just about every major city had a temple to Augustus, including Caesarea, the city built by Herod the Great along the coastline of Judaea, which was also the imperial capital of Pontius Pilate. The Roman governor traveled to Jerusalem only three times a year to oversee the three main Jewish festivals: Passover, Pentecost, and the Day of Atonement festivals. Sitting at the fire looking at the gimbal, I calculated that Pentecost (Shavuot in Hebrew) had ended about a week before we left Jerusalem.

The next day I was ordered to stay with the horses and wagon while my Spartan teacher accompanied the two gimbal salesmen. This continued every day until Sabbath eve. Just before sunset, which marked the beginning of the Sabbath, I spotted a horseman riding down the road toward us. Amcheck told me to signal him to come join us. Reaching the road, I discovered it was Saben, the captain of the Jerusalem Guards.

Amcheck-Belkin slapped his friend on the back as he dismounted his inky-black horse and asked him why he was functioning as our messenger. "Herod Antipas does not trust too many people these days. I was nominated to visit you before each Sabbath and pick up the young fugitive scholar's report. I understand you have plenty of ink and pens," he said looking at me with a crooked smile. "Do you have any papyrus?"

Chapter Eight

"Actually, we do," answered Nicodemus-Batana, who was sitting with Grillius next to the fire. "We have a box full of papyrus to be used for demonstration purposes for the gimbals we are trying to sell. There are also several sheets of vellum." Everyone laughed at Nicodemus, including me. The old scholar looked befuddled until he saw me laughing and realized no one meant any malice. This was his first meeting with Saben, and Nicodemus did not know about Saben's caustic wit. Before springtime arrived, he would have him figured for the scoundrel he was.

"Why does Herod need a report each week?" asked Nicodemus-Batana with keen interest.

Saben scratched his beard and shook his head in bewilderment. "Perhaps Herod does not have any excitement to entertain him these days. Oh, I just realized, once I deliver Achilles' scroll, I will have to turn around and go find you fake salesmen. Except, each time I will have to hunt for you somewhere else. This is going to be a long summer, winter, and spring. I hope Foul Breath takes good care of the palace in Jerusalem while I am on these fool errands. The only time I will have any relaxation will be on the Sabbath with one Jew and three Gentiles, or is it two Jews and two Gentiles? I did get a good look at our young Achilles' Jew markings before that Roman was flogged by Amcheck. Now I believe I got the dirty end of the stick – excuse my lavo humor, Lord Nicodemus – but riding all over Judaea and Samaria each week is going to wear me as thin as an old sheet of papyrus." Everyone except Nicodemus laughed again, and a clay jug of perhaps the best wine in the world started around our campfire that also had a skinned rabbit cooking on a spit.

Amcheck-Belkin was an excellent shot with a little Parthian bow we had in the wagon. The bow was the type that was used to defeat Crassus at Carrhae when the Parthians rode around the Romans on their horses. Pontius Pilate had referred to this battle when speaking to Amcheck before Demos was flogged.

Sitting by the fire my mind drifted over to Zoe, my dog, and how his breed had been bred for centuries to have long legs and viciousness that enabled them to drag men from their horses and tear out their throats. This most likely explained why Zoe hated anyone walking strangely or running, but he mainly hated horses. My thinking was, had the Romans used a hundred Zoe dogs at the battle of Carrhae, the Romans might have won that fight.

After our meager meal, I asked Saben what I was supposed to write about since we hadn't sold any gimbals nor met anyone who has seen Jesus.

"Not true. I sold two today," commented Nicodemus. "He was a rich man who was fascinated by the gimbal's mechanics. He wanted one for a friend and one to take apart to see how the thing worked." We all laughed because now I could write we sold two gimbals. We also were happy to learn we were to leave Hebron as soon as the Sabbath ended. Our orders were to go north on the Ridge Road until we reached the little city of Bethel. "Remain there until we meet next Sabbath. Now tell me. Have you run into anyone hunting for Cata?" asked Saben.

Amcheck-Belkin said he talked to two slave hunters. "These were hard men who had been hunting down runaway slaves for years. Now they said they were looking for a Venustus Vetallus, the murderer of Claudia Pulchra Vetallus, the ex-wife of General Varus, who lost three eagles during the reign of Augustus."

This was news to me, and I asked Amcheck if the bounty had grown. "It has doubled from whatever it had been – something to do with that Roman I whipped with the *phagellow*. This rich kid has a father who has added to the pot. My name was also on the bounty hunters' lips. Now we know that this kid's father, Senator Treverorum, is working in tandem with Senator Vetallus. This is apparently the largest bonus award known in history. You better watch your step, Star; I might just change my mind and turn you in myself."

"Be my guest, but I will turn you in first," I said reaching for a dagger. Amcheck lifted his empty hands up with a broad smile saying he was only being flippant.

Saben added, "Do not turn each other in because each one of you will be paid at the end of your summer whatever the bounty is. That includes me in that payment if you all behave until then."

"That is four million *sestertii* if what you are saying is true," Amcheck added. "And does Star also get paid his own bounty?" Again, everyone except Nicodemus laughed thinking this was high humor.

Learning about the doubling of the bounty confirmed that Demos had reached Rome alive, and now the hunt for me would become fierce and aggressive. When Grillius asked who Senator Treverorum was, Amcheck retold the entire story when Demos and his men brought me unconscious into Herod's palace. He continued telling the tale with great relish and details, even the gory particulars of Demos's severed eye soaring across the room causing a Roman officer to faint after he was struck in the chest. I noticed Nicodemus looking uncomfortable during this part of the story, and he excused himself to go check on the horses.

After the long, detailed tale, we all grew quiet until Grillius-Leonidas said, "With that kind of prize money floating around for anyone to take, we may

Chapter Eight

have a fight on our hands. Does anyone in Herod's palace beside us think Star is really Venustus Vetallus?"

No one said a peep, but I kept my eyes on Saben and Amcheck to see their reactions. Both remained very stoic in their expressions, which told me they were both guilty of talking or doing something despicable. Once I obtained my unspoken answer, I made a deflecting declaration that I did not want to be called Star any longer.

"Why?" asked Amcheck-Belkin.

I explained, "Star or *Aster* in Greek could mean a heavenly object, or it is also slang for a woman. Do I look like either?" Everyone including Nicodemus-Batana, who had returned from checking the horse, smiled at my words. Then Saben broke out laughing at my amusing comment that caused the rest to also double over in laughter.

"Well," said Amcheck-Belkin. "We surely would not want anyone to think us a woman," he declared returning to his old way of slaughtering Aramaic by referring to everyone in the plural, which Grillius did not yet understand.

I said, "Let us use Greek so we all can understand what all we mean." Again, there was laughter at my witty impersonation of Amcheck; but I did it in Greek and not Aramaic.

I observed Amcheck carefully that night and decided he was more loyal to Herod and Saben than to Grillius, Nicodemus, or me. Besides, the three of us had all been threatened by Herod's whip to obey Amcheck. However, we all appeared to be in good spirits; and I commented on the fact my life was like Job. "So just call me Iob or Job." That was not acceptable to the Gentiles in our group because it was a Semitic name. It was finally decided that I would go back to being called Aristarchus. A Parthian with a Greek name was not uncommon. In the middle of our conversation, Saben said something to the fact that Demos now knew I had converted to Judaism.

"You don't have to be a genius to know I am now a Jew after I stood naked before God and everyone in Jerusalem at Herod's throne room," I said with a little bitterness showing in my voice.

Saben spoke next. "He knows you are in Judaea as a Herodian guard; that is, if he thinks you survived the skull fracture he gave you. Just in the last week, some bounty hunters had concentrated their efforts at Herod's Jerusalem palace. After the force left Jerusalem, Herod the Fox had me leak the news of your death to all the guards at the Jerusalem garrison. That is why I am the only one visiting this merry group once a week."

With Saben now staring at me over the fire, I said as I looked back, "I was born at night, but it was not last night."

"I see what you are thinking, but banish it from your mind. Herodias will never allow her husband to turn you over to the Romans. She has a hold on him like no woman I have ever witnessed. I am safe in saying that woman has some kind of a motherly infatuation with you, Cata."

"A grand reward today is better than a promised bounty tomorrow. Why wouldn't you or even Sicarius turn me in?" I asked since we were on this straight-edged subject.

Saben then looked at Amcheck and said, "As for Sicarius, Demos is never going to forget who almost killed him with a whip. Demos knows full well a Herodian guard and close friend of Venustus Vetallus was the one who blinded him in one eye and disfigured his face forever." Saben then looked at me to answer my question. "Amcheck will not want to betray Aristarchus-Cata to Demos." Saben stood to show this conversation was over. I decided to employ my favorite trick, changing the subject. Looking at Saben, I asked if Herod had any news from Rome.

Returning to the fire, he said, "Nothing except that maybe next week at Bethel I might have some interesting news from Rome. A dispatch from Rome is late coming, and that usually means something is brewing in the imperial capital. I am sure I will know about the contents of this dispatch before next week."

During the Sabbath, I busied myself with writing a lengthy report to Herod using the gimbal that was our demonstration example for hopeful buyers. It was quite a device no matter how it worked. After a dip of the bamboo pen, I would spin the gimbal; and when it stopped, it always ended with a hole on top to re-dip the pen. It was fun to play with giving me something to do while I was thinking about what to write next. I rotated the gimbal and watched it gyrate a few turns as I waited for words to come into my mind. I immersed the pen into the top hole, and the power of words just appeared on papyrus sheets leaving my thoughts to be preserved and transmitted into the future.

When the sun dropped ending the Sabbath, Saben mounted his dark horse for Masada. The next morning our merry group of gimbal salesmen packed up and struck out for Bethel. When we passed through Bethlehem, Nicodemus was able to sell one gimbal to the head rabbi of the synagogue. This was the only gimbal sold that day, but we spent only a few hours in the small village. No one threw rotten fruit or rocks at us since they pictured us as foreigners and not mercenaries of Herod Antipas. I concluded gimbals were going to be a hard sell to Jews. Even though the gimbal is hundreds of years old, it is something to be suspicious of, particularly for an anti-Hellenistic

Pharisaic rabbi. A good Jew, like most ancient, archaic-thinking people, believed, whoever the Creator is, He never changes. His laws and His ways always remain the same. So why should mere humans invent something new and try to sell it? Hopefully, the Samaritans in Samaria would see things differently.

By early afternoon, staying on the Ridge Road, we passed Rachel's little stone tomb and later bypassed Jerusalem by half a mile since the Ridge Road misses David's city to the east. Close to nightfall we reached Bethel and made camp on the southern outskirts of the town. Bethel is located high in the Judaean hills about twelve miles north of Jerusalem and situated between two wadis. The history of Bethel rivals that of Jerusalem. The Scriptures makes reference to Bethel dozens of times. Once called Luz, Bethel is where Abraham built an altar to Yahweh. This altar was located somewhere on a hill east of Bethel and west of Ai. I never found this altar, and today it seems no one knows where it was exactly. Besides, even the famous city of Ai is also lost to history. All anyone knew was Ai was not far from Bethel, somewhere to the west. I am sure with some digging Abraham's altar foundation stones could be found along with the city of Ai, but I never had the time to look for either.

Bethel was also the location where Abraham's grandson Jacob used stones as pillows when in the night he had a dream of angels ascending and descending from Heaven. This occurred while Jacob was making his escape from the wrath of his twin brother Esau for stealing their father's blessing after Jacob used chicanery to gain from his elder brother the family blessing. In the night, according to the Scriptures, Yahweh said, *"The land on which you lie I will give it to you and to your descendants."* Jacob said this was a dreadful place since this is the House of God and the Gate of Heaven. He made a pillar of stones, from the ones he used as pillows in the night, and anointed them with oil before he left. This pillar is also lost to history. Bethel is mentioned again in the Scriptures as the town in which the ten tribes gathered to fight against Gibeah because of the Benjamites' sexual sins and the ruthless murder of a man's concubine.

Bethel is located on high ground, which covers most of the area on the low hills between two wadis. Because the time of the year was early summer, there was some water in both wadis; and that is why we camped next to one of them to wait for our next visit by Saben. We placed the wagon out of sight off the road, but an interested person could see massive wheel tracks and horse hooves turning off at that point toward a downward slope although the wagon was hidden by trees and bushes.

The first day after we camped outside Bethel, Nicodemus, Amcheck, and Grillius went into the city to try to sell gimbals. When they returned, no gimbals had been purchased. As we ate our evening meal, I moved over to Nicodemus-Batana and quietly asked when he would start answering my questions he was told by Jesus to explain. I thought I should capitalize on this mandate from Jesus. Grillius seemed to be curious and moved over to where he could hear. "What do you want to know?" asked Nicodemus in Greek for Grillius's sake

I thought for a moment and then asked, "Why do people say and think John the Baptist was Elijah?"

My new teacher shook his head and asked, "Why is it you want to start with that question? Do you realize that the answer is perhaps one of the hardest to answer, let alone understand?"

I told him I would table the question for later if he felt I should know more of the history written in the Scriptures starting with Adam. He agreed but said it would be easier if we had the use of a *scriptorium* for that. However, his concern was how it would look if a Parthian nobleman were reading Hebrew and teaching a mere Persian bodyguard in a *scriptorium* that the Pharisees controlled. I looked over to Amcheck-Belkin and waved him over to our conversation. "What do you think, Belkin?" I asked trying to show submission to Amcheck's authority. He seemed to relish in his new power and said he would sleep on it but first he had to go and find a rock for a pillow. We all laughed except Grillius-Leonidas, who knew nothing of the Jews or their history. After the laughter had died down, Grillius asked if he, too, could be a student of Nicodemus-Batana. It touched my heart knowing Grillius wanted to learn about the Jews.

"It would be my pleasure to teach an old Spartan," declared a delighted Nicodemus.

With a rare smile, Grillius asked, "Start with explaining this road we must not leave, and what are the other roads crossing through *Palestina*?" I suspected Grillius had other plans in his mind other than just curiosity.

"Perhaps we should start with the Transjordan Highway or Jordan Rift Road, more of a muddy, winding byway, which follows the Jordan River between the Dead Sea and the Sea of Galilee."

"Sea of Tiberius," Amcheck-Belkin corrected with a scowl that could be clearly seen from the campfire.

"Sea of Galilee," repeated Nicodemus-Batana with a rare rebellious smirk; and it did not look like he was joking. I remembered the Rift Road as the one Amcheck and I took after we left Machaerus and returned to Jerusalem from

Tiberias. "The King's Highway is the most principal road used by foreigners from Mesopotamia to Egypt. It follows many miles east of the Jordan River starting from Damascus in Syria. This well-maintained road cuts south below the Dead Sea into Egypt via the delta region known as Lower Egypt."

Grillius-Leonidas confessed, "Egypt is one place I have never visited. What does the term Lower Egypt mean?"

The old scholar gave a satisfactory grin and began instructing. "The greatest river in the world flows from south to north into the Great Sea. At the point where the river empties into the sea is Lower Egypt. It is also the lowest elevation point of Egypt."

"Why do you call it the greatest river in the world?" asked Grillius.

"It is the only river that does not have bridges spanning its width, and depending on the season, the Nile is 7 to 20 miles wide."

Grillius held up his hand to stop Nicodemus-Batana. "You are saying there is a road running between the Dead Sea and the Sea of Galilee called the Transjordan Highway or Jordan Rift Road? Then far out to the east of *Palestina* is a well-maintained road running from Babylon to Alexandria called the King's Highway?"

"That is very observant, and you are correct on both accounts. Now the only other major artery that armies usually take when moving from north to south is the International Highway. The International Highway comes out of Damascus but runs to the north of the Sea of Galilee passing through Capernaum, the adopted home of Jesus and the town where many of his disciples resided before leaving to follow him. The International Highway then goes through the Jezreel Valley passing by Megiddo, where over forty battles in the past have been fought, due to its perfect, flat terrain for soldiers and chariots to effortlessly maneuver. It is also considered the most fertile place in the world, perhaps 10 feet of topsoil due to the hundreds of thousands of bodies that have rotted into the ground over the past 3,000 years."

I interrupted and asked if this was the location where King Josiah was struck by an arrow and later died in Jerusalem from his wound at the hands of the Egyptian King Necho. Nicodemus winked at me before he nodded yes and began again. "Passing Megiddo, just a small, walled city on a hill next to the Valley of Megiddo, you run into the International Highway that goes to Joppa, paralleling the Great Sea to Alexandria. The Romans maintain both the King's Highway and the International Highway keeping these ancient roads in perfect condition. There are respectable bridges over streams and rivers along with comfortable rest stops every 15 miles just like the Persians had incorporated into their vast highway system in the past, such as the Susa to Sardis or Royal Road that ran for over fifteen hundred miles. The Romans planted sycamore trees on both sides of the *Palestina* highways so that travelers would be in the shade during most of their travels. Unfortunately, most of the trees planted out on the Transjordan Highway died due to lack of rain."

Grillius-Leonidas added, "The idea of rest stations and trees for shade was also an innovation adopted over three hundred years past by the first Emperor of Chin in the Far East when he ordered imperial roads to be built, but he had the fast-growing mulberry trees planted for shade."

"How would you know that?" asked Nicodemus.

"I traveled in the land of the Hans when I was younger. The first famous emperor was the emperor of Chin. That is where the word Chin comes from. His name was Shih Hwang Ti but pronounced Shir Hwahng Dee. He was the emperor of the Chin Dynasty about a hundred years after Alexander the Great died. He was the one who started building the Great Wall of Chin. He also regulated coins, weights, and measures. The complicated picture writing of these people was also standardized by this otherwise ruthless dictator. He hated scholars and feared their knowledge, such as you, Batana. He had 460 teachers beheaded on one day and burned all the books in the land except law manuals and works on horticulture." Everyone was amazed at this old Spartan, and we all sat speechless.

After a short silence, Nicodemus nodded and said, "We should never judge a man by his scars." Amcheck thought this was hilarious; but, when we all became quiet, Nicodemus continued. "The Way of the Sea Road is just an extension of the International Highway that goes off to Caesarea, Ptolemais, Tyre, Sidon, and Antioch."

Amcheck-Belkin chimed in saying, "I know about Antioch; it is just south of the famous battle of Issus where Alexander the Great defeated Darius the III and captured the Persian king's family and the royal banquet tent."

"Very true," complimented our old teacher.

The other old man in our group, still wanting information about roads asked, "Now tell me about the Ridge Road, this road we must stick with for the next nine to ten months?" I still wondered why Grillius was interested in this subject. It would not be many days later when I learned why.

This time the old scholar picked up a stick and started drawing lines in the dirt, which were illuminated by the fire. "The Ridge Road starts out of Damascus but meanders around the Sea of Galilee toward ancient Dothan and then to Sychar, which used to be Shechem in the days of the patriarchs and perhaps my favorite city on earth. Sychar is a quaint little town situated in a beautiful, fertile valley between Mount Ebal to the north and Mount

Gerizim to the south. The patriarch Jacob and his sons dug a well located today just on the edge of the city. The well itself is the deepest I have ever drunk from; but, believe me, the effort of cranking up the wooden bucket hundreds of feet is worthwhile. The water is always cold as ice and the best water you will ever sample."

"Why all these details about the Ridge Road?" I asked the old scholar.

"Well, all you really need to know is that the Ridge Road or Route of the Patriarchs follows the east-to-the west watershed of the Judaean and Ephraim mountains. I am giving all these details because Abraham, Isaac, and Jacob walked its length repeatedly just as the four of us are going to travel. I would not be lying by saying most of the stories of the Jewish Scriptures have the Ridge Road as the backdrop. The Ridge Road is not the most direct road from the north to south, but it is the easiest to travel. It may not be the best-maintained road in *Palestina* but, since it follows the mountain ridges, there is very little going up and down steep valleys and ravines. Plus, the Ridge Road rarely floods during the rainy season because it runs along the watershed line high up in the mountains for most of the time. In the summer and warmer times, the Ridge Road is cooler than the other three routes running north and south because it is the highest road of the three."

Amcheck-Belkin interrupted into the narrative just as Nicodemus stopped talking. "Tradesmen and merchants usually use the Way of the Sea Route or the International Highway but not the Ridge Road. Those Jews living in the Galilee going to Jerusalem for one of the three major festival periods each year take either the winding footpath down along the Jordan River or go further out of their way to the two nicer and safer roads – either the International Highway or the King's Highway. But, the truth is the most direct route from Galilee to Jerusalem is the Ridge Road, however that means passing through Samaria. The Samaritans are a mixed people of Jewish and Assyrian blood. They are considered unclean and pseudo-pagans by the Jews. This has been the Jewish attitude since Sargon conquered this land of Israel about seven hundred years ago and when he removed most of the ten tribes of Israel into Syria. One would think attitudes among the Jews living in this land and half-Jews in other areas would have waned by now."

Nicodemus jumped back into the conversation by saying, "But this is the case among different Jewish groups. All Jews have memories that go back centuries. The only Jews to travel openly up and down the Ridge Road have been Jesus and his disciples. Jesus has been reviled for this along with doing miracles on the Sabbath; eating with sinners; and not washing his hands before eating, which would include seven shakes to allow excess water to drip down the fingers until dry. There is a host of other things against Jesus, which are just as petty. Apparently people do not understand his sayings, which causes many to continually slander him."

I decided to add to the conversation. "Especially the religious rulers in Jerusalem and Pharisee leaders of the synagogues,"

Nicodemus did not disagree with me considering he identified with the Pharisees' way of interpretation over the Sadducees'. He held up his hand indicating he wished to continue speaking. "The loss of the ten tribes by deportation to Assyria and the ones who were left to intermarry with the Assyrians brought into this land led to the creation of a new international trade and diplomatic language we use today called Aramaic. For this reason, Aramaic became a mixture of Hebrew and Assyrian. Both languages were considered as being birthed from the same Semitic mother tongue but different enough before Alexander the Invincible to demand Aramaic be replaced by Greek. Thus, today Greek is the new diplomatic and commerce language of the Roman world." Looking now at Grillius, Nicodemus explained. "The average Jew today speaks Aramaic and only reads Hebrew. Most Jews in *Palestina* also understand common Greek, even if they do not speak it very well."

I added, "I should state that the Greek spoken and written today is different and exceedingly diluted from what is sometimes called the Classical Greek, the language used hundreds of years ago during the times of Pericles when the *Parthenon* was being constructed in Athens."

"You are quite right, young man," said Nicodemus allowing his compliment to find its target before he continued. "All Jewish children who are males attend synagogue schools located in most villages to learn Hebrew so they could read the Scriptures themselves when they became adults once they reach the age of 12. Only a few parts of Ezra and Daniel have some Aramaic included in the Hebrew Scriptures. Since Aramaic has been the international language for over seven hundred years, this is why Jesus himself speaks Aramaic. It is the standard language most Jews speak and understand, even in Judaea as well as Galilee."

"Maybe it has survived as a protest language to the Greeks who were Hellenizing their Jewish culture," added Amcheck.

Nicodemus looked at him and responded quickly by saying, "However, if this were the case, why not turn to pure Hebrew?"

There was now a period of silence as we all thought about this. Finally, I broke the quiet moment by asking Nicodemus about taking me to a *scriptorium* in Bethel and translating Hebrew into Greek or Aramaic. Amcheck jumped in immediately saying someone had to remain at all times with the

Chapter Eight

Parthian carriage. No one responded as we tried to respect his position of leadership. After this uncomfortable moment, we all prepared for bed.

Grillius came up to me and said, "I will take the first six hours." I nodded, remembering this was the same hourly rotation for the galley slaves on the bireme I traveled on from Athens to Rome just a few years back. During the daytime when no one went to sell gimbals, Grillius and I took either morning or afternoon shifts for the other person to get sleep or to do whatever. On days the gimbal sellers went into town to sell, I always guarded the wagon; and Grillius accompanied the two Persian-looking men into town. I didn't mind this arrangement because it gave me some time to catch up on sleep even though this was dangerous to do. I was a light sleeper, and any noise could frequently wake me in an instant. I would not sleep in the wagon but would find a hide in the bushes with the camp in sight. My reasoning was, if any curious person started investigating the wagon and its contents, he would inevitably make some noise, which would alert me in my hide, and I would have an edge of surprise upon the intruder. Even if I were not sleeping, I still secreted myself in a hidden position. One man guarding a wagon in sight could be at a disadvantage even if he were awake and visible.

Over the next few days, no one from Bethel bought a gimbal. The salesmen even knocked on rich people's front gates with no success. On our third evening outside Bethel, we received a visit from two men walking out of Bethel. The four of us were sitting around our fire, each roasting some grain for our evening meal. Grillius and I both became quiet when we heard some strange banging noise coming from above us up on the road. Since I was technically on my guard rotation, I went to investigate. I discovered two poorly clad Jewish men standing in the middle of the road beating dust off their sandals by slapping them together in their hands and muttering something about Bethel. I closed the face doors of my helmet and surprised the men coming at them from behind as I appeared out of some bushes.

"Who goes there?" I challenged once I was behind them out in the middle of the road.

The two men were startled and defenseless. The older one answered in Aramaic, "We have no money and are only trying to get home, for we are the victims of a great deception."

I had spoken in Greek but changed to Aramaic. "What deception do you speak about, and what are you doing with your sandals?"

The older one did the answering. "We are shaking the dust from them because the people of Bethel rejected us. We used to be disciples of the one called Jesus of Nazareth, and Bethel is no longer friendly toward Jesus." I studied the talkative, more-aged man and concluded he was maybe thirty years of age making him somewhat older than I. The other was closer to my age.

"Why do you say Jesus of Nazareth is a deception and a deceiver?"

"We have been following him off and on now for perhaps two years; and we believe he has now lost his mind, or maybe he has been a false prophet all along. About a year ago, he said something in Capernaum to thousands of people after he fed them in the wilderness far above the Sea of Galilee; and everyone stopped following him after he spoke... well, mostly all, if you do not count his sycophant inner circle of 12 and a few silly women."

"I believe I heard that story over a year ago. Why are you still following him if that is your reason?"

The elder one spoke but did not answer my question. I wondered if he just wanted to stay on the same subject. "Not long ago this Jesus did the same miracle again, but this time he fed maybe four thousand Jews with some Gentiles like you. These people came from the pagan cities from the north of Galilee wanting to hear him speak. Jesus did not send them away; and, after about three days, these people did not have any food; so he did the same thing with a few fish and a few loaves of bread."

"You said twice Jesus fed thousands? Was it the same miracle as he did shortly after the death of John the Baptist?"

"Yes, exactly the same miracle a year ago, right after John the Baptist was beheaded by Herod Antipas. The talk of the first miracle was in our hometown, and that is the reason why we left everything and started following him.... but no longer."

"Where is your home?" I asked.

"We are brothers who left our elderly parents to follow Jesus. No telling what condition our poor parents are in since we left them to fend for themselves. They now need us to plant and bring in the barley harvest. We are from Azotus, down near the coast. It is the best land for growing crops in the fertile, flat lands of Shephelah."

"Is not this a rest year for the land? Are you not supposed to plant barley or wheat?"

"What is it to you, Gentile mercenary, telling us Jews about our laws?"

"I may be a soldier, but I am not stupid."

The two brothers looked at me strangely and wondered if I was going to become violent. "Our apologies. We had no right to accuse you of not understanding our ways; and, yes, it is a land rest. But we do not know of anyone who follows that old rule. You see, we were raised in the synagogue, of which the Pharisees are the teachers; and they do not practice land rests or even

Chapter Eight

Jubilees. It is only the Essenes down near the Dead Sea who believe in that old rubbish. It was the Pharisees who fought the encroachment of paganism, both religiously and politically, for centuries, not the Essenes. The Pharisees are the champions of godliness and true religion. However, just in a few years, Jesus shows up and has nothing good to say about the teachers of the synagogues, who taught us all that we know. It is utter chaos. He does not walk with the Essenes either, I might add."

The younger brother finally spoke for the first time. "Jesus does tell us to do what the Pharisees say but not what they do." The older brother looked at him as if he were annoyed for his interrupting.

"I have two questions before I invite you to our camp and some refreshment before your journey home."

"Ask away, friend," said the elder Jew. "But first, why do I have to talk to a man with his face covered." Thinking that these men were followers of Jesus, I thought that there would be no harm if I opened the side that did not show my scar. I reached up and opened the right side of the face shield of my helmet. "You are younger than I thought. What are you, maybe 21 years old?" I did not answer as I wondered what he meant and why my age had anything to do with anything. If I told him I was now 23 years old, soon to turn 24, he might figure out I was the age of the fugitive many were hunting. After a long, awkward moment and my staring at the older man, he finally asked, "What are your questions?"

Giving a slight smile after my long stare, I asked, "Was there a woman named Messina following Jesus?"

"There was, but she no longer follows. She became ill not long ago, and we left her with a kind woman in Sychar. That is strange that you ask because we stopped and looked in on her a few days ago on our way home. If you keep on the Ridge Road and head north, you will run into Sychar; for it is the largest city in Samaria."

"How will I find Messina? I have never been to Sychar, and this is still my first question."

The older man asked, "What route did you take to get here if you came from Parthia? You must have passed through Sychar if you came from the north."

"No," I lied. I began thinking of the map Nicodemus drew in the dirt a few nights back. "I came down the International Highway, and my master is making a full circuit of this land before we head home."

He seemed satisfied with my lie and asked for my second question. I decided to just ask again how I was to find Messina in such a large city, reminding him it was still my first question. He told me she was staying at a large house next to the tomb of Joseph the patriarch. "There are no other homes near the tomb, but it is a large estate with high walls around it. The color of the villa plaster is painted a strange pinkish color. It is the only home in Sychar or all *Palestina* that is that color. You will have no trouble finding it."

"My last question: what exactly convinced you of Jesus's heresy?"

"Heresy?" came a voice from the bushes. Ambling onto the road from the bushes was Nicodemus-Batana.

"This is Master Batana," I said to the two. "He is a merchant from Sardis; and I, his guard."

"I repeat. What heresy are you talking about?" demanded Nicodemus-Batana with a stern look on his face and speaking in Aramaic, since that was the language he heard us using.

"These two men were followers of Jesus of Nazareth for the past two years," I said to Nicodemus-Batana. "They have witnessed miracles and listened to Jesus's words, but recently Jesus said something that convinced these men that Jesus has become... shall we say... unhinged."

"Speak out; we will not harm you," said Nicodemus-Batana. "What exactly did Jesus say that made you think he was deranged or unhinged?"

The older of the two disciples hung his head in shame and then realized he was holding his sandals. He bent over to place them on his feet as he thought of what to say. After we patiently waited, he finally began. "Thousands heard this, so we are not making this up as slander. Jesus performed a great miracle of feeding thousands of people. He has now performed this miracle twice. Just recently, he has started feeding Gentiles and not the people of the House of Israel. These Gentiles came down from the north looking for Jesus. When they found him, they were without food for perhaps three days. Jesus took compassion on them and fed them with a few loaves of bread and some fish. There were baskets of leftovers after everyone ate. After the first miracle of the feeding of thousands, he instructed his special 12 disciples to beware of the leaven of the Pharisees, Sadducees, and Herod. We have grown tired of Jesus attacking the Pharisees, for we consider ourselves of that school. Both of us attended the synagogue school in our village of Azotus for years. It was the Pharisees who taught us much of what we know about the God of Israel."

"And what do the Pharisees say about Jesus?" asked Nicodemus-Batana.

The older man lifted his head up and to his right as he thought; and, after lowering his head and looking straight at Nicodemus, he said with venom in his voice, "They say Jesus refuses to adapt to their established system. He overturns their sacred concepts. He is from 'vile' Nazareth, for no Messiah could come from there. He is self-educated – not schooled correctly – and teaches by telling stories no sane person could ever understand. He talks to the outcast, tax collectors, and sinners. Finally, they say, if he is not checked, his teachings are going to bring the Romans upon this land to destroy everything the Pharisees have built since the return from Babylon. Besides, the Scriptures teach the Messiah is like an Alexander the Great, who will surely come and dash the Romans to dust. However, Jesus says we must love and pray for our enemies. He says, 'If a Roman asks you to carry his pack one mile, you should carry it two miles.' I tell you the man is a heretic, and I am sorry we wasted two years with him."

"Anything else?" asked Nicodemus-Batana in an unexpected, gentle voice.

"Well, we never really got over what he apparently said in Capernaum after the first miracle of feeding thousands. He said, if anyone wanted eternal life, one had to eat his flesh and drink his blood; that to us is his chief blasphemy. Those were his exact words. People should have stoned him right there, but they were too shocked. My brother and I were not actually present when he said it, but we did ask him privately not long ago to explain himself. The problem was it took so long to ask him because anyone who wishes to speak to Jesus must make it through the 12 bodyguards, especially the fisherman named Simon or "Little Rock" in Greek or "Little Pebble" in Aramaic. The 12 guard Jesus as if he is a king. But he did commit his cannibalistic blasphemy two Passovers ago, shortly after John the Baptist was beheaded. Thousands of disciples left Jesus and are now speaking poorly of him. We were some of the last to leave. He is now almost alone, except for the 12 who have been with him from the beginning, the ones he wanted, not the ones who chose him."

Nicodemus-Batana spoke now with authority. "I met this Jesus of Nazareth outside of Jerusalem when he started his ministry, over three years ago, and long before you started following him. I must confess that I made the same mistake you two are making."

The older man seemed insulted by Nicodemus's words. "What mistake is that, Parthian? First, what was a Parthian doing in *Palestina* three years ago? There is something strange about you two, but I apologize if I have offended. We should show more respect since you are an older man, even if you are a foreigner from Parthia. But perhaps you do not understand the ways of us Hebrews."

Nicodemus crossed his arms in his colorful robes to gather his thoughts while I noticed the younger brother move slightly away from his own brother to put on his sandals. Finally, Nicodemus spoke. "I am a long-time secret student of the Jews and the Scriptures, which I believe have come down from

Heaven. Hence, what if a man is from far away? That does not make him any less than a Jew. I will tell you both now that I am a follower of the true Elohim, and I have submitted to circumcision late in my life. Understand what I am about to say. We humans speak one of two ways – either figuratively or literally. Jesus told me I had to be 'born again' to have eternal life. I asked, 'How could a man enter his mother's womb and be born again?' He rebuked me because I took him literally and not figuratively. If he said, 'You must drink his blood and eat his flesh,' then he was speaking figuratively and, of course, not literally. He was using a metaphor. How else can he teach heavenly things except to use worldly examples that we humans can understand?"

"I disagree; and how is it that you, a foreigner, speak Aramaic almost like a Jew from Jerusalem?" questioned the older ex-disciple, who was becoming visibly angry with his face flushing.

I jumped in taking Nicodemus-Batana's side in this argument, "Did Jesus take a knife and cut off his little finger and offer it to anyone to eat and drink?"

"Of course not!" said the younger man standing out by himself.

"There, you see, he was speaking figuratively, not literally," I said. "Because you two don't understand the things of this world, how will you understand the things of the spiritual world unless someone who knows of that realm is forced to use figurative speech?"

The older one held up his right hand and said, "We will forego your kind offer for food and be on our way. Besides, we Jews are not to eat with foreigners anyway. It is against our laws. But before we go, let me tell you both one last incident that turns my stomach about your friend-idol Jesus. I was present at a home of a Pharisee, who graciously fed Jesus and his disciples. A woman who was obviously a sinner came in unannounced and began weeping; she washed Jesus's feet with perfume from an alabaster vial along with her tears as she wiped his feet with her hair. Jesus told her that her sins were forgiven. Tell me now; is it not true that only God can forgive sins? Then Jesus went on to insult his host by saying he did not wash his feet when he entered his home but this woman washed his feet with her tears. I am telling you this story to show you Jesus is *mega-luna*, and he is unbalanced and disturbed in the head. All the people flocking around him for years has gone to his head. He actually thinks he is something beyond human!" The two brothers then turned away from us and walked south as fast as they could.

"Stop!" ordered Nicodemus-Batana.

The two obeyed Nicodemus, but I am sure they would not have stopped for me if I had commanded them. Nicodemus and I walked down the road to them. It was apparent they wanted to get away from a man who had an armed guard. In a calm voice, Nicodemus-Batana asked one last question. "Tell me, what story is it that upset you the most?"

Without even thinking, the older brother spoke from his heart. How Nicodemus-Batana even knew there was another problem I never understood. "One day Jesus was eating with sinners and even tax collectors in a small village. Some Pharisees and scribes came up and rebuked Jesus for this action. Jesus answered with one of his long stories. Actually, it was three stories in one. The first story was about a man who lost 1 sheep, and the man left 99 sheep to find the lost one and found it. The second story was a woman in a house who lost a valuable coin and swept the house thoroughly until she found the coin. Then his third story was about a well-to-do man who had two sons. The younger wanted his inheritance early, and the father gave it to the boy. He left and went to a faraway land and spent it on harlots and other sinful things. After he was destitute, he found work feeding pigs for some Gentile. It was then he decided to return home. When the father saw him on the road coming home, he ran to this wayward son and gave him his ring and cloak along with new sandals. He also slew the fatted calf and had a party for his son. When the elder son, who never left the father, came in from the fields after working hard all day and asked one of the servants what was going on, he was told that his younger brother had returned broken and penniless and that the boys' father was throwing a party for the younger son. When the father found out the elder brother would not enter the house, the father went to the elder son and said, 'All that I have is yours, but your brother was lost and now is found. You should be happy and join us.' The elder brother refused. That was the end of the three stories."

"And how did you interpret what Jesus meant?"

"It is obvious: God is unfair. Why should the younger brother get a party when he spent the father's money on harlots?"

The younger man said, "And the son who stayed home and worked received a stern lecture."

Nicodemus crossed his arms and blew some air out of his mouth before answering the two. "The story had to do with whom Jesus was addressing. It sounds to me the story was directed to the Pharisees and scribes. Did you not tell me Pharisees and other religious men were attacking Jesus for eating with sinners? Furthermore, the three stories all have something to do with something lost. The first had something lost out in the wilderness, that being a sheep. The second had something lost in a house, that being a coin. The last story had two things lost. The younger boy was lost in the wilderness, but where was the elder son? He was in the house. However, by his actions, he was just as lost as his younger brother was, if not worse. The father was not lying when he told the older boy that he stayed home and had everything, but his heart was lost because he would not rejoice when the younger brother had repented and returned home. The Pharisees and scribes all stayed home, but they are lost; do you not see that? They did not rejoice that sinners and tax-gatherers are listening to Jesus and are repenting. Did not John the Baptist teach that people needed to repent, for the kingdom of God was at hand? Warning about the leaven of Herod is also a correct statement – but so is the hypocrisy of the Pharisees and the Sadducees."

"We have heard enough. We do not agree and are returning home."

"Did Jesus say you could go home?"

The elder turned and said over his shoulder, "No, he rebuked us with another story."

The younger brother from a distance said, "Jesus said to us as we were leaving, 'A man who puts his hand to the plow and looks back is not worthy of the kingdom of God.' If a man cannot leave his wife or parents for Jesus, then he is not worthy. I am sorry, but we cannot follow a man who encourages a man to leave his wife just to follow a poor stonemason who will not talk plainly."

I just had to throw one last dart from my "ugly bag." "Why is it that you two Jews think of yourselves as righteous and yet you walked through evil Samaria? And if Bethel is not in Samaria, certainly Sychar is in Samaria." They did not answer and walked away.

After they had disappeared over the rise in the road, I asked Nicodemus-Batana who he believed Jesus was. "I believe it has something to do with what Jesus told me near the gate to the Garden of Gethsemane. He said he was going to be crucified by the Romans. He asked that I help bury him for just a short time. He quoted a prophecy from King David that is recorded in Psalms that goes something like this: *'For You will not abandon my soul to Sheol, nor will You allow Your Holy One to undergo decay.'* Now I think I understand a little more. If a person wanted eternal life during the time of Adam and Eve before they were ejected from the Garden of Eden, what could that person do?"

I answered the question with the only ideas I possessed on the subject. "The Scriptures speak of two trees; one was the Tree of Life, and the other was the Tree of Knowledge of Good and Evil. Adam was told not to eat from the latter tree or he would die. For this reason, it should be clear to see: one tree was for eternal life; and the other, death."

"Are you speaking literally or metaphorically?"

Chapter Eight

"Splendid question," I answered with delight in my voice. A fire burned deep inside me as I looked at Nicodemus smiling at me as if he were back in his home in Jerusalem. "But, you tell me the answer."

Nicodemus smiled from ear to ear. I could see his delight in giving me the answer. "It has to be literal. We are here because of Adam and Eve. We literally came from Adam's seed. After our ancient parents ate from the forbidden tree, they were cast out of the garden; and cherubim with flaming swords prevented entrance to the Garden of Eden. That had to be literal. The cherubim were there to prevent Adam and Eve from entering the garden again and eating from the Tree of Life. Had they eaten from the Tree of Life, they would still be alive today. They would have gained eternal life and not died, but they would have lived forever in their sins. It makes perfect sense that Jesus will be lifted up on a tree; and, thus, his body is the fruit from the Tree of Life. God has been telling us throughout the Scriptures that God Himself will visit this world and that only His blood will be the perfect sacrifice to take away our sins. The sacrifices we perform at the Temple in Jerusalem only cover our sins, but God's blood would definitely make a difference and forever take away our sins. But we first must somehow go to the Tree of Life and eat and drink his blood. Of course, this would all be symbolic, the drinking of his blood and eating of his flesh; yet, literally, he will die in our place. Yet, somehow, we will eat and drink his blood. This remains a mystery to me at this juncture."

"Are you saying Jesus is God?"

"That is exactly what I am saying. It all makes sense; do you not see it? I do not think Jesus wanted thousands following him for the wrong reasons. This is what I have heard: every time a demon-possessed person is in Jesus's presence, that person begins screaming, 'He is the Son of God; Jesus is the Son of God.' Why is it, when a demon-possessed person encounters Jesus, the demon speaks through the person declaring who Jesus truly is? Jesus then rebukes the demon or demons and casts these evil spirits out of the human host. You see, my young disciple, Jesus was speaking to people who wanted him to be a king, not because He is the son of God. They wanted Jesus only because he would feed them. They wanted him for the wrong reason; they wanted him to be a bread-king, and then they could sit around and never again have to work. It makes excellent sense to me that Jesus understood their hearts. Thus, He challenged them with the brutal truth of who He is. Most rejected Him, including those two brothers now leaving us."

"How could he be God?"

"Didn't God appear to Abraham as a human just before Sodom was destroyed? Moreover, when this becomes apparent to the authorities like the Sanhedrin, what do you think they will do to Jesus?"

"They will kill him because they will never accept him for who He really is."

"Precisely! Yahweh Himself has stepped out of time and entered into the very time we are living. Yahweh decided from the very beginning of creation to enter into His own handiwork as one of us. And He knew what it would cost Him. Yes, He is with us right now. I agree, when the Sanhedrin learn of this, they will order His death. What is sad is the Sanhedrin will be worse than those two men with whom we just spoke. Did you notice they would not even eat with us? Hatred has filled their hearts. A hard heart, according to Jesus, equals a lack of understanding. Did those two young men understand a thing we said to them? How could they? They both had hard hearts. Neither of them could see that the son who stayed home was just as lost as the coin in the house. That is the danger of a hard heart. They have lost their faith in Jesus. Maybe they never had any faith to start with. They will join all the faithless ones who will cry for the death of the one they think is a false prophet. The book of Job says, '*They have gaped at me with their mouth; they have slapped me on the cheek with contempt; they have massed themselves against me. God hands me over to ruffians and tosses me into the hands of the wicked.*' When did that happen to Job? Never! It was a picture of the future Messiah. Jesus knows what is going to happen because, from outside of time, all of this has already occurred. The Scriptures are full of descriptions of the plight of the Messiah. We all have free choice, but God already knows our hearts and what our options will be. Jesus knows your heart. It is not where He wants it today, but He must know where it will be in the future. Why else would He tell me to disciple you? I will not be wasting my time with you, for God has wonderful plans for you in the future. Understand this, He told me what was going to happen to Him when He spoke to me on the Mount of Olives. Therefore, He must know your future."

Wanting to change the subject, I asked, "Why do you think the Romans will harm Jesus?"

"Only the Romans have the authority and the power for the deed He talked about. The Sanhedrin will have to convince the Romans to do their dirty work, but it will be the Romans who will carry it out. Still, Jesus's death is all part of Yahweh's plan. Do you not see? If I only had my scrolls, I could show you a passage by the Prophet Isaiah that is even more precise and convincing than what Job said. It talks about the suffering servant, a man of sorrows. What is strange is that the text is written in the past tense, as if the event had already happened, yet Isaiah wrote the prophecy seven hundred years ago."

"What kind of sorrows?" I blurted out in the waning light of day standing in the middle of the Ridge Road. I lowered my head because I was dropping deeper into confusion and bewilderment by trying to process all that this old scholar was saying.

"The Romans use trees and make crosses out of them. Jesus will be lifted up just as He told me, figuratively and literally. You see, Jesus will become the snake on Moses's staff. Sin is the snake, and that is figurative. Unless we believe and partake of the fruit of the Tree of Life that will soon somehow be taken out of the Garden of Eden, we will not have eternal life. To believe, indeed, requires a massive conversion or as Jesus said, 'To be born again,' requiring each human to become a new creation if he or she wishes to have eternal life with Him. It is all figurative, yet literal, all at the same time. I cannot believe it took me so long to understand," remarked an excited and enthused Nicodemus. Yet, Nicodemus had a new and profound understanding, which he had been trying to figure out for his entire life and now it was all being tied up neatly in a tiny box.

I looked at this man in his colorful robes as the evening colors become most vibrant. "You said the Scriptures do not give us eternal life; they only speak of Jesus!"

Hearing my words, the old scholar threw his arms up to heaven and said, "Jesus is Yahweh, and now I can see how that statement is true. Tell me, my young disciple, what do the Scriptures talk about over and over?"

I stood on the road and had memories of my happy years at the Lyceum. With a smile, I said, "I would surmise that the Scriptures are stories, poetry, and prophesies all talking about Yahweh."

"You see, Jesus is Yahweh. He says He has come to us from Heaven to give us eternal life."

"He actually said that?"

"What he told me over three years ago when I went at night because of fear from my fellow Pharisees and those of the Sanhedrin is now something I understand for the first time. You see, three years ago Jesus said to me, *'If I tell you earthly things and you do not understand, how will you understand and believe if I tell you heavenly things.'*"

"Tell me what you understand?"

"God has come from above to give us a new birth from above. If you and I do not understand that Jesus left Heaven for this world, then we will not be able to live with Him forever. This is so simple; yet it is hard!"

"Very hard, but let me make sense of what you are saying. Jesus is God and now walking in this world for just a little time, perhaps until next Passover when he will be killed by the Romans on a cross made of wood. The wood is important because it is a picture of the Tree of Life being placed outside the Garden of Eden for all to approach and eat its fruit. And the fruit somehow is his body and blood."

"You have just hit the spike and driven it home in one strike! But, in order not to live forever in a fallen state, we first must believe in who He is to be born from above before we eat of the Tree of Life. Only God's Spirit from above could have had you say what I just heard. The very first prophecy in the Scriptures states the seed of the woman would crush the head of the viper, the very same viper Moses made of bronze and put on a wooden stick in the wilderness. Moses then told the Hebrews to look at the snake on his wooden staff and live. Jesus is going to become our sin or take up our sin somehow, and we will need to believe with faith to live. He came to destroy the works of the devil, who is just as real as you and I. This eternal life is free and has always been free. It is so simple; I do not know why I missed it all these years. I want to blame it on the teaching of the Pharisees, but that is only an excuse. You see, believing the Messiah was coming to destroy sin is vital. Perhaps later He will deal with the Romans as the King of Kings – first things first. He has openly and repeatedly stated that He has not come to judge the world but to save it. However, all this sin must be purchased with bloody wages. It has something literally to do with His body and His blood. It is sad those two ex-disciples did not stick with Jesus. They have become slanderers of the kingdom of God, and now both are in Satan's camp. I wonder if the younger brother, who did not say much, took his inheritance early and if the older brother is still angry. Just a thought."

"This is hard for me to understand even if it is literal," I said with a chuckle before becoming serious because I felt more in Satan's camp than God's. Once again I changed the subject to protect my mind from imploding with all that Nicodemus had just revealed. "Can you tell me now why people say John the Baptist was Elijah?"

The old scholar turned and looked at me with a funny expression on his face. Then he started to laugh and said, "I have a plan that will help explain the Elijah mystery and everything else."

"That is excellent news. Now, shall we return to camp and eat, and I will try to learn patience?"

CHAPTER NINE

Bethel – Early summer in Tiberius's 18th year. Pontius Pilate's 6th year as Prefect of Judaea. Jesus of Nazareth's 4th and last year of his public ministry.   *(32 AD)*

After watching a small boy pull a mouse out of its hole turn around and bite him on the hand of its captor and escape, King Agesilaus said, "When the tiniest creature defends itself like this against a giant aggressor, what ought we to do?"   A Spartan king as recorded by Xenophon

"Life is what happens after you make your plans," said Grillius-Leonidas. My old Spartan teacher did not talk much; but, when he did, we usually listened. Mercury Day and Jupiter Day had passed, and no one bought any gimbals at Bethel making it four days in a row where no one wanted a new way of inking pens. While we were still camped at the wadi south of Bethel, Nicodemus-Batana declared on the fifth evening at the wadi (two days since our encounter with the two disgruntled disciples of Jesus on the Ridge Road) that he was not going to try selling any more gimbals in Bethel. Instead, he made an ultimatum to Amcheck-Belkin that he was taking me into Bethel tomorrow on Sabbath Eve (or Venus Day) to answer my question about Elijah and John the Baptist. His logic was that Saben was due to arrive anytime on the Sixth Day (Venus Day) and that it was best if more people were at the wagon listening for his arrival. "Aristarchus has had been guarding the wagon all week, and now he needs a break. Just the two of us will go to that *scriptorium* next to the synagogue on the south side of town. We should be safe, and Star will dress like a Jew." Amcheck was clearly upset after hearing Nicodemus's plan, but the old scholar persisted. Finally, Nicodemus-Batana convinced Amcheck to take a day to rest and stay with the wagon and horses. "Besides, we would only waste our time trying to sell gimbals," remarked Batana. "There is no one else to approach whom we haven't already."

On the morning of the sixth day, little did I know this day was going to be one of the most anomalous days of my life. By the time the sun set, my life would be moving in a completely different direction than I could have ever predicted. Looking back on that day, I can now say that the change of routine most likely saved all of our lives. The morning started as usual except Amcheck-Belkin with an air of authoritative bearing ordered Nicodemus and me to be back by the middle of the afternoon and to only go to the *scriptorium*. Grillius never talked much when others were around, especially when there were disputes. I tried to follow his example and stayed out of the few heated arguments that on occasion blew up between Nicodemus and Amcheck. Just as we were leaving the camp by foot was when Grillius made his statement about life. It was odd, but by the time this day ended it made great sense.

Nicodemus and I were wearing simple Judaean garb; and I covered my head and face with a *shimla* like a sheepherder. Over my clothing, I wore a long peasant cloak, which hid my cuirass as well as my sword. I did not want to enter a dangerous situation and not be prepared. In my hands, I carried a gimbal, still in its box, while Nicodemus took a cloth bag containing a new scroll, one bottle of ink, and pens. He told me I was going to make notes and write down some scriptures to discuss in the afternoon once we returned from the *scriptorium*.

No one seemed up and around the synagogue when Nicodemus and I found the *scriptorium*, a simple, one-room affair that was adjacent to the main gathering place of worship. The sun was just cresting over the hills when we entered, and Nicodemus found a particular scroll in a wall niche near the back in the early light. He unrolled it on a long reading table instructing me to sit. Just as I sat down with the gimbal and other writing instruments, in came the chief rabbi of the synagogue. "What are you two doing?" the indignant little man asked. "And what is that device on the table?"

Nicodemus kindly ask the Pharisee his name; and the little man said he was a Benjamite, and his name was Saul. He also said he was not the principal rabbi of the synagogue but was filling in until the leading rabbi returned from his long trip to Rome on urgent business.

Chapter Nine

"I want to show this young sheepherder the Word of God," stated Nicodemus very softly. "The object on the table is a unique ink pot called a gimbal."

"Oh, yes, you are one of the Persians trying to sell that evil 'devil' device. But today you are dressed as a Jew. Are you Persian or Jew? And how do you think you know how to explain the Scriptures? To understand the Scriptures, one must be adequately trained."

"I am a Jew. Years ago I studied under Gamaliel. Do you accept his authority as being acceptable?"

"Gamaliel, the doctor of the Law from the Jerusalem Temple school?"

"The same scholar, but it was a long time ago."

"I, too, studied under Gamaliel but not that long ago. If you sat under Gamaliel, I would be a fool to say you could not teach this shepherd boy. But, on the table is that demon inkpot, you are not planning on making a copy of the Scriptures? It is not allowed," he remarked pointing at the gimbal.

"We are only copying Malachi in Greek, not Hebrew. That should not be a problem. The boy only knows how to read Greek and not Hebrew. You know shepherd boys are uneducated in Hebrew."

"Oh? Are you telling me you are only making a copy of the Septuagint? Is that what you have on the table?"

"Yes to both questions," explained Nicodemus.

"Go ahead; that scroll is worthless. I hate the Septuagint; I feel like burning the whole collection."

"You feel it has errors?"

"Any translation from the original source has errors. I think it is *Beelzebub's* biggest trick on humans."

"Perhaps I could take the entire collection off your hands for a price. I am sure the synagogue and this *scriptorium* could use the money."

With a new gleam in his eye, the rabbi asked, "What would you offer?"

"Since the Septuagint is full of errors, I am not sure what it is worth," negotiated Nicodemus. "Did not 72 Jewish scholars translate the Torah in only 70 days? There must be many errors. I would be willing to pay the price of the papyrus, and you can have this writing device along with all our pens and this bottle of expensive ink."

"You make a convincing argument. That copy of the Septuagint looks very old, and the papyrus most likely will crumble in your hands. Let's say 10 *denarii,* plus that devil device along with the pens and ink."

"I will give you eight *denarii* and, of course, the gimbal along with the pens, ink, and that new papyrus scroll resting on the table. Do we have a deal?" asked Nicodemus before the rabbi could change his mind. The short, balding man popped his head up and down looking like a funny bird. Quickly Nicodemus pulled eight coins out of a money bag, which I realized was a little over a week's worth of pay to a Roman soldier or one of Herod's guards. Nicodemus waved his hand at me to gather up what seemed to be more than twenty-four scrolls.

"I think there are more scrolls here besides the Scriptures," I commented while I was gathering up the collection.

The bird-looking rabbi answered, "That is another problem I have with the Septuagint. A couple hundred years ago in Alexandria, as your teacher said, 72 Jewish scholars transcribed the Torah in 72 days, not 70. Apparently the rest of the other books in the Scriptures were translated later for the Great Library in Alexandria. I am guessing it was necessary since many Jews living in Alexandria had forgotten how to read Hebrew. Well, anyway, many of the later books were split into parts. That is why there are more scrolls than the original; but you have the entire collection of the Scriptures there on the table, and what is left in the shelves behind you. Just take all that is in Greek. How accurate the collection is I am not sure. You will find some differences in Amos, Job, and Jeremiah. They are also a little shorter than the Hebrew texts. Why? It is a mystery to me."

"It will be sufficient to our needs," uttered Nicodemus.

"You will also never find Y-H-W-H in the LXX as the Greeks call the Septuagint; but, instead, the Greek word *kyrios* or LORD is used. This is blasphemy in my thinking since the name of God is the one crucial principle in the Scriptures. Here we are today hundreds of years later; and you can attest, old man, that many Jews have already forgotten the real name of our Creator; and I blame this partly on that Greek translation. You see, many foreigners today think God's name is LORD or just *Theos* in Greek or *Deus* in Latin. Who knows why this happened other than Satan is attacking the precious name of our Creator. It must have been a sad time for us Jews living under the Seleucids with the start of Hellenization in our Holy Land. Our Temple became desecrated with temple prostitutes and pig sacrifices. Judas Maccabee rose up and fought the heathens, but he was later killed. Then Judah's son took his place until he was martyred. This forced his brother Jonathon to build an army of over ten thousand, but he made an alliance with one of the weaker Seleucid kings to ensure our independence. In return, Jonathon became high priest and king. We were a free nation again until Pompey, the Roman blasphemer, entered Jerusalem. He slaughtered many priests in Jerusalem after brazenly walking into the Holy of Holies and finding nothing in the most sacred room. What kind of people are these Romans?" declared the little rabbi as if he wanted to understand the mind of the Gentiles; yet, he realized he had answered his unattainable question.

Nicodemus said, "Did Pompey not know we had lost the Ark of the Covenant years before the Babylonians razed Solomon's Temple, the most magnificent structure man had ever constructed?"

"I would agree with your question. It must have been a grand sight to have seen Solomon's Temple before the Babylonians destroyed it. It took Solomon seven years to build the Temple, the same number of years it took Pericles to build the *Parthenon* in Athens."

I kept my mouth shut, for I was taught that it took Pericles nine years to build the *Parthenon*. I did not want to correct the little man and lose getting the entire collection.

However, Nicodemus added, "Some Babylonian scholars and ancient Jewish writers say the seven years was the number of years it took to just lay the foundation stones."

A strange peace came over me as I found this discussion quite refreshing. Here were two men of great learning talking about ancient events most did not even know. It had been years since I sat and listened to such a discourse. I found myself trying to memorize everything I heard. Nicodemus slightly smiled before he commented next. "I believe Solomon's Temple was not a massive structure but more of a magnificent work of art in all the details that only the priests and Levites were able to see. For instance, Solomon had built his own palace on Mount Moriah and built a palace in the far north of Moriah for Pharaoh's daughter, one of his many wives."

"You are correct. There were three others that I know of. The House of the Forest of Lebanon, the Hall of Pillars, and the Hall of the Throne, all located on Mount Moriah."

"Therefore, the Temple must have been more of a royal chapel in the midst of all those monstrosities," commented Nicodemus with a twinkle in his blue eyes.

"I never thought of it that way, but you must be right," commented the rabbi.

Now I could not contain myself any longer, and I asked a question that came from nowhere. "Rabbi, you mentioned the *Parthenon* in Athens. It just dawned on me that the translation of that pagan temple in Greek was the 'temple of the virgin' or 'virgin's place.' Do you find that odd considering the prophecies of the Messiah being 'virgin born'?"

"I never thought of a pagan temple having anything to do with us Jews," replied the little rabbi now looking a little perturbed. "Besides, how would a shepherd boy know such a thing? Who are you really?"

Nicodemus smiled from ear to ear. "He is more than a shepherd, and that is why I have taken him as my disciple."

"Where did you find him, and how long has he been your student?"

"That is a long story, and he did make a splendid observation. Does not the Scriptures tell us that, when King Solomon prayed at the Temple's dedication, he reached out to pagan nations to consider worshipping Yahweh? Therefore, why wouldn't the pagans have some truth buried in their blindness?"

The little proxy scholar looked puzzled not knowing the answer. Then his coloring became dark; and spittle emitted from his mouth as he said, "You just said the word that is not to be said! We humans are not allowed to utter the real name of God!"

Nicodemus smiled before it disappeared. He then held up his hand to show he was going to talk and for the bird to listen carefully. "You said yourself the name of God is being forgotten. Where does it say we are not to use the name of the Creator given to Moses at the Burning Bush? His name is written in the Hebrew Scriptures repeatedly. How are we to read the Scriptures and not pronounce God's personal name? Besides, you said the Greek translation is going to cause the future to not know the personal name of God. According to your logic, the same will occur even with Hebrew-speaking Jews."

After a long time of thinking, the little rabbi conceded to Nicodemus's logic. "You have made a strong argument. I will think about what you just said. Perhaps we Pharisees are a little legalistic over some matters. You see, I am a Pharisee, and you must be of that persuasion if you studied under Gamaliel."

I wanted to start laughing and then screaming when he said "little," but Nicodemus must have known what I was thinking; and he put his hand on my shoulder along with a nod toward the Scriptures on the table we had just purchased at a steal. I understood and kept quiet. Nicodemus just smiled, but his eyes told me to begin gathering up the scrolls. While I started gathering the scrolls, Nicodemus turned back to the rabbi and skillfully changed the subject. "Most of the Jews from Jerusalem were exiled by the Babylonians, and Solomon's Temple was burned on Av 9 of that year. Am I correct?"

The rabbi nodded with a smile.

Nicodemus then asked, "Then could it be plausible that the Ark of the Covenant had been hidden before the city fell to the Babylonians and that no one today knows where it was hidden?"

Chapter Nine

"Perhaps you are right. That would explain why nothing stands in the Holy of Holies today in Herod's Temple. Nevertheless, Pompey the pig, believed we had an idol of some god in there; and he was displeased when he discovered nothing in the Holy of Holies. Still, he had no business in there and no right to slaughter our priests that day."

"I agree; Pompey had no right entering the Temple. Remember what happened to Uzziah the king of Judah when he entered the Temple and offered incense, a job only a Levite priest is allowed to perform. Was he not struck down by God with leprosy that he had until he died. However, we could go on and on, but we must be on our way and, I thank you for the most stimulating history lesson," said a crafty Nicodemus, who also started to pick up some rolled scrolls.

"Hold on. I want to know how a young shepherd boy would know that the *Parthenon* in Greek means 'virgin's place.'"

Nicodemus touched his own head and said, "I am guilty. I talk too much, and the boy has a never-ending memory. He spouts out everything I say. I have to be careful around him – If you know what I mean." The little rabbi giggled with the absurd explanation at my expense. I just stood there with scrolls in my arms and purposely crossed my eyes thinking that would make me look stupid. Stupid or not, had the rabbi been a fish, he had a hook that Nicodemus had buried in his gills. For one more *denarius*, the rabbi provided a second large cotton bag to carry all the tightly rolled scrolls.

I had a smile on my face as we walked down the streets of Bethel with two hefty bags over my shoulder. I could not believe we actually had our very own collection of all the Scriptures in Greek. From now on, Nicodemus could answer any question I had by pointing to the Scriptures. Once we reached the edge of town, I said, "Do you think that rabbi knows he was taken for a trip and dumped into a wadi?"

"One man's trash is another's treasure."

"Are you quoting Menander?"

"Maybe," was all Nicodemus grunted. I noticed his breathing was labored from the long walk in the heat that was going to be intense by afternoon.

"Do you at least feel guilty about cheating him?"

Nicodemus, the old, half-blind sage and a member of the Sanhedrin, just smiled and said, "He is the one who set the price. How is that cheating someone? If anyone was cheated, it was the rabbi who deceived himself with his own fallacious preconceptions."

"True; but when I was a child, you should have seen how my father operated. He would have made you look like a child in business negotiations. He would have taken the entire *scriptorium* for less than what we paid for these Scriptures." Nicodemus laughed for the first time that I had ever witnessed. Apparently comparing Nicodemus to Gaius Vetallus in business dealings was a high compliment to his ears.

Before long, Nicodemus wanted to stop at a beautiful grassy place under a giant oak and look at the scrolls he bought. I felt it was a grand idea. Nicodemus quickly found the scroll containing the Psalms, and a funny look came over his face.

"What is the matter?" I asked.

"Do you know the 22nd Psalm?"

"I have it memorized only in Greek. The rabbi in Rome, who circumcised me, gave me some of the Psalms to memorize. They were all in Greek."

"That is wonderful. Do you remember where it says, '*they pierced my hands and my feet*'?"

"That is what the Greek says," I agreed. "Does the Hebrew say the same?"

"The Hebrew says, '*like a lion my hands and my feet.*'"

"Is not a lion that is killed skinned and stretched out by its feet? Is it just a literal translation into Greek from a figurative in the Hebrew?"

"Perhaps you are right but maybe not. I always took this literally as the Messiah being a metaphoric lion. Now it makes great sense to me even more than ever that Yeshua is going to be crucified on a Roman cross. He is the Lion of Judah, and he will have his hands and feet stretched out." Nicodemus rustled through the bag until he found the scroll named after the prophet Zechariah. With the manuscript at arm's length, he pointed to a passage for me to read.

I was careful with the old scroll and read where his finger had pointed. "*And they shall look upon me because they have mocked me.*" I looked up and asked, "Is that what the Hebrew says? And who are 'they'?"

"'*They*' are Jerusalem; and the Hebrew Scriptures says, '*they look upon the one they pierced and lament.*' This is just another prophecy of the death of the Messiah at the hands of the Jews."

The hours flew by as I listened to Nicodemus. When the sun was a little past high in the sky; I remembered we told Amcheck we would be back to the camp by mid-afternoon. After pointing to the sun and its location in the heavens, Nicodemus agreed that we should pack up the scrolls and start back to camp, which was not that far down the road.

Once we reached the spot where we had encountered the two ex-disciples of Jesus, we heard shouting coming from near the gimbal wagon. I immediately sensed trouble and grabbed Nicodemus and pulled him into some

Chapter Nine

bushes across the road. I whispered to him to stay hidden with the heavy bags full of scrolls. I quickly pulled off my Judaean robe and coat that concealed my black cuirass over my black soldier's tunic. I was glad I was not wearing those long purple pants and Persian jacket. It is strange how the mind works, especially during a crisis. I touched my two throwing knives and my falcata, which was still tied to my back. If there was trouble, I was going into battle without a helmet or shield; so be it. As long as I had on my high Spartan boots, which were tied securely to my feet, I felt ready for whatever was to occur.

"What is happening?" asked a frightened Nicodemus. I gave him the universal sign to be quiet, the same sign I had taught Zoe when I wanted him to stay and not bark. He understood by shaking his head in the affirmative. I left him and hurried down the left side of the Ridge Road to the spot our wagon had turned off the road down near the wadi. I then crossed the road quietly on my belly. Being flat on the road, I looked down at our camp and counted 12 men with swords and Amcheck and Grillius trapped next to the wagon. The 12 must have surprised Amcheck and Grillius because Grillius had his falcata in its scabbard still hanging at his side. I had a hard time trying to understand how anyone had the edge over Grillius. Maybe he was getting old and slow. I also wondered about his hearing since he was getting on in years. My surprise turned to confusion when I noticed another man holding 13 horses just a little ways behind the 12. "Grillius allowed 13 men and 13 horses to get the best of him?" I said to myself. "If we get through this alive, you, Grillius, will never live this one down."

With a quick study of the horses, I realized they had been ridden hard. Each mount was wet with soapy sweat and had their heads down looking for grass. The 13 animals were not giving any trouble to the man holding a few of them by their reins. Looking closely at the saddles, I concluded these were Roman soldiers. My suspicion was confirmed when I noticed the right front quarters of each horse had a well-defined SPQR brand. Also, the men who had Grillius and Amcheck surrounded were holding Roman-style swords. However, no one was clothed like a Roman soldier. They were hard-looking men with short hair and only a couple days' growth on their faces; yet, all were wearing bits and pieces of Roman gear. All of them looked old to me; perhaps all appeared to be in their late forties or early fifties. I concluded they must be a group of bounty hunters of ex-legionaries formed into a small army of thieves. The leader, or whom I perceived as the leader, was the oldest-looking with an ugly X scar on his face and doing all the talking. Comparing his scarred face with mine, I thought he made me look handsome.

"Come out of the wagon, whoever is in there!" yelled X-man in Greek with a foreign accent. Then he called out loudly in Latin. All 12 were formed into a semicircle with Amcheck and Grillius trapped with the wagon behind them. It reminded me of that dark night in Rome when Demos had his *thags* fan out to surround me.

I had to do something quickly to free my friends. I noticed Amcheck had his *sicarius* in the waistband of his Parthian robes. I did the math, which meant 3 against 13, which was over 4 to 1. However, we had the element of surprise; and Grillius was a master warrior. It could be done I concluded, but I had to come up with something quick. I realized all these men had to die, and no one was to escape. The horses had to be the key to the strategy I was forming. Once I had my plan, I crawled back across the road and ran some ways to get behind the horses. When I thought I was far enough, I crossed the road at a run and quietly entered the wooded area. I moved as fast as I could without making noise trying to get behind the horse holder. He was at a distance from the rest and hidden behind some trees. While I was moving, X-man's voice helped cover any noise I was making.

"I am not going to say it again; come out of the wagon!" screamed X-man.

Amcheck spoke Persian acting as if he did not understand Greek or Latin.

"Speak Greek, salesman; no one comes to *Palestina* not knowing Greek! Who are you trying to fool! Besides, those scars on your face portray you as something other than a salesman."

"There is no one in the wagon!" Amcheck finally answered in Greek. "It is just the two of us, and we are not this Venustus person you are looking for!"

"That is not what those two misguided disciples on the road told us yesterday! They said there was a young soldier with an old Parthian merchant, which must be you in the purple robes! They said he was older than I am; and you, Spartan, are the only one who looks older than dirt! But you are not a Parthian merchant. Where is this young Venustus fugitive? Where is the young guard if he is not cowering in that monster wagon? I am not going to ask again! I believe the two disciples said the young guard was wearing purple pants," and all the bounty hunters began to laugh thinking someone wearing purple pants was quite a joke.

What happened next was fast and violent. While all the men were laughing, I came up behind the horse holder and simultaneously placed my left iron knife into his left kidney area as the other knife cut out his vocal area in his throat. Both blades entered at the same time. The knife to the throat was a quick, deep strike into the side, and then I pushed the sharp edge forward. My tactic worked because the man dropped back into me without a sound, even though he was struggling as I held him. When he finally went limp, I quietly lowered him to the ground and then cleaned my knife blades on his tunic. I knew he was dead when I smelled what had been in his bowels. This trauma was something a person had to experience firsthand to understand the horror of taking a life, especially in such a fashion. It was horrific and something that plagues you for the rest of your life. I am only giving these details to persuade anyone from choosing a life of violence and thinking there is some kind of glory in it. Leaving him crumpled on the ground, I stepped away replacing my throwing daggers into their side sheaths. With them back in place, I crept back through the bunched-up band of horses, and hoped they would not smell blood and become spooked. Oddly, I could smell the blood; so they must have been too tired to care. After I was behind the horses, I found a good one, a gray gelding; and he looked like he could run. I jumped up allowing my stomach to rest on the saddle for a few moments so the horse could get used to my weight. When he didn't move, I quickly pulled my right leg over the back of the saddle and straightened up into a sitting position. Holding the reins, I quietly talked to this gray beast telling him what we were going to do. After I had explained what was going to happen, I shouted, "Yee Haw"; and I put my heels to his sides. The gray gelding jumped forward as if he understood all that I had said. His sudden bolt caused the other 12 to spook and stampede toward the *thags* and the wagon. There was nowhere for the horses to go except toward the wagon with me behind driving them. With my falcata still in its scabbard, lashed to my back, I pushed the band into a frenzied state. Everything was going according to my plan when I placed the reins in my mouth. With both hands now free, I pulled out my two throwing knives, one in each hand. I tried to control the horse the best I could with my head and body pulling back while using my thighs in a death grip trying to stay in the saddle.

The 12 men in their semicircle all turned at the same time staring at the charging horses. I again jabbed my heels hard into the sides of the gray pushing the other horses toward the men and the wagon. Each man stood frozen for a split second as each one tried to figure out what was happening. Pandemonium then ensued as the horses continued to rush toward them and the giant gimbal cart. When I spotted the leader, I threw my right heavy throwing knife over the horses' heads into the middle of the X on his face; the X-man went backward to the ground. From the corner of my eye, I saw Grillius pulling his falcata and rolling to his left. In a unique, graceful, and fluid motion, especially for someone his age, Grillius had performed a quick and subtle swipe cut into two men's tendons from behind their ankles disabling them both. While the two men were slowly falling forward into the path of the horses, Grillius jumped away from one of the charging beasts. The two wounded men's screams could be heard for miles when several of horses ran over their bodies.

For some unknown reason, my horse suddenly lowered his head and braked to an unexpected bone-jarring stop. I braced myself with my knees and thighs as the other horses kept going forward. Mysteriously I held my seat. When I righted myself off the gelding's neck, I noticed Amcheck over to my left dashing forward with his *sicarius* toward the last man standing on his end of the semicircle. In a well-used technique, he put his blade into the man's lower back near his right kidney. The man had not seen Amcheck as his attention had been directed toward the horses stampeding into his friends.

To get the gray horse moving again, I jabbed my booted heels hard against his sides. The gelding leaped forward back into a driving run behind most of the other horses that were now turning away from the wagon and moving in a mass escape in the direction of the Ridge Road. In my mind, I calculated eight men were remaining. By this time, everyone was moving in what seemed like a blur but not so fast that I could not miss with my second throwing knife. My left hand spun the dagger toward my intended target. It hit home into a man's right thigh. I had aimed for the leg since he wore a thick leather chest protector. I planned to strike the limb between the knee and the hip. Most of the *thags* were wearing the same short white tunic, which was standard for Roman legionaries in this part of the world. My blade drove through the bottom of the material of his tunic, high and inside of his thigh, right where a large artery ran down the man's leg. A few years back in the death-house, Grillius had taught me exactly where this artery traveled in a man's leg. The man with my dagger in his thigh started falling in front of a turning horse, which caused the animal to perform the most beautiful and elegant jump over the wounded man. Before the jumping horse had cleared the man, someone yelled out, "*Tortoise*!" Obediently, the remaining *thags* boxed together around the man that yelled, which placed everyone in front of the wagon wheel performing this Roman tactic that looked to be a walled box minus shields.

Just moments before the man yelled, "*Tortoise*," and while the horse was in its graceful jump, two men charged Grillius, who was on his feet waiting for their attack. The closest one tried to thrust his sword into Grillius's face, which was quickly blocked by his falcata. That man stepped back to gather himself allowing the second to attack. He rushed in perhaps thinking his opponent was old and slow. Instead, he discovered the old warrior was very nimble; and Grillius struck unexpectedly with an effortless-looking kick that

Chapter Nine

shattered the man's knee. The now injured man began collapsing as Grillius spun in a circle building up momentum with his falcata to counter the first man's second sword thrust. Not only did Grillius's sword block the man's sword thrust; but Grillius's body momentum carried through in an elegant, dance-like spin. This was something he never taught me, but it was similar to the move I used on Marius with wooden swords. I looked away when I realized Grillius was going to shatter the man's right knee with his Spartan boot. Everything was happening in a shadowy haziness yet in slow, dreadful, discernable details. Now I understood when I trained in Athens why Grillius repeatedly told me to keep my feet moving in a fight. "Never find yourself flat-footed in a battle with a sword, knife, or your hands. Your legs must be pumping up and down driving you forward continually." I was glad I was not fighting Grillius.

By my count, Grillius had his four; I had put down three; and Amcheck, one. That left four or five men now standing in the box formation and still dangerous. Unfortunately for me, all the spooked horses had veered off to my right moving up toward the gentle grade and the road. Now alone, I lashed my horse's flanks with the long reins, and the gelding continued forward heading straight toward the remaining men bunched shoulder to shoulder in their little box formation. Whatever this *tortoise* tactic was, it looked well organized. If they held large Roman shields, they would have been unbeatable. This was definitely a well-practiced maneuver; I concluded these men had to be Roman soldiers or auxiliaries. I just could not understand the reason they were all out of uniform. I also determined that Roman soldiers were trained in using their gladiuses only in a thrusting maneuver. This thrusting with their gladiuses in an underhand movement was all they had to know since they always fought as a unit like a stabbing machine. They were never allowed to hack or parry with their short, double-edged swords. Since Roman soldiers were mentored in this underhanded thrusting technique, they would always aim for a man's midsection, upper legs, throat, or face. This was the only maneuver necessary for a cohort engaged in combat. Hence, they all lacked the art of proper swordsmanship since Rome only wanted a massive wall of shields boxed together always moving forward with everyone thrusting their swords quickly with this pumping underhanded action. It had worked for centuries and wreaked havoc on any phalanx that could not stand up to this cohort box-stabbing-machine. Therefore, all these men were predictable fighters who did not stand a chance against someone like Grillius or even me.

Forging forward, my animal continued in his suicidal attack into this human wall. As soon as contact was made, I felt more than heard a sword go into my horse's chest, but the beast carried on into the mass of men as he stumbled down on top of several, including the one who had pierced his chest. Even before my horse hit his knees, I went flying out of the saddle over the horse's head. I did a heel-over-head flip and landed on my back on the other side of the wall of men next to the wagon wheel. My back hammered the ground with a great thud, which jarred my innards into a nauseating mutiny. I tried to blow out all my air precisely at the moment I hit the ground. As I have already explained, this was the technique learned at the Lyceum when learning how to ride horses. "When thrown from a horse, take a deep breath while in the air; and blow it out at the exact moment your body hits the ground" were the words of Grillius from years ago in Athens and were the very words I heard in my mind as I flew through the air. "If executed correctly, it will be like landing on a bed of soft hay. If your timing is off for just a mere mini-second, you could suffer broken bones and be gasping for breath because your wind was knocked out of you. If the latter happens, the body temporally paralyzes until the lungs come out of spasm and begin to function. This state of immobilization could render you helpless or, in the case of combat, dead." I had timed the maneuver correctly, except I forgot my falcata was still strapped to my back. Therefore, I did not factor that into my timing. Once my back hit the ground, I knew the scabbarded sword was going to leave an ugly bruise; but, luckily, I still had most of my air.

From the ground and looking backward, I saw the gray gelding rise up off the man who had stabbed him. The semi-crushed man reached up and pulled his sword out of the wounded gray's chest causing my horse to snake-bite him in the face. Even though a horse has only flat teeth, its jaws are stronger than a lion's. The man went down as the wounded horse flipped his head up with a flap of the man's face whipping about from his mouth. The horse then reared up and began stomping the faceless man with his front hooves.

The remaining men were painfully slow in rising from the ground after they all had been knocked down by my horse's collision. Still on my back, I saw Grillius quickly moving toward the disorganized *tortoise* formation. One man was standing when Grillius reached him, knocking away the man's sword thrust that was aimed at my teacher's chest. After Grillius had circumvented the soldier's gladius, Grillius pushed his sword onward and into the man's throat while also kicking with his right-booted instep into the face of a second man who was on his hands and knees trying to crawl to safety toward the wagon. I noticed my throwing knife sticking out of the upper thigh of the man Grillius had kicked. By now I felt my air had stabilized. Without thinking, I told myself to get up. I wondered why no one had come over and finished me. Perhaps the remaining *thags* thought I was out of action and no longer a threat. Trying to stand my eyes noticed Amcheck still near the front of the wagon in a frozen position holding his wickedly curved knife. His eyes were wide, which gave him a look like this was his first major battle and panic had finally set in. I wondered whether all his stories of fighting in the Parthian Wars were false; yet, how did he receive the long scar on his face? When Amcheck saw me looking at him, he began screaming for help. I spotted what seemed to unhinge him, and there was one of the pseudo-soldiers coming toward him with a sword in hand. I guess a gladius versus a *sicarius* was not a fair match. After his cry for help, Amcheck tried to block the Roman sword; but the heavy weapon was too much for his smaller curved knife, and the man's double-edged gladius continued into Amcheck's side. When the blade was pulled back, I saw Amcheck howling in pain and blood spurt out in a long jet. He sounded like a wounded rabbit after an arrow has struck its hindquarters. My lungs were just starting to work as I watched Amcheck fall to the ground dropping his curved knife and grabbing his side with both hands to stem the bleeding. The soldier was not practiced in swinging a sword down from above his head, and I laughed slightly when the blade hit the wagon instead of Amcheck. This gave my Herodian friend time to roll under the front of the wagon and get away from the man and his sword.

Taking in a gasp of breath, I started to move forward to give Amcheck aid; but, oddly, I felt my legs give out after I slammed into the huge wagon wheel striking my forehead against the iron rim. Bouncing away after my head hit the wheel, I felt warm blood flowing from a wound above my eyes. Once again I was on my back. From the ground, I wiped away the blood with my left tunic sleeve; I felt like a turtle turned upside down. Doing what a turtle would, I rolled over and did a push-up maneuver; ascending once again to my feet. I reached back and pulled out my falcata from its scabbard. It took only a few wobbly steps to reach the man who had stabbed Amcheck. In the time it took to get up and reach the front of the wagon the attacker had bent down and stuck Amcheck again while he was under the wagon. Now the man had Amcheck's foot and was pulling him out to finish him. Had I not run into the wagon wheel, Amcheck may have not been struck the second time. Realizing this old *thag* had not seen me coming, I filled my injured lungs with air and made a loud roar trying to sound like a lion as I ran toward him. The trick worked: the soldier stopped and turned his head toward me. I had already assessed my target in the few steps it took to reach him. He was wearing a thick leather cuirass that covered his upper body leaving me only one option. With the man still on his knees and holding Amcheck by his foot, I brought my right hand down and slammed my sword's hilt into the top of his skull while I was still in a full run. I hit the man as I went flying over him, and found myself for the third time this day on my back. I felt like I was spending more time on my back than I was on my feet. All I could see was the man I had struck crumpled on the ground smelling like bad garlic and *garum*. I decided to catch my breath. It wasn't a long rest – just a few seconds – all before I rolled over and got back on my feet. Standing now, I could see Amcheck under the wagon and rolled up in a ball moaning from his wounds. Since he was now safe, I looked for Grillius. He was cutting the throat of one of the men he had first hamstrung. The wounded man was in extreme pain and was slowly trying to crawl to safety from the old Spartan. I was shocked to see Grillius dispatching this man without any remorse. Behind Grillius was another lying on his back with his knee dislocated by a horse, and his throat freshly opened. Looking away from this violent scene, I felt Amcheck's hand on my foot. He had crawled out from under the wagon on his hands and knees and was now holding his retrieved *sicarius* in his other hand. He let go of my foot and crawled toward the man I had knocked down with the handle of my falcata. The man was lying oddly with his head bleeding, but he was not moving. I quickly stepped forward and grabbed Amcheck's wrist when I realized Amcheck was going to cut the man's throat with his *sicarius*. Using my left hand, I pushed his thumb back causing him to drop his knife. It was executed just like I had done to Demos back on the Roman bireme.

"What are you doing?" I yelled more than asked.

"By the breath of Mithras, let me at least cut his throat; for he may have already killed me!"

"You are not going to die!" I declared not really knowing how severe his wounds were.

I fixed my eyes back on Grillius and roared again like a lion at the top of my lungs to get his attention. It worked; and, when he looked at me standing near Amcheck, I shouted, "Stop cutting their throats; we need to interrogate at least one *thag!*"

Grillius stood still for a moment and then gave me a lopsided grin. Instead of cutting the next man's throat, he kicked the man in the head. Grillius appeared to be enjoying himself, something I had never seen before in him.

I wiped my eyes of fresh blood coming from my forehead. I decided to leave Amcheck, who was trying to assess his wounds and moaning at what he saw.

My old teacher looked back at me and yelled while pointing at a man on the ground. "You get this *thag* to talk, the one with your dagger in his leg!" I nodded my head as Grillius swiveled his head around and started counting, "alpha, beta, delta." Each time he counted he touched a new finger to his thumb. "Oh, no! There are only 11! Two of them got away!"

I started counting myself, and I only came up with 10 *thags* dead or dying on the ground. I counted again, and this time came up with 11. "Are you sure there were 13 at the start?" I called back.

"By Apollo's *effeactus*, there were 13 if you include the one holding the horses. I am telling you two men are missing. They must have crawled under the wagon after you crashed that gray horse into them. Two are definitely gone. If we do not find them, you are a dead man, Eunus."

It was strange hearing my old school name used by Grillius. "How many did you take down?" I asked trying to calm him. I could see him running everything through his mind as I, too, was doing. "Five, I believe. And you?"

"I got four if you count the horse holder, and Amcheck got one; so that adds up to ten!"

"That does add up to ten. Hold it, we forgot about the warhorse stomping the eleventh," stated Grillius pointing to a bloody, faceless man crumpled on the ground. "That still leaves two missing."

"I forgot about the horse... bless his soul," I said with a warm smile.

"Who is Eunus, and what is an *effeactus*?" came the words from an extremely agitated Nicodemus. We looked over toward the old man who stood at the other end of the wagon with two heavy cotton bags over his shoulder. "What did a horse do? And what in heaven's name happened here?"

"Batana, where have you been?" asked Grillius in Greek.

"Hiding in the bushes like Aristarchus told me."

"Did you see anyone running away from here in the last few minutes?"

"Yes. That is what I came to tell you. After I saw a bunch of horses come running onto the road, two men came dashing out of the bushes on foot right across from where I was hiding. They appeared like crazed madmen running down the road after the horses. The whole group was going south away from Bethel. One of the men looked wounded because he was moving differently from the other. It was more of a side-to-side rolling stride; and he was not moving as fast as the other, who was outdistancing him."

"Going toward Jerusalem and not Bethel you say?" asked Grillius very loudly, who I guessed was hard of hearing. I then noticed blood dripping out of his left ear. I pointed to his bleeding ear; he touched it with his left hand and did not seem to care about examining the blood on his fingertips. "They should have gone to Bethel if they wanted help!" yelled Grillius, again unusually loud.

Nicodemus looked around some more, and his mouth hung open; apparently he was a stranger to this kind of butchery. He squinted his eyes toward Grillius and asked, "Why would someone run away toward Jerusalem? That direction is too far to get help even if you were going to Adasa or Bethany."

Grillius still talking too loudly finally yelled, "Wherever they went, it is going to be dark before we catch up with them! They most likely think they can catch up to their horses!"

I kept my eyes on Grillius watching him look up toward the sun, which I figured to be a little past midafternoon. It looked to me like we had plenty of daylight. I wondered what he meant. Grillius turned to me like a general during a great battle. "Eunus, I will saddle Zeus! He is hobbled somewhere over there! You get your knives and be ready to ride! You are going after them, and do not bring either back alive! Now move!"

When Grillius went to get my horse, Nicodemus said to me, "The sixth commandment demands we are not to kill. You are not going to murder those men if you find them, are you?"

I retrieved my knife from X-man's face without looking at Nicodemus. Noticing his shadow behind me, I said, "Last time I followed that rule, because of you, I got my brains smashed in. I do not have time for this, Nicodemus. Now listen to me. Leonidas is going to need your help over there to save Belkin's life. Belkin is seriously wounded." I pointed toward the front of the wagon where Amcheck was now rolled over in a ball on the ground moaning.

"Oh, my!" exclaimed Nicodemus. This was the only response from the old scholar, whose eyesight apparently was not as bad as I first thought. Maybe it was the loud moaning coming from a blurry form by the front of the wagon, but Nicodemus dropped the cotton bags and rushed to Amchech's side. I stumbled to the other unconscious man on his back and pulled my throwing knife out of his leg. Spurts of blood shot out as soon as I removed the knife; and every time his heart pumped, another long red-line flew out. I knew he was going to be out of blood in a few minutes, for my knife did hit the main artery in his upper thigh around the inside of his leg. I realized I had to stop the bleeding if I wanted to interrogate him. I put both my hands on his leg and applied pressure, and this caused the man to quickly sit up and grab one of my wrists. I pulled away and said, "Fine! Bleed to death for all I care!"

"What happened?" he asked speaking slurred Latin.

"You tell me!" I said scooting away from him. The man seeing his blood shoot out at intervals from his wound began to apply pressure himself. I could see he was dying just from the paleness of his skin and the glassiness growing over his eyes.

Chapter Nine

"Who sent you, and why did you threaten us?" I asked pointing my dagger at his face.

"Are you Venustus Vetallus?" he asked almost in a kind voice.

"I am. Why are you looking for me?" I asked thinking it was a stupid question.

"We are all Roman legionaries or auxiliaries from Caesarea. All cashiered after 20 years serving in the legions. We heard that you were in Judaea, and your capture is worth over four million *sestertii*. That split with a dozen men is close to 250 years of payment for being a soldier for each one of us. What would you do?"

I said nothing realizing my reward had grown astronomically. Four million *sestertii* was a lot of money and a reason to die for, especially if you worshipped money, which most men do without realizing it. I remembered a statement a man told me he heard from Jesus. "*The love of silver is the root of all evil.*" This is a maxim that has been proven to me over the years to be correct. Without a doubt, humans have a problem with money; yet, it is not silver but the love of such that is the problem.

"You all knew each other?" The dying man lowered his eyes indicating they all knew one another. "From what legion are you?"

"We are all from the Italian cohort out of Caesarea. As I said, we just got our discharge for honorable service of 20 years. None of us has any family, and this seemed like a way to make some easy money to buy a little land in Asia or Greece. Some were going to acquire citizenship and go to Rome to retire."

"I'm sorry your actions have led to your death, especially after so many years of faithful service to the Empire."

"Do you really mean that?"

"I do. And do you forgive me for killing you?"

"It was not your fault; it was my own greed that did me in. The man with the X on his face was the real evil one among us. He had been our centurion for the last ten years, and he was a mean cuss. He was the one who needed killing; and for killing him, I forgive you for killing me." He slowly lay back down, and soon the blood stopped spurting out his leg. I was amazed at the man's honest remorse. If things had been different, this man could have been an honest and sincere friend. He seemed brave and decent. He just fell in with a wrong group of men and made a wrong choice to follow X-man to get rich. It was strange to have a man forgive me moments before his death. I knew this would be a memory that would last until the day I died, which it seems now to have done just that. As strange as it sounds, as I tell this story to my scribe almost seventy years later, it seems like this man was just talking to me only yesterday.

As I was sitting on the ground looking at the peacefulness of this man who had just died, Grillius come up to me. "Here is your horse and mine. There is a day's ration of roasted grain for you and the horses. Take your horse and mine for a spare to move faster when your horse becomes fatigued. Remember, do not come back without our runners; or we are all dead, especially if they catch up to their horses."

I quickly told Grillius what the man next to my feet had said before he died. Grillius stood silent for only a few seconds and then said, "I am betting that the runners will go back for help to what is familiar to them. That would be Caesarea, not Jerusalem. They will think they have some time since we have a huge wagon to pull. I will give my boots away if I am wrong. Those two runners must be Roman soldiers and will suspect that their tame horses will also be going back to what is familiar to them. Their only smart option is to follow the animals, which is what Nicodemus saw them doing. Roman soldiers are men who have followed orders all their lives without much thought involved. They are just as predictable as the rising of the sun each morning. Their horses are the same, and any stupid horse soldier understands the behavior of a tame animal. Once the spooked horses feel safe, they will stop together and think about food and water. As the sun starts to set, those horses are going to begin looking and smelling for grass and water along with a safe place to bed for the night. Those were some tired horses. I bet they do not go very far."

Grillius could be right about everything he was saying. The horses would look for water and a place for the night since horses were not nocturnal creatures. They typically lock their knees at night and sleep standing when it is dark. Once they are well grazed by sweet grass and full of water, then they will want to go home for better food and protection.

"You head south; take that cut-off a few miles or so down the road that leads toward Azotus. It is the road those two ex-followers of Jesus had to have taken – those two who talked to you and Batana the other night. They are the ones who must have told all these dead *thags* about you. Am I right?"

I nodded at Grillius and was amazed by his quick and logical deductions from the little information he possessed. What astonished me was his ability to understand and assimilate all of this on the spot. I wanted to be like Grillius in his ability to assess and make evaluated decisions under enormous pressure and tension. My experience up to this point seemed to be the opposite. I was like most men finding it hard to think precisely after a significant ordeal because of the effect of stress flowing through my veins and the physical fatigue after a life-and-death battle. All I wanted to do was fall down and go to sleep.

After I had acknowledged Grillius with "*ave*," normally a Latin greeting, he continued. "The two missing are on foot but will try to catch at least two of the horses. If they get their horses, you are going to have to run them down, even if it means going to Hades. You will be able to do it. That is why you have two horses." Grillius handed me my helmet and told me to conceal myself when people were about. "If anyone asks why you shut the face shield, say that your face was burned and that you are uglier than Pluto himself."

I tied my sweat rag from my neck around my bleeding forehead and then put on the helmet. I rocked my head indicating I understood before I asked, "Where do I find you when I return?"

"You will find us, or I will find you. Once I get rid of these bodies and close up the wounds on that coward friend of yours, the old Jew and I will head into Samaria and stay on the Ridge Road or not far from it. The moon tonight will be full, and the sky looks like it will be clear: But don't worry; you should be able to run them down before sunset."

I took his arm, hand to elbow, and asked if this is what war was like. Both our arms were covered in mud, sweat, and blood. He answered, "Just like this except an enormous battle goes on for hours. Once it is over, if you are not bleeding too badly, you lie down on the battlefield and sleep for about an hour hoping some scavenger does not kill you. When you wake up, it takes another hour to get your fingers off your sword because your tendons are frozen to the handle. Now hurry; we do not have time to talk."

It would be years later in Gaul when I experienced exactly what Grillius had described. Yet, this little battle outside Bethel was a skirmish I never forgot since it was my first real battle against an enemy that outnumbered me and I lived to tell about it. I absently felt for my two throwing knives at my side and touched my falcata still scabbarded to my back. I was ready to mount up and go after the runners. From atop Zeus and holding the second horse by its reins, I noticed both Nicodemus and Grillius, working on Amcheck's wounds. I loudly announced I was going. Grillius just grunted without looking at me. I then called out, "Do not tell Amcheck-Belkin how much I am worth, or he will turn me in himself for the reward."

"He already knows how much the bounty is," stated Grillius. "What are you really trying to say?" he asked, now looking at me with a questioning look.

I motioned for him alone to come over and join me. Grillius told Nicodemus to keep pressure on the wound and started for the back of the wagon. Once we were away from listening ears, I said, "I'm not sure I can trust Amcheck, and I am not thinking about the bounty."

"Do not worry, Eunus. Belkin will not be a problem for weeks with his wounds, but I will keep a clear eye on things until you return. If you find the horses, you are going to have to destroy them as well. Maybe run them off a cliff. One last thing: you are going after cowards because only cowards will leave their friends in need. This is a fact, pure and simple. Remember, cowards are the most dangerous creatures a man will ever hunt. To beat a coward, you must think like a coward. Think like Deva would think because he is the greatest coward I have ever known, and you know him better than I."

I thanked him for his advice and turned Zeus toward the Ridge Road. Looking back, I noticed Grillius walking very stiffly back toward Nicodemus and Amcheck. I was a little confused trying to digest what Grillius had just said, and I didn't really want to kill all the horses if I found them. Reaching the road, I decided to not think about it while I put my heels to Zeus, and we began a leisurely three-beat lope heading south in the direction of Jerusalem.

For the next mile, both horses did not break stride at our steady pace. Zeus and Amcheck's horse seemed to be happy that they were back out and working again. Being hobbled for over four days will do that to any domesticated working animal. Zeus was a big, black, strong, gelding bred to be active all the time. He had been procreated as a warhorse, much like the gray gelding that killed the soldier who put his gladius in his chest. The bravery of that horse to keep fighting as he was dying was remarkable. This was something else that would never leave my memory. After the first mile, I stopped to give the horses a rest; and I started scanning ahead for any movement. The road so far had been emptied of any travelers. It was the late afternoon of a Sabbath Eve, which explained why the road was void of people. I remembered that Bethel was on the boundary line of Samaria and I was now back in Judaea. Zeus's sweat had turned soapy-white where the leather reins rubbed his neck, and there was also frothy lather around his bit. The insides of my legs were also wet from Zeus's sweaty sides. I could feel him heaving for air, and his nostrils were flared as far as they would open. Looking at his neck, I noticed large veins protruding up toward his head and down the sides of his long jawline and nose. I thought of changing mounts but instead decided to do so once I reached the turnoff to Azotus. It had to just be around the bend and a little up ahead. I noticed the temperature was starting to get colder as the wind was kicking up coming in from the direction of the sea. Sitting on Zeus in the middle of the road, I could not believe it when I noticed the sun was only

Chapter Nine

a few hours from setting. Time had gone by quickly ever since Nicodemus and I encountered the 13 bounty hunters at our camp around midafternoon.

I lightly tapped my heels to Zeus's sides and clicked my tongue to urge him forward. The turnoff was not at the next bend nor the one after that. I was now just walking the horses slowly; but, finally, after several more curves in the road, we reached the junction to Azotus. Zeus acted like he knew I was going to change horses and walked to the left side of the road where there was a patch of green grass growing. I guess he thought he was also going to be able to get a mouthful of grass when I dismounted. I pulled up on his head with the reins next to a rock cliff to my left to keep him from eating, and I looked to my right at the road snaking down toward the sea. It looked like it had many switchbacks that descended to the flat plains of Judaea that stretch out to what the Romans call *Mare Nostrum*, "Our Sea." A burst of refreshing wind came blowing from that direction. Sniffing the air, Zeus pulled back his ears and gave a low noise coming from his throat. I tried to understand what had his attention until I faintly picked up the scent of horseflesh. Zeus wanted to pull around facing the road to Azotus with his hindquarters facing the rock wall. Whatever he was smelling was overpowering his desire to grab a mouthful of fresh grass. The words of Grillius came back as if he were standing next to me and talking. "Think like a coward; think like Deva," our old name for Demos back in Athens.

The day I left Nicodemus's *domus* in Jerusalem, Demos must have concealed himself from behind a pillar; and after I had passed, he stepped out and caved in the back of my skull with the flat of his sword. I quickly turned in my seat looking behind me at the side of the rock wall, for that would be where the coward Demos would come from. To my surprise and horror, a person above me came jumping at me. It was a small form dropping from the cliff above holding in both hands a leather cord to loop around my head and choke the life out of me. In that split second, I pulled on my left rein while putting my left heel into Zeus's ribs. The warhorse spun around in a quick, tight half-circle giving me time to use the heel of my right hand to crush the attacker's nose as the assailant missed my head only by inches with the leather cord. The villain-coward fell hard to the ground with blood already flowing down from the nose. In one graceful motion, I slid off my horse; and, as the coward moaned in pain, I heard quick footsteps crossing the stone road from what had to be the other coward, who had been hiding in the bushes on the other side of the road. It was a well-planned ambush.

I pulled my right throwing knife and threw it at the soldier running toward me with his gladius in his right hand. He saw what I was doing and stopped dead in the middle of the road as my arm was moving forward in its throwing arc. When my knife left my hand, the stationary man ducked down; and my dagger spun harmlessly over his head. We both watched the iron dagger hit a rock wall near where the man had been hiding. It reminded me of when my father moved his head to avoid the spinning knife on that stormy night in Rome over three years ago. There was the unmistakable clang of iron hitting rock. My heart sank as I watched the thin blade fly apart into two equal pieces. I clicked my tongue in the loss of a good knife.

Remembering the person behind me, I quickly turned back. The groaning had stopped and there was this form crawling for the leather strap that was lying on the road. I took one step back and in a looping kick connected with the crawling person's face. I saw and felt the person receive the full brunt of the bottom of my boot heel. While the victim flew backward, blood started to appear along three long lines on the person's face from chin to forehead. I guessed three sharpened nail heads on the bottom of my heel cut the three long strips. Once the coward rolled to a stop, I heard a horrific scream of what sounded more like a woman than a man.

Still holding both reins of my two horses in my left hand, I quickly turned my attention to the now-spooked horses, which tried to bolt at the strange scream. Both horses spun and danced in an attempt to get away from the high-pitched shriek coming from the coward on the ground, who was now rolled up into a ball. I tried to calm the horses with words until I felt a sword tip punch through my thick leather cuirass low into my left side. I had forgotten about the soldier I had missed with my knife. I was exhausted; and my mind was drained, which caused my thinking to be fatigued. However, everything came back into focus in a flash of self-condemnation. I had made the mistake of not taking in fluids and food after the wagon fight and this long ride hunting these two runaway *thags*. My salvation came not from me but because the attacker wore sandals with spiked nail-soles. This section of the Ridge Road was constructed with large square, flat stones. Running in to stab me, he lost this footing when he tried to slow his charge at the last moment. If he had not lost his balance, my bowels would have been run through; and I would have been the one on the ground. I watched in surprised awe as his feet flew up and he landed flat on his back. My fatigue and surprise somehow kept me from taking appropriate action against the fallen man who was still holding his gladius. It was then that I noticed about an inch of wetness at the tip of his sword. I now realized he had cut me through my leather cuirass. In an incredible move, the ex-soldier was up and getting ready to finish what he intended before he lost his footing a second time.

Chapter Nine

Still fighting with the frightened horses, I turned my head to exam the whereabouts of the one I kicked in the face. Noticing that one was still in a ball whimpering, I turned back to the one getting ready to thrust me with a second underhanded move. This had to be the only maneuver he knew. Realizing I didn't need the horses any longer and if I continued to hold them, they were going to get me killed. Dropping both reins, they both bolted toward the ex-soldier holding his sword causing him to move away as they passed him and giving me time to place my hand on my falcata handle that was over my left shoulder. Gladius Man predictably stepped forward with his right foot as I was still pulling my sword. Twisting away from the tip of his sword was all I could do to get away from his attack. Apparently, I had not moved fast enough as I felt the tip enter my left hip, which was an acceptable sacrifice if I wanted to win this fight. Stepping sideways and rolling with the stab of the sword, I was able to grab the man's sword hand with my left hand that was now free of the horses. Holding Gladius Man's wrist, I pulled back allowing his forward momentum to cause him to continue past me. I could smell his sweaty odor in his clothes before I released his hand causing him to lose his balance and fall forward face first onto the stone road. Knowing he would jump up like he did before, I pivoted around and brought my freed sword's hilt crashing into the top of his head as he tried to rise. It was precisely the same as I had done to the man at the gimbal wagon when saving Amcheck. Gladius Man crumpled back down to the road with his iron blade clanging away from him. Following Grillius's orders, I had to make sure the ex-soldier would not rise from the road one last time. Using both hands forming a fist around the handle, I expertly swung my falcata. The end of my sword cut into about an inch of the back of the man's neck. I heard and felt the vertebra bones being severed. It was a quick, fatal blow I practiced many times on a log with Grillius watching out in the Lyceum courtyard during our late evening training sessions. I would not typically have used two hands on the sword, but I was fatigued beyond anything I could remember other than when I was ten years old running for hours through the sewer-filled alleys of Rome to lose my pursuers. Now I understood why Grillius said, after a massive, all-day battle, a man dropped and fell fast asleep. I desperately wanted to lie on the road and go to sleep.

The other runner was still rolled up into a ball and crying like a girl. I tried to get my breath when I remembered the two bolting horses. There was only dust hanging in the air toward Azotus. Both had disappeared from sight, but I let out a loud whistle for Zeus to return. To my surprise, here came the black warhorse up the Azotus road trotting with his ears back toward the Ridge

Road. I turned back to the screamer and told him to shut up. To my surprise the runner became silent. I was thankful my horse had obeyed my whistle along with the screaming to have ceased. Zeus walked up and stood in the middle of the Ridge Road. Slowly walking toward Zeus, I started talking in a soothing voice saying, "Good boy. You are a good boy." I wanted to calm him and encourage him to stand right where he was. Getting closer, I slowly reached up and gently took hold of the bridle straps. Once I had his reins in hand, I looked back across the road toward the cowering runner. It took a few moments to realize the person rolled up into a ball might be a woman and not a man. The small size and the whimpering just did not fit my image of an ex-legionnaire. With this realization, I sheathed my falcata.

I continued patting Zeus on his neck with my free hand and talking to him with soothing words. Animals are no different than humans; kind words and compliments mean a great deal to people when they do something right. Once I had his fear under check, he began to settle down and seemed happy. I removed the leather hobble ties that were attached to the rear of the saddle and placed the leather device on his two front legs. Once the ties were on, Zeus could not run. He could walk but not far. Grillius had hobbled all our horses each night instead of securing them to something, and Zeus was familiar with this hoof device. Besides, a frightened horse could tear any tie-down regardless of how it was tied; but hobbles would keep a horse standing, or the creature would fall not being able to stand until the hobbles were removed. I had made a mistake at the Lyceum many years ago attaching a horse with a rope to a bronze ring screwed into the wooden side of a building. The horse was frightened by a slave woman who accidentally dropped a huge, clay water jug; and after the explosion, the frightened animal tore off half the wood siding of the building in its attempt to flee. Fight or flight is what horses will do when scared, but usually they do the latter. A well-trained warhorse will do the same unless it is schooled to break its fear of becoming frightened by some unusual sound. The best technique is to ride back and forth next to someone who hits a bronze gong or blows a ram horn. It usually does not take long to get the animal accustomed to loud sounds. Zeus apparently needed more work in this area, or maybe no one had ever trained him in this fashion.

After the hobbles had been attached, I pulled out my falcata once more. It was at this moment out in the road that I realizing the wind had stopped blowing, but the temperature was pleasant. With my sword in hand, I carefully crossed back over the stone road. If this was a female, I knew I was going to have to be especially vigilant since I had just permanently disfigured a woman's face. There was no telling what she might try to do to me. It was highly probable that she could turn into a lioness of rage at any moment. Once I had my sword between her and me, I gently asked if she was with the men at the large wagon. She sat up with her hands on her face. She nodded yes but would not look at me. This runner was a woman who was wearing men's clothing. I had never seen a woman dressed as a man; but, as I studied her, I could now see she was, indeed, a woman, and much older than I. I used my falcata tip to flip off the red cloth cap she was wearing, and her dark hair came falling in a tangle below her shoulders and cascading over her bloody face.

Grillius had told me not to bring back the runners, and that meant only one thing. Yet, I could not kill a helpless woman, even if she had tried to choke me with a leather cord. I turned away and walked to the center of the road to see if anyone was coming from any direction, and I found myself asking Yahweh what to do. There was no one in sight except the dead soldier lying in a pool of blood. The sun was quickly falling toward the horizon; therefore, there would be no one on the road at this hour, it being Sabbath Eve. I returned to the woman. She finally looked up at me and started begging for her life knowing I was going to kill her.

"Give me one reason why I should not kill you," I said in Aramaic with agitation in my voice.

"I have no reason. I should die because the holy man saved me from a stoning death and told me to go and sin no more. I disobeyed, and now I should die."

"What are you talking about?"

Between sobs she said the religious leaders in Jerusalem had tricked her. "It is a complicated story. I was taken to the holy man named Jesus to be condemned. If Jesus had said 'yes,' I would have been stoned to death; and the Romans would have arrested him for murder. If he had said 'no,' then he would be discredited as being a holy rabbi of the law."

"Stoning for what?" I asked.

"Adultery! I am a whore! Why do you think I was with those men you killed back at the wagon and the one lying out there on the road!"

"Are you the woman who was taken to Jesus at the Temple by the religious leaders last winter; and Jesus said, 'He who is without sin should throw the first stone?'"

She put her hands back to her bloody face and began shaking her head to acknowledge that she was that woman. Was I to kill her since she disobeyed Jesus when he told her to go and sin no more? I stood thinking for a long time when I heard a horse whinny down the road toward Azotus. Thinking someone was coming, I picked up the leather strap that was meant to kill me and roughly tied the woman's hands. I then dragged the dead soldier into the bushes on the other side of the road close to where he had been hiding when the woman jumped me. Looking to where the man had died, I realized this was a bigger mess than when I cleaned the Altar to the Unknown God in Athens the night I met Eli's Uncle Anab. I scuffed the road the best I could to hide the dark bloodstains and then kicked dirt over the stains. Still, some stains needed more soil to cover the blood. I made several trips to the side of the road carrying dirt to the spot where the blood had been. After I was satisfied, I went to the woman and lifted her to her feet and pulled her to Zeus. After helping her up into my saddle, I removed the hobbles and pulled myself up behind her. With my arms around her, I turned Zeus toward the hide across the road and went into the bushes behind a huge rock next to the dead man. I planned to stay concealed in the bushes until what was coming passed. We quietly waited both leaning against one another.

"This must be the smell of women," I said to myself under my breath. Even though she smelled of horse sweat and human perspiration, it was, indeed, different from a man. Her smell was surprisingly pleasant, which was mostly coming from her long, tangled hair. She must have washed it recently. I whispered to the woman to keep quiet, or I would shove a cloth into her mouth. I poked her in the side near her right kidney with my remaining throwing knife to make my point. She nodded indicating she would keep silent, and I put my last remaining dagger back into its sheath.

The next thing I remember was waking up from a deep sleep, and it had gotten very dark. The woman in front of me was shaking her head to get flies off her face. The quick movement awakened me, and I realized that I had slumped forward onto her and had fallen asleep from exhaustion. I did not know how long I slept, but I could hear a strange buzzing noise. Looking down to the ground from where the buzzing was coming, and I barely made out what looked like a million flies all moving around on the dead *thag's* head. His body lay next to us in the bushes, and a stench was beginning to rise from his corpse. It was then that I realized flies were landing on my blood soaked side as well as the woman's cut face. I wondered how long the sun had been down in the west. I calculated that it had to have been at least an hour or more that I slept on the horse with the woman in front of me in the saddle. I was surprised she had not tried to escape during this time. All she had to do was push me off the horse while I was asleep and ride for it.

Both of us just sat quietly in the bushes on top of Zeus. We both heard the same horse whinny and some neighing sounds that I had heard before I fell asleep. Wherever these horses were, they had not moved for the past hour

Chapter Nine

or so. Now that I was awake, Zeus started to get nervous to the point he was going to begin whinnying as well. I had no choice except to slowly leave the hide and turn down the road toward Azotus. About a hundred yards to my right on my way to Azotus and about fifty feet off the road, I counted 14 saddled horses in the light of the full moon. They were all eating green grass next to a spring in a small meadow not far from the road. I realized the extra horse was Grillius's horse, which I released during my fight with the ex-soldier on the Ridge Road. I started to laugh aloud at the absurdity of such a beautiful sight. They were all there standing around in the small field, full of purple hyacinth flowers and saffron crocuses of the same color. It is hard to describe the relief of sitting there looking at such a vista. At first, I felt as if I were having a vision; but the display of satisfied horses before me was real, not a wishful illusion. Not only were all the horses there, but they were trapped by the road and cliffs that surrounded the other side of the meadow. What a location for an abode! If I were a rich man, this would be the spot where I would build a small, comfortable villa; but it would be selfish of anyone to destroy the natural beauty of this place. When the moment passed, I noticed one horse bleeding from a horrible chest wound. Sadness came over me when I realized that was the gray, which saved my life by chomping off the soldier's face and stomping the man who stabbed him. At that instant, I had a love for that gelding I could not define, even if I had a hundred years to analyze it. I knew this horse and place would be a treasure in my mind for the rest of my life.

"Did you know the horses were here?" I finally asked the woman in front of me.

"If I did, I would have grabbed one and escaped long before now."

"Why did you not run when I was asleep?"

"Your body had me trapped with your leaning into me. I had no advantage to push off and get away. I did think about it until I, too, went to sleep. Those horrible flies awakened me by crawling all over my face."

I rode into the meadow and then told her we were going to get down. I then removed Zeus's bridle and let him wander in the little field of flowers and grass. He was too tired to run; and with water, green grass, and the other horses resting and grazing, I knew he would stay put without my hobbling him. I walked with the woman toward the other horses. The full moon was up in the east providing a bluish light that was almost as bright as daytime. I told the woman to sit. She complied with my command. I went to Grillius's horse and removed his bridle. I removed my helmet and then took off my black sweat cloth that was tied around my head. I put the neck scarf into a little brook of running water coming from some spring up near the rocks to the west. Following the flow of water with my eyes, I could see it meandering across the meadow where it spilled over a cliff forming a small waterfall. After gently cleaning the cuts on the woman's face, I concluded she had to be in her late thirties. She was very striking if I looked beyond her facial wounds. However, she was never going to be beautiful again because of what I had done to her face. To me, a young man in his early twenties, I thought she was a little past her prime, most likely from hard living; but she was still somewhat stunning. Today, considering as an old man, I can say she was rather beautiful and in her prime. After cleaning her wounds by moonlight, I started to like her looks over those of Salome, who was always wearing makeup; and yet, this woman had her nose smashed to one side and long slashes on the left side of her face, from chin to forehead. After cleaning her wounds, I realized I had torn the dried-blood scabs; and her face was bleeding again. It must have hurt, but she said nothing. It was apparent I had broken her nose when I had hit her first with my hand. I asked if she wanted me to straighten it. She nodded, and I went to find a wooden stick for her to bite on. Using both hands, I then took her nose and quickly snapped it back into place the best I could in one move. I knew, if I did not get it back in one try, she was not going to allow me to try again. I looked at her nose, and it was straight; but there was going to be a slight bump in the middle. I realized that was better than having her nose heal to the side of her face.

"What about you?" she asked.

"What about me?" I replied still speaking Aramaic but using a different dialect.

"You are bleeding down your legs in at least two places, and your face is almost as bloody as mine."

I looked down at my left thigh, and she was right. I had forgotten that the man on the road had stuck me twice and that the wound from the wagon wheel must have started bleeding again after I removed my helmet. I placed my hand on my forehead, and it came away bloody. I got to my knees and lapped water from the spring like a dog until I thought water would come out my ears. The woman also drank after I untied her hands with the leather strap. As I watched her drink, I felt like a barbarian. She, like a well-bred woman, used one hand taking small sips with her one cupped hand to her mouth. I then took off my cuirass and examined my stomach and left hip. Both wounds were not bleeding much but still needed attention. I washed all three of my injuries in the cold, spring water with my sweat cloth. After several rinsings, I ripped the black fabric into three equal parts. One part I shoved into my stomach wound; and another, into my hip. I then picked up the remaining

Chapter Nine

piece and tied it around my head injury. I then asked the woman to put her hands together, and I wrapped the leather cord around her wrists. She did not appear happy to be placed back in restraints, but I ignored her and strapped on my cuirass. Looking around, I noticed little flashes of light that appeared just above the ground. "Did you see that? There it is again!"

"Those are fireflies. You have never seen them before?"

"Flies on fire? What are they?"

"You are just a child in a man's body. They appear this time of the year just after sunset. They apparently like places where there is grass and water. Maybe they are mating, but soon they will be gone."

"You are smart for being a *luna*," and I noticed her head drop from my name I called her. After watching the fire show for a few moments, I decided to strip the horses of their gear.

I left the woman sitting and walked over to the first horse that was busy eating sweet grass. I removed its saddle and bridle. I soon had the saddles and bridles off all the horses except Zeus and Grillius's horse. I then carried each saddle and bridle to the cliff just a little distance from the small waterfall. Without knowing why, I began throwing the saddles and bridles over the cliff. For some unexplainable reason, I did not throw two of the best bridles off the cliff along with two of the best saddles. When this was finished, I returned to the spring pool near where the woman sat. She had been right; the fireflies were gone. All the horses were either grazing or just standing still when I noticed the woman had been watching my every move. She was sitting there looking like she was content with her hands tied. I was thinking about approaching her when I heard a loud voice calling from the Azotus Road. "Is that you, Eunus?" When I turned, I saw Grillius sitting on the gimbal wagon with four horses out front.

"It is I," I yelled back. "Come here and see our coward."

"I think I already found him in the bushes up on the main road."

Under my breath I uttered, "So much for my stealth in hiding dead bodies."

"The stain on the road, the flies, and the smell gave you away," he answered back.

I watched him slowly climb down from the wagon seat and amble over to me. When Grillius saw the woman in men's clothing, he gave her a big smile. "Well, if Vulcan and Venus aren't into something strange and tricky, this is certainly the work of Hephaestus to get back at his wife Aphrodite. This is a first for me. I have seen many strange things but never a woman in the outfit of a man."

I noticed the woman was visibly scared until I realized she perhaps thought this old scarred-up Spartan was going to kill her. If I were she, I would have been worried as well. Grillius clearly had a hardness in him, which could mean he would not hesitate to murder a helpless female; yet, there was another side of Grillius I was soon to experience. Grillius was speaking Greek in an accent she must have had a hard time following. When Grillius stood there looking at her and giving her a rare smile, I guess his speech must have portrayed a kind heart from many years of suffering; and I even noticed a change in the woman sitting on the grass.

In the moonlight Grillius stopped smiling and finally asked the woman, "Give one good reason why I should not kill you, right now!"

Even with her facial cuts, the strikingly beautiful woman said in passable Greek, "I am a good cook. Moreover, for your sparing my life, I will be the young one's slave for the rest of my life. And unlike you, Greek warrior, I believe in only one God, the God of Abraham, Isaac, and Jacob. I also believe in the resurrection of the dead; and, if I were to die now, I am afraid I would go straight to Hell. I need more time to make things right. You see, the holy rabbi Jesus told me to 'go, and sin no more.' Please allow me to follow you, whoever you are; and I will sin no more. I give both of you soldiers my solemn word."

"She is a talker, I will say that," said Grillius. "I will leave that decision to my young friend. That is because he found you, not I. In the meantime, we will keep you tied up while he thinks about your proposal. Right now we both have a lot of work to do."

With her hands tied, she looked at me with pleading eyes and I don't know if I gave her any hope or not before I followed my old *paidotribes* out of the meadow. When I reached the Parthian wagon, I spotted Nicodemus sitting on the driving seat with all the reins in his hands. He was looking at me without any sign of recognition. I wondered if he were angry with me. I nodded, and he slightly lowered his head. Then I spotted someone else on the wagon seat. It was Amcheck leaning against the old man and looking pale in the moonlight. I wondered why he was not resting in the back of the wagon. Circling around the foreign cart, I opened the back flap. Flies buzzed everywhere, and a horrible stink came rushing at me. Now I understood why Amcheck was up with Nicodemus. The entire area was piled with dead bodies, including the one I had hidden in the bushes. Throwing the tarp back into place, I turned; and there was Grillius. "Where did you deposit all the saddles from the horses?"

I told him I tossed them over a cliff. He scratched his bearded chin and asked after waving his hand toward the back of the wagon, "Do you think we could throw all these bodies over the same cliff?"

"The smell will be atrocious for about a week. However, the vultures and wild animals should clean up the mess within that time. It is a place no one can get to unless you are a goat or a dog."

"Let us hurry before someone comes down this road," said Grillius.

An hour later all the bodies had been tossed over the cliff, and Nicodemus used a bucket and cloth to clean up the blood on the inside of the wagon. When I looked for Amcheck, I found him lying in the meadow where the woman was tied. I broke a mustard tree branch from the side of the road that looked more like a bush than a tree and messed up the dirt, blood, and tracks where we dragged the bodies to the cliff. It appeared to be the middle of the night, but I knew it had to be only a few hours since sunset. Dark clouds were scudding in front of the bright moon; and a strong, cold wind began chilling the sweat on my body. After a while, gloomy darkness settled in; and so did our night vision, which slowly adjusted to the lack of light.

About an hour later, I awoke from a dead sleep near Amcheck and the woman. I didn't realize I had fallen asleep; but, when I woke, there was a brilliant full moon that had reappeared between breaks in the clouds. The moon had moved quite a distance westward over the southern sky. Grillius came up to me and told me to strip and throw all my bloody clothes off the cliff. I told him I was not going to wear those Persian pants and red coat ever again. I said I would wash my bloody tunic and wear it when it dried. I reminded him of what the Roman said before he died about looking for this Venustus character dressed in a Parthian outfit of purple pants and red coat. Grillius quietly said, "I understand. I, too, would rather die than wear those purple pants. But we do not have any other options. Either wear bloody clothes or purple pants. Just do not wear the red coat unless it gets colder or rainy."

I agreed; and, after changing into the purple pants and wearing my cuirass over my bare skin, I untied the woman and ordered her to wash my tunic in the spring. While the woman worked on my tunic, I washed my hands, face, and hair. Grillius did likewise after he had stripped down to a loincloth and also had the woman wash his bloody clothes. Grillius and I used the wagon wheels to dry our tunics, and Grillius covered up with his long purple-red *chlamys*. As I looked at him in the dark, there was no mistaking him for anything other than an old Spartan soldier. Standing there in the moonlight, Grillius said, "It is a miracle only two of us were wounded in that little battle we had today."

"Do you believe in the gods of Sparta?"

"Let me answer your question this way. I noticed the two saddles and two bridles where we threw the bodies over the cliff. Why did you spare two saddles and two bridles?"

I stood for a moment trying to come up with a reasonable explanation, and I could not. I decided to tell the truth. "To be honest, I do not really know why."

"I think you do," answered Grillius. "Let me ask you another strange question. Did you at any time during our battle this afternoon up until you were throwing the saddles over the cliff openly talk to your God Yahweh?"

I thought again collecting all the past events and running them through my mind until I remembered out on the Ridge Road asking Yahweh what to do once I discovered the woman knowing I had to kill her. "Yes, after the fight with the coward-runner on the Ridge Road, I knew I had to kill the woman. I did ask Yahweh what to do. Why do you ask?"

"You tell me, what did you ask?"

"I just asked for guidance. I did not want to kill a woman."

"I would say your God Yahweh is stronger than all the other gods put together. The two saddles tell me more than anything else that He is the one true God," Grillius explained. "First, you should know one thing. While I was with Hector and Anab in the stone house far above Thermopylae, I listened for hours to their theological discussions. I was entertained for many days by their deep dialogues. I think this God named Yahweh might be the one true God. I started to believe this Yahweh to be more powerful than all the other gods of Rome, or anywhere else in this world. Just maybe all the other gods are fake, fabricated conceptions of man's own foibles and pernicious ideas. Just as you told me you needed to talk to the Baptist, I would like to meet and ask this Jesus a few questions. I am starting to believe nothing happens by accident – nothing. I also believe, like your slave girl, there is going to be a resurrection of the dead; and we all have to give an account of all our thoughts, words, and deeds. Your faith in this Yahweh is at the core of everything, but we will have to discuss all this later. Second, as the girl said, we all need time to repent. But until then we still have to see if more miracles are going to come upon us before we take our last breath."

"Sounds like you are becoming a Jew; but when did the girl say she needed time to repent?" I said more as a statement than a question.

"That is where the friction of my belief comes into the view of things. I would love to talk more about this, but it will have to wait. But, no, I don't want to become a legalistic Jew. That is one of the questions I wish to ask Jesus. Can someone follow Yahweh without becoming a Jew?"

Grillius motioned with his head for me to follow him, and we both walked very stiffly over to the front of the wagon where Nicodemus sat quietly. I looked back into the meadow, and the woman was sitting on the ground near Amcheck, who seemed to be asleep. There was a sound of insects that was almost deafening. It was odd that I hadn't noticed this noise until now. Grillius broke my spell as he started talking, so only Nicodemus, and I could hear. "I know Herod Antipas put Amcheck-Belkin in charge, and we are to follow his orders. As I see it, we got away with a nasty situation; and now things have changed. We cannot stay at or remain near Bethel and wait for this snake of a human Saben to arrive tonight or tomorrow. Now, this is going to be our plan. I want both of you to use the moonlight and travel through Bethel and make some distance until morning or until the moon goes down. Perhaps you can make it into Samaria. Try to get as near as you can to that town called Sychar. When you do stop, you will need to hide the wagon from the road and keep a lookout for Saben. I am sure he will figure out something happened when he arrives at our last camp, where our little skirmish occurred. He is smart enough to go into Samaria looking for you along the Ridge Road."

I nodded my agreement as did Nicodemus, but I had a question. "What about all those horses in the meadow?" I asked. "We cannot leave them there, or someone will become suspicious of a dozen animals with SPQR brands on their shoulders. That person will wonder why these horses are out in the middle of nowhere, especially when the sky will be darkened by all the vultures circling around this area by tomorrow morning."

"There was probably a bill of sale in one of those saddles you tossed over the cliff, but it is too late now," responded Grillius. He did not mean any malice as he was smiling when he mentioned the bill of sale in one of the saddles. "You did spare two saddles; maybe there is a bill of sale in one of them. You go check. Maybe that will be one of our needed miracles. However, before you check and I leave, I need all the leather straps you have in the wagon."

"What do you mean before you leave?" asked Nicodemus.

I could see that Nicodemus was readily accepting the leadership of Grillius over Amcheck. "I will kill the one wounded horse in the meadow, which should explain the circling vultures that Eunus believes will be circling here by morning. A dead horse will also account for any smells from the dead bodies down at the bottom of the cliff." Grillius looked away from Nicodemus and placed his eyes on mine. "It is the humane thing to do, Eunus. That horse will be dead by morning. He performed a courageous act, but his days in this world are up; he has lost too much blood. I will spare the rest of the animals by driving them down toward Azotus, which is on the International Highway. From there I will try to sell them to some foreigners going to Egypt hoping they do not ask too many questions about the SPQR brands on the shoulders. If I have time and a little acid, I can alter the brands to look like 8ROB or something else. If that does not work, I will give them to some poor farmer and tell him to change the brands himself with a hot iron. Other than the gray, who is already dead, there is no need to slaughter those innocent horses. I don't think your Yahweh would bless us if we ran them all over that cliff."

Nicodemus seemed to grimace but then said, "Or some Zealots will take them off your hands along with your life before you get to Azotus. This is their favorite wilderness hideout area. I would say run them over the cliff and come with us."

"After what I did at the camp, you do not have faith in my ability to defend myself against a few Zealots?" said Grillius in a rebuking fashion. I wondered who was older, Grillius or Nicodemus.

"Are you really doing this because you do not want to kill all the horses?" asked Nicodemus.

"If they are God's creatures, why should we run them off the cliff just because their masters were evil and greedy," answered our new general, who had just declared he was now leaving us. "I will leave Star in charge now that Amcheck-Belkin is out of commission. Besides, I do not trust that Parthian. There is something he is not telling any of us." Grillius turned to me and said, "You can keep your horse Zeus. Back at the camp, I stitched up your friend Amcheck before we packed up and followed you. I should tell you that the Parthian almost died a couple of times. I am surprised he is still alive. Maybe that woman will nurse him back to health." Out in the moon-bathed meadow, Nicodemus and I looked to where Grillius had pointed his chin. The three of us quietly watched the woman place a wet cloth over Amcheck's sleeping head, and I now knew she was going to live.

Nicodemus broke the moment when he spoke to me. "Aristarchus, after I helped with saving Amcheck from his wounds, I told Amcheck-Belkin that Grillius-Leonidas was the best surgeon I have ever seen. I believe Amcheck-Belkin realizes that Leonidas saved his life and will not argue with any decisions Grillius-Leonidas makes tonight."

I assumed Grillius's words must have stung Nicodemus, and this must have been Nicodemus's way of repenting. I looked at Grillius and asked, "When will we see you again?"

Chapter Nine

"I will find you somewhere on the Ridge Road, but you must understand one thing: I suggest you get rid of that wagon as soon as possible. Those two disciples who stopped following Jesus might have seen it when they were talking to you two up on the road. Without a doubt, other bounty hunters are coming this way looking for someone in purple pants, an old man, and perhaps a huge wagon. Herod Antipas is going to have to forget about his investment of gimbals, which was a ridiculous plan from the start if anyone were to ask me. Remember, Eunus, four million *sestertii* will turn even grandmothers into killers. However, you are going to need that wagon to move Amcheck for the time being. Just head north into Samaria, and get as far away from Bethel as you can before daylight. Then hide or destroy this death trap of a wagon."

Nicodemus and I agreed to the wisdom of Grillius, and I said to myself I was going to get rid of these purple pants as soon as he left even if I had to wear a wet tunic in this cold wind. I walked out into the meadow and gently guided the woman back to the wagon. I asked her if I needed to tie her up and gag her. She looked hurt by my question, so I let it be.

"Is your name Eunus?" she asked since I did not gag her. Maybe she did not understand I was the one her group was hunting. She was only asking because of the name Grillius had called me.

"Just call me Aristarchus, and I will call you Euna since you are now my slave." I could see her plainly from the one oil lamp, the one Nicodemus must have used when he was cleaning the back of the wagon. After I had given her a new name, I noticed a sparkle in her eyes and a slight smile form on her full lips. She had lovely white teeth that totally changed her appearance when she showed them.

Amcheck now seemed to be asleep in the grass, for he did not answer when I spoke to him. Euna came up beside me and helped half-carry Amcheck back to the wagon. I instructed Euna to take the blankets from one of the cots and place them on the floor. After she had obeyed, we rolled him over onto them. I pulled back his bloody tunic and used the lamp to inspect his wounds. They did not look good. Grillius had closed them up with a dozen dark horsetail stitches. I guessed Grillius did not have time to boil the horsetail strands before he stitched up Amcheck. Based on the redness developing at the edges, I believed infection was going to be a problem; but we had bigger tribulations than contamination to deal with tonight. I told Euna to take care of Amcheck; and, honestly, I didn't care if she stayed or escaped. Down deep, I hoped she would just run away.

I felt utterly stiff and exhausted when I slowly stepped off the great wagon to the ground. Grillius was tieing Zeus to the back of the two-wheeled cart with the saddle in place. My old teacher then took me by my arm out to the meadow to speak to me alone. Standing not far from the gray gelding, he said, "A multitude of dangerous people are looking for you. They are not hunting for me or those other three in the wagon. Get away if necessary and leave your friends. Get yourself to Thermopylae and try to find that hidden stone hut where Hector and Anab are staying. I will find you if I discover that you are missing. Let me warn you: Herod Antipas and any of his capricious friends will turn on you and me as well. With that said, we now need all the lead straps you can find in the back of the wagon for the horses."

I touched Grillius on the shoulder to let him know I understood. I then returned to the wagon. In the back, Euna was tending to Amcheck, who still appeared to be asleep. I searched up front for any long lengths of leather. I found several that were about 24 feet that could be tied together to make two 40-foot leads. After I found Grillius and gave him the two lines, he then ordered me to select two of the strongest horses, saddle them, and check for any papers and money hidden in the two saddles I had spared. There was no bill of sale or anything else of value. If there were a bill of sale, it was down below with the dead bodies. Now I felt foolish for not checking any of the other saddles before tossing them over the cliff. I also began to realize there might be a good deal of money down there. Generals and *prefects* regularly gave a fixed payment of 20 years to a soldier who just ended 20 years of service. That was a great deal of money paid out to a dozen soldiers. There had to be a fortune down at the bottom since Grillius did not find any money on the dead bodies.

Grillius quietly came up to me at the edge of the cliff. "I know what you are thinking and do not worry." He then privately handed me a leather bag full of coins. "I went through each man's clothing before I loaded them into the wagon. The one with the X on his face was the only one with any money. He had this money bag tied to his battle belt."

"Yes, I remember X Man," I said, showing I was listening.

"I then checked the two saddles you did not throw over the cliff before I asked you why you threw all the horse gear over. Both saddles held these coins," and he showed me two more bags of coins. "I am guessing all those dead soldiers had some kind of severance pay on their saddles, except X Man. Those saddles down at the bottom of the cliff contain perhaps a large fortune in silver. That is why I know the God of Israel is the one true God. He had you remove and save only two saddles. The rest He had you place in the perfect repository. When you need that money in the future, come back here; and bring a long rope. Tie it off up here, go down, and collect the rest of the silver when you need it. It should still be there amongst the bones of all those *thags*. What I just gave you has to be about twenty years of wages for one legionary. However much it is, use it wisely, especially if you decide to run for Greece. You see, you do not have to live off the sale of those gimbals. Get rid of them and the wagon as soon as possible." He shook my arm in the old Spartan fashion and said I did well today. "If you were my son or even my grandson, I could not have been prouder."

After Grillius had spoken, I went and saddled the two best horses I could find out of the bunch in the meadow. When I led the two horses to Grillius, he had his herd of horses tied together with the leads, minus the wounded horse. "It looks like I will need about ten more lines 30 foot each," commented Grillius. I suggested that we start cutting strips of the oiled tarp that was to be used when it rained. He agreed and after cutting the tarp, we had ten more 30-foot lines. Grillius took the leads and walked stiffly back into the meadow. He was one tough, old warrior; but, as I watched him hobbling around with the horses, I realized his fighting days were growing short. Age and past wounds will do that to us all.

I climbed up onto the wagon and sat next to Nicodemus, who was curled up and fast asleep on the large padded seat. I picked up the four sets of reins and snapped them and gave commands for the four horses to move. I went down the Azotus Road looking for a spot to turn the great wagon around. Just before the first switchback in the road, I found an open area. Once I had the two wheeled vehicle back on the road, I drove it back toward the meadow, and Grillius was waiting with the horses. I waved to my old teacher wondering if I would ever see him again. Standing next to Grillius was the bravest horse I had ever known, and there he stood with his chest covered in blood. He let out a whinny and tried to follow but stumbled when he took a step. I wanted to cry but choked back the feelings as I set my jaw and eyes forward. I did not want to watch Grillius kill the gray horse that saved my life, and I looked away as I drove the horses toward the Ridge Road. It was one of the saddest moments of my entire life. Once I reached the Ridge Road, I turned left; and we headed north toward Bethel.

Within a couple of hours, we passed by the small but infamous Bethel Battle Site as I would call it for the rest of my life. Every soldier always remembers his first battle, a form of a baptism every soldier goes through before he considers himself a true and tried warrior. There was nothing glamorous about what happened in that tree-covered wadi; what happened was quite the opposite.

Within a short time, we passed through a dark Bethel. The glow of the bright moon, which had moved higher in the sky, made traveling at night almost like traveling by day. This night was better than when Amcheck and I traveled the Jordan Valley Road over a year ago. Going slowly through Bethel proved to be uneventful as we did not make much noise and most of the residents were asleep. Not even a dog made a sound and I thought about the Children of Israel leaving Egypt with Moses as the Scriptures said the same thing: not even a dog barked. This was very strange.

According to Jewish standards, we were breaking the Sabbath; but no one threw rocks at us or yelled any curses. Nicodemus sat up and asked where we were. I told him we just exited Bethel. He said, "Bethel was once called the "house of God" but later it was known as the "house of idols."

"What are you talking about?" I asked but then remembered Bethel once housed the Ark of the Covenant in the days before King David.

Nicodemus being in a rested state began to teach by answering my question. "The prophecies of Amos and Hosea. Hosea called this town *Bethaven* or the 'house of wickedness.' This was after Jeroboam had placed one of the two calf idols here after Solomon died and Judah and Israel divided. Remember I told you how King Josiah removed the idols from Jerusalem; well, he also removed them from here. Now that we are leaving Bethel, we have now entered Samaria; and we are no longer in Judah."

"I assume those two prophets lived before Josiah removed the idols?"

"You are learning, young man."

When we passed the wadi on the opposite side of town, I felt like we were going to be safe now that we were in Samaria. It was at this time I thought of Jacob, who almost two thousand years ago, had his vision in Bethel as a gateway to Heaven, but I did not see any door or entrance to anything.

For the rest of that night, the Parthian wagon was the only vehicle on the road going deeper into Samaria. After many hours, the moon dropped over the horizon; and everything became pitch black. The best I could tell we were on top of a mountain, and way down below were some torches and lights in windows of a large city that had to be Sychar. I would have gone down into the city; but it was now dangerously dark, and I was not feeling very well. I felt tired and weak. Even my hands were shaking while I held the reins of the four horses. Nicodemus was fast asleep, and I got out of the wagon to lead the horses by walking in front of them to a well-hidden place far off the road into a grove of holm oaks and tamarisk trees along with a few acacia and almond trees. I felt this was the best I could do to hide the wagon. I brushed our tracks with a branch from a broken oak raking the road and the deep grooves that had been cut into the hard ground when the wagon went off the paved road into the grove of trees. After I had finished, I found everyone still asleep. I was surprised to find Euna had not jumped and run away. I returned to the road, crossed over, and found a hide in some rocks and bushes. With a wool blanket over my shoulders, I, too, fell fast asleep.

A READING BY EPAPHRODITUS GIVEN AT THE GREAT LIBRARY OF ALEXANDRIA

Given in the year of the four emperors. During this year of civil war, the great fire broke out on Capitoline Hill destroying much of Rome's archives.   **69 AD**

SAMARITANS AND THE TEMPLE ON MOUNT GERIZIM

The Samaritans of Palestina existed on the altering spectrum of the Jewish religion. Today the Samaritans occupy the land that lies between Judaea and Galilee, and they are considered only part Jewish. The other part is mostly Assyrian. A thousand years ago after the death of King Solomon, the name Samaria referred to all of Palestina north of the town of Bethel. In those days all the inhabitants were full-blooded Jews who broke away and set up a new kingdom known as the Ten Tribes of Israel.

There is confusion about the word Samaritan. The Greek feminine name Sebaste is the equivalent of the Latin Augusta. Rome adopted this name Sebastia for the largest city in Samaria, which today is called Sychar. The name was a way of giving honor to Caesar Augustus and later to Tiberius Augustus. From Sebaste comes the word Samaritan. In ancient times Samaria was the name of the capital of the Ten Tribes of Israel, which was then located only a few miles north of the city today called Sychar. In ancient times where Sychar is today was formerly known as Shechem. In those times it was occupied by Canaanites, the people living in this land before the Jews arrived under Abraham. Today Jews and Romans call the people living in Sychar or Sebastia Samaritans. These people are part Jew and part other Semitic people (mostly Assyrians), but there are many other groups also mixed in. Rome incorrectly believes the Samaritan people are more loyal to the Romans than the Jews in Jerusalem. It is true the Samaritans and Jews are hateful to one another, but that does not mean the Samaritans are pro-Roman. As a young man, I spent some time in the city of Sychar; and I discovered that the Samaritans have more in common with the Jews of Judaea and Galilee over any sympathies for Rome, but Rome was apparently unaware of this fact until the great revolt started a few years ago.

Chapter Nine

The Jews of Judaea and Galilee have only one monumental issue toward their half-Jewish brethren called the Samaritans. That matter was a temple that once stood on Mount Gerizim near the city of Sebaste (Shechem to the Canaanites) but today called Sychar. The Samaritans have always claimed Mount Gerizim as the correct site of Abraham's offering of his son Isaac. The Jews of Judaea insist the site Abraham tried to offer his son in sacrifice occurred at Jerusalem on Mount Moriah at the highest point, today located north of the Castle of Antonia. The very hill Jesus of Nazareth was sacrificed on a Roman cross. To both Jews and Samaritans, Mount Gerizim was the mountain-hill where Joshua, after capturing this land from the Canaanites, gave the blessings of Moses and where the curses could be heard, which were being yelled across the valley from Mount Ebal. In those ancient days, this land was called Canaan after the children of Ham, the middle son of Noah. These people became evil in those ancient days; and, after four hundred years of the Canaanites not changing their ways and mixing their seed with the Nephilim, Yahweh dealt with them by sending in the 12 tribes of Jacob under the leadership of Joshua, their general, prophet, and successor of Moses. (Regarding the Nephilim, I will in the future deliver a talk about who they are.)

Once the land was subdued, Joshua divided the territory among all the tribes of Jacob by lots. In time all the tribes eventually turned away from the worship of Yahweh and returned to calf worship. Secretly many adopted Baal worship with Nimrod and Semiramis as god and mother goddess. Just like here in Egypt where Isis and Horus are still worshipped. I am sure you are aware that the story goes that Horus's mother is Isis and, when Horus matured, Horus married his mother. It is the same story with Semiramis. She like Isis married her son Nimrod. As time passed the name Tammuz became interchangeable with Nimrod.

Yahweh turned the Israelites (the ten tribes) over to Sargon II of Nineveh, the king of the Assyrians, after a few hundred years of no sign of repentance from their spiritual adultery. One hundred and thirty-six years later the tribes of Judah and Benjamin (the remaining two tribes of the original twelve) were turned over to Nebuchadnezzar, the Babylonian. The majority of the Jewish population was then deported to Assyria and Babylon. Over many years, both Assyria and Babylon sent in many of their own people who in time populated with the remaining Children of Israel who had not been exiled. Within a few hundred years of intermarriage, the result was a new people called the Samaritans.

The tactic of intermarriage has been a frequent practice by kings over the centuries to destroy a people and their customs. You are all aware of Alexander the Great ordering his troops to marry the women of Susa after he returned from the Indus River. According to the Jews, Yahweh was very clear concerning intermarriage unless the Gentiles converted to Judaism. For instance, many Samaritans who mixed their Jewish beliefs with those beliefs of Assyrians built a blasphemous temple to Yahweh on Mount Gerizim. The reason was that the Jews would not allow the half-breed Samaritans to offer sacrifices in Jerusalem. Thinking of themselves as part Jewish, the Samaritans solved that problem of sacrifices by celebrating all the festivals and sacrifices prescribed in the Torah at their new temple on Mount Gerizim. All Jewish sects today reject the Samaritans as corrupt people and followers of an evil cult that co-opted Judaism with paganism. Any good Jew these days will have nothing to do with Samaritans, even if it means not joining together to fight the Romans.

A few hundred years ago a tribe of Levi calling themselves the Maccabees captured the Temple in Jerusalem from an anti-Jewish Syrian-Greek king who was sacrificing pigs at Zerubbabel's Temple. This king was Antiochus Epiphanes IV, who also claimed to be Zeus in the flesh; and he demanded worship by all those in his Seleucid Empire including the Jews of Jerusalem. To honor Antiochus Epiphanes required pigs to be sacrificed at the temple in Jerusalem. This was a great blasphemy and insult to the Jews' one-god worship. In response to this profane act, a priest and his sons, the Maccabees, physically drove out Antiochus Epiphanes' troops to the north. Approximately thirty-five years later, Yahanan Hyrcanus, a high priest and descendant of the Maccabees, had the temple on Mount Gerizim demolished to stop the blasphemy of the half-Jews and half-Syrians worshipping on the wrong mountain.

It should be noted that today Aramaic, the language of the Samaritans, has spread to all Jews as the universal language of Palestina. What is a mystery to me is why one group who hates the other still adopts that group's language. Perhaps this is the height of hypocrisy. To see how deep the animosity between Jews and Samaritans has become, all one has to do is observe those Jews living in the Galilee region. Due to their twisted hatred, the Galilean Jews will travel on feast visits to Jerusalem many miles out of their way to bypass Samaria. For some Galilean Jews, an extra day of travel is the result of this hatred.

Besides the Samaritans worshipping at a different temple than the Jews, the second major issue between the two groups is the Holy Canon *of Scriptures. Today, the Jews accept the 22 biblios in Hebrew, which are divided into the Law, the Prophets, and the Psalms or Writings. Samaritans, on the other hand, accept as their holy writing only the five books of Moses, which both groups call the Torah. It is such a shame the Hebrew people are not united in their common faith but, instead, have such revulsion for one another.*

CHAPTER TEN

Mt. Gerizim and Sychar - Summer in Pontius Pilate's 6th year as Prefect of Judaea. Jesus of Nazareth's 4th and last year of his public ministry.   (32 AD)

And I will pour out on the house of David and on the inhabitants of Jerusalem, the Spirit of grace and of supplication, so that they will look on Me whom they have pierced...   Prophet Zechariah

When I woke up in my hide next to the Ridge Road, I was broiling hot. The sun had been up for hours, and I was still wrapped in a wool blanket. After I had thrown off the blanket, I discovered I could not stand. Feeling the urge to void, I rolled over to my side to relieve myself. After considerable effort, I noticed my urine was mixed with fresh blood. I began to worry about a multitude of problems. I was not paralyzed since I could move my fingers and wiggle my toes, but perhaps I was having a heat stroke along with kidney injuries. I suspected damage to my back must have occurred when I landed on my falcata when I went flying over the gray gelding's head. Besides my lower back, my head was also throbbing. After gently touching my forehead, I remembered staggering after running into the wagon wheel; and I wondered whether there was something wrong with my head.

    I next began thinking my stab wounds had become infected. I unlaced my black leather chest protector and then pulled out the ripped neck scarf shoved into the holes the night before. My examination revealed swollen, pus-filled redness around both wounds. What seemed strange was I did not feel thirsty or hungry. Now I began to worry. This was abnormal since I had not eaten for over twenty-four hours. I barely had any fluids since drinking in the meadow. I needed to get some fluids into me. I did not care if I missed Saben riding down the road; I was going to return to the wagon. Conceivably Saben had already ridden by while I was asleep, but I doubted it. Looking up at the sun, I guessed the time had to be around noon; and Saben most likely was at Bethel. Looking both ways down the Ridge Road, I did not see anyone traveling. Was it still the Sabbath?

I tried to stand again and began to panic when I fell down. The pain in my back was beyond my ability to stand. I started doing Grillius's breathing exercises he learned in the land of the Panchatantra. I stayed on the ground and put the blanket over my face to keep the sun out of my eyes. The breathing seemed to help keep me from panicking about the unknown. I found myself praying to Yahweh. I asked the same thing repeatedly. "God of the *cosmos*, please help me; God of the *cosmos*, please help me."

An hour went by in the haze of my suffering and sorrow when I heard a horse coming down the road from the south. I tried to lift up; and, sure enough, I saw Saben approaching. I looked for a rock to throw when he went by hoping it would get his attention. Before his horse got close to me, I tossed a fist-sized rock over onto the road. I heard the horse blow out as he came to a sudden stop. Saben yelled, "Who threw that rock?"

"I did!"

"Who is 'I did'?"

"Cata threw the rock!" was all I could think to say.

He found me and could not believe his eyes. His only words were, "What happened to you, and where is the wagon?"

"The wagon is across the road and in the trees."

"Stay here, and I will be right back," he said sounding more like a guard dog yapping at a soldier on a parade ground.

There I lay for almost a second hour until Euna came with a wineskin. Her face was infected and swollen and nearly twice its size, and I repeatedly apologized for hurting her. She was very kind and said it was meant to be. "Yahweh is showing me that He loves me and that I have a second chance. I am the one who should thank you."

I did not understand what she was talking about unless she believed in some form of providence that dictated all affairs in this world. Still mulling over my ideas regarding man's destiny, I asked, "How is the man on the cot in the wagon?"

"He is not doing well. All of us are in bad shape, except that kind, older man."

"I am glad that malcontent on the black horse found you."

"Yes," she answered with a gentle smile. "He said you sent him to find us after you had thrown a rock at him."

"I have been out here in the sun for over an hour since he rode by. He said he would be right back to help me."

"That is not true. That bellyache of a man named Saben just found us. It has not been an hour; it has only been a few minutes. Do not be angry; it must be your fever. Once I learned of your whereabouts, I grabbed a wineskin and came to find you."

I stared up at the orange, fiery orb above me. She was right; the sun had not moved very far across the sky. What was wrong with my mind? "How did you get untied?"

"You did not tie me up last night. Don't you remember? When the old rabbi found me sleeping in the back of the wagon this morning, he asked who I was. I told him I was your slave, and I would not run away. He said I was no one's slave, and I could run away if I wished. He spoke of the Year of Jubilee, and said I was free."

I began thinking that Nicodemus was going to get us killed before this was all over; but, then again, maybe he was the only sane one among us. I took a long drink of wine and handed the skin back to the woman. "Listen, Euna; there is a girl in Sychar if that is the city down in the valley below us, and she is with a friend of Jesus of Nazareth. She is staying at some woman's home. I learned this bit of information from a couple of disgruntled followers of Jesus the day before you and your friends showed up outside of Bethel. Saben or 'Lord Bellyache' is going to have to find them. I am sure they will take us in and care for us if they are faithful followers of Jesus. If we stay out here, we will all die."

"God will care for all of us. This I know, but do not ask how. Would you please stop suggesting those men were friends of mine? It is a long story how I ended up with them, but I cannot talk about it now. However, they were not friends of mine."

"Amcheck, the wounded man inside the wagon – have his wounds infected?"

"Yes," was all I could hear her say in a low voice with her head down in what appeared to be shame, the look when a small child has been caught lying. I had no idea what was going on with Euna. I dismissed it as a womanly thing.

Chapter Ten

Many months later I would discover exactly why she had this expression of dread, but on this day I just waited until her boldness returned; and she said, "He is delirious and dehydrated. You also need to drink some more; and I will ask that new man, who scares me if you do not mind me saying, to ride down into Sychar and find help. Can you stand and walk back to the wagon?"

"If you help me, maybe I can."

After taking a second long drink and with all my renewed strength, I was able to roll over to my hands and knees. From that position a sharp pain slammed into my back, and I found myself heaving up the wine from my stomach right in front of this woman I barely knew. It was embarrassing; yet, she showed compassion and did not seem to mind. Again, I tried to stand but fell to the ground losing the rest of what fluid I had just taken in. Finally, I was up and stayed up, except I could only take baby steps, which were the most painful steps I had ever made. I could not understand why I was in this much pain, and I did not think it had anything to do with my wounds. It took a long time; but, with Euna's help, I got to the wagon, which was well hidden in a stand of trees.

On the shady side of the wagon, I collapsed onto some soft grass. From the ground I looked around and spotted all the horses unhitched and grazing out on green grass. All the horses were unhobbled or tied to anything. Saben came up to me asking about the girl I knew who might be staying in the city of Sychar. He also wanted to know what happened outside Bethel since Nicodemus refused to say much. I did not know why Nicodemus was evasive, but I told him everything starting with the ex-disciples of Jesus. I did not say anything about Euna being associated with them, and he did not ask. Saben agreed with my evaluation concerning the ex-disciples as the ones who gave us up to the band of former Roman soldiers. "There is no other logical explanation for those soldiers finding you that quickly in the wadi outside of Bethel. Tell me more about the house in Sychar? The slave woman said something about a place where all of you can hide and heal."

"All I know is the house is the closest dwelling near Joseph's tomb. That would be the Jewish patriarch, Joseph of old. I do not know the name of the woman who owns the house, but she is a follower of Jesus of Nazareth according to the two ex-disciples. Jesus teaches his disciples to love their enemies, so this woman at Sychar should be kind to us."

"I know it is the Sabbath, but I will ride down into Sychar. Samaritans are not as legalistic as other Jews. Amcheck is in a bad way as well as you are. You both might die from your wounds out here or from the bands of men hunting for the richest bounty ever known. And, if this woman knows Jesus of Nazareth, that will serve the tetrarch just fine; for he now wants to personally talk to this Jesus. Maybe everything will work to the best."

I understood precisely what Saben meant, and this news was not good for Jesus. Pain ripped through my lower back, and Saben apparently made his decision as he stood there watching me heave what was left in my stomach. Saben made a disgusting noise and wagged his head showing nothing but antagonistic antipathy. He mounted his sweaty horse without saying a word and rode away out of the grove of trees toward the Ridge Road.

When Euna came to check on me, I asked if there was anything to eat. For some strange reason, I felt hungry and thirsty even though I had just thrown up. I took a long gulp of wine when she returned with the skin and a handful of burnt grain in a cloth she held in her hand. After consuming the food, I lay back down and went into a deep sleep. Several hours later the pain woke me up. It had now moved, and it was lower and more in front. Lying asleep next to me was Euna.

"Wake up, Euna," I said pushing her as gently as I could. She rolled over; and I noticed her bruised, swollen face. I felt horrible for doing all that damage to her sweet face. Then, when she smiled at me, I felt even worse. I attempted to return the gesture and then asked where the old man was.

"I do not know. Perhaps he is asleep in the wagon with your friend."

"Could you find him please?" I asked trying to be polite. I think I was starting to realize women were delicate creatures who needed to be handled with kindness, not with a swift belly kick in the guts, much like some grooms would do to a misbehaving horse.

It was as she said. Nicodemus had been resting in the wagon. She had roused him, and he came out to see me. "What is it, Aristarchus?" Nicodemus asked. Euna was standing behind the old scholar.

"What were you doing in the wagon?" I asked.

"I have been trying my best to keep the flies away from Belkin's wounds."

"That is what I wanted to talk to you about. Let the flies do their thing. They will lay eggs in his wounds, and the eggs will hatch; and little white maggots will eat all the infection away." He looked startled; to him, flies were symbols of Baal, the Lord of the Flies. "You, too, Euna; let the flies land on your face, and try to stay still. If you both do what I say, there is a good chance no one will die from infection. I will do the same with my wounds."

"I do not know, Aristarchus," moaned Nicodemus.

"Euna, you go into the wagon and lie on the cot; and you, Nicodemus, stay right here with me. Euna, do as I say," I ordered but trying not to sound rude. This was actually hard for me because all I remember was how my father talked to his slaves when I was a little boy living in Rome. Every time he spoke to any slave, it always sounded rude.

"Yes, master, I will do as you ask," she answered politely before she quickly walked toward the back of the wagon.

Nicodemus was now outraged. He was visibly upset about allowing flies to lay eggs in our wounds and went off to be by himself. Euna returned after a little while and said the man in the wagon seemed to be unconscious but was still breathing. "I did remove his bandages so flies could produce those little white-worm things in his injuries."

"Good; now, if you could, help me take off my cuirass. I also need to expose my wounds to the flies." She seemed skilled at undressing men. I gathered this was not the first cuirass she had untied. She even insisted on removing my purple pants. I was glad I had on a loincloth, for the humiliation of being naked in front of a woman would have mortified me. It did not matter to me whether this woman was a *luna* or not; she was still of the opposite sex. It may be hard to accept; but, even at my age, I was still naive in this area. She commented on my stomach muscles being as tight as iron as she undressed me. I did not respond. Afterward, I lay back down; and the flies started to land all over my forehead and the two open wounds, one on my left hip and the other low in my stomach.

"Euna, lie next to me; and allow the flies to land on your face. And, Euna... I was rude to you earlier; and I want to make an apology to you." She said she did not know what I was saying but did as she was told.

Later, when I looked at her, she was weeping as thousands of black flies were amassed on her face; and she tried to remain still. I reached out, took her hand, and held it to comfort her. This gesture seemed to help.

When the third star appeared, Nicodemus had not returned. I commented, "The Sabbath has ended, and we should see Saben at any time." Moments after I spoke a new pain struck me. It was a horrible pain in my male area.

"What is wrong?" asked Euna after I moaned slightly.

"I do not know, but I have this pain." It was hard to tell her where the pain originated until she guessed and smiled. I asked why she was laughing at me, and she said I was passing a kidney stone. She told me to turn over onto my side or get on my knees and let my water blow out the stone. I told her I could not roll over. With gentle hands almost as tender as those of Herodias when she cared for me in Jerusalem, Euna helped roll me over and loosened my loincloth. She must have seen the horror on my face when she told me to release my water as hard and as fast as I could. I was relieved when she said she was going to the wagon to check on the other man and get more wine for me to drink. Sure enough, right after she left, I had a strong stream going; then, all of a sudden, a little brown, jagged rock came out in my urine stream. I picked it up and looked at it. I could not believe such a little thing as this had the power to render me to the point I was throwing up from pain. I marveled how Euna understood about tiny rocks coming out in someone's stream. I began to wonder who this woman was. When Euna returned, I showed her my stone; and she clapped her hands in delight. She wanted to hold it, so I gave it to her. She cheerfully exclaimed, "We will call it Beelzebub. It is not the largest stone I have ever seen but large enough to cause great pain."

"How is it you know about kidney stones?"

"I had seven brothers. Two of my brothers were afflicted with the same problem." She gave me the startling news that I would have these stones off and on for the rest of my life, and she was right.

Euna asked if she could keep the stone as a memento; and I said, if she wanted Beelzebub, it was hers. "How is the man in the wagon doing?" I asked now that my "stone ordeal" was over.

"He is not good, I am afraid to report."

I realized my two small inch-deep wounds were starting to infect, and I could only guess how bad Amcheck must be since his injuries went to the bone below his lower rib and the second was on top of his hip. I asked Euna about her face, but she did not answer. She seemed to be a selfless and noble, who worried about others rather than herself. My mother's words rushed back like a mighty wind: "Think of others as more important than yourself." After all these years, now almost 70 years later, I still have not entirely conquered the last words of my mother. Such a simple request became a massive boulder of a burden, the monumental struggle of my entire life. Others would tell me I was a selfless man. However, they did not know my heart; and selfishness was always to be my companion. I never stopped working on this problem; but it was always a particular weakness, just like the stones that came around from time to time and caused me great pain. And like the sun and the moon looking entirely different from one another, so are humans struggling with various problems.

"The man in the wagon is awake, and I gave him some wine with gall mixed in it. He will be out until morning. His fever is still present, and you look a little flushed yourself."

She held out the wineskin for me to drink.

"Is it wine with gall?" I asked. She nodded; and knowing she needed to get a good night's sleep, I told her I would rather have just everyday wine but she should drink the wine mixed with gall. She did not question me and took an enormous gulp from the wineskin. Afterward, she brought me a different wineskin and placed it next to me. She also held out a round roll of barley bread and broke off little pieces for me to eat. We sat there in the dark for about an hour until she fell asleep on the ground. I covered her with a blanket and went to the wagon where an oil lamp burned on the floor next to Amcheck's cot. I picked it up and checked Amcheck's open wounds.

I was startled when I heard a voice behind me. "Has Saben returned?" There stood Nicodemus out in the dark. He had finally returned to our camp.

"No. We will have to wait here until he arrives. In the meantime, we should try to stay warm; for the temperature of the air on top of this mountain is dropping. Why not lie on this cot next to Amcheck? I will wait for Saben outside the wagon." Nicodemus did not argue and asked how Amcheck was doing. I shook my head as if only time and God were the answer to that question. When Nicodemus was on the cot that had been erected next to Amcheck, I covered him with a blanket. After I blew out the lamp, I went back out into the night. I picked up a wool blanket and lay next to Euna. In the night she rolled me over on my side away from her and put her body next to mine. I stayed still as her arm came over me as we remained on our sides. I must admit this was one night I knew I would treasure for the rest of my life. It was the first time, in a platonic way or otherwise, I had actually slept next to a woman. It did get cold that night, but we both stayed warm by holding each other. Today, as an old man, I can still say it was one of the most pleasurable nights I have ever enjoyed. The smell of a woman is different from a man, and it was gratifying just lying there with her arm around me. It was true that we both reeked of blood, sweat, and other unpleasant odors; but the smells did not matter as her womanly scent overpowered the others. It reminded me of the other time I slept with her in the saddle of my horse.

The next day Nicodemus spent his time organizing the Greek translation of the Jewish Scriptures. Happy that he was preoccupied, I was able to get up and move and was even able to go off and do some bodily business in the bushes some ways from the wagon. Euna looked very pale, and I felt a fever on her forehead. Both Euna and Amcheck were not doing well with their wounds, even more so than yesterday. Euna's face was now hard to look at as her eyes were beyond black and blue and partially closed. The three long black-scabbed lines ran from her left chin to her forehead. I checked Amcheck and discovered two red lines under the skin running upwards from his wounds, which indicated blood poisoning. I knew this from reading medical manuals at the Lyceum and at Hector's house, especially the ones written by Hippocrates. Grillius had also taught me a great deal regarding battle wounds and what to do to save someone's life if infection developed. There were several tricks he had taught me. One was pouring hot honey into the wounds, but we did not have any honey. A second remedy was available. I went into the forest and gathered green tree moss on the north side of several trees. After mixing the moss with wine, I applied the gooey stuff to all our wounds. I told Euna and Amcheck I read about this cure from Hippocrates, but the truth was Grillius had shared this with me. My thinking was, if I told them Grillius had taught me, they would have doubted its effectiveness. By giving credit to the great Greek physician of old, the remedy would be accepted. Later, because of the teachings of Jesus, I learned to refrain from lies no matter my motive. Whatever the other person's reaction to the truth was God's business. I have since concluded that all truth is God's truth. Plato said, "The things we see will pass away, but the things we do not see are forever." A famous disciple of the Way plagiarized Plato in one of his renowned letters that today is accepted as one of the books of the canon of Scriptures by most followers and believers in Christ. Interestingly enough, Plato was not a follower of the God of the Jews; yet, his statement is correct and accurate. Therefore, all truth is God's truth, no matter the source. I have also learned that the "Father of Lies" uses many correct facts to deceive after he drips a few drops of deadly poison into the pot of truth.

    I spent most of that day resting in the shade of a large oak or under the wagon. Late in the afternoon Nicodemus went into the cart, and I heard angry screaming above me when I was under the carriage. I crawled out to find what was happening. As I looked into the back of the cart, Nicodemus was screaming about maggots. Seeing me, he pointed his finger in my direction and shouted, "This is unclean and a violation of the law!"

    "What law are you talking about?" I inquired.

    "Flies are unclean, and now their eggs have hatched. Look at Belkin's wounds. They are crawling with maggots."

    "That was the point of letting the flies land yesterday on all our wounds! I wanted them to lay eggs! The worms will now eat up the infection and rottenness of our wounds! Are there any maggots on Euna's face?" I asked. I noticed she, too, was not able to get up from her cot. Nicodemus looked carefully and started screaming again. "Yes! They are all over her face. This is impure and disgusting!"

    I was now wearing my black tunic, and I pulled it up after undoing my tie to examine my wounds; and, sure enough, maggots were crawling around in my two wounds. "Come here, Nicodemus; and check my forehead. Do you see any worms?"

He did as I asked and said sarcastically, "I hope you are happy." He stormed out of the wagon mumbling something like this was the worst day of his life. We did not see him again until a few hours after sundown. I assumed he returned because he probably was hungry even though all we had left for food and drink was wine and some bread.

That night I was beginning to feel better, and I resumed my guard duties. I slept across the Ridge Road in the same hide I was in when Saben found me. Shortly before sunrise on the next day, I wandered down the road and came upon the most beautiful valley I had ever seen. I concluded we were on top of Mount Gerizim; and across the valley was Mount Ebal, the most prominent point above the small *polis* of Sychar. Homes were spread out in clusters forming what I would refer to as design by grand accident. If there were walls protecting the many domiciles I could not see them, and the fertile fields spread out as far as the eye could see. Wheat seemed to be the primary crop growing golden in the early morning sunlight. Based on the height of the grain, harvest was still a month or so away. I said to myself I could build a stone hut right here and be happy for the rest of my life; yet, I would get bored after a few years since farming was not in my blood. If I had my choice, I would rather have that house in the meadow next to the Azotus cutoff that had the fireflies shortly after sunset.

For a long time, I just stood and enjoyed the sight until I heard my name called. Toward my left was Nicodemus sitting in what looked like the ruins of an old temple complex. I went over to where he sat, and Nicodemus smiled. Apparently he was over his tantrum about the maggots.

"What is this place? I asked sitting next to my old teacher.

"This is the temple the Maccabees destroyed many years ago saying the Samaritans were heretics for worshipping Yahweh up on this mountain where the men of Joshua called out the blessings after they took the Promised Land. As you can see, I believe this is the most beautiful spot in the land Yahweh first promised to Abraham."

"I would agree with you on that point, but how well can you see to make such a judgment?"

"I am making my assessment from when I was younger, and my eyesight was not as bad."

"Do the Samaritans still worship here?"

"They still come here on festival days, but no longer do they sacrifice any animals. They claim they are blessed that their temple was destroyed by the demon Jews. Surely, one of the biggest issues between Jews and Samaritans is this very place where we sit."

Letting my mind wander, I noticed a lone rider in black coming out of Sychar and heading this way. "Look down there," I said forgetting Nicodemus could not see where I was pointing. "It must be Saben on his big black horse. He is riding out of Sychar toward us."

We waited for about an hour not talking but just sitting with our own thoughts. Finally, we both stood and wandered back to the wagon to let Euna and Amcheck know that Saben would be arriving soon.

Amcheck was awake and in good spirits. Nicodemus apologized as he said the maggots might have worked because both Euna's and Amcheck's fevers had broken. I checked their wounds and my injuries, and he was right. Euna's facial swelling had gone down, and her face was now scabbed up from her chin to forehead. Her eye bruising was now turning green, which was also a good sign. I examined her nose; and it looked like it was going to heal straight, except for the cute little bump in the middle. It was good to see Amcheck sitting up and talking, and Euna said she had helped him go into the bushes to take care of his bodily functions.

When Saben returned from Sychar, I hobbled and unsaddled his horse. Saben had a considerable cotton bag full of supplies and some salves and therapeutic oils. Nicodemus-Batana told him of the maggots; and he was not impressed, most likely knowing how Herod's Greek physician saved Demos's life with the same trick. Amcheck on his own decision had left a few remaining worms that were still eating around the moss dressings and getting fat. I cleaned my wounds with water that Saben had with him in a waterskin. I then pulled several strands from the tail of Saben's horse and boiled them in a copper pan over a fire Euna had built. After I had found the sewing needle that Grillius had used on Amcheck back at Bethel, I threw the needle into the copper pan of boiling water. After a good boil, I took the pot with a rag around the handle and gently drained off the hot water. I cleaned my hands with the cloth around the handle before I threaded a long strand of horsetail in the needle. Both my puncture wounds were about two inches long and no deeper than an inch. I closed up both wounds and then applied some salve and oil after pouring a little wine over the stitched area. Amcheck's injuries were much more profound and needed to be irrigated. I had already removed the stitches Grillius had placed on Amcheck to allow the maggots to eat deeper into the infection. After a few hours, I pulled off the remaining fat worms and cleaned his deep wounds with wine before I stitched up his injuries.

I asked Euna to examine my forehead and asked her if she needed to stitch it. Both Saben and Euna said it was too late to sew it and I was going to have an ugly wide scar on my forehead. Generally, a person would not wait this long to sew up a gash or slash; but we were not under ordinary circumstances. Yet, as I said, Grillius had sewn up Amcheck's wounds before leaving the campsite outside of Bethel. Nicodemus told me that Grillius did not have time to boil the horsetail hairs he used as stitches. I was hoping the infection was only on the surface areas where the maggots ate. I would later learn that the disease had gone deeper because of Grillius's lack of time to boil the horse hairs.

When Euna asked about her facial wounds, I applied oil and several salves on her facial injuries to soothe her pain. Her cuts could not be sewn together because the tears were not that deep and skin pulled together by stitches would scar her face more than if I just left them alone. Besides, her slashes were already scabbing over. I told her the cuts were not profound and tried to assure her they would heal without much scarring. She looked at me with a smile and a twinkle in her eyes believing everything I said. I silently prayed to Yahweh that her beautiful face would be restored because she was turning her direction in life.

Before it got dark, we ate to our full all the food Saben had brought. We also drank a good deal of wine. Once we were comfortable, Saben gathered us around a warm fire with Amcheck propped up next to the wagon wheel. We had been gathered together for what I assumed was Saben giving us our future orders besides wanting to tell us what he found in Sychar.

"I found the house," started Saben. "The one nearest the tomb of the patriarch Joseph, who was carried out of Egypt about fourteen hundred years ago. What was strange to me was that most of the residents I asked to give me directions to Joseph's tomb knew where it was but did not know who Joseph was. Some Samaritans even came daily to pray at the site, but those I asked did not know why. The home nearest the tomb belongs to a single woman named Photina, who had five husbands but not all at the same time. Her last husband had been quite wealthy and left her the large estate when he passed away. The home is more of a small villa with high walls running around and behind some storage structures, a metal workshop, and some nice horse stalls. However, Photina was not there. I learned that this Photina has been away for some time, but she has allowed Jesus of Nazareth and his disciples the use of the villa anytime they are in the area. I was told there had been a sick woman, not yet 30 years old, staying with another woman who was not the owner. No one knew the sick woman's name or the one caring for her. Someone said the young one had recovered and the two women left to find the Nazarene prophet, who was reported to be back in the Galilee region. I found the house unattended with no one watching, nor were there any slaves keeping an eye on the place. It was locked up when I found it; but I went over the back wall, opened a large gate, and bunked in some stalls in the back with my horse. I stayed there all night and most of yesterday sleeping. It was not until the afternoon that I started to question a few neighbors after telling them I was a relative of Photina and was there to watch her home while she was away. I am sorry I could not get back sooner. The healing oils and the rest of the supplies I liberated from the main house. I did leave a few coins on a table for the owner when she returns."

"The neighbors believed you?" asked Nicodemus.

"Why would they not? I borrowed some men's clothes from the house and looked like a respectable Samaritan. For some reason, there was an extensive collection of men's robes and such. Now for the details of my plan; or, to put it more bluntly, what is going to happen."

Everyone except Amcheck looked at one another, but no one said a word. It was at this moment a strange thought came to my mind that maybe Herod Antipas was in contact with Tiberius at Capri. It was possible that Herod the Fox was keeping me safe until the right time to confess to Tiberius of my father's treachery, which was directed toward the emperor. If this was what Herod was planning and Tiberius believed my story, then Herod could become king of Judaea; and all of my father's wealth could be confiscated for Tiberius's coffers. It seemed to me to be the perfect plan, which Herod certainly had to have considered. Why else was Saben going to such lengths to make sure I was safe until spring time?

Maybe my ideas were a little wild and off the main road; and over the years many have called me somewhat delusional, irrational, and over-suspicious at times. My only defense is my "out-there thoughts" have saved my life more than once; but, for most of us, the things we tend to worry about never happen. To understand your enemy is to think like your enemy. Grillius was right about that bit of advice concerning Demos being a coward and thinking like him. His words saved my life when Euna jumped me from the rock wall and the other man charged me from his hide across the Ridge Road. If I were not thinking like the *Deva* coward, I would have died on the Ridge Road at the Azotus cut-off.

This idea of treachery had also crossed my mind many times concerning Amcheck even before we left Jerusalem. Learning about the gimbal adventure at Herodium sowed more seeds of suspicion. Someone had spent a great deal of time, treasure, and thought in keeping Nicodemus in Samaria as well as me. Paying Grillius to have him as bait to get me to go along with this crazy plan was also reason for concern. I always considered Saben and Herod as enemies and not allies, no matter what they said. The reward for my capture had grown to four million *sestertii* or more; and that would make anyone a potential foe including Herod, who needed a great deal of coinage to pay for an army of mercenaries to fight King Aretas. I felt my days were numbered; and to stay alive was to trust no one, not even Nicodemus, Euna, or Grillius. Deep in my heart, I wanted to believe the latter three were loyal friends, except Grillius was now gone. However, upon Mount Gerizim with those sitting around the fire, I was not satisfied with who was and who was not an enemy. Certainly Herod, Saben, and Amcheck, in that order, were people to watch with a clear eye.

Saben waited for any resistance to his order; and, when no one voiced any objections, he continued. "When it gets dark tonight, there should still be some good moonlight by which to travel. We will start out around midnight, travel together down to this Photina's home, and hide the wagon in the back. It will take a couple of hours to get there, and no one is usually up at those hours. The gate is broad enough to drive the wagon in with the four horses abreast, and the walls are sufficient to hide it from any inquisitive neighbors. We will use the house since Cata seems to know something about the sick woman and will explain who she is when this Photina returns if she ever does. I am sure it will all be fine. The neighbors I talked to said Photina is a very generous and kind woman. However, many commented on the fact she was not always that way but that she had changed ever since the Nazarene stayed with his disciples in her home for two days a few years back. This Jewish prophet apparently first met her at Jacob's well not far from her house. After everyone is settled at Photina's villa, I will return to Masada and see what Herod Antipas wants you to do. As I said last time, some major problems are coming out of Rome."

"What kind of problems?" I asked.

"To start with, Quintus Naevius Cordus Sutorius Macro is now Praetorian *Prefect* of the Imperial Guards in Rome. About half a year ago or maybe even longer than that, the Roman emperor was convinced by his sister-in-law Antonia that his life was in danger from the then-Praetorian *Prefect* Sejanus. Tiberius had been in denial until then. Tiberius thought to live on the island of Capri a safe haven. He had moved to this island five years earlier thinking it safe. Little did he know that was not the wisest of decisions."

"Was his life really in danger?" asked Nicodemus, somewhat interested in this gossip.

"I would say all of Rome knew he was not safe, no matter where he lived. He was the only one who thought he was safe on Capri."

"Sounds like a plot from some Egyptian story where the pharaoh was the only one deceived," commented Nicodemus.

"In danger of whom?" I queried.

Saben answered, "The average Roman knew that the former *prefect* of the Praetorian Guard, Lucius Aelius Sejanus, had poisoned Tiberius's only son, Drusus Julius Caesar, many years ago. Moreover, it was well accepted that Sejanus apparently had help from Drusus's wife Livilla, who was also Sejanus's secret lover. Even though Drusus's death occurred maybe nine years ago, most knowledgeable people guessed the truth shortly after Drusus died. A couple of years after the mysterious death of Drusus, Sejanus asked Tiberius for the hand of Drusus's widow in marriage. Tiberius said no because Sejanus was of equestrian rank; and tradition, not law, prevented one from rising to a higher social rank through marriage. You see, Livilla did come from the Cornelii Lentuli clan on her mother's side, which connected her to a senatorial family. Just on those grounds alone Tiberius refused, and the question of marriage was tabled until about three years ago."

Nicodemus raised his finger, and Saben looked angry but allowed his comment. "I thought Tiberius did allow them to marry."

"True, three years ago; but first wait until I get to that point. Now the citizens of the streets of Rome expressed their feelings about Sejanus and Tiberius by scrawling graffiti almost on a daily basis on any blank wall to what the truth was. However, Tiberius knew nothing about the graffiti because he was living on Capri and never came to Rome even for his mother's funeral. Sejanus was furious about the graffiti and had a small army of slaves repainting walls almost every morning. The people of Rome knew Sejanus had become emperor in everything but name since Tiberius had moved to that lecherous island. Slowly and assuredly, Tiberius was giving all authority to Sejanus including Livilla as Sejanus's wife. Yes, Lord Nicodemus, Tiberius finally allowed the marriage between his dead son's widow and Sejanus, the final sign that the emperor of Rome was totally blind to the truth."

"This is a bizarre story. Is it really true?" Euna asked surprising everyone who thought women were not interested in political rumors.

Saben scrutinized her with a look on his face then asked, "Are you mocking me?" She seemed to hold her ground with this mean-looking soldier. Finally, he gave up and continued with more details without answering her question. "Sejanus and Livilla had an official marriage ceremony on Palatine Hill in the Imperial Palace about three years ago. Shortly after the wedding, coins began showing up in Rome with Sejanus's image, not Tiberius's. I am talking about silver denarii coins, not low-level bronze semis or quadrans that turn green after a few years. I believe this is the first time since Augustus that a denarius had been stamped with any profile other than that of Augustus or Tiberius. To top that off, Sejanus's birthdate became a holiday in Rome; and prayers were to be given to Sejanus and Tiberius at every religious ceremony. Tiberius a few years ago conferred *tribunician* power on Sejanus, which, in reality, made Sejanus joint-emperor and Tiberius's successor at Tiberius's death. Therefore, at the death of Tiberius, who becomes the next emperor had become a foregone formality." Saben looked at everyone except Amcheck and Euna and asked if we understood his critique of Roman politics.

Euna leaned over and whispered something into Nicodemus's ear. It looked like she was having a hard time understanding all that Saben had said. Nicodemus whispered something back like "I will explain later."

"Anyway," said Saben looking at me with his narrow, beady pig eyes. "Tiberius was warned by Antonia, a woman who never involved herself in Roman politics until then; she informed the emperor either by letter or her presence on the island of Capri. I am not privy to which way she informed him. But, in the end, Tiberius believed in Sejanus and Livilla's crimes against his dead son Drusus. Evidently, the aged and diseased emperor understood that Sejanus was going to soon arrange for Tiberius's death and proclaim himself the next ruler of the Empire."

"Now this sounds like some tale about the kings of Israel or a few of Judah," commented Nicodemus.

Saben did not even smile at the old man when he continued. "When Tiberius's rage had subsided, the emperor hatched his nefarious plan to block Sejanus. He placed Quintus Macro, a Praetorian officer below Sejanus, to personally arrest and execute Sejanus. But it was more ingenious than what I just said. Herod's spies had a hard time sorting out all the details. First, a letter was delivered into the hands of Macro to be read to the assembled Senate during one of its sessions at the *Curia Julia* or Senate House in the *Forum Romanum*. Sejanus was led to believe that the letter to be read before the Senate was to make him emperor or co-emperor before the death of Tiberius. Sejanus was dressed in his finest military uniform, the metal shined on his cuirass and helmet, and his leather wristbands had been oiled. Second, Macro read the emperor's letter aloud to about two hundred gathered senators including Cata's father, Senator Vetallus Crassus, as well as the infamous Senator Treverorum." Saben now looked at Amcheck and explained Treverorum was the father of the Roman tribune Amcheck had flogged last

Passover. Amcheck looked concerned, but Saben just laughed saying Herod would protect Amcheck. I wasn't so sure about Herod protecting anyone, especially if that person stood in Herod's way to becoming king of the Jews.

"Returning to the story. Macro had circled the Senate building with Praetorian Guards who were all loyal to him. Then, as Sejanus stood before all the noblemen of the Senate, the imperial document was read aloud. It started out saying that the new *prefect* of the Praetorian Guards was Quintus Macro, and then Tiberius's windy words went on to describe Sejanus's extensive inventory of treason. A shocked and paralyzed Sejanus was immediately placed under arrest and later executed. Sejanus's corpse was dragged through the streets of Rome to great rejoicing, for the people thought the reign of terror of Tiberius and Sejanus was over."

"Was life really that bad in Rome before all this happened?" asked Nicodemus.

"Rome has been living under a plague of fear for years. For many years Tiberius had issued thousands of decrees of death warrants that were viciously enforced by Sejanus. On top of Tiberius's old edicts, there had been laws enacted, orchestrated by Sejanus, stating that anyone who said anything ill about Emperor Tiberius was guilty of treason and was to be executed. Rome has seen thousands of senatorial trials. At first, Tiberius sat through some of the early ones. But, actually, how could anyone, day in and day out, sit and listen to what a rat you are? Much of what was said was probably true, and it most likely affected Tiberius. But Sejanus always had long lines of witnesses repeating what so-and-so said, and thousands of people were beheaded or crucified depending on their Roman status or non-citizenship. Thus, thousands perished in these slander purges during the reign of Sejanus. This alone was what many said was the reason Tiberius left Rome for Capri. Still, Tiberius could not escape the trials in Rome. Each morning for the next five years on Capri, hundreds of accusations were read aloud to the emperor."

"Is it correct to believe all these trials have ceased?" Nicodemus asked with his forehead furrowed in the tragedy of what he was hearing.

"Everything changed after the death of Sejanus except the purges soon swung the other way. All supporters and family members of Sejanus were rounded up, recalled, and killed. So far, only a few hundred have died including Sejanus's 11-year-old virgin daughter, who was raped first by Praetorian Guards before she was hacked to death. Roman law says a virgin cannot be killed by the state, and that technicality was circumvented before she was murdered in her father's home."

Chapter Ten

I noticed Euna put her hand to her mouth in horror and asked to be excused from the discussion. Saben gave a cruel grin and dismissed her with a rude wave of his hand. After she left the fire, Saben continued. "Now even darker days have been occurring in Rome since Sejanus's death. Oddly, Tiberius is still at Capri; but now he personally makes new lists daily of people to be killed. What has changed is now Macro has become the new Sejanus. Macro is a fat buffoon of a man but not as ambitious as Sejanus; yet, he is still a danger."

I had to interrupt this unbelievable revelation of what was happening in Rome. Much of what Saben had said I already knew from my evening conversation with Felix the Praetorian when I was last in Rome a few years back. "I have two questions." Saben stopped and place a dried fig into his mouth, which was his way of allowing me to speak. "Since Judaea is an Imperial province, was not Pontius Pilate appointed as governor by Sejanus? Also, how has my father survived all these purges? A couple of years ago I had it on good authority that he was on one of Sejanus's lists."

"Excellent observation, Schoolboy. Back when you were recovering in Herodias's bedchambers with a smashed skull, you might remember the golden shield incident."

"Yes, I remember it around the Passover time when Antipas and his brothers were protesting the hanging of the shields in Herod's throne room at Jerusalem."

"Did you know Pilate had the shields removed from Herod's Palace shortly after that protest?"

"No, I did not know; or maybe I did. My mind was not thinking well back then," I confessed.

"Well, Pilate did. He was quite angry, but the incident is what saved him. He had the gold that covered the wooden shields melted into bars. He sent most of the treasure straight to Capri with a letter to Tiberius. Pilate clearly offered the gold to help finance the Sejanus purges, a brilliant move on his part to distance himself from Sejanus. You see, the gold and letter must have arrived after Sejanus was dead; but the trick must have worked. How Senator Treverorum and your father have survived is beyond me. But you know how your father can escape any problem. People in Rome say that he has a *genius* or *jinni* spirit received at birth that protects him. Now that brings us to the present. Mysteriously, your father, young Cata along with Senator Treverorum, the father of that schoolboy-tribune flogged by Amcheck in Jerusalem, have both survived the latest purges. Surprisingly, so has Pontius Pilate, who, as you guessed, was a Sejanus appointee here in Judaea. But, Herod Antipas is waiting and hoping Pontius Pilate will be recalled and executed. If that happens, then Herod's dream of becoming king of the Jews could be his reward. How Pilate has escaped and has not had to answer for almost killing Demos Treverorum is the secret of all secrets. Some mysterious power is at the center of the despicable interweaving of politics in Rome. Yet, what it does tell me is that your father, Cata, and Senator Treverorum have lost some influence with Tiberius."

Amcheck lifted his head and said, "Maybe Pilate has the same *genius* spirit Cata's father has. How else could he achieve anonymity in this faraway hole in the Roman Empire?"

I was amazed at the word usage of both Amcheck and Saben. Both spoke as being well educated, especially Saben, who related all these details extemporaneously using the standard Greek of the day. I was amazed at his improvised choice of words that were precisely used. During Saben's aspects of Rome's sickness, I had been thinking; and I finally voiced my opinion aloud. "How hard would it be to gather an army to storm Capri? Herod could do this and be king of more than Jerusalem or Judaea."

"That is insane to think such thoughts," blurted out Nicodemus as his scolding eyes locked onto mine. "You should be rebuked for even voicing such an evil proposition!"

He was right, and I looked down in embarrassment. Nicodemus then looked at Saben and asked, "What do Rome's intrigues have to do with us, those of us who are sitting around this fire on top of Mount Gerizim?"

Saben smiled at the question before answering. "Let me say this, Judaea's distinguished member of the Sanhedrin, that is where it gets interesting." Saben's tone and words were noticeably patronizing toward Nicodemus, and why he was condescending toward the old scholar I had no idea. I slowly moved my gaze to Nicodemus, and I wondered if he knew why; but, if he did, he kept his mouth tightly shut. "Like I said, Pontius Pilate was placed as *prefect* of Judaea during Sejanus's reign. Tiberius might remember and recall Pilate back to Rome. It is well known that Sejanus was a Jew hater and would send a like-minded person to rule Judaea. Sejanus hated the Jews more than any other person in the Empire. I am sure Master Nicodemus remembers when Pilate first came to *Palestina* six years ago carrying out an agenda that baited many Jews and caused the death of thousands of your countrymen. More than one delegation in the past six years has tried to reach Tiberius's ear, but thanks to Sejanus I doubt anyone actually spoke with Tiberius. Now those days are over. If just one delegation or even if the Sanhedrin were to send a letter to Tiberius today, Pontius Pilate's governorship would soon end and permanently."

Nicodemus hung his head as Saben beamed a huge smile. Remembering that Nicodemus was in charge of the water project during the aqueduct that was built to bring water to the Temple, I began to wonder if a delegation concerning that event was sent to Capri. I remembered very well that hundreds of protesting Jews were stabbed to death in the square before the Castle of Antonia. To me, it was still quite vivid as Amcheck and I witnessed Pilate giving the signal atop the rampart of Antonia. Watching from the roof of the house of the Jerusalemite never left my mind. I can still see the silver *denarius* on the edge of the wall that Amcheck had left so that we could watch the carnage in safety. Now I felt guilty because I did nothing to help even though there was nothing that could have stopped any of the murders. A sharp shiver ran up my spine as I thought about Nicodemus being the Sanhedrin member responsible for the water systems in Jerusalem. What did Nicodemus know about the slaughter of the Jewish protestors? Looking now at this old scholar, I saw a broken man saying nothing to the sarcasm directed at him by this captain of Herod's Jerusalem guards. All of this told me that maybe Nicodemus was living with some guilt about what happened that day.

Listening to Saben explain about all these political details, I realized that, despite my young age, I already had become hardened to political doings. I had already learned to hate any type of government, may it be secular or religious. For example, the Roman Senate or the Sanhedrin making decisions as if they understood the needs of all people. It all seemed to me as a false leviathan charade. In reality, only a few influential men or women, here and there, make most decisions and are manipulating the others when the time comes to vote. That is if there is such a time when people are allowed to vote. Nicodemus could have been the chairman of the Water Committee in Jerusalem and still not have the final say in any decision.

"You see, Master Nicodemus," continued Saben's insipid attack upon this old and kind man. "Herod Antipas is overjoyed at the idea of Pilate being called back to Rome and executed because Sejanus had appointed him *Praefectus of Judaea*. I can assure you that many letters in the past few days have been sent to Rome by Herod's hand. He has even sent a delegation of some noblemen and powerful Herodians to Carnal Island to use their sources to help Herod get back his father's kingship of Judaea. It looks like Pilate will eventually be implicated with Sejanus, and this will not be that hard to prove. Unfortunately, Pilate's gold gift to Tiberius so far seems to be the only logical reason Pilate is still governor of Judaea. If this is true, then

Herod made a major mistake in demanding the shields be removed from the Jerusalem palace."

I finally asked, "Is it certain there is a purge of all of Sejanus's appointees? And are you sure Pilate was placed as *praefectus* by Sejanus and not the Senate?"

"Well, you are a smart one, Cata; but you are still young. You see, I am the son of a Roman father and a Carthaginian mother, one of the last Carthaginians. Most Roman scholars today believe the Carthaginians are no more. That is not tactically accurate. Besides, I grew up in the province of Africa without a father because he served in the legions. When I turned 18, I joined the auxiliaries in Africa. After my 25 years were up, I came to work for Herod Antipas. Therefore, I know a little more of the structure of provinces than any of you. So first, a little lesson. Augustus established the first imperial provinces where he alone appointed the provincial governors, who held *imperium maius* with *lictors* and have the power over life and death. When the Empire began under Augustus, he first decreed that ten provinces would be controlled by the Senate. This was designed to make the Senate seem like it still had some power. Since then, the Senators have been responsible for selecting and sending a *proconsular* for a term of five years to each of their provinces. Their *proconsular* answers only to them, and all the rest of the provinces fall under the emperor's control. Any territory acquired by the might of the legions by definition is an imperial province. Therefore, those provinces under Augustus and now Tiberius, receive their *prefecti* from Caesar alone. Even if Sejanus appointed Pilate, removing him now would show the world that Tiberius is not in control during the years Sejanus was pulling the strings of the puppets in a *gypsy* show. Since Judaea was first taken by Rome's legions under Pompey the Great during the time of the Republic, Judaea, along with all of what is now referred to as *Palestina*, by definition is an imperial province. However, only Judaea is maintained by the emperor, who has appointed a *praefectus* or *proconsular,* and not the Roman Senate. According to common practice, when Rome began accruing provinces, local kings remained if possible, especially when they supported Rome with taxes and gave fidelity to Caesar. Since Herod the Great was king over Judaea and loyal to Rome before his death, why is it that Judaea is now an imperial province? This is the argument Herod Antipas is making. He should rightfully be king of Judaea and not just a tetrarch of Galilee and Perea."

Nicodemus raised his finger indicating a question. When Saben consented after shaking his head in frustrated dismay, the old scholar humbly asked his query: "What is a *gypsy*?"

Chapter Ten

Saben threw up his hands and said, "What does that have to do with what I have been trying to explain?"

I interrupted because I understood Nicodemus was someone who always wanted to learn. He most likely had never heard the term '*gypsy*.' "Allow me to answer, and then we can return to the subject at hand."

Saben crossed his arms in a gesture that screamed, "Whatever!"

"First, let it be known I learned this in a class at the Lyceum. The word '*gypsy*' is believed to have come from the Greek word *Aigyptos*. It was the Greek writer Herodotus who used this Greek word *Aigyptos*, which loosely translates as 'The Gift of the Nile.' About the time of Moses during the time of the ten plagues in Egypt, an ancient story told of a lower class of people living in the delta region on the Nile River decided to leave Egypt before they all died under the god of Moses. That group of individuals secreted themselves out of Egypt by ships and landed in *Italia*. These people became rejected people who had no choice but to wander. Thus, these displaced ones were turned away by most settled people, making them a people of great mystery. The name *gypsy* and their strange language kept them separated from others. Also their unusual forms of Egyptian divination, such as palm reading, placed them in a category of fear. It was believed these *gypsies* could curse any person with an 'evil eye' and frighten people into giving coins to the *gypsies* when they begged on streets of a *polis* of any size. Over time, these *gypsies* became skilled horsemen and ironworkers. Coming out of Africa, they all had dark skin, hair, and eyes. The only oddity to the belief they came from Egypt was the fact these *gypsies* all had wavy hair and not tightly coiled hair like the Burnt-faced Men living in the Hamitic lands of Africa. Their skin color, eyes, and hair looked more like people living on the other side of the Khyber Pass. Thus, I would rather believe they are people who entered this part of the world from that region and not Egypt, say 1,500 years ago. It is possible they were living in Egypt, but they were not Egyptians. These *gypsies* are also famous for making money by putting on shows when they entered a new city with little wooden people on strings, which they controlled from a covered area above a small stage. That is what Saben meant by saying 'pulling strings' such as the *gypsies* do with their wooden character dolls."

"Thank you, Aristarchus," said a smiling Nicodemus. "Very interesting. Now, Captain Saben, you may continue."

"I am sorry, but I forgot where I was," remarked Saben, who was apparently perturbed.

"You were explaining the position of a *proconsular* and that Herod was only a tetrarch," Nicodemus stated in a kind voice to help Saben return to his subject. The adage proved true: *a soft answer turns away wrath*.

Saben wagged his head in his frustration and pursed his lips before he started speaking. "To be *proconsular*, one first had to be a senator with one year as a *consul* in Rome. It should be noted that Pilate came from the equestrian order and served in the legions before he went into politics. However, he was elected for one year as a Roman *consul* coming from the tribunes out of the equestrian order, which allowed him to sit with the Senate with the power to only yell '*veto*.' Once Pontius Pilate arrived, he had possession of one legion to keep the peace in Judaea. According to Roman law, having command of one legion designates that person as a *legate*. Therefore, all *legates* have control of at least one legion; and this gives any *legate imperium* power, which also makes Pilate a *propraetor*. At the end of Pilate's first five years, Sejanus gave him a second five-year term. At this time, I do not think Tiberius is going to change a *propraetor* in the middle of a river. For you, Master Nicodemus, that was a word picture, not a literal changing horses or mules in the midst of a river."

"Thank you, Captain, because I, being a non-military man, would have wondered about that very thing if you had not cleared it up for my understanding."

Was Nicodemus pulling Saben's robes in jest? Being truthful was hard to tell by the old man's stony expression but sweet tone. Saben did not take offense because he continued speaking. "Two things to remember. First, one man running the Empire requires a great deal of time. Second, it should never be forgotten that Judaea is at the edge of the Empire; and who cares what goes on out here. Rome only wants its goods of pleasure moving to Rome without any interruption. That brings us to the problem with King Aretas and Herod Antipas. Most of the perfumes and other treasures that come from the Chola region must pass through his kingdom. Chola would be the southern part below the Ganga River, where Cata thinks the *gypsies* came from," he said with a little laugh. "Anyway, if there is war, that would put Herod Antipas into that copper pan full of hot water, much like Cata boiled earlier with the horse hairs and needle." Saben began to snicker again at his own analogy.

When Saben was finished with his own mirth, he took another fig and a drink of wine before he continued. "Therefore, what we have in Judaea is an equestrian *praefectus* as governor with *imperium* power. Here is where it gets tricky. Pilate is also considered a *procurator* due to his past rank as a *consul*. I am sure this sounds like mud to all of you including you, Master Nicodemus;

but all we need to know is our Pontius Pilatus, or Pilate as he is called, is a dangerous and unpredictable man. If he came from the class of senators, then we could better understand and predict his political moves. Being in a powerful position with an equestrian pedigree is why he is unpredictable and dangerous. Think of a lion with a huge thorn in its front pad. Do not get close to that lion even if you want to help him. Understand this: Pilate has most likely bought himself a few extra years with that gift of gold from the shield incident. Thus, we now know what Herod knows concerning Pontius Pilate except this: *Prefect* Pontius is of equestrian rank from the house of *Pontii*. Rome is like a 'snake-pit' with its peculiar oligarchical structure. Just remember, equestrians in Rome are lower than any patrician aristocrat or senator."

I nodded as if I agreed. I felt this lecture was over and above what was asked of Saben to explain.

"Here is Pilate holding only equestrian rank; yet, he has possession of such a powerful position," stated Saben as if he were not done.

"In a faraway province," I said with some sarcasm.

"You have a point," conceded Saben. "Rome seems to care about this desert wasteland only for obtaining taxes and commodities. Still, Herod Antipas is making his move against Pilate with his representatives in route to *Italia* as we speak. The only problem is everything must go through Macro, and he is an unknown to Herod Antipas."

I finally gathered where Saben was taking us; yet, I wondered if he really understood the final piece. To discover whether my theory was correct, I had only one question to ask. "Tell us; who is Pontius Pilate's *patroni*?"

Saben looked at me with the grandest smile showing missing teeth among green and black posts in his mouth. Maybe his teeth were not as bad as the firelight made them. "That is brilliant, Cata. Even Antipas missed that question. The simple answer is the key to everyone's problem concerning Pontius Pilate. There must be someone of enormous power behind Pilate who is protecting him. In some ways, it is as if he has a *genius* spirit guarding him; but, no, it has to be his *patroni*. I do not think anyone has asked that question. Besides, no one here in *Palestina* or maybe even in Rome knows who Pilate's *patroni* is. But, it must be some powerful clan in Rome. Maybe it is your father, Senator Vetallus," he said with a drunken sneer.

I decided to change the direction away from my father. "Yet, if it can be proved that Sejanus appointed Pilate, then the days will soon be over for Pilate's ruling from Caesarea."

"Correct you are," answered Saben. "No matter how far away this province is located from the center of power, his days are numbered. Besides, as

I said, Rome is dependent on the trade that passes through the lands of the Nabateans. Most in Rome think it is the Nabateans who are the ones who provide Rome with most of its luxuries. It may all come down to how Antipas prevents the war that is looming over the horizon. This one issue is what might be keeping Pilate in play."

I jumped on that statement by saying, "I have a question. Why would Herod's family in Rome wish to help him? Did not Antipas take Herodias from his brother Philip? If I am not mistaken, Philip is one of those family members still residing in Rome."

There was a long anomalous silence by everyone after I made my pronouncement. While Saben was digesting my statement, I broke this singular moment by asking one other important question that would bring my father back into the conversation. "What about my father's plans to seize the throne? My half-brother Julius with his bloodlines to the Julio-Claudian dynasty must be old enough to be considered; that is, if Tiberius were to soon die prematurely. Do you understand my question? Now, if you will allow me, Batana, consider a small but powerful mercenary army storming Capri. That would change everything. I am only thinking like my father would think," I said looking at Nicodemus. I knew this was a new concept to my way of thinking, but Grillius had been right when he told me to think like Demos when I was hunting the two runners after the battle of Bethel.

Nicodemus now refused to gaze at me since he had already expressed his opinion on my previous point of an army taking Capri. Instead, Nicodemus was looking at Saben, whose countenance was of anger and delight mixing together. Noticing I was eyeing him, he looked away responding in a high voice. "If we had that scroll from Senator Carnalus, then Tiberius would have your father executed; and that problem would vanish."

"Just like a war would open the doors of all Janus temples?" I asked with a fake smile.

"Maybe that is why we are talking on this historic mountain. No scroll, no proof. Besides, your half-brother is still too young for most Romans. They would know who was ruling, and some people should not have all power."

I wondered if Saben wanted an answer or if he was just having a flight of ideas. I assumed it was the latter, and just maintained eye contact with Saben, who continued. "Unless your father forms an army of mercenaries like you suggest to march on the Praetorian Guards in Rome as well as Capri, he has no hopes for his imperial dreams. I am sure your father realizes money can buy blood, power, and sex but not the throne of Rome. Julius Caesar, Augustus, and Tiberius have established to some extent who will rule this world we live in. With the executions of Sejanus and Livilla, I would venture to say murdering the next in line will continue. Your father does have the resources to assemble an army of mercenaries, much like his namesake Crassus did during the Spartacus slave uprising; but, at this moment in time, I doubt he would dare such a bold move. Besides, I am somewhat skeptical about your father recruiting and properly training an army of that size. Remember he would need to accomplish such a task before Macro and his spies discovered what he was scheming. If he could, it would be quite a feat. Nevertheless, I will relay all of this to Herod to ponder. You, Cata, are more than a young, simple soldier. I can now see what Herodias, as well as her husband, sees in you. Your mind was decently-trained at the Lyceum, unlike that one-eyed fool, Demos Treverorum."

"Can you bring something back from the dead?" I asked once I concluded that Saben had exhausted his thoughts on politics and succession in Rome. I wished to explain something once again. "Remember the scroll everyone wants was in the house my father's men burned to the ground in Athens. Herod most likely knows this; but, if it slipped his mind, planting that seed could not hurt." I could see my words went deep into Saben's thinking. "I know Herod believes he could create a fake scroll, but that would be spotted for what it is and could bring down the tetrarch before he could become king of the Jews."

Hoping my words would accomplish my desires, I realized the truth was in the scroll. Could the scroll still be intact? It was hidden in the corner of my room at the floor level inside a stone hole. The hot stones might have scorched the outer edges, but perhaps the main body could still be read. At this time, I felt that the scroll was my only insurance for staying alive; and now was not the time to give up my one roll of that dice. Declaring the manuscript might still be intact was something I should keep to myself.

Saben's assessment of who was going to be the next ruler of Rome was erroneous, to say the least. Knowing my father as I did, I believed the heir could possibly be my younger brother. My father building and training an army, too, was not a problem. My father certainly would not do anything that would reveal such a dangerous plot. He could easily recruit a mercenary army on the other side of Parthia if that is what it took for secrecy. From there he could train the mercenaries for months and then transport them by using a pirate fleet to *Italia* but first stopping at Capri to capture Tiberius. Did not Julius Caesar bring an army, perhaps small at first, into Rome by first crossing the Rubicon violating all senatorial laws about such matters? Clearly, Julius Caesar eventually destroyed the Republic; but my father would not be destroying the Empire. He would only place himself at its head. Since the Republic was long gone, what Caesar did and got away with so could my father. If my *patra* did such a bold act, he might be considered a savior of Rome. He could be the man who would end the inexcusable cruelty of Tiberius and Sejanus that stretched back over some years. Tiberius allowed Sejanus to do all that happened, so why would anyone trust Tiberius now that Sejanus was dead? Macro was the new Sejanus in charge of a new reign of terror. To the people in the streets of Rome, nothing had changed with the murder of Sejanus. Any mob leader could overthrow the Roman Empire from within if that leader only promised to end the bloodshed.

"Perhaps I am a little too harsh about the Carnalus Scroll," stated Saben now in a level voice but still a little brisk to hide his anger. "But Herod Antipas mentions that blasted Carnalus Scroll almost every time I am in his presence, especially when he talks about his future!"

I began wondering again what Herod's plans were for me now that the events in Rome were changing like the winds in an open cave during a violent storm. The recall of Pontius Pilate might still give Herod the title, which is the lust that drives his every decision; but I needed to change the subject for my own protection against what this rat of a captain could relay to Herod Antipas and his wife. "Should you remind Herod that Nicodemus and I are hunted men by roving armies of bounty hunters? This wagon idea of openly selling gimbals in Samaria is not going to work anymore. I suggest we follow your plan; go to Sychar, hide out at this home of the woman Photina, and wait to see what happens to Pontius Pilate by springtime. Until then it is not safe for Nicodemus to be in Jerusalem because that is where Demos Treverorum most likely will start looking for me; that is, once he recovers from his flogging and returns for revenge. When he does, he will also go after Amcheck since he is the one who blinded him with the *phagellow*."

"You are perfectly right on that point, Cata. The word is the two senatorial families of Treverorum and Vetallus have joined to avenge everyone including Pontus Pilate and Herod Antipas concerning the flogging of Treverorum's son. That is why it would be a disaster if your father did take over the throne in Rome. That would be the fly in the ointment that could prevent Herod from becoming king of the Jews. It could lead to his execution."

"You are right. I guess I never thought about my father and Demos's father regarding Herod and Pilate. Those two must still hold a great deal of power in the Senate."

"Yes, they do. Those two senators alone could block the appointment of Herod by the Senate or the Emperor. The word coming out of Rome is

Demos Treverorum will be returning in the spring personally looking for all three of you: Nicodemus; Amcheck; and you, Cata. I can tell all of you that this is trustworthy information. Herod is working on precisely what you just alluded to, Cata. Those two senators are an obstacle to Herod's personal desires. However, many factors must be considered. Herod Antipas has mentioned in my hearing about sending Amcheck to Rome to assassinate Demos and the two senators. Nevertheless, as you can see, that is not going to happen. Perhaps you will be sent to Rome in the spring, Cata, in Amcheck's place. But that would fail if Herod were to ask me."

All of this was a great deal to digest, and I wanted to hear no more of Demos or my father. "I agree with your plan, Saben. We leave at dark and go to Photina's home. We stay there. We can use Euna to go out and purchase all that we need; and, if anyone asks, Euna will tell the neighbors she is a long-lost relative of this Photina woman. Euna can say she received permission to use the home until Photina returns. You said no slaves are watching this small villa. Besides, Amcheck will need several months to heal."

"That is my plan but with some added features," confirmed a smiling Saben. "I will convey all that has been said here today to Herod; and, when I have his wishes, I will let you know the next time I arrive at Photina's villa. If she returns and throws you out, then send this slave woman to Masada, Machaerus, or Jerusalem to find Herod Antipas; that is, if you are sure she will do as she is told. Besides, where did you pick her up anyway?"

"It is a long story," said Nicodemus. "Think of her as my slave to help me with my work and affairs while I am away from my home."

Why was Nicodemus putting his head on the chopping block with this lie? Maybe he liked Euna. Yet, under the present circumstances, staying and healing at Photina's villa seemed like a safe plan. I decided to reassure Saben. "We will wait until you give us new orders. In the meantime, we will all try to heal. And remember to suggest to Herod that he send some spies into Caesarea and see if the Romans know what happened to those ex-legionaries who attacked us outside of Bethel."

Saben smiled at my words and then added, "Since we are on that question, how is your Spartan friend going to find you in Sychar? And why did he abandon you all with the captured horses when he could have just as easily run them off the cliff with the dead men?"

I decided not to answer any of his questions other than to say, "He will not find us if the bounty hunters cannot locate us. But perhaps he will discover you at Masada or wherever the tetrarch is staying. If he does show up, just tell him to go to the house next to Joseph's tomb in Sychar; that is, if you want him here to help us – if he reappears. On the other hand, he could also be sent to Jerusalem to wait for us there. As you know, he might be old; but he did kill five of those legionaries by himself. If I were Herod Antipas, I would want him as close as possible as a bodyguard. That is only my opinion."

"Using that logic, you, Cata, could make an advantageous bodyguard. Did you not kill the same number the Spartan killed?"

"I killed five, but I will not take credit for the one the horse I rode stomped to death."

"I will mention that as well," said Saben with his smile of unpleasant teeth. "I believe Herodias would love it," he said with a wink. Saben must have discerned I did not like his wink, for his visage turned dark. After puckering his lips while thinking, he finally said, "You, Cata, killed five; the old Spartan killed five; and the horse, one. I assume Amcheck stuck his knife into the back of another. That adds up to 12, and I thought Nicodemus told me there were 13 bounty hunters. Did I miss something?"

"I am afraid Amcheck ambushed two, not one with his *sicarius*. Is that not right, Belkin?"

Amcheck, who had not spoken a word since Saben told us his father had been a Roman, looked somewhat confused. At that moment Euna returned to the fire, and Amcheck looked at her with a smile in his eyes before answering me. "Two of those Roman mutts felt my curved *sicarius*, but two is closer to what the horse killed compared with five each like Leonidas and Cata." Saben began laughing accepting the lie as truth. After he had stopped his cackling, he picked up a stick and bent over to draw something. We all watched and waited with relief that we had thrown Saben off the scent. It seemed even Amcheck wished to protect Euna. After he finished drawing in the dirt, Saben stood and said, "You might be right about everything you said, Cata. And just now thinking things over, I will tell Herod that I believe that you would better serve Herod as a counselor as well as a bodyguard."

That last statement was loaded two ways, and I was not sure which way to take it. My life depended on what Saben meant. Whatever, I was going to consider the statement of Saben as a direct signal to find Messina and head for Greece. Perhaps it would be safer to go to the land of the Indus River or the land of Chin. Every day in *Palestina* was a day closer to a painful death for my friends and me. I was sad that Grillius was gone but glad he was safe from these demented people that circled around Herod Antipas. Saben finally slapped me on the shoulder to communicate that he meant nothing by what he just said; but Grillius always said, "Be careful, for a man's actions sometimes speak so loudly you cannot hear a word he says." Saben was a dangerous ally; and, unfortunately, until next spring my life was in his hands. For a little while longer, but I could see nothing by trusting him. My thoughts at the time were to think only for the sake of the very people I did care about; nevertheless, in the meantime, I was going to have only "fear" as my old friend.

A few hours after the moon came up on that cloudless night, Saben gave the order that we were going down the mountain. It wasn't warm nor cold but a bright, perfect cloudless night filled with stars along with the moon. It was one of those rare evenings we all get to experience from time to time. There was no traffic on the road as we began descending this famous mountain. The trees, rocks, and all the blades of grass looked magical in the muted moon and starlight. Even the night sounds were intoxicating. By the time the moon reached its southern zenith, I realized it would stay up as it slowly moved into the western sky. Saben was leading the way on his black horse while I was driving the wagon with Zeus tied to the rear. Euna sat next to me on the cushioned seat, and Nicodemus stayed in the back of the wagon with Amcheck. At times when the cart jumped a bump in the road, Euna would slip her arm around mine to keep herself steady in her seat. I did not mind, and I think Euna sensed as much.

It seemed eerie going down from the top of Mount Gerizim toward the ancient capital of the ten tribes who broke away after the revolt when King Solomon died maybe nine hundred years ago. That kingdom lasted for a few hundred years until the Assyrians under Sargon removed many of the descendants of the ten tribes north to what is today Syria, Cilicia, Cappadocia, and beyond. The ancient Jewish prophets called this land Ephraim, and the ten tribes supposedly ceased to exist because of Yahweh's punishment. Ephraim had been unfaithful to the One God of the Jews and guilty of committing spiritual adultery. The tribes' first king after the death of Solomon was Jeroboam; and he gave the ten tribes two golden calves to worship, one erected in Bethel and one in Dan. The cause of the revolt was launched like an arrow to its target when Rehoboam, Solomon's son sitting on his deceased father's throne, drove a wedge into the people's heart because of his malicious intent and incorrect perceptions of the people's condition under the rule of his father Solomon. With Solomon dead, Rehoboam could have eased their burden; and history would have gone in a much better direction.

This new religion of the golden-calf worship by Jeroboam was a throwback to the time of Moses when God's prophet was away on the mountain in the desert receiving the law written by the finger of God on tablets of stone. This later would be a dramatic picture of what God was soon going to do to human hearts. Calf worship by the Egyptians, Arameans, and Canaanites plagued the Hebrews after the Egyptian Exodus and up until the death of Moses. When Moses came down Mount Sinai 40 days later holding two stone tablets, he discovered his older brother Aaron had erected a golden-calf to be worshipped in place of Yahweh. In his righteous anger, Moses broke the tablets and destroyed the golden-calf idol. Yahweh was going to kill all these people who had passed through the Red Sea into the wilderness, but Moses repented for the people. Repentance, the theme of the Scriptures, saved the children who escaped out of Egypt. It was strange that Yahweh allowed a good man's repentance for all humans if it was genuine and was given before destruction began. Yahweh's goodness started with Adam and Eve with the promise of a virgin born male to correct the sin problem that kept Yahweh's humans from fellowshipping with their Creator. All that humans had to do was believe Yahweh was going to send His Redeemer to save them, and they would have eternal life even after death. I should reiterate that faith comes from the heart or spirit of man and knowledge originates from the soul. Yahweh looks upon the heart first.

Repentance, an act that comes from the spirit of man, was the message of John the Baptist and was and still is presently the core teaching of Jesus of Nazareth expressed in almost every parable. Jesus even spared Euna, who had supposedly been caught in the act of adultery; yet, even though the law's remedy was stoning, he forgave her. I truthfully could not understand Yahweh and his many facets. Whenever I contemplated Yahweh, I felt like I was staring at a well-cut diamond. On the one hand, God would destroy entire cities or nations due to their collective sins; but, if there were just a whiff of repentance by one person, He spared all the people. According to the Scriptures, the prophet Jonah went to the Assyrian capital of Nineveh to deliver Yahweh's message that the city of Nineveh would be destroyed if the people did not repent within 40 days. In Nineveh during those days lived the meanest people perhaps in history. Yet, they repented and were not destroyed in the days of Jonah. At first, Jonah ran away from Yahweh via a sailing vessel. I can understand why Jonah did not want to go to Nineveh. Don't warn them; and then, in 40 short days, Israel and Judah's greatest enemy would be no more. However, Jonah was thrown into the sea during a great storm by the sailors of the ship; and a giant fish consumed him. The wayward prophet himself repented while in the belly of the fish; and, after three days had elapsed, this prophet was vomited up on a beach not far from the Assyrian capital. Once Jonah reached the great city, he began preaching to the people. He told them they had to collectively repent of their wicked ways or Nineveh would be overthrown in 40 days. By the third day, Jonah had covered the four-city complex of Nineveh, Rehoboth Ir, Calah, and Resen, together forming a 60-mile circumference. The people followed the lead of their king, who arose from his throne, laid aside his robe, and covered himself with sackcloth while sitting in ashes. If I were alive at that time and lived in Nineveh, I, too, might have repented because the sight of a foreign man, partially digested from being in a fish's belly for three days, would have made an impression even on my hard heart. Someone with rags for clothes, perhaps parts of his face digested, showing his teeth and bleached white hair – surely anyone seeing this fish-food prophet would have repented and changed his or her ways.

Once we came off the mountain, we were in the suburbs of the sprawling, historical city of Sychar. Many events and battles had occurred here in the past. It was once the capital of the Hyksos and the place where Abraham built an altar when Yahweh promised the land to Abraham and his descendants; thus, the term Promised Land first started here. This was the city where Yeshua or Joshua of old gave his farewell speech and made a covenant with the Children of Israel. I thought I could live here for a hundred years and never learn all the historical events of this city that is situated in one of the most beautiful valleys I have ever seen. To the south is Mount Gerizim; to the north, Mount Ebal. The valley is fertile for wheat and other grain crops that are fed yearly by only the rains.

Traveling quietly through the dark streets of Sychar, we soon reached the far edge past the outskirts of this ancient city where the famous well had been dug by Jacob and his sons. We all stretched our legs, and each had a drink from the oldest and deepest well I have ever visited. There was an old, wooden crank with a wooden bucket for bringing water from perhaps a subterranean river hundreds of feet below. This water was the most excellent refreshment I ever remembered. Once we finished drinking this cold, delightful, water we continued until we reached Joseph's tomb.

After Joshua led the Children of Israel out of Egypt into the Promise Land, Joseph's embalmed body came to this place as his final resting place. Why Joseph was buried here instead of Hebron with the other patriarchs is a mystery. Many years later after much research, I learned that Jacob, the grandson of Abraham and the father of Joseph, purchased this portion of land from the sons of Hamor for a hundred pieces of money. It was the only piece of land Jacob had ever purchased with any form of currency. Therefore, a part of this beautiful valley was bought by Jacob and later given as an inheritance to his favorite son Joseph. It is a little odd to think a claim on what God had already given to Abraham could be obtained with some kind of script, but this spot was purchased. Yet, it makes sense to be buried in the land that belonged to you as your only inheritance from your loving father. Besides, the cave in Hebron was purchased by Abraham to entomb his wife, Sarah. This valley was the single other piece of the Promised Land ever purchased by Abraham, Isaac, or Jacob. Many years later the threshing floor of Ornan, the Jebusite, on Mount Moriah was bought by King David for 600 shekels of gold by weight. After the threshing floor was purchased, King David wanted to build a permanent temple on that spot, which today is the exact location of Herod's Temple in Jerusalem.

Just a short distance from Joseph's simple stone crypt was our final destination for the rest of the summer and coming winter. Photina's home was a sizeable walled dwelling from the outside and was the only structure near the simple tomb of Joseph. It was, indeed, painted a strange pink color, a sign I took to show only a woman lived in this huge home. Comparing this *domus* to my father's in Rome, I would not call it a villa like Saben had. Yet, it was a large estate, nonetheless. We found the back gate unlocked and large enough to drive the four-horse wagon through just as Saben had earlier stated. Once we settled ourselves inside, we went to sleep until noon the next morning when Saben left for Masada after we all had a hearty meal cooked by Euna. With Saben gone the four of us were left with the protection and obscurity of Photina's vacant home.

During the next number of months at Photina's *domicile*, Nicodemus taught me everything anyone wished to know about the man buried not far from where I studied. I learned that Joseph had the faith of Abraham, the gentleness of Isaac, and the courage of Jacob. Joseph stands as one of the most admired men in the Scriptures just behind Moses, Abraham, Isaac, and Jacob. I grew to see Joseph as a man after my own heart. I actually began to relate to him beyond anyone else in the Scriptures. He was a remarkable man starting with the almost-unbelievable story of his brothers selling him into slavery at the tender age of 17 because of their envy and jealousy. I, on the other hand, left Rome at age 10 due to the murderous will of my father and Claudia. Families at times become someone's greatest enemies, and perhaps Joseph's story is not that unbelievable. Jacob being at odds with his twin brother Esau is a prime example. Even today the descendants of Jacob (the Israelites) and his brother Esau (the Edomites) are still at enmity with each other. This is one key reason why the Jews of *Palestina* reject Herod Antipas since his father was part Edomite or a descendant of Esau.

I had other observations concerning Joseph. Starting at age 17, Joseph was sent by his father from Hebron to check on his brothers who were watching

Jacob's flocks of sheep. Joseph's Ridge Road adventures started in Hebron and ended here where Joseph's body now rests. The Scriptures state that the evil brothers had traveled with their flocks about fifty miles from Hebron to Shechem and even a little further to Dothan. I have indicated that Dothan is about eighteen or more miles from Sychar or Shechem as it was known then. Joseph was sold as a slave for 20 shekels, the price of a slave 2,000 years ago in this part of the world; this transaction happened at or near Shechem. The Scriptures say Joseph's brothers recognized Joseph while he was still some distance off near Shechem before they disrobed him and threw him into a pit. Selling him to merchants destined for Egypt is also reminiscent of the life of Jesus, for Yeshua lived in Egypt for some years as a child because of Herod the Great trying to kill him.

The brothers of Joseph lied to their father by taking Joseph's clothes, covering them with goat's blood, and deceiving their father by saying Joseph had been killed by a wild beast. I could relate to this event because my old *didace* Zeno took my clothes to my *Pater* in the amphitheater to fool him for a short while that I was dead in the Tiber.

From this point, I began seeing other parallels. While Joseph was in Egypt, he was a victim of unwanted sexual advances by the wife of his master Potiphar. I, too, felt like a sexual prey of Herodias, the wife of my employer, Herod Antipas. Joseph ended up in prison; and currently, I was imprisoned in Photina's home, however, in a friendly way, I should add, with good friends and excellent food. Joseph was removed from prison by the pharaoh of Egypt and given a new name. On that score, if my theory and observations remain in line, I, too, may be declared innocent and freed in some strange way by some future king; and I have received many new names. I first went by Venustus, then Venu, Eunus, Little *Sicarius*, Little Si, Little Carius, Little Car, Curus, Leopard Man, Leo, Falcata Man, Cata, Achilles, Little Yoc, Star, Iob, and now Aristarchus. Oddly, the only name that meant anything special to me was the one Jesus of Nazareth called me, Epaphroditus, the Greek pronunciation of Venustus. I eventually took that name given to me by Jesus, and it has remained my name until this present time at age 91.

A READING GIVEN AT BY EPAPHRODITUS AT THE GREAT LIBRARY OF ALEXANDRIA

Given in the year of the four emperors. During this year of civil war, the great fire broke out on Capitoline Hill destroying much of Rome's archives. Due to this loss, the scholars of Alexandria's Great Library requisitioned anyone with past knowledge to recreate the history of Rome. These short lectures were delivered on the afternoon of the seventh day of the week for a fee of 25 denarii. I have incorporated several lecture readings that I personally gave during this pivotal year.   **69 AD**

THE INTRODUCTION OF MONEY INTO THE WORLD SYSTEM AND HOW IT RELATES TO THE PRESENT-DAY ROMAN CLAIMS ON PALESTINA

The Jewish patriarch Jacob purchased some land in Shechem at the value of 100 pieces of some kind of currency. Today the value of 100 pieces of money is unknown to anyone of knowledge I have asked or researched. Back in ancient times, a piece was just a unit of money by weight before coinage entered into common usage. It would be the Persians who started an extensive use of coins, most likely borrowing the practice from the Lydians and their famous King Midas a half-century ago. There are several stories of King Midas. I lean toward the Greek writings of Aristotle and Herodotus regarding Midas. Both men say Midas was initially from the Phrygian capital city of Gordium and was the person responsible for tying the Gordian Knot that Alexander the Great could not untie. However, Alexander removed the Gordian Knot from the chariot lead, where the knot was tied, by hacking it to pieces with his sword. Herodotus goes on to say that this member of the royal house of Phrygia named Midas, fled from his grandfather Adrastus after Midas had killed his brother. Midas apparently took asylum in Lydia during the reign of Croesus. Phrygia was under Lydia's protection in those days and may have been a city of refuge to the Phrygians.

Did Midas become a king of Lydia and start the idea of money, or is it a myth? This question is one about which I never learned the truth. Yet, the introduction of money by the Persian Empire was perhaps borrowed from

Lydia. That one little change in history altered the world in several significant ways. It should be noted that the Greeks of Ionia and the mainland were using coins of different metals about the same period, but they may have also learned about it from Lydia.

It should first be noted that the barter system was soon to become a practice of the past. Second, money transformed the legal systems. The old eye-for-an-eye and hand-for-a-hand laws, first practiced in ancient Babylon, were also to pass away from all civilizations except the Barbarians. The point is that today eyes are now considered to be worth specific amounts of money, and a guilty person could pay for that eye and not lose his own. Third, I believe women benefited greatly from the introduction of money. If a female were able to sell products she had created or to perform labor she had a new power, which she never held before. For instance, let us say a man's wife mended torn tunics and amassed some money. Then, let us say her husband needed that money for a land transaction. Would he not have to treat his wife differently if he wished to borrow from her? Therefore, this idea of money gave new empowerment to women. This is only my observation, and I might be incorrect in my remarks about women and money; but I believe I am on solid ground in this observation.

It is true that the world acquires land by conquest. Rome today holds the title to Palestina, but the Children of Israel took the Promised Land through much more blood and warfare. The Scriptures are clear: God used the leadership of Joshua, the man who replaced Moses after Moses died on Mount Nebo at the edge of the Promised Land, to destroy the wicked people living in Canaan. Yahweh used Joshua to lead the children of Jacob-Israel back to their homeland that they had left 400 years earlier. This man, who took the Children of Israel across the Jordan River, hastily conquered 6 nations and 31 city-states that existed at that time in Canaan. This Joshua, who led the people into the Promised Land, ironically had the same name as the stonemason from Nazareth, which is Yeshua in Hebrew or Jesus in Latin. This is just a side observation on my part.

However, there could be a second motive why Joseph wanted to be buried in modern Sychar or ancient Sychem and later known as Shechem. The first ten sons of Jacob sold their younger brother to some Midianite traders who were passing by after Joseph found his brothers with their father's flock of sheep about eighteen miles north of Shechem in a place called Dothan. This small village is located near the Ridge Road; but it is also the closest spot to the International Highway, the route running toward the sea and on toward Egypt. Being sold by his brothers not far from Shechem may have been a motivation why Joseph wanted his body to be buried there. I believe the Children of Israel, who carried Joseph's remains out of Egypt and for 40 years in the wilderness, were perchance making a grand statement that may be lost to the Jews today when they placed his remains in Sychar, the name of the city today where Joseph's body rests. The message from Yahweh is that in His time He will correct all wrongs done one way or another. This burial spot in Samaria, a place the Jews will not venture into because of their fear of uncleanness, shows generations into the future who truly owns this land; and Yahweh will not tolerate the robbery of His land forever from anyone including the Samaritans. Someday they, too, will be displaced for the rightful owners to occupy this valley and the rest of this land promised to Abraham and his descendants through Isaac, his first son by his favorite and legitimate wife Sarah.

For all of those listening to this lecture, a short history lesson will help to more fully comprehend. The brothers of Joseph were pasturing their father's flocks in Shechem when Jacob, who was staying in the valley of Hebron, asked his son Joseph to find his brothers and report back to him. The Scriptures tell us the brothers had moved the flocks from Shechem (now Sychar) to Dothan, which was a good day walk from Shechem. Thinking their father loved Joseph more than them, Joseph's older brothers sold Joseph into slavery to some Midianite-Ishmaelite traders coming from the east out of the land of Gilead on the other side of the Jordan River. The traders apparently were heading toward the Way of the Sea Highway using the Ridge Road via Dothan as a shortcut. These traders were carrying aromatic gum, balm, and myrrh bound on hundreds of camels. The Ishmaelites are the descendants of Ishmael, Abraham's eldest son by the concubine Hagar. The Midianites are the descendants of Abraham through his second wife Keturah, whom Abraham married after the death of Sarah. By this time in the land the Romans now call Palestina, the Ishmaelites and Midianites had begun to intermarry among themselves; yet, they maintained their own identity. Midianites and Ishmaelites even today travel together in large caravans for their personal protection since the items they carry are priceless. Myrrh is used for many purposes; but just the use of it as labdanum, an aromatic gum that comes from the leaves of the cistus rose, produces an oil used in beauty treatments; and, when it is mixed with wine, it relieves pain like no other product of which I am aware besides gall. Ishmael was the first son of Abraham and the father of the Ishmaelites. Ishmael was never officially adopted by his father since Abraham's wife Sarah forced the concubine Hagar, mother of Ishmael, out of the camp making Ishmael *forever an illegitimate. I should point out, however, that, after Sarah had died, Abraham did recognize Ishmael as his son by giving him blessings and promises, not typical for a son of a concubine, other than Jacob adopting all his sons from concubines. However, Ishmael, the eldest son of Abraham by a slave woman, was never officially adopted in the fashion I was by my Roman father, who, too, had me by a slave woman or concubine.*

After Joseph was sold to a mighty captain of the guard to Pharoah in Egypt, Joseph became a slave himself and ended up in an Egyptian prison. Eventually, Joseph was miraculously removed from prison to become one of two viziers of Egypt because of a special gift Yahweh had bestowed upon Joseph – the ability to interpret dreams. By correctly understanding several of Pharaoh's troubling nightmares, Joseph benefited by being appointed vizier, the leader of Egypt just below Pharaoh himself. There was a severe seven-year famine coming according to the interpretation of the dreams; and, before the famine arrived, Joseph was in charge of collecting wheat along with other foods to sustain the entire population of Egypt and more. "To be able to offer substance to your enemies during a famine makes for future peace" were Joseph's words, and logically he shared this with Pharaoh. Feeding the Semitic people to the north of Egypt proved Joseph's point. When Pharaoh allowed Jacob's clan, who numbered more than seventy in those days, to live in Egypt, they provided skills of sheep herding that were lacking in Egypt. Hundreds of years after Joseph's clan settled in Lower Egypt, the Hyksos, another Semitic people living to the north of Palestina, attacked Egypt, which led to the enslavement of the Hebrews. By the time Moses was born in Egypt, the Hebrews had numbered over a million people. Once the Egyptians reacquired the Delta Region from the Hyksos, the Egyptians kept the Hebrews in bondage solely because they were Semitic people like the Egyptians' archenemies, the Hyksos. The cry of God's Chosen People, under the leadership of Moses, led to ten plagues and the humiliation of all the false gods of Egypt. Due to the plagues, the Children of Israel were able to leave Egypt. This great and ancient nation now lost an available workforce that was very lucrative to the Delta Region of Lower Egypt.

One result of this One-God concept led to a future pharaoh of the same dynasty Moses had served under and fought against. This Egyptian king took the name Akhenaton because he started the worship of Aton. This new god's name must have been a corruption of the Hebrew name Adonai (or Lord). Adonai – Aton. It made perfect sense at the time that the true Creator of the universe had punished the Egyptians for their false, idolatrous beliefs and practices. Once it became apparent that the Egyptian pantheon of gods was fallacious, why not rectify the situation by worshipping the one and only God? Under Akhenaton, Egypt became monotheistic for the first time in its long history. However, after the death of Pharaoh Akhenaton, the Egyptians, who are the most conservative people in history, returned to their old ways of worshipping the many false gods that failed them during the time of Moses and the exodus of the million-plus Hebrew slaves out of Egypt. Time and distance do have a way of eroding people's faith in something that is foreign to their past experiences. There is also the problem of traditions replacing revealed truth in God's Word, something I had a hard time understanding starting with the first time I entered the Jewish Temple complex in Jerusalem in my early twenties.

After Joseph's brothers had sold Jacob's beloved son into slavery, the other sons had conspired to construct a tale to deceive their father Jacob into thinking Joseph was dead. Many years later, when the famine reached the Promised Land, Jacob sent the ten guilty brothers into Egypt to buy food; by this time, the world learned the Egyptians were the only people who had prepared for this disaster. On arrival in Egypt, the brothers did not recognize Vizier Joseph when they first asked to purchase food. However, Joseph did know his vile brothers. Joseph sold the guilty brothers what they wanted even though he had secretly placed the price they paid back into the tops of their bags of grain.

It was not until the brothers returned to Egypt on their second visit to buy more grain that Joseph finally revealed who he was. After their guilty eyes and minds had been opened, the brothers understood the power of this God who chose them – not the other way around. To see their brother Joseph not dead but, instead, standing before them with the rank of vizier of Egypt placed them in his power, which could have easily been death for all of them. Let it be understood, once again, the theme of repentance or meta-neon in the Scriptures continues. Instead of executing all of them, Joseph forgave his brothers for all their lies and treachery.

Repentance, undoubtedly, is the most significant, if not the greatest, theme of life. This was the message Yahweh had been communicating from the very beginning of time to Adam and Eve up to John the Baptist. "Repent, for the Kingdom of God is at hand." Therefore, if a man repents, Yahweh will forgive him; or, if a man does not repent, there will be destruction. It is that simple and that hard for all people, one way or the other. There can be no in-between; all humans have a free choice to make before they leave this world in death. If I am offending any pagans present today, so be it. Let it be understood I am offended whenever I listen to pagans explain their cosmology.

Part of the act of repentance in the story of Joseph was for the brothers to tell the truth to their father and suffer the embarrassment of their evil deeds. Jacob, a repentant deceiver himself as revealed in the Scriptures (the meaning of his first name Jacob or "grabber"), had a choice to make himself. He, too, forgave his repentant sons of all their past deeds and deceptions. Sometimes we reap what we sow in this life, and sometimes we reap in the next life what we sow in this life. I personally would rather repent here in this life and not have to suffer eternally. To admit you have a hardened heart and a stubborn mind is not easy to confess. Once we do, God is faithful to soften our hearts, which leads to understanding all the other deep things of God.

The final story in the first book of the Torah tells us that the family of Jacob did relocate to Egypt and lived in the grandest part called Goshen located in the Delta Region of Lower Egypt. Joseph made a request of his descendants that he be buried in the Promised Land at Shechem. Approximately four hundred years later when Moses led the children of Abraham, Isaac, and Jacob to their Promised Land, Joseph's mummified remains were carried out of Egypt and throughout the desert wilderness for 40 years.

The Great Exodus happened the day after the first Passover, the death of the first-born males of Egypt. Those homes which had the blood of a lamb painted on their doorposts and lintels did not lose a firstborn male. Every detail in Scriptures is essential. There is a specific reason for these directions. Changing anything and calling it a tradition becomes a sin that is on the level of witchcraft, divination, or even the worship of the Evil One. When John the Baptist called Jesus the "Lamb of God" at the time of Jesus's baptism in the Jordan River, the metaphor had finally become a reality. It would be years before I would understand what I know today, but I have learned one thing that is important to comprehend: Yahweh is a patient God as long as a person is seeking to understand the world around him or her. Once a hardened heart is softened by Yahweh through our repentance to Him, then God's extraordinary revelations in the Scriptures open like a spring flower opens showing its glory.

CHAPTER ELEVEN

Sychar ~ Summer, fall, winter and the start of spring in Tiberius's 18th to 19th year of rule. Pontius Pilate's 6th to 7th year as Prefect of Judaea. The final months in Jesus of Nazareth's 4th and last year of his public ministry. (32-33 AD)

To know your Enemy, you must become your Enemy. Sun Tzu, Art of War

In Samaria during the summer until winter of Jesus of Nazareth's last year of public ministry, the weather went from hot to rainy and then to cold. Jesus was not as open to the public as the previous three years. During this period Jesus was exclusively teaching by parables. Those who were faithful understood the deeper meaning behind the stories, but for his enemies they only heard something that was entertaining. There were more controversial sabbath healings during this period, which turned the religious leadership of all Judaism against him. Jesus was always on the move and hard to find. He even disappeared from Galilee because the religious elites had now turned many of the common people against him. The adage "a prophet is not welcome in his own home" kept coming to mind. I believe I first heard this statement from Jesus's grandfather Eli when I visited Nazareth. The first time Jesus disappeared, he went north into Phoenicia, Decapolis, and dropped back south into Perea. It appeared from all the rumors that he and his few disciples always seemed to be slowly moving toward Judaea in a roundabout way.

Chapter Eleven

There were over 200 villages and towns for Jesus to visit in *Palestina* and not all of them turned him away.

Living at the home of Photina in Sychar was the opposite of what I had anticipated. While the days turned from hot to rainy and then to cold, it was really a blessed time. When this Ridge Road trip began, I thought I would be camping in and around the huge gimbal wagon. Instead, I found myself in a warm and dry place. This was beyond my expectations as I waited for spring to arrive. The only surprising drama or *fabula* we experienced was Amcheck, whom we thought might die due to his wounds sustained in the fight outside Bethel. For a while after we arrived at the villa, it looked like he was getting better; then he took a turn for the worse.

His condition came to an apex during the last days of summer on one rainy night. We were all worried because his bout with infection had returned. Euna came looking for me in the back of the villa at a late, dark hour. She found me in the stables where the horses were located, which was my hide just in case we were compromised and I could either defend my friends or escape if necessary. She had run from the house and was soaking wet in a borrowed powder-blue *palla* that reminded me of Messina. Underneath, her white *stola* of fine Indian cotton was also wet. I could see her shivering from the rain while she stood before me with her left hand cupped over the flame of the oil lamp in her right. Each of the five horses had its own individual stall, and there was plenty of hay to make their lives comfortable. The sixth and remaining stall served as my quarters; I had liberated one of the wagon's cots, which sat in the corner of the last stall on the left from the entrance. It was not as comfortable as a queen's feather bed but was a safe place to sleep, which was off the ground. On some moonless nights, Zeus kicked the boards in the next stall; but the boards never broke. I let him be when he was like this and tried to sleep through his kicking. It was one of those nights with Zeus busy kicking when Euna entered looking for me.

Euna, Nicodemus, and Amcheck had taken up residence in the sizeable and mysterious villa of Photina, each having their own private room. We later learned the townspeople only referred to this building as the home of the "woman at the well." I still felt responsible for the battle that occurred outside Bethel because I openly talked to the two ex-disciples of Jesus on the Ridge Road, which led these men to reveal our location to the ex-legionaries. Our lives were still in danger, and someone needed to be on guard. The *stabulare* or stables were perfect for this task. I told everyone I was in the stalls to keep an eye on the horses, a half-truth that was not questioned, since horse thievery was common but not normally from a walled villa. Samaritans did not have a problem with the riding of horses since they were not readers of the prophets or other histories of the Jews' Scriptures. On the day after asking Nicodemus concerning the question of why I never saw a Jew riding a horse, he quoted a passage from the prophet Hosea. "*Assyria will not save us, we will no longer ride on horses.*"

"What does that have to do with today?"

"You see, my young friend, Hosea paints a picture of repentance by saying a man who rides a horse develops a sense of superiority over other men. I also believe it has something to do with King Solomon breeding horses for chariots, and this among other iniquities led to his downfall. Therefore, one man's evil deeds cause horses to be hated by all Jews. And that started almost a thousand years ago. So sad."

"Cata, come quickly!" came the worried voice of Euna calling from the door of the *stabulare*. "It is Amcheck; I am afraid he is dying. We are going to lose him unless you know of some way to help him!" she cried shivering in her wet clothes. It was a wet, inky-dark night. I realized Euna had started calling me Cata because that was what Saben called me on top of Mount Gerizim. I believe Cata was more comfortable to say instead of the four-syllable word Ar-is-tar-chus. She never asked what Cata meant, and I never asked her for her real name. In the shadows of my stall, I tried to be gentle with her and told her I would come to the house shortly. She begged me to hurry, and I wondered what relationship had developed in the past few weeks while Euna was caring for Amcheck. Could it be she was becoming attracted to Amcheck, and he was as well toward her? She was a good fifteen years older than I, and Amcheck was closer in age to her. Maybe Amcheck had found his life's partner. I smiled at these thoughts as I buckled on my cuirass by habit and laced my boots in the dark. I stumbled around until I found a piece of wood in the harness room along with an armful of leather from some old harnesses. Finding the door, I ran toward the light in the house and found Nicodemus already awakened and standing in Amcheck's room; and, as soon as I entered, I detected an accusatory look.

"I told you those maggots were unclean, and now look at his wounds!"

I said nothing to Nicodemus; instead, I could smell the infection before I saw it. In some ways he was right, for the maggots did not ultimately do their job. Maybe I had closed up the wound too soon, or perhaps a missing worm had been left inside Amcheck when I sewed him up and it had rotted inside his injury. With the aid of an oil lamp, I looked at the first wound in his side where the ex-soldier's gladius had gone in below his last rib. The tip of the sword must have scraped the last rib bone, and the point of the sword

Chapter Eleven

had stopped at Amcheck's hipbone. The other wound was not as infected as the deeper one.

"I was afraid this was going to happen," I said as I looked at Nicodemus in the lamplight.

"Why do you think that?" questioned Nicodemus.

"Did Grillius have time to boil the horsehairs before he sewed up Amcheck after the skirmish at Bethel?"

"No! Why?" asked Nicodemus still acting flustered.

"That is what was unclean. Look where the infection is. All the redness starts and spreads out from the old stitches Grillius had first put in. You can easily see that the disease has spread from there into the wound. The maggots worked; but now we do not have time for that, or we will lose him. Besides, he is running a high fever as you can see; his bedding is all wet from sweat even though it is quite chilly outside." I placed my hand on Amcheck's forehead in the lamplight and noticed he was semi-conscious and moaning like a sick dog wanting to go out and do his business.

Looking toward Euna who had followed me into Amcheck's room, I ordered her to bring to the bedchamber a brazier with hot coals and several lamps for better light. Once the brazier was brought into this very spacious room, I could see Amcheck much better in his ornate, wood-framed bed. Turning away from him, I pulled my last iron throwing knife from my cuirass and placed it in the coals.

"What are you going to do?" asked Euna with worry in her eyes. Her face still had small scabs as did my forehead; but, as each day went by, I could see she was healing up nicely. She was a lovely woman to gaze at even though she was much older than I. When looking at her, I would never forget who had scarred her beautiful face. My evaluation of her appearance had changed since my first assessment when I saw her in the clothing of a man. After we arrived at Photina's villa, she never dressed in a man's tunic again; and I can say I did not see her sin anymore, which was true to her words. Her new look was beautiful. She had turned into a proper woman wearing costly garments that most likely belonged to Photina, which fit her as if they were her own. This night she had on a long, dry *stola* that she must have changed into since she came to me at the *stabulo*. She also had on a long head covering; her long, dark hair was falling out of the covering that hid part of her face. In a moment of time, she reminded me of my mother sitting on the stone bench in my father's garden before the fight with Claudia Pulchra that hot morning in Rome.

Gazing back at Amcheck, I spoke to Nicodemus. "We are going to need to open up this mess and re-stitch him after we clean his infected wounds."

Looking up toward Nicodemus, I did not ask; but with urgent authority I ordered him to go to the stalls with a lamp, get a dozen long horse-tail hairs, and boil them in water in the unattached kitchen. Nicodemus picked up a small palm light and left the room without making any more accusations.

With Nicodemus gone, Euna asked what I was going to do. I kindly stated we were going to try to save Amcheck's life. Amcheck, who was partially awake but barely, whispered, "Do not worry, my Little Kitten; Cata will not allow me to see the ferryman tonight." He then reached out and grabbed Euna's hand. "Do what Cata asks, and I will be better." She smiled at him confirming my suspicions of something developing between these two while I had been living in the stalls. I left them holding hands and took the longest leather straps I had carried in from the stables. I began to tie Amcheck's upper body to the bed frame. I then tied his hands and feet as snugly as I could without cutting off the blood circulation. I finally put into his mouth the wooden end of the broken hay rake I found in the stalls before I came to the house. I tied the two ends of the round wooden stick with a leather strap going behind his head. Now he had something to bite into instead of screaming and possibly biting off his tongue.

"What are you doing?" asked Euna. She seemed beside herself with concern for Amcheck. I told her I did not want him to wake the neighbors. I also asked if she could find a strip of cotton. "Bring it to me wet so I can tie down his tongue."

"Why?" she implored.

"Just do what I say; we do not have much time."

She obeyed; and, in a few minutes, I untied the stick in his mouth; tied the wet strip of cloth around his tongue; and looped the ends tightly under his chin. I replaced the rake handle in his mouth and again tied the two ends of the round wooden stick with the leather strap going behind his head. "The wet cloth will keep him from swallowing his tongue when he screams and passes out."

"Passes out? What are you going to do that will cause him to lose consciousness?"

"When someone is in excruciating pain, the body shuts down to protect itself. The person normally passes out and goes unconscious. When that happens, as you lie flat on your back, you can sometimes choke on your own tongue. We need to keep his airways open. I have never read about humans swallowing their tongue, but it can happen to a horse. Grooms at the Circus Maximus sometimes do the same thing with horse tongues before chariot races. You see, some horses try to spit out their snaffle bits and, in the process,

Chapter Eleven

can swallow their own tongues. I had witnessed horses spitting out their bits but I never saw a horse swalling their tongues. Perhaps this is a false legend. To save my friend, it would be best if he passed out and stayed motionless for the duration of what I have to do."

With the stick in his mouth, Amcheck said with muffled words. "Euna, do what he says; it is going to work. I trust him. He is very smart. He has read many medical books. I know he looks like a killer and was trained by that old Marauder Spartan, but he will not kill me tonight."

I pondered his words "not kill me tonight" as if he knew something that would cause me to want to kill him later. I noticed tears in Euna's eyes as she looked at Amcheck, and my unpleasant thoughts vanished. I left them alone for a moment to hunt for some rags to grab the handle of my iron knife that was still in the brazier. When I found what would work, I returned and saw that the blade of my knife was red as any berry I had ever seen in the springtime. "Well, my knife is as red as Vulcan's tongue; and it is time."

"What did you say?" asked Euna.

"I was just using a pagan metaphor. Everything is now ready." I rechecked the knife in the brazier, and the blade looked like the center of a volcano; and, if I left it in the fire any longer, the blade would lump off from the handle. After placing the rags around the handle, I told Euna to put a lamp near the wound but not on Amcheck. Nicodemus entered the bedchambers, and I asked him to hold Amcheck's head down from behind his bed. When everything was ready, I noticed Euna closed her eyes; and I went to work. Amcheck began screaming as he felt the heat from my knife cut open all the stitches. His screams were not loud but muffled by the wet cloth holding his tongue and the wood rake handle he was biting. In less than a minute, Amcheck went limp as I predicted; and he remained this way until I was done. After all the stitches had been cut, I pulled each one out with one hand after I returned the knife back into the brazier to turn red again. The pain of removing the stitches was nothing compared to what I was going to do next. I ordered Euna to help Nicodemus with the boiling of the tail hairs and to get them to me as soon as possible along with a large bone needle that I had given her earlier and asked for it also to be boiled. She did not want to leave Amcheck, but I gave her a look that caused her to obey my words.

When she was gone and I readjusted the lamps for better light, I took the fire-red knife out of the brazier again and began cutting out the rotten, putrid skin of the deep wound. The burning of pus and blood was overwhelming, and I tried to hold my breath to the best of my ability. The searing knife also burned the central blood vessels near the wound. Why Roman doctors bled patients when they were ill was a practice that made no sense to me. The room quickly stunk as the heat of my knife fried all the pus, skin, and blood near and in the wound. I raked out all the burnt refuse with the cooling blade. When the knife was red once again, I cleaned the second wound. Shortly after I had finished, I yelled for Euna and Nicodemus. When they both came in carrying a dozen long horse tail hairs in a clean bowl, I asked Nicodemus, "Did you boil the Hades out of them?"

"I did, but that does not make them holy hairs," said Nicodemus. This was the first time I had ever heard him make a joke. When I looked over at him, he was not smiling. His facial expression actually said the opposite. Euna held the large, curved white bone sewing needle in a clean cloth and I dismissed Nicodemus altogether. I decided to leave the room to find some water to wash my hands before I sewed up the wound. This was a practice from the land of the Hindu people I had once read about in a Gupta medical journal at the Lyceum. Grillius had also told me about this method when he was a mercenary around the Ganga River, where the Gupta-Hindu kingdoms still stood. The other major river in this land was called the Indus River. The word "Hindu" was an ancient Persian word for that river when the Persians controlled this region 500 years earlier. After the Indus people drove the Persians out of their land, the Persians continued to refer in their literature to the word Hindu. Therefore, since that time, these people on and beyond the Indus River have been called by the Persian word Hindus; and that is how all the people west of their land refer to them. The word Indra was once the name of an ancient pagan rain god. Today, from the Indus River to the Ganga River down to the Chola Kingdom live the Hindu people. This Gupta medical book, which I had read in Greek, had been brought to the Lyceum by orders of Alexander the Great for his personal *didace* Aristotle. Still, I had never seen a Roman or Greek physician wash before doing any medical procedure, and I stopped speculating on the cause of my own infection. That was when the back of my head had become infected after Herodias's physician performed surgery due to the wound Demos had inflicted on me at Nicodemus's front door in Jerusalem. Phoneinus, Herodias's Greek doctor, as good as he was, never washed his hands from what I remembered. When I asked Nicodemus to re-boil the needle after I returned with clean hands, he must have deduced that either he or Euna had touched it after it was boiled the first time. He smiled at me when he understood I was finally concerned about cleanliness.

We waited until Nicodemus returned with the needle cradled in a clean cloth. Euna carried in extra-hot water in a clay bowl. I tried to irrigate the charred holes of the two wounds with the hot water that I had mixed with some wine. Now, with clean hands, I took the needle and horsehairs and began sewing up two ugly wounds. About half an hour later, both injuries were closed up tightly. Amcheck did not feel any pain during any of this since he had remained unconscious. I said to both Nicodemus and Euna, "These are going to be two awful-looking scars, which I am sure Amcheck will not show many people." When I was finished, I announced, "These wounds should heal properly now, and I am going back to bed."

"Is Amcheck still alive?" asked Euna before I left. I nodded and told her she could untie him and take the cloth and wood out of his mouth before he woke up. I instructed her to let him drink all the wine and gall she could find after he wakes. "I am sure there is some gall in the house somewhere as Photina is a wealthy woman. If not, you will have to purchase some gall when the shops open in the morning." After we first arrived and Saben had left, I had given Euna and Nicodemus plenty of gold coins to pay for any expenses. When she asked where I got the money, I told her it was mine to give.

It was still raining when I walked back to the stables. I did not care if I got wet, for I was already soaked with my own sweat. The rainwater took away some of the smells that covered my body, and I just stood in the cold summer rain thanking Yahweh for His help. I had not prayed like this except on the Ridge Road after Euna tried to choke me with her leather loop. Of course, I should not forget the prayers when I was passing my stone. After I finished my prayer, I realized I was asking for help after the fact. Then I realized something profound. Since God was so powerful, I could pray now and He could answer the prayer in the past thinking He knew what I was going to pray for in the future. I know this sounds strange, but that was what I was thinking while taking a shower in the rain and praying at the same time. I also realized I had not actually lost all my faith in this God of the Jews. Apparently, the simple faith I had when I submitted to circumcision was still present within me. I guess I had always believed since my baptism in the Tiber that Yahweh was the one true God. I think it was John the Baptist who taught me who God really is – a Creator who categorically cares about us humans more than we actually care about ourselves.

Jesus, on the other hand, terrified and perplexed me. I did not understand what Jesus meant when he said we are to love our neighbor as we love ourselves. Jesus knew the heart of us humans very precisely. We all have self-love that makes us selfish most of the time. It is this self-love that also makes cowards out of us. Only when we put others ahead of our needs do we have a chance of being courageous. Standing in the rain was like standing in the Garden of Eden talking to the Creator. The presence of the one who allows the rain seemed so present. When the rain changed to a drizzle, I wondered if it were possible for the Creator to enter time as Nicodemus had previously explained to me. He was convinced that the Scriptures alluded to this and the future was also written about. No other book or scroll I had ever read or seen talked about the future as did the Scriptures. Even beyond this idea, the Hebrew Scrolls read as if everything has already happened and we humans are living out that future in the present; yet, while we live in the present, we never lose our freedom to choose. God not only knows what we were before the creation of time; but He will judge each one of us at the end of this age based on our words, works, and thoughts. I started to shiver when my mind contemplated this weighty subject of "freedom of choice and God's providence." How amazing is this? This concept alone makes the Jewish Scriptures the utmost immutable and matchless writings in the world. To have this freedom requires faith in the Creator, who gives equally to each human who believes. Besides, if we could not choose, how could the Creator judge anyone at the end of time? Therefore, life is what we do moment by moment; and this determines our eternity. I could learn knowledge but where did wisdom come into the picture. I found myself asking for wisdom since I seemed to lack in this area. Maybe now I would stop uttering everything that comes to mind and instead speak appropriately at the proper time.

I looked up into the dark, gloomy heavens; and my mind turned to the quandary of the sin nature as transmitted by Adam's first sin and passed along to all the children of Adam. The Dragon in the Garden of Eden deceived Eve but not Adam, who had been a witness to all that occurred between the Dragon and Eve. Adam apparently chose to disobey the words of God and ate the forbidden fruit in order to remain with the woman whom God had made from Adam's rib. She had been tricked or deceived in her disobedience against the one law of the Creator but not Adam. Therefore, his open sin was far more significant over Eve's deception. Adam was guilty of worshipping the creature and not the Creator. This idolatry seems to be a significant problem with most humans, along with all the other forms of idol worship.

Let us consider a male child being born today without the curse through Adam. Take, for instance, the claim that Jesus of Nazareth is the promised, virgin born Redeemer. Therefore, the Son of God would have to be virgin born to be the Son of Man and in an unfallen state in this world. Would that not make Jesus a sinless human? Add to that the idea of being conceived by God's Spirit through a human woman. Could Yahweh Himself be born and now living in the body of a physical man? Jesus's mother had confessed to me on the Mount of Olives that Jesus was a miracle-birth child, and she did not

Chapter Eleven

seem to be telling a lie. The mother of Jesus had decades to ponder this concept; and, still, she developed a spot of uncertainty regarding her eldest son when she thought he had lost his own senses a year ago. Yet, her own father Eli, or Heli, knew she would return to her original faith roots; and this, too, was beyond understanding. When I spoke with her on the Mount of Olives, she seemed to have returned like her father had predicted.

Now comes the most sobering question of all: if the mother of Jesus lost faith in who her son was, what hope was there for the rest of mankind? When I spoke to her just a few months earlier, it was evident to me she had repented of that misgiving and passionately wanted me to understand the true nature of Jesus. Messina had also become angry with me on that day when I turned the tables on Jesus's mother about her own reservations just a year earlier. Yet, on that sunny morning on the Mount of Olives, Jesus's mother was solidly set concerning the identity of Jesus by showing me she had repented. Perhaps she had been a prodigal daughter.

Consequently, my question is very straightforward. If the mother of Jesus stumbled at this marvelous work of God, what would the rest of humankind do when this concept was presented to the minds and hearts of those who did not have the experience she had? The only conclusion was that it was up to God Himself to draw someone to Him and not the other way around. Even hundreds of years in the past when the prophet Isaiah called this virgin born child *Immanuel*, meaning God with us, what will happen if the Jewish scholars and leaders hear Jesus himself openly claim to be *Immanuel*? Will they understand what was written as an explicit prophecy, which all Jews accept as inspired by Yahweh's Spirit? Undoubtedly, the Scriptures declare God will walk among us mere humans. Once again, I ask, "What will the Jewish leaders do when this fact is revealed?" I have a good idea what the Gentiles will do; but, for those who have God's Word and have read it, what a tragedy that will ensue if they refuse to believe. What would be the outcome of such a sin by the chosen ones of God? I can only see the destruction of this evil generation along with Rome's pseudo-empire, both built on the foundation of shedding blood. It was enough to make a man, especially a warrior-stoic like Grillius, weep.

The Scriptures, however, do reveal in the prophecies of Ezekiel that the chosen ones will be removed from their land and will return in the far future. The Spirit of God had the prophet Ezekiel write about the distant future where the Promised Land was a valley of dead bones. Then God tells Ezekiel these bones will in the far future be given physical and spiritual life. God explains that these dead bones will come alive and that they become the whole house of Israel. The Spirit of God will fill them and take away what was cut off from them after bringing them back to the land of Israel from the far reaches of all lands. God explicitly says there will no longer be two nations but one. They shall be God's people, and Yahweh will be their God. The hope that was lost will be rekindled and will be found by a new nation of Israel in the future. All of this will happen, but not until there is repentance.

John the Baptist, when he was in Herod's prison, had also doubted whether Jesus was the Promised One; so why couldn't Jesus's mother enter into doubt? It would have been suspicious had she and John never doubted. Both were fallen humans unlike a virgin born child without Adam's sin. As I stood in the wet drizzle, I tried to close down my thoughts as I began to shake with all these revelations spinning through my mind and spirit. Had God's wisdom come upon me, and could it happen this quickly after I had asked? Having no answer, I returned to the stables, where I dried myself with a horse towel before I lay down on my cot wearing a dry tunic. I closed my eyes and willed myself to fall fast asleep.

It was late the next day when Euna awakened me with a kiss on my cheek and thanked me for saving Amcheck. She said she did what I had commanded about the wine and gall. She commented that even Nicodemus was now singing praises to Yahweh and that he included my name in those praises. I asked her what food she had in the kitchen. After a long list had been recited, I said I would be in the house shortly to eat. She smiled and told me to be in the house in about an hour.

For the rest of that summer into the cold and wet winter, Amcheck slowly recovered; but I noticed he would always walk with a noticeable limp. I hoped his wounds only injured his flesh. I have seen over many years men who have been severely wounded by arrows, spears, or swords. Long after these wounds were healed, strange anger replaced a pleasant disposition that hadn't been present before the injury. My conclusion was bitterness sometimes enters the heart of a kind, gentle soul after a great trauma; kindness and gentleness are replaced by something dark and evil. Perhaps the person realizes he will never be the same and allows the pain to never leave but to control. Amcheck became more pleasant after his recovery; and I understood it to be because of the growing relationship with Euna. She and Amcheck would spend many hours together talking and laughing while I spent my morning hours walking the horses in a circular circuit inside the walled yard. Afterward, Nicodemus schooled me with the Greek Scriptures he purchased on that momentous day in Bethel.

Chapter Eleven

Nicodemus was an excellent teacher; and I, the dutiful student. I allowed Nicodemus to explain the complete history of his people and the history of the Scriptures. We started with Adam and went up to the time the Jews returned from Babylon to rebuild the Temple that had been destroyed by Nebuchadnezzar. I did not want to study Job, or Iob, nor the Psalms. I still had the first 33 books of songs that were given to me by Rabbi Issachar, but they remained in my hidden hole in Jerusalem. When the time was right, I would take a long look at all 150 Psalms and Job; but now I was not ready.

Besides learning of the history of the Jews, I desperately wanted two good throwing knives. After the operation on Amcheck, the heat did something to the balance of my remaining iron blade. I tried reheating it and beating on it, sticking it in water, and repeating the process; but the knife just was never the same again. A few weeks after Amcheck's operation I came upon a plan. I found some bronze nails, a few old bronze snaffle bits, and other pieces of bronze in the horse stables and workshop. I decided that, if I put my mind to it, I could make two good bronze throwing knives. I used a block of wax that Euna had in the house and spent hours forming what I wanted in wax. I then vented the wax knives with thin wax tubes to provide air holes. Next, I mixed plaster and created a cast around the wax with an air vent on top along with a pour hole. About a week later when the plaster shell was hard, I placed it over a warm, burning fire and melted the wax out of the mold. Inside the workshop that stood next to the horse barn, I discovered a stone crucible. I placed all the bronze items inside of the crucible and used the metal shop blast furnace to melt the bronze items into a glowing gold-color liquid. The discovery of the metal shop next to the stables was unbelievable. I next buried the plaster mold into a sand pit next to the shop, and with Nicodemus's help I poured the molten bronze into the plaster mold pour hole. A few hours later I pulled the mold out of the sand pit. With an iron hammer, I broke the plaster off the bronze, even while it was still steaming. It took days to cut away the metal air vents and polish and sharpen the two bronze knives. Both were identical to each other; and, as throwing knives, they rivaled the two I once had when I left Athens.

After practicing for days, I found Nicodemus and told him I was ready to study with him if he wouldn't mind. This time we left the history of the Jews and started going through the prophets. When we reached the seer Malachi, my questions concerning the return of Elijah before the coming of the Messiah resurfaced. I asked Nicodemus, "Can you now tell me about Elijah and John the Baptist being Elijah?"

"I believe it is time to chip away at your question," stated Nicodemus. From this day forward, I never used his name Batana again. Maybe this was my way of disobeying Amcheck as our leader, or maybe it was not necessary to hide our identities while we were at Photina's home. Nicodemus moved around in a wooden chair to make himself comfortable but I believed he was just hunting for a place to begin. When a smile came to him and he settled down, I knew he found his starting point. "To start, Elijah's and John the Baptist's lives have many parallels," explained Nicodemus. "Now remember there are many ways to interpret the Scriptures; yet, there is only one correct interpretation to any passage. Once you understand the correct interpretation, then you will have proper applications and principles. Wrong interpretations divide Judaism into all the many sects that exist today. For instance, the issue of the Essenes who divide over the dates of the festivals that Moses gave in the Torah is just one significant disagreement. I am not saying they are wrong; but we should look with an open mind to what God, the author, is telling us. Therefore, we must know the author. If I were to write a letter to you, since you know me, there would not be any problem understanding what I might be saying to you. The Scriptures are like that – messages from God to whoever wants to be his children."

"How does someone know he has the correct interpretation?" I asked with my heart on fire realizing I was finally going to receive some of the deep knowledge that Nicodemus possessed.

"That is the issue. I foolishly interpreted the Scriptures one way until I met Yeshua one dark night. Knowing him personally changed the way I viewed everything. He had given out one little diamond publicly in the Temple at Solomon's Porch to many religious leaders and groups listening; yet, many threw it away as if it were a chip of glass. He had said, 'You search the Scriptures for eternal life, but the Scriptures only speak of me.' That became the key to understanding the Scriptures. Read; and have faith that the Scriptures are talking about the Messiah, whom Jesus claims to be."

Nicodemus told me that, during the days I was working on casting my daggers, he had spoken to many people here and there, in Sychar; and they told him Jesus several years previously openly confessed to the woman who owned this villa that he was the promised Messiah. "Jesus came to this city a few years back and rested just outside at Jacob's well after he had sent his disciples into Sychar to purchase supplies. Jesus remained at the well with his youngest pupil, that being the one named John. The other disciples did as their master asked; and, while Jesus was at the well, Photina, the mistress of this house came to fetch water. It was in the middle of the day and, obviously, not the standard time women came to the well. You see her peers did not respect her because she had been the wife of five men and was living at that time with a man who was not her husband. This beautiful home had become her personal property after one of the five husbands had passed away."

"So she was not a respectable woman, even according to Samaritan standards."

"Just because a Samaritan is part Jewish and part Assyrian, that does not mean they do not hold to the Law of Moses. Even the Barbarians live by a set of values, morals, and ethics. But we must return to the well and day when Jesus spoke to Photina."

Just as Nicodemus was about to continue this story, Euna appeared at the door and asked if she could join our study. Nicodemus, being the gracious man that he was, agreed. She seemed happy to come into our study room and listen. I pulled up a tall stool for her to sit next to me. After she was settled at our Scripture table, Nicodemus picked up where he left off. "What I learned was this story happened only a few years ago. Jesus asked Photina to give him some water. She was surprised a Jew was even traveling in Samaria; and men never addressed strange woman in public, especially when they are unaccompanied. There are many customs or practices that Jesus violated that caused many to reject him as a prophet, let alone the Messiah. But remember that most customs are man-made behaviors. Yet, when Photina was told by Jesus to go get her husband, she said, 'I do not have one.' Jesus then said, 'You spoke the truth. You have had five, and the one you now live with is not your husband.' She perceived only a prophet would know such intimate details of her life. When she spoke of the coming Messiah, Jesus stated to her that he was that person. She then ran leaving her water pitcher and told the town about the prophet at the well who told her he was the promised Messiah. The people of this city came to hear Jesus speak. Afterward, they implored Jesus and his disciples to stay and teach them more. He stayed for two days speaking and healing the sick. Jesus is still respected by many in this town, not like what is happening up in Galilee and to the south in Judaea, where the Jews are losing their faith and are taking the kingdom of God by force. What this means is there is a real danger someone will try to kill Jesus. The sad truth is, if this happens, they will think they are doing God's bidding."

"Tell me about Elijah and John the Baptist," I asked once again thinking we had gone off subject.

Nicodemus just smiled at me and for a long time looked skyward searching for a new starting point. When his eyes twinkled and when I noticed a slight smile, I knew he was ready. This reminded me of dangling a fishing line and waiting for a strike. The last time this happened was in Nazareth with Eli, the father of Miriam, Jesus's mother. "To start, one must look at the similarities. John and Elijah both came from obscurity. They were country boys from nowhere important, and both did some of their work for Yahweh down near the Jordan River. Elijah verbally attacked Jezebel, the queen of King Ahab, and almost lost his life to her wiles. John the Baptist verbally attacked Herodias, the queen of Herod Antipas, and did lose his life to her wiles. Both men had spiritual doubts at the time they should have had their greatest faith. Elijah defeated the Baal worshipers upon Mount Carmel, and John had hundreds come to the Jordan River to be baptized unto repentance to identify with the movement that was calling for reform because many had grown sick of the ritualistic Temple system in Jerusalem. Today, many ordinary Jews believe the traditions in Jerusalem can be compared with paganism, causing them to participate in Temple activities without any heart. As King Solomon said, 'there is nothing new under the sun,' and so Elijah confronted paganism in his day of Baal worship. After killing all the Baal prophets, Elijah ran from Queen Jezebel and ended up on Mount Horeb where Moses received the Ten Commandments. It was there that Elijah told Yahweh he was the only one of His prophets left and everyone wanted to kill him. Remember we are talking about a man to whom Yahweh gave the power to call fire out of heaven to burn up his sacrifice at Mount Carmel. He also could call down fire from heaven and destroy his enemies, which he did twice to King Ahab's captains and troops of 50 men who were trying to arrest him. John the Baptist, similar to Elijah's lapse of faith, while lingering in a stinking pit at Machaerus, sent some of his disciples to Jesus to ask if he were truly the promised Redeemer-Messiah. When his followers returned, they told John, 'Yes, because of the miracles of Jesus, He is the Messiah.' Doing miracles was one of the signs of the coming Messiah as stated by several prophets in the Scriptures. I would guess that the reason you want to know about Elijah is perhaps due to what you read from Malachi, the last prophet to write in the Scriptures."

I nodded my head yes.

Looking now at Euna, Nicodemus said, "You see my dear, Malachi said the greatest sign of the coming Messiah was that the Lord himself, not just the Messiah, would come to His earthly Temple and cleanse it of its wickedness. Jesus-Yeshua did that three and a half years ago on a Passover. He came and turned over the tables of the moneychangers and those selling sacrificial animals in the Court of Gentiles. This was the start of Yeshua's public ministry. Everyone who has read Malachi should have understood what Yeshua was doing and who He is. I must confess at the time I even missed it. I was angry with Yeshua, falsely thinking he disturbed the Temple activities during the busiest time on the liturgical calendar for his own glory. Yet, it was precisely the sign that Malachi prophesied would happen."

While Nicodemus talked about the Temple money business, I remembered when I first visited the Temple. I could not shake my feelings of the Sadducees, Pharisees, scribes, and lawyers and all their hypocrisy and pretentiousness. It was disheartening to me that all the corruption I witnessed had returned to the Temple shortly after Jesus had cleansed it and rebuked the Levites, just like the prophet Malachi said would happen. Why did they return to business as usual so soon after Jesus had turned their tables? That was a sure sign that the leadership in Jerusalem suffered collectively from a stony heart. Even Nicodemus confessed he was once within that hard-hearted group as a proud Pharisee.

"Yet, Elijah has to come first," continued Nicodemus not knowing what I was thinking. "Jesus as the Messiah must fulfill the prophecy of Malachi, yet Elijah must come first. John would have assumed that role had the people accepted Jesus at the start. However, due to the people's collective rejection of Jesus as the Messiah, the death of John was inevitable. I have been told that Jesus now says Elijah will still come; but it will be the real Elijah, who never died, and not John, who did die. On the other hand, maybe he will be another Elijah, like John the Baptist. When you think you know the future, you do not. That is how God works. Why? I do not know, but it does humble those of us who study the Scriptures about the future."

"What do you think will happen?" asked Euna still in the room listening. She had been so quiet I almost forgot she was with us.

"I believe that the Messiah is going to be rejected as we read in the scroll by Isaiah, where Isaiah states that someone will take upon himself our infirmities and will die a horrible death. I believe Jesus knows this will happen at the next Passover as I am sure we will witness this great tragedy. It was said just yesterday in the marketplace here in Sychar that Jesus told his disciples that he will go to Jerusalem and be tried by the Sanhedrin and be put to death by the Romans. Remember last Passover?" asked Nicodemus looking at me. I nodded, and he continued. "Jesus gave the parable of the fig tree. Afterward, I wanted to retake you to my study and show you the book of Leviticus. I still feel horrible I chased you away to almost death at my doorway. I am a foolish man at times."

"You are forgiven," I said trying to be gentle with this old man.

"That means a great deal to me, my young student. Here is what I was going to show you on that day in my study. We look at the third book of the

Torah where it says, when the Children of Jacob come into the Holy Land and plant all kind of trees for food, then they shall count the fruit as forbidden. The people are not to eat any of the fruit on the trees for three years. In the fourth year, the people still are not to eat of the fruit because all the fruit will be holy. The fruit will be holy only during the fourth year but not for consumption. Finally, during the fifth year, the people can then begin to eat from the fruit trees. It is straightforward if you use the code. Yeshua-Jesus is the real fruit tree, or better said, Yeshua is the Tree of Life. Yes, he is the Tree of Life that was in the Garden of Eden. He has been teaching and doing miracles for over three years; yet, the House of Israel, as prophesied, has rejected him as their long-awaited Messiah. Most of his disciples are abandoning him like the two we spoke to on the road outside of Bethel. Why? It is straightforward. This is the fourth year, and we still cannot eat of the fruit tree. You see, this is the holy year, the year of offering. After it is over, then we will be able to partake of the Tree of Life. I believe Yeshua-Jesus will go to Jerusalem at the end of the fourth year as he told me when we met him on the Mount of Olives a week before Passover. This is the fourth year. This is the holy year because of what is going to happen in Jerusalem after Yeshua-Jesus returns to the Temple. I believe the Scriptures are correct, and Jesus will be rejected and killed by the Jews and the Gentiles this coming Passover."

"What are you talking about?" uttered Euna looking disturbed. Her eyes were bulging, and her hands were grasping the table as if it were going to fly up through the ceiling.

"Aristarchus and I were witnesses to Yeshua's entrance to Jerusalem before last Passover. However, he never entered the city; but he did ask me to bury him."

"Bury whom? Jesus or Cata?"

"Jesus was talking about himself. He knows the future because he is God. He will die upon some kind of tree just as Moses used a wooden pole to lift up the bronze serpent in the wilderness."

"Do not the Romans use trees to crucify Rome's enemies?" asked Euna still gripping the edge of the table.

"Perhaps you are right. Jesus the Messiah will die just as King David said in the Psalms – naked, with his clothes being gambled for, dogs barking, and his hands and feet pierced. It has all been foretold. However, the good news is he will not stay dead even though he asked me to bury him. The Scriptures are very clear: the son of David will not decompose or rot in his tomb. King David rotted in his tomb; all the other kings of Judah did as well. Most of Judah's good kings are still buried together in that horseshoe tome down in the Valley of Decision, east of Mount Zion. It is important to understand that Jesus is in the line of Judah, the line of David, and is David's son by his mother's genealogical side and even on Joseph's line, his adopted father, the stonemason of Nazareth."

Euna was beside herself. She looked like she wanted to cry and scream at the same time. "What are you saying? Are you talking about Jesus being crucified by the Romans?"

Nicodemus apparently did not understand Euna's emotional state, and he continued. "Jesus is going to be crucified. I am sorry, but that is the only way to interpret the Scriptures regarding the Messiah. Jesus told Cata at the Temple that he was the Christ. He told the woman at the well here in Sychar he was the Messiah, and I believe all those claims."

"Jesus is going to be killed by the Romans on a tree?" she cried. "That means he is going to be crucified as some kind of criminal. Why would he allow this if he is who you say he is?" questioned Euna looking like she wanted to run away and cry.

"If Israel were to have a revolution and overthrow the Romans, it would not be Herod Antipas who would be the rightful king of the Jews; it would be Yeshua or Jesus because he is the *descendens* as the Latin says. He is the eldest ancestor through Joseph and Mariam coming through King David. Jesus is the real biological owner of the throne of the King of the Jews. That is why Herod has our Aristarchus and me looking for him. Herod wants to kill Yeshua as Herod's father tried killing Yeshua almost 40 years ago in Bethlehem. However, Herod will not kill him; but the Romans will. Most likely his death will be by crucifixion if the Scriptures are to be accepted as the Word of God. The Romans are the only people today who have the authority to kill any Jew, and they use crucifixion on non-citizens in their Empire. To me, this seems very clear. Jesus, as the Romans call him, will be put to death on a *xulon* or tree. Are not Roman crosses made of trees?"

"Euna, Nicodemus might be wrong," I said trying to calm her. "No one knows until it happens." I began to wonder why she felt this strongly about Jesus. It was as if she knew Jesus personally and he was her good friend. Then I remembered, she did meet Jesus in Jerusalem; and he did forgive her when she should have been stoned to death. This apparently had left a profound impression on her as it should.

"Euna," said Nicodemus. "Jesus talked to me for the first time about three years ago, a few days after the cleansing of the Temple. I met him one dark night at the Garden of Gethsemane on the Mount of Olives. You see, I perceived that he was a prophet sent by God. Yet, I was a coward. I went at night so that my colleagues would not see me talking to him. But I wanted to know how I could get into the kingdom of God. He told me how without my even asking. Can you believe that? Only Yahweh can read minds; and Jesus said that, unless the Son of man is lifted up as Moses lifted up the serpent, no one could have eternal life. We all are separated from Yahweh because of the sin of Adam along with our own sins. Yahweh loves the world and all He has created. He decided at some point to become a snake or sin and lifted on a tree. Moses raised the bronze serpent on a wooden pole in the wilderness after thousands of poisonous snakes in the Desert of Sin attacked the complaining Israelites. This is not a myth as the Sadducees, scribes, or even some Essenes would want you to believe. The Sadducees, who control the priesthood and the Temple, do not even believe in the resurrection of the dead. What a confused and evil world we live in," stated Nicodemus stepping away from the table and placing his hands on his head.

Here was an old man with his hands on his head, and Euna had hers covering her open mouth. I could see she now heard words that made sense, and she wanted to hear more but if she did she looked like she would die. I stood watching her until a strange peace came over her; and I thought of the psalm that said, even if we travel through the valley of death, God will be with us.

Just as Euna dropped her hands, Nicodemus regathered himself and said, "Now listen carefully, Aristarchus, and you as well, Euna. Whoever controls the information controls the future. Satan, the evil leader of the fallen host of the third heaven who can interfere with us here in the first heaven, wants to distort God's truth at every corner and byway. The Sadducees control a great deal of the ways their students are educated at the Temple schools. Jesus said their father was the devil, and that says it all. These students at the Temple schools are going to infect future generations with lies, and those lies will grow like leaven in bread. It looks like a world without hope except for us."

I raised my hand as I did at the Lyceum. I would do this only to slow a lecturer so I could think longer upon his words. Not only did I need to stop Nicodemus but I needed to make one comment. Nicodemus nodded for me to speak; and I first reached for a clay cup of watered wine but pulled back empty-handed because I realized I was not hungry for physical food or drink. "I believe I understand thoroughly; and, if I learned one thing from my adopted father Hector in Athens, it was to question everything. This way I would cover all the angles on a particular subject, but it was something I had to do for myself even if a teacher's thesis sounded solid and convincing. My father Hector always said, 'Do not put your mind on a shelf and accept what someone says no matter what title he holds or how old he is.'"

"I would like to meet Hector and his new friend, this uncle of your deceased friend Eli. His name was Anab if I remember correctly."

I nodded in affirmation to his response feeling pleased with Nicodemus as not an arrogant man who only listened to himself. He just showed me what my mother was trying to say on the day she died: "Think of others as more important than yourself." Nicodemus was one of those few men who listened and remembered little details about someone else. I realized I was a selfish young man and had miles to travel before I could be what my mother wanted.

Nicodemus now looked like a young man on a raft in a swift river. His eyes were twinkling with delight as his thoughts were rushing him along at a speed only he could appreciate. Euna and I both looked at each other as if we knew Nicodemus's words were going to be like a blur once he started talking. I loved listening to whatever he wanted to say about the Scriptures and Jesus, but this was almost like sitting at the feet of the King of the Universe telling a child what life was all about and why. I pointed to the tall chairs and we all returned to the table located in the center of the lovely *tablinum*, which served as our study room.

"Well, let's take King David's first son who was given to him by the wife of Uriah, the Hittite. When his attendants were worried that David would harm himself when they told him his son died, David surprised everyone moments after the child's death by saying he, King David, would join his son in the next world. Even Job, the book you do not want to read right now, Aristarchus, ends with Job receiving a double portion of everything he lost after he repented in dust and ashes or in Latin, he sat in the *cinis*. If we now look at a small detail, it will reveal a great mystery. You count all the livestock numbered at the end of Job, and all the figures are increased by two from what he lost to Satan's attacks at the beginning of the story. However, let's look at what happened to Job's lost children. Job had only 10 children returned to him after his trial, which is the same number of children he had before his trial. You might ask, how is that being doubled? He lost 10 children at the start and only received the same number at the end of the story. Yet, if he had 10 camels that were killed at the start, he received 20 at the end. Why did Job receive only 10 children at the end of the story and not 20? Well, the mystery is answered in the resurrection."

"The answer is the resurrection?" I asked in a bewildered tone.

"Precisely. You see, all of Job's children will be resurrected from the dead on the day of resurrection; and then Job will have 20 children or double what he started with who will go with him into eternity. Yahweh does not hide the truth in His Scriptures for anyone with eyes to see. The prophet Daniel at the end of his book tells us we will sleep and then we will rise from the dead. What a glorious promise! We were not created just to live a few bad years in this corrupt world and then go into oblivion. God loves us and wants us to be with Him for eternity. We were all created in His image for fellowship with Him, who placed all the stars in the second heaven and everything else that our eyes see, noses smell, ears hear, and fingers touch. Above all of this is our ability to think and discuss the past, present, and the future. No other animal we know can do that. It seems to me all animals only live in the present. That is not the situation with us humans. We worry about the future, dread over the past, and strive in the present. This is not what God wants us to do, but we do anyway. He wants us to believe He exists and to obey Him. It is all quite simple; and, yet, extremely hard to accomplish in our own power. Sometimes the truth is so simple that it is hard to see. The Sadducees are filled with heresy when they teach that there is no resurrection of the dead. Faith in the Scriptures is the only way a man can have true wisdom. I always told my students: 'Facts plus faith equals knowledge. But correct facts combined with correct faith equals truth.' What do we humans want – knowledge or truth?"

Nicodemus loved to pose his own questions so he could answer them himself. Both Euna and I remained still and patiently waited for his response. I loved this type of teaching, not the way Zeno taught where you had your hands beat if you did not respond quickly enough. This way I could relax and listen while I processed the information. Sure enough, Nicodemus came forth with his conclusion and analysis of his own question. "The answer is what Adam and Eve wanted when they ate from the Tree of Knowledge of Good and Evil because that is what we would have done if we had been in their place at the start of life. The answer is always knowledge, but knowledge will never save you; only truth will save anyone. Truth is the door to eternal life, not knowledge. Knowing where the door is will not get you through it; only truth will provide entrance into the realm of eternal life. What Yahweh is doing and telling all of us is the truth. That truth is as fantastic as it is simple. Yeshua is Yahweh. To say it plainly, Jesus is God walking in the flesh among us, just like the prophet Isaiah said would happen. If Yeshua walked on water, then Yeshua can walk us through that eternal gate. Do we Jews accept the truth of the Scriptures? Not really. We humans know for a moment; then we doubt what we know. To know and believe are two different arenas. A gladiatorial game or a chariot race at a circus both provide entertainment; but, clearly, both are two separate types of venues of entertainment. The religious leaders and the people look for guidance but reject Jesus for who he really is. They are only looking at the many prophecies saying the Messiah will be a king.

Yeshua-Jesus will not be accepted by anyone this last year as the promised king. No, not one. Why? Because he does not fit our human expectations of a worldly king. If anyone wants him as a king, it is only as a bread-king. Yeshua has said as much. We must love our enemies and pray for those who misuse us. The Zealots have rejected Yeshua as a king because they know Yeshua will not kill all the Romans and throw them out of the land given to Abraham. Remember Yahweh's land has always been the property granted to Abraham, who gave it to Isaac, who gave it to Jacob, who is the real owner of this physical land, including Samaria, where we are now as we sit in this mystery villa. If you do not believe me, tell me who is buried next to this house; and you have your answer."

"Joseph the patriarch, of course," I answered trying to remember all that Nicodemus was saying and letting him know I was listening to his mostly rhetorical form of teaching. Zeno, as well as the teachers of the Lyceum, had drilled into me to respect an elder. All learning techniques were universal. Even the teachings of Siddhartha, or the Buddha as he was called, used rhetorical questions and storytelling from the little I could gather from the *Pali* and *Sanskrit* texts that had been translated into Greek. One of his illustrations was "Life was like a raft crossing over and not to carry once you reached the other side. One must leave the raft after crossing for someone else going the other way."

Euna surprised both Nicodemus and me when she said, "Yes, it is Joseph the patriarch. Of course, Joseph the son of Jacob!"

"You both are correct!" exclaimed Nicodemus. "The only piece of property purchased by Jacob was given to Joseph. David was an adulterer, murderer, liar, and thief. He broke perhaps all the Ten Commandments with his affair with the woman Bathsheba; yet, King David was a man after Yahweh's own heart. Now I am not saying patriarch Joseph, Enoch, or even the prophet Daniel were sinless; the Scriptures are just silent about their sins. However, come to think of it, Joseph may have been involved in pagan practices with his cup of divination he had put in Benjamin's sack on the brothers' second visit to Egypt. Having a cup of divination is a sin, so there you have it. Even Joseph was a sinner, something I missed all these years until now."

It was fun watching Nicodemus teaching Euna, me, and even himself. He loved the Word of God and accepted every inch of all the scrolls we purchased for only eight *denarii*, plus one for the bag. Since Nicodemus knew Hebrew, I was confident he was careful when reading a translation in Greek that was somewhat different from the common Greek, even used today. I noticed Euna was very agitated with all she was hearing, but she was also excited when she answered correctly about Joseph. I asked her if she understood all that Nicodemus was saying.

"Understand? 'Drink this water, and you will never thirst again.' Do you know what that means?"

"Not really," I confessed.

"Well, I understand; and that is why I sit here. If I were to leave this table, I would lose my mind and perhaps eternal life." She again stepped away from the table with her hands to her mouth. I looked over at the walls and noticed all the Roman-style reclining couches. Nicodemus must have pushed them all against the walls. The long eating table in the center now looked like a high *scriptorium* desk. When I was looking at the tall eating beds pushed up against the walls, Euna unexpectedly ran from the room.

"Her actions are contradicting what she just uttered," I remarked in astonishment.

"Something caused her to leave but what, I am not sure," said Nicodemus; yet, her behavior did not bother the old teacher as he seemed to dismiss her action as something to be expected out of women. He just looked at me and asked if I wanted him to continue.

There was a part of me that wanted to go and comfort Euna, but I just didn't. "Of course, I want to hear more," I finally declared. I did want to hear more, even though I honestly would not understand what Nicodemus was saying for many years. Today, sitting in Rome dictating this story, I still wonder why I didn't go and try to help Euna. Had I gone to her there was a good chance the future would have unfolded differently. Knowing what I know today, I am sure things would have happened differently, but either way, I should have been thinking of her over myself.

Staying with Nicodemus, he assumed all was well and just picked up where he had ended. "We shall return to Enoch. You remember he never died because he was a righteous man, but the Scriptures never said he did not sin. Do you understand all that I just said?"

"I think I am satisfied with your explanations, but it will perhaps take time and maybe years to truly understand all that you are trying to tell me. All I know is I am lost spiritually; and I need salvation, which only Yahweh can provide. I cannot do anything on my own, and the Law alone will not save anyone. I believe Yahweh gave Moses the Law to define sin, not as a means of salvation. Without the definition of sin, we will never know what is evil and wrong with us. However, I see the Law as evil in a strange way because it is entirely contrary to what is proper behavior for us humans. You know, do not do this; do not do that. Yet, before we can repent, we need to know what sin is; and sin is harmful, and that is why the Law is negative. Does not the Law teach us we are all sinners? Yes. Yet, why do the Pharisees, Sadducees, lawyers, and scribes reject Jesus and want him dead, other than he convicts them of their sins and hypocrisy? He is not breaking any laws that I can see – only their interpretation of the Laws of Moses that they have defined incorrectly. The way it appears to me is they have made the Laws of God into an idol above the Creator. They have turned Moses and the Law into God. Am I not right, is not Moses a god to many Jews? Maybe that is why God Himself buried Moses so no one would know where his grave was, to keep people from worshipping his dead body as some people do to Joseph just outside these doors of this pink villa."

"That is correct. I have witnessed people bowing down at his tomb; and it appears they are praying to a dead man," said Nicodemus with a slight smile.

"I know they deny that they are worshipping Joseph; but, if Moses's body was next door, well what would be going on with most religious leaders, along with most of the common people? Now I understand why I carry this scar under my left eye. I did not bow to Moses's representative, High Priest Caiaphas. Tell me if I am correct in what I just said?"

"Your understanding is beyond your years, especially for a proselyte Jew. It is a pleasure to teach someone who will carry my ideas long after I am dead. Your scar under your left eye is a mark of honor in the eyes of Yahweh. So is your friend Eli. God's love for him is greater because Eli sacrificed himself for you to live. Now you have to live out the legacy of two men, not just one. Do you understand what I am telling you? Now explain to me what man's greatest sin above all sins is?"

Nicodemus was silent and waiting. These two last questions were not rhetorical questions, but I did not know the answer. Therefore, I made a facial jester showing I needed his insight on the issue. He understood and began to help me. "Man's greatest sin of all is something that we all possess and commit more than any other sin. I am talking about the sin of 'pride.' If the Sadducees, Pharisees, Levites, scribes, priests, and lawyers accept Jesus-Yeshua, then they will lose all their power and positions, which they love and worship above God. This is all pride and vanity. They think this world is their empire and not the coming kingdom of God. Envy of Jesus is their fundamental problem. Does that answer agree with you?"

"Only partially; I still think the religious leaders are still guilty of a new golden-calf, and it is the worship of their view and interpretation of God's Word. I do understand what you mean concerning my dead friend. I will honor him in some way because I know it is God's will to do so. However, in the second book of the Torah, it says something interesting after the law was delivered to the Children of Israel."

"Oh, yes, let me find it and read it aloud." I waited patiently until he said, "Here it is. *And Moses says to them, be of good courage, for God is come to you to try you, that His fear may be among you, that you sin not.* What does this say to you?"

"We are to fear only God and nothing else. If we fear God properly, we will not sin. Following the law will only cause us to sin. Fearing God will keep us safe."

"Brilliant observations. Absolutely brilliant. The Children of Israel were afraid of God speaking directly to them from Mount Sinai, and they begged Moses to approach the Living God as their mediator. You see, Aristarchus, if God does not cloak some of His attributes, we would die. Think of Moses in the crack of the rock when God passed by him."

"Then if Jesus is God, how is it we can look upon Him?"

"Perhaps coming into this world as a human, God has laid aside His glory. Adam and Eve looked upon God in the Garden before the fall. Abraham talked with God and did not die. It is only when the full essence of God is manifested would we die."

Nicodemus gave out a long sigh signaling he was exhausted, and I asked if it was time to rest and return later to this subject. He nodded looking over to one of the couches against the wall. "A nap would be in order," he finally said.

Before I left, I asked him why Euna left the room. He told me in a quiet voice: "She is indebted to Jesus as no other person. My talking about Jesus's possible death disturbed her. In her heart, she knows what I said is true; but her head tells her otherwise. She could not stand any more light on the subject. That is how a woman is created. Women are more sensitive, where men can be too harsh. Maybe both need to move away from each edge and meet in the middle."

As I closed the door to the *triclinium,* I noticed Nicodemus climbing up on one of the beds to take his nap. Walking down a hallway I passed an open door next to the dining room. Looking inside I recognized that it was a small library. I spotted a strange little red covered book sitting on a table looking out of place among the many books and scrolls in this place. There it was a small bound book on a low table next to a comfortable chair. I entered the room and examined the unusual red-colored binding. It was then that I noticed it was a book from the Chou Dynasty; but it was a Latin translation from its ancient language. I took it and stealthily carried it back to the stalls and sat on a tack box where there was plenty of light coming in through an open window. I noticed the book was full of strange words from the Chin language mixed with Latin. The title was peculiar as well because it had to do with warfare. The author called himself Sun Tzu or Master Sun. I started to read a story by this Master Sun and understood it was about a man who went to the king of his land and interviewed to be the king's top general. The king asked the man being questioned how he could take thousands of peasants and make them into warriors. "Easily," said Sun Tzu. "I will show you by making your hundreds of concubines here in this throne room obedient soldiers."

Everyone laughed including the king. After everyone had grown silent from what they thought was a ridiculous statement, Sun Tzu was allowed to speak. He merely asked the king: "Who are your two favorite concubines?" When the king pointed out the two most beautiful women out of the hundreds who sat on silk cushions, Sun Tzu swiftly pulled out a long sword from a nearby soldier-guard and with only two expertly practiced moves cut off the heads of the two favorite concubines. There was great horror at what the audience witnessed, and all froze with shock and surprise. Sun Tzu barked out orders for all the other concubines to form a line immediately. The king was outraged, but the women all moved as one according to what Master Sun had instructed. There before the stunned king stood all the concubines in a straight line. Sun Tzu turned to the king and said, "Remember I told you two things about war. One, if you go to war, you must be sure that, when it is over, you will be richer than before it started. Second, if you want to win the war, you have to allow your chosen military commander complete control of the upcoming war. Now I have just shown you that I as general have authority over you regarding war by killing your two favorite concubines. Also, as you see, I now have total control of these previously giggling girls. Does this not answer your question on how I can take peasants and make them into warriors?" The king agreed and appointed Sun Tzu as his top general.

Master Sun had commanded obedience by using fear. Jesus was demanding obedience, but he was not cutting off heads and making threats. He was offering living water to any who wishes to drink. I looked up and asked all the horses, "Who would you follow?" Only Zeus answered by bobbing his head up and down as if he agreed. "Well, do you choose Jesus?" Zeus stomped his right hoof three times. I let out a laugh and read on speaking the words aloud as if Zeus understood all that I was saying. After about an hour, I stopped and looked for a blank papyrus scroll in the wagon that I had hidden between the stables and the metal shop. I found several sheets along with pens and a gimbal. Back at my little table near Zeus, I sat to write. I wanted to record everything Nicodemus had said and what I just learned from Master Sun.

This was a moment in my life I still relish. It was a moment frozen forever in my mind and triggered every time I reread what I had placed on the papyrus. I hope today that I captured the Sun Tzu story correctly from my memory since I do not have my notes with me as I sit in this Roman prison. However, I believe I captured the true essence of it.

When finished, I took a short nap until I began thinking of the ministry of Jesus. The fourth year of Jesus's public ministry would soon be over. This had to be the holy year or last year. In a few months, Jesus would graciously and freely offer himself to his enemies, the ones he said were trying to take the kingdom of God by force. In some strange way, Nicodemus believed Jesus was going to resurrect the lost Tree of Life and somehow die on it. By doing this, Jesus was going to make his body the fruit that would blossom from this long, lost, gnarled tree at the start of the fifth year. This Passover had to be the end of Jesus's fourth year of ministry. If anyone had faith in who Jesus was and believed his words, then that person could eat the fruit that somehow gave eternal life. I still could not entirely understand Euna's words or behavior in the *triclinium*. She left the discussion by saying something about drinking water that would cause the partaker to never thirst again. I did not understand what she meant, nor did Nicodemus. Euna must have comprehended more than I because she realized what this fruit or water would cost. In her deepest part, she understood the cost was the life of Jesus whom she must have secretly loved. As I looked at Zeus staring at me, all I knew was Jesus was the one responsible for saving her from being stoned to death in Jerusalem. However, before the fifth year ended, I would understand Euna and her behavior completely. She was a mystery woman, and it would take the rest of my life to completely understand her. However, on this day, all I realized was the fifth year – the year the fruit could be consumed – would soon arrive. This metaphor was not hard to miss once you got over the shock of how the Creator Himself was going to humble Himself to die on the tree. In time this understanding would guide me up till today. Jesus was the fruit of the Tree of Life coming out of the Garden of Eden and becoming available to anyone; yet, it was a faith move each human had to make. It went beyond intellectual assent to understand Jesus was the eternal fruit that was the only way to eternal life. Even a child could have this faith, and in many ways a child's innocence allowed the child to accept this truth long before the great scholars of any age.

Once the Chou king got over the shock of Sun Tzu's beheading of his two concubines, the king became a believer in the abilities of Master Sun as a general. The Creator can do anything He desires to draw us to Him. However,

Chapter Eleven

at present, the Creator was using a gentle approach, not the beheading of whom we loved. Instead of killing two innocent concubines, the Creator was allowing Himself to be killed. Then the world would see and understand, much like the king understood Master Sun. We must have faith to see all the small and abundant details of life. Most of the things the Creator has shown us humans in nature are quite spectacular and beautiful. Yet, He is not slow in providing something that is surprisingly shocking if that is the only way to get our attention. God allows extraordinary events in life, such as the destruction of the cities around Sodom and Gomorrah or the destruction of the evil Canaanites, because there is no other way for us humans to see the truth. I know my analogy is weak because the concubines may have been innocent victims where the Canaanites were not. Still, the overall idea stands. Come in on your own to the presence of God or fall alone into the ditch along life's highway. I wrote down this thought to end my scribblings on the Egyptian paper using a pen from Sirca and ink from Indus Chola.

I placed the pen on the top of the gimbal and realized that this life is temporary and fragile. Death could come at any moment, and people feared death more than anything else. Humans would do anything to resist pain; but death was almost unspeakable, especially an early end. John the Baptist was only arriving at middle age when he died at Machaerus; yet, he was the only person I knew who did not fear death. He wanted something better than this fallen world of vanity. His faith told him there was a higher reward awaiting him somewhere else. When I spoke to him in his pit at Machaerus, he had more hope than any ruler or rich man I have ever encountered. I believe his hope came from the psalm he quoted by heart to me, which cut deep into my spirit and explained the nature of Yahweh as a loving Creator; yet, in many ways, Yahweh would do what Sun Tzu did to the concubines, but then maybe not. Except, He would allow Himself to be murdered to accomplish the impossible. Someday this wicked world would be put to Yahweh's sword, in a literal way. Not only would concubines be beheaded, but perhaps millions if not more would be beheaded to get the attention of the remaining humans or even the ones not yet born. I have no doubt that there is going to be a day when all people will prostrate themselves to Yahweh but not before something horrible happens to shock the world into repentance.

A READING AT THE GREAT LIBRARY OF ALEXANDRIA GIVEN BY EPAPHRODITUS

The year of the four emperors. 69 AD

Jewish Feasts

To a Jew, the world is divided between the Chosen People and all others, or respectfully Jews or Gentiles. I assumed, as a Yisrael, I was somewhere in the middle. I was born a Gentile but converted to Judaism in my early twenties. The one factor that holds the Jews together are the seven feasts. The great lawgiver Moses gave the Jews seven feasts, which ended up being grouped together into three festival periods. The first three feasts became one festival period that repeated itself year after year. The fourth festival remained by itself, and the last three again grouped together to form a third festival. The reason the first three and last three formed one long celebration was because of the proximity of these feasts falling around one week. One landed in the spring and one in the fall of each year.

Considering that the festivals of Moses held the Jews together, these feasts also caused much of the sectarian strife in Judaism. The conflict revolved around what day to celebrate the major and minor festivals. The Torah is clear when to start the first feast which is Passover. It was always to be observed in the Jewish month of Nisan on the evening of the 14the day. Nisan 15 was the beginning of Unleavened Bread, the second of seven festivals. The third festival was always to be observed on the first day of the week after Passover. This was called the Feast of First Fruits. Starting with Passover, it was celebrated with a sacrifice of a lamb and it was then eaten at dinner. This special meal was to occur sometime on Nisan 14 to remember the last day the Israelites in Egypt were slaves and the first Passover supper eaten back in Egypt. This activity was a remembrance of salvation and release from the bonds of this evil world if the Jews obeyed God. On the first Passover in Egypt, a lamb had to die. Its blood had to be painted on the sides and tops of the doors of the homes of the Hebrews to protect them against the Angel of Death, who killed all first-born males, humans or animals; thus, the term Passover. The Angel of Death passed over the homes with the blood of lambs painted on the doors. The only protection from

Satan and death was blood from an innocent lamb. The next day in the time of Moses, the last or tenth plague caused the Egyptians to demand all the Children of Jacob to leave Egypt. The Israelites had to hurry and were not able to leaven their bread before they went; thus, the Feast of Unleavened Bread on the next day. Today, according to the Law of Moses, the first day of Unleavened Bread was a Sabbath, no matter what day it lands.

The third of seven feasts was First Fruits, which began after the first Sabbath after Passover at sunrise when priests opened the Temple for the worshippers to enter and present baskets of their first fruits of the year. These baskets of fruits were an offering to Yahweh. At the Temple, each person was to place before the Lord first barley and then wheat, olives, dates, pomegranates, figs, and finally grapes. If any worshipper was not poor but wealthy, then the baskets were made of gold or silver; and the baskets were left in the Temple treasury. All the food went to the priests and other offerings to Yahweh. This was also the marker day for the beginning of harvest, which would end 50 days later at the start of the Feast of Harvest, Feast of Pentecost, or Shavuot. First Fruits and Pentecost always landed on a Sun Day, 49 days after First Fruits, which was rounded off to 50 days. This was the only feast all sects of Judaism agreed on. What they disagreed with was what day was really the correct Sun Day or the first day of the week after Passover. This had been a debated point of contention for centuries. First Fruits, once again, always fell on the first day of the week, which is always Sol Day or Sun Day. This was more than a start of the growing season but also was in memory of Noah landing on Mount Ararat in the Great Ark, the Children of Israel passing through the Red Sea when they left Egypt with Moses, and their passing through the waters of the Jordan into the Promised Land 40 years later under the leadership of Joshua. Therefore, fifty days after First Fruits, Moses instructed the Hebrews to celebrate Pentecost or Shavuot, which also always landed on a Sun or Sol Day, the first day of the week to the Jews. This festival celebrated the day Moses returned from being on Mount Sinai or Mount Horeb for 40 days when he came down with the two stone tablets with the Ten Commandments written by the finger of Yahweh. Yet, Shavuot is also a harvest celebration associated with the spring harvest of the barley crop along with the other fruits I have already mentioned that were starting to sprout fifty days earlier. This festival landed in the days of Sivan to the Jews. Once again, it is important to remember this is always a feast that fell on the first day of the week or Sun Day.

Today, as I am speaking to those gathered here at the Great Library under the rule of Rome, we have a new sect called the Way. Those who follow the Way believe that Jesus of Nazareth was the promised Messiah and all the feasts are a picture of him. For instance, it was Jesus who led the Children of Israel into the Promised Land. Egypt to the Jews was always a picture of bondage in a fallen world. It was Jesus who baptized the Children of Israel in the Red Sea as they passed out of slavery into something new. The literal interpretation of any passage in the Scriptures could also have a figurative explanation. Knowing which way to understand goes beyond human contemplation. Those who follow Jesus see Jesus all over the Scriptures. Thus, to use the Messiah Code was always to watch for a figurative interpretation but to never forget the literal meaning. Jesus was present when the Hebrews crossed the Red Sea. The name Yeshua or Jesus means "to save." Understanding the meaning of names in the Scriptures is also very essential to understanding the Biblical stories. Just picture Moses lifting a wooden staff with a bronze serpent and comparing that to the Messiah dying on a tree was a classic mosaic of figurative interpretation. These double meanings in the Scriptures make the Scriptures an ageless work of art.

Moses gave instructions for three more festivals which are observed in the fall. This one long festival period began on what was called Trumpets, the blowing of trumpets from sunup to sundown. This became a noisy celebration to honor the day Yahweh began creation or time. The Essenes always celebrate this festival on a Wednesday or fourth day of the week, which was the day God hung the sun and the moon for all men to begin counting time. On this point, I could not find any fault with the Essenes. It was as if each sect had some unique truth buried in a pile of untruths. To not look at each faction was to not discover the insight that was correct within each sect. Since all sects may have some different truths to share, yet the danger is all the deadly, venomous, and lethal substance that can spiritually shipwreck anyone, including someone like my old Jewish teacher and friend Nicodemus. The problem is not being entangled by lies and falsehoods. The question is how does someone drink a cup of water with a single drop of poison mixed in and not die? To drink and not die was genuinely a miracle. Yet, the challenge is well worth it if you are successful in your discovery of truth over any evil. To spot a counterfeit denarius, one must correctly know a real denarius. Only then can one quickly spot the fake. Yet, how to have a calendar that is not divisible by seven so Trumpets always lands on the fourth day each year was a mystery the Essenes refused to discuss openly. Years later I learned how the Essenes did it, but it is too long for me to explain today. But, it is essential to understand that it does require a little tinkering with numbers.

The Feast of Trumpets lasted two days because the sects in Jerusalem were covering all the angles regarding the start of the first day according to the phases of the moon sited in Jerusalem. For instance, if it were cloudy one morning, how would you correctly know if it was the start of a new moon? Celebrating for two days would ensure one of the two days was the start of the first day of creation. The danger here is the loss of accuracy over a long period of time. The Essenes were the only ones to claim to have the solution with their calendar. For instance, the Feast of Atonement, according to the Essenes, always had to fall on a Venus Day, Frigg Day or the sixth day of the week. This is another trick of math that is quite creative. However, I can tell you it was on Frigg's Day when Jesus did go to the Tree of Life and became the ultimate atonement for all of humanity; yet, the miracle for that year Passover landed on Frigg's Day. Can I safely say today that it was the sixth day of the week when on that Passover when the Lamb of God provided a way for the angel of death to pass over any human covered with the Lamb of God's blood? Timing, once again, is just as crucial to a miracle as the miracle itself.

The Hebrews are required not to eat during daylight on the Day of Atonement, or Yom Kippur in Hebrew. That is because the high priest is to offer a sin sacrifice of blood in the Temple in the Holy of Holies for all people. I will always remember the day my good friend was murdered in the Temple and how hungry I was. I stand here today and confess to all of you that this day became my darkest day of the year because that was the day I walked away from organized ecclesiastical Judaism. This all happened in the first year of Yeshua's public ministry. My Jewish teacher named Nicodemus said, "The Day of Atonement is the only time the high priest is to enter the Holy of Holies room of the Temple, where the Ark of the Covenant used to rest before the ark disappeared hundreds of years ago before the destruction of Solomon's Temple. Today the Holy of Holies is an empty room in Herod's Temple, the replacement temple of Zerubbabel's Temple, the one constructed after the Persian King Cyrus freed the Jews from Babylon."

The last festival ordered by Moses begins only a few days after the Day of Atonement; it is called Tabernacles, Sukkot in Hebrew. This feast is where all Hebrews are expected to camp in tents or tabernacles for one week in memory of their forefathers' wanderings in the wilderness and living in temporary shelters for 40 years before the Jews entered the Promised Land under Joshua, or Yeshua in Hebrew, or Jesus in Latin and Greek.

There are other festivals that came after Moses, such as Wood Gathering, Lights, Purium, the fast over the destruction of the Temple by the Babylonians, but I will explain these in a future lecture if there is any interest.

CHAPTER TWELVE

Sychar – Summer, fall, winter and the start of spring in Tiberius's 18th to 19th year of rule. Pontius Pilate's 6th to 7th year as Prefect of Judaea. The final months in Jesus of Nazareth's 4th and last year of his public ministry.   *(32-33 AD)*

Thousands of candles can be lighted from a single candle, and the life of the candle will not be shortened. Kindness never decreases by being shared.   Buddha

The next morning Nicodemus declared he was fasting because it was the Day of Atonement. I remembered my first Day of Atonement in this land, the day Eli was murdered. I, too, fasted on my first Day of Atonement and decided once again to resume the practice. However, I honestly fasted this time to honor Nicodemus more than Yahweh. The day after our fast we continued our lessons in the *triclinium*. It was a cold morning and I remember wearing a heavy coat. It was Venus Day or the sixth day of the seven-day week. Nicodemus was beyond excited because he had discovered news in the Sychar market early that morning concerning Jesus of Nazareth. He told me he had learned of a great miracle that occurred only a few miles southeast outside Jerusalem. Actually, not much was heard of him until this miracle. According to Nicodemus, a man was brought back from the dead, someone he knew. His name was Lazarus, and Jesus had called him back from the dead after four long days. All I knew concerning Jesus before this was he had left *Palestina* with his small group of disciples. I guessed it was due to the many death threats against him. The Sadducees, Pharisees, scribes, religious lawyers, Herod Antipas, Zealots, and the Herodians all wanted Jesus dead. I understood how he must have felt since I had a four million *sestertii* bounty hanging over me. There was a rumor spreading that perhaps over a couple thousand bounty hunters were now looking for me in *Palestina*. I was sure Jesus did not have that many bounty hunters looking for him because the authorities had some idea where he was. What Jesus had that I didn't was many followers providing protection. When all his followers dwindled to just a few, I was sure his days, like mine, were numbered. Yet, this news of Lazarus was beyond my understanding. I still struggled with understanding much like a man who has fallen overboard a ship at sea and did not know how to swim. Strangely enough, before the next Passover, I would meet Lazarus, and he personally told me in great detail about his four days while his body was in the grave. After talking to him, I was convinced that there had to be life after death even though our body was in the grave.

During the many months at Photina's home, I never left the security of the walled estate. Euna, Nicodemus, and eventually Amcheck ventured out to buy food and other items of need. We had plenty of money, which I secretly provided from the coins Grillius gave me in the meadow before he killed the mortally wounded gray horse. No one asked where I got the money; and, at the first signs of spring, Nicodemus and Euna believed we were running out of money to live on. Only I knew where all the money came from, and we were not in need of coins. Twenty years worth of wages for a Roman soldier would take a long time for four people to spend. Considering we only bought food and other necessary necessities, I wondered why Nicodemus and Euna questioned the problem of money. When I was once alone with Nicodemus, he told me he knew there was plenty of money but that it was wrong for me to support everyone. I still decided not to reveal to him the source of the coins because I knew he would certainly refuse to use blood money. I assumed he thought it was from my personal savings and I was guilty of allowing this idea. Had he directly asked me I would have told him the truth. A few days later after that money conversation, Nicodemus suggested that we remove all the alabaster ink bottles and pens from the gimbal boxes in the wagon and sell them at the weekly market in Sychar's *agora*. I said nothing allowing him to feel like Herod should contribute to our needs. This idea worked and provided funds to alleviate the problem of using all my coins. I later learned Nicodemus began purchasing extra items to replace what we had used from

Photina's storage rooms during the end of summer and the long winter. This act taught me that Nicodemus was an honest man worthy of emulating. If everyone for just one day thought of others over themselves, this world would never be the same again.

One early spring morning when I could not sleep, I entered the kitchen area and discovered two *sestertii* coins resting on a counter that had to be the ones Saben left on his reconnoiter of this house months earlier. This was more of a gesture and not even close to paying for what Saben took from this house and brought up to Mount Gerizim. Yet, even this step made by a hard man such as Saben was a move in the right direction. We did not see Captain Saben again until a week after my discovery of his coins in the kitchen, making it at least nine months since we last saw him. When he finally arrived, he acted as if he never left. I realized it had been nice not having Saben show up every week but kept this to myself. It had been a period of freedom not hearing all his gossip from Herod and Rome. The day he returned the weather had changed over to something beyond spectacular. It was when the budding of leaves began to pop and flowers appeared from nowhere. It was also the time birds were increasing their chirping, and insects were on the move. True to form, Saben arrived on a Sabbath Eve. I heard someone knock at the back gate; and when I checked, it was Saben in his Herodian uniform sitting on his black horse. I quickly opened the gate to allow his entry. After he dismounted, I told Saben it had been a long wait. He did not answer but instead handed me his reins like I was a lowly stable boy. I took this action as an ominous sign. Silence is a form of communication and sometimes speaks louder than words.

After the Sabbath meal that night, we were all reclining in Photina's *triclinium* or dining room. Nicodemus and I had rolled up all the scrolls and placed them in the small *tablinum* or study library, where I found Master Sun's *Arts of War*. Euna had decided that for this one night we should eat Roman style in the prone position using only fingers to eat. Each person had his own coach, and we all were resting on our left sides with a pillow under our left arms. Euna did all the serving that night. Euna, Amcheck, and I had fully healed from all our wounds which we received nine months earlier; and even my skull fracture with the gold plate was wholly cured and caused me no problems. Amcheck, as I predicted, limped noticeably when he walked; and Euna's facial scars blended into her skin's coloring and few wrinkle lines. Scars or not, she was still a beautiful woman. She knew how to use makeup purchased in the market to cover most of the visible injuries. No one begrudged her this little vanity. My wounds were nothing compared to Amcheck's although I had a new scar on my forehead from striking the wagon wheel after my spill over the gray gelding's head. I imagined my new scar might keep me safe in a strange way. In future years, most angry men wanting to fight for one reason or another stayed away from me because they could see something in my eyes, framed by my facial scars, which must have screamed, "Do not bother this one!" Whenever I did gaze into a bronze mirror, I felt like I appeared quite ugly and fierce. Females, I later learned, experienced the opposite toward my looks. Many told me, even as I grew older, my facial scars added a strange attraction; and females never seemed to fear me as men did. This has always been a mystery to me. It is true to say, when I was younger, I could turn heads; but in my later years, all I could do was turn stomachs. However, about the time I reached age 60, my facial injuries became great story starters: younger people wanted to know how I got such marks on my face. By then there were very few people with facial wounds as the world moved into a more prolonged period of peace, which became known as *Pax Romana* or Roman Peace. Only boxers, gladiators, and a few ex-soldiers sported facial scars. Perhaps this placed me in a tiny and exclusive group.

Once dinner had ended and we stayed on our couches for evening wine, Amcheck asked the question all of us wanted to ask since becoming somewhat prisoners in Photina's home. "What news do you bring from Masada?"

"Herod has moved back to Machaerus since King Aretas is still building and training a large army of Arab soldiers gathered from many desert tribes. Since King Aretas is at the hidden city of Petra, he has a considerable number of trade routes funneling through this isolated city. Due to taxes on all the goods passing through his lands, Aretas has unlimited funds to pay for an army that makes Antipas more nervous by the day. Even if Rome were to help him, he would not be able to gain the title he desires, king of the Jews. Because of this unrest in Petra, I understand Rome might be moving a second legion to Judaea and keeping it permanently at Jerusalem. This is just in case there is trouble if fighting breaks out. Herod is doing the same by enlarging his mercenaries, and this is costing him a small fortune along with too many men sitting around Machaerus doing nothing. I have been there instead of Jerusalem over the winter training all the new recruits. Too bad Cata is not with me, for you and that old Spartan are worth a hundred of what we are getting these days. And to think all this war business is keeping me busy because Herod married his niece and brother's wife. If Herod had just listened to John the Baptist and sent Herodias back to Rome, this would not be happening right now. I really cannot blame King Aretas. If I were he, I would be doing the same thing. Herod Antipas left the king of Petra with no other choice when Herod scorned Aretas's daughter and caused her to return to her father."

I could not believe I heard Saben say such things. Before dinner I had instructed Euna to make sure Saben had all the wine he wanted. Euna had agreed with my logic and kept filling his cup with Photina's best wine from Hebron. I had found a large clay *amphora* of Hebron wine stored in a basement room, which was colder than the upper house. I had a couple of cups myself since it was also my favorite but stopped after two cups.

Amcheck lifted his wine cup and said, "I guess the moral of the story is to be careful whom you marry." There was a long burst of mirth coming from Amcheck at his own statement, and I looked toward Euna and saw a hurt look on her face.

Saben gave out a hearty laugh with Amcheck, and I joined with a show of good cheer. I wanted both men to feel at ease and mostly to loosen Saben's tongue.

"What about this holy man named Jesus?" I asked.

Saben strangely stared at Nicodemus before he answered my question. "There may be war in Perea, which is where the rumors have Jesus of Nazareth hiding. But that is all we know of Jesus. He is missing in action. Most think he is hiding out somewhere in Nabataea. Philip's spy named Y'hudah from *K'riot* has been silent for months regarding Jesus, and this is disturbing."

K'riot in Greek was Iscariot, and I remembered Y'hudah was the one called Judas. I am mentioning it now because of his later activities as one of the twelve disciples of Jesus. Today, as I am dictating this story, Judas Iscariot is an infamous name; however, many do not know its origin. Some people say he was part of the group Amcheck was supposed to have worked for called *Sicarius*. The word Iscariot or *K'riot* is not even the same root word for *sicarius*. Judas was from the little village of Iscariot, south of Jerusalem and beyond Bethlehem. He most likely is known as Judas Iscariot in the same way Yeshua is, Jesus of Nazareth. The Hebrew method, back before the fall of Jerusalem and the Temple, was to take the name of their origins as their family name, primarily if a male was illegitimate. Since Jesus was virgin born, he carried the title Jesus of Nazareth, not Jesus ben Joseph. On the other hand, Jesus's half-brother, James was known as James ben Joseph, or James son of Joseph. Never did I hear that he went by James of Nazareth. Just a few years before the Jewish Wars began with Rome, a leader of the Way, he was brutally murdered by the Jews under the name James the Just. Fugitives or the fatherless, such as myself, are identified by only one name – Venu or Cata. Since I rarely gave a family name, most understood and never probed this sensitive subject. Much information is learned by hearing someone's family name and the family's occupation. Having just one name made you a bastard of bastards with no family or home to identify yourself.

Saben continued talking after his inebriated laugh, which caused him to release some wind. Only Amcheck laughed with him when Saben asked if the villa had a nest of mice running around. To hide the fact I was not joining in this indecent hilarity, I lifted my cup to Euna acting as if I wanted more to drink and appeared not to hear Saben's rudeness.

When Amcheck and Saben settled back down, the crude captain continued. "However, there was one report concerning Jesus. We did hear a few months back about a healing in Phoenicia's port town of Tyre. It had to do with a non-Jewish woman's daughter. You see the Jews are now angry that a Jewish teacher has left the Promised Land and is now healing foreigners." Saben now gave out a sniggered hoot, thinking it funny the Jews might have lost their long-awaited and promised Messiah to the Gentiles.

"A few years back, Jesus healed a centurion's slave," Nicodemus added.

Saben looked across the table at him for a short moment before he responded. "But that Gentile was in Galilee and not Phoenicia. Tyre is not one of those Chosen One's city."

"True. Now tell us more of this Jesus," inquired Nicodemus.

"Are you one of his disciples?" queried Saben with a slight smirk in his voice. "That is what the Sanhedrin thinks."

"In my opinion, contrary to most of my colleagues in the Sanhedrin, Jesus has done nothing wrong. Performing miracles on the Sabbath is not a sin, just as it is not a crime to help a poor animal injured on the holy rest day. Would you not pull your horse out of a mud bog on the Sabbath?" This seemed like one of those rare times I had seen Nicodemus show his fangs.

Saben threw up his hands as if he were surrendering on some faraway battlefield. "I am not a Jew; and, if an animal needed help on any day, I would see what I could do."

"You see, even a non-Jew understands miracles that help people on the Sabbath are appropriate," proclaimed Nicodemus with a thump of his fist on the top of the table.

"I will concede to your illustration. What about Jesus's claim to rebuild the Temple in three days? That sounds like sedition to me," argued Saben, who seemed to know more than he had previously said about Jesus. "And what about raising a man from his tomb who had been dead four days? What business is it for Jesus to bother the dead?"

Chapter Twelve

Nicodemus arranged his robes from his prone position indicating he wished to speak. Everyone waited for him to respond. When he looked over to Saben, out came his words wrapped in high authority. "The answer to your first question is that Jesus is clearly speaking figuratively. Since when are figurative statements seditious?" Nicodemus came across as being very stern, something I had never seen before, except when he was angry about the maggots.

"Are you sure Lord Nicodemus?"

"I do not believe Jesus is promoting that we Hebrews or even the Romans are going to destroy the Temple and that he will rebuild it himself in three days. That would be impossible. Therefore, he must be speaking of something else. Do we Hebrews have freedom of speech in the Roman Empire or not? Apparently not," answered Nicodemus using his usual rhetorical method. "Raising a man after four days tells me Jesus will not remain in his tomb after his four years of ministry is up, and that is the answer to that."

"Wait a moment. Did you say Jesus is going to die? And die soon?" questioned a surprised Saben.

"You can tell Herod Antipas that Jesus will be at Jerusalem this Passover, but it will be the Romans who will kill Jesus on a cross and not Herod. Ask Herod if he actually gained any friends after killing John the Baptist. I am sure Herod will leave it to Pilate to do this dirty work. Besides, Herod should think twice before he destroys Jesus if he even gets the chance. I am sure the Sanhedrin, not Herod, will give Jesus to Pontius Pilate. Herod does not have the power to put someone to death in Judaea. If Jesus is sent to Herod, he would be wise to transfer him to Pilate. Now, before we leave this song, I would not wish to be in the *prefect's* position on that day."

"This miracle worker has not been to a Passover for a couple of years. What makes you so sure he will appear in Jerusalem in a few weeks?"

Nicodemus threw up a hand indicating he had the answer. "This is not true. I personally saw Jesus last Passover in Jerusalem or at least outside the walls. So did Aristarchus," said Nicodemus waving his eating hand toward me. "This will be the fifth Passover since Jesus turned over the moneychangers' tables on a Passover. Jesus also gave a parable on the Mount of Olives last Passover, which both Aristarchus and I heard. Jesus, in essence, declared without any doubt that he would be attending Jerusalem openly this Passover festival. You can tell Herod the Scriptures are clear. Jesus as the Messiah will be present at the Temple a good week before this Passover is over."

"Are you telling me I can tell Herod that this is a fact? Of course, showing up in Jerusalem this Passover is nothing compared with Jesus raising people back from the dead."

Euna had been standing behind Saben with a silver pitcher full of wine, and after she overheard Saben's words, she began refilling Saben's cup. After it was filled, she boldly asked, "Who was raised from the dead?"

Saben looked surprised that a servant woman would dare talk during a dinner party. He looked at all of us, and not one person seemed astonished while Euna waited for an answer. Finally, Saben shrugged his shoulders and replied, after he gave a hard look at this unusual serving woman. "There was a little girl in Capernaum raised from the dead. Also a widow's son in the village of Nain. This Jesus raised both on the same day they died. The little girl had just died before she came back. The next question is, was the little girl in Capernaum just sleeping and not dead when Jesus woke her?"

I was surprised that Saben knew these things about Jesus. Nicodemus with all his persuasive authority of age and position declared, "Believe what you want, Captain; but bringing back a man after he is rotting in a hot tomb for four days is a fantastical miracle. The question is, was he just sleeping for those four days in his grave clothes?"

No one answered for Nicodemus was right. Who was this Jesus? I now had a new desire to speak with Jesus, a greater need than what I had when I went to find John the Baptist a few years ago.

"I agree, Master Nicodemus," Saben finally uttered in a defeated tone as he sucked on his two greasy fingers. "Yet, if this Jesus becomes a threat to the Romans and there is no longer tranquility in the Empire, Jesus will be dealt with seriously. I have it on good authority that the Zealots are hiding in the hills around Jerusalem just waiting to see if this so-called Messiah will come to Jerusalem this Passover. The Romans have patrols right now hunting them out of their caves going as far as around the Dead Sea region. Judaea is a hotbed of rebellion more than I have ever witnessed since I came to this land and, might I add, that you, Nicodemus, may remember."

"Oh, I am old enough to remember 40 years ago when Rome crucified thousands of Jews who went into rebellion."

"Any word of my Spartan friend?" I asked, changing the subject because I perceived this argument was becoming too dangerous for Nicodemus. It appeared to me that the old scholar was openly making himself a friend or even a disciple of Jesus.

Saben scratched his beard with his left hand before he answered. I recognized this behavior when Saben encountered a dilemma he wished to avoid.

Chapter Twelve

Usually after stroking his beard, Saben would deliver only a half-truth if he did answer. I was surprised at what he said once he stopped stroking his beard. "All Herod has learned from his spies, who were sent to Caesarea as you suggested, was a Spartan mercenary was intercepted a day after that battle in Bethel down on the plain near the town of Azotus."

"Intercepted by whom?" I asked, waving for Euna to fill Saben's cup again; but this time she had mixed his wine with a touch of gall. I had held up two fingers, the prearranged signal to her when I wanted his tongue and mind well lubricated with gall. We had earlier spoken privately in the kitchen, and I was behind the idea of serving the best wine. I was also the one behind the idea of giving him gall but only when I gave the signal. She understood and did as I asked. My plan was to introduce the drug once Saben was too drunk to know or to care he was tasting gall in his drink. I must admit that my decision was based on Jesus's first miracle when Jesus made wine out of water in the town of Cana. After the water had turned into wine, the steward of the groom's house asked Jesus, "Why waste this excellent wine on drunk people?" The point being, drunk guests are not aware of what they are really tasting.

"A Roman cavalry patrol of a dozen or so came in sight of him on the road to Azotus, which is part of Judaea and under Roman control. It had to be the Spartan because the rider was wearing a Laconian cape that flapped in the wind. He released most of the herd of horses he was pulling by long leads. After the released horses separated, the Spartan stayed on the road traveling south with only two ponies in tow. The Roman patrol took chase until they realized all three horses were saddled. The ones running free were not. That Spartan friend of yours is one smart character. He changed mounts every five minutes by jumping from horse to horse without stopping. The Roman horses could not match his speed since your Spartan friend was using a fresh horse every five minutes, and his purple cape was flapping at them as if he were giving them an obscene jester. One Roman witness told me personally that the Spartan would stand on the horse he was riding before jumping at full speed onto the next horse. This is a feat I have never seen but would love to have witnessed. When I told the Roman how old your friend was, he said I was a liar. I then said he had recently killed five ex-Romans at Bethel. He did not believe me, and I left one frustrated Roman calling me all kinds of filthy things. If it had not been true, I would have returned and fought the foolish man."

I was upset that our secret at Bethel was now known. Perhaps Jesus was correct when he said that when something was done in secret, it would be yelled from the rooftops. From that day forward, I learned it was a waste of time trying to keep secrets. "Then Grillius got away?" I asked, hoping he did.

"Well, the only problem for your Spartan friend is that the Roman patrol had a Hindu archer with a recurve bow who could shoot 400 yards and hit a melon. The archer stopped his horse and pulled out one of those *sigma* or S-curved bows that curve away from the archer when unstrung."

"It is true that the Hindus use such a bow; and I think they call this bow the deceitful bow because, if not strung properly, it could snap back and break a man's arm. It could also be because the bow looked backward when unstrung," I added.

"Of course, you are always right, Cata," replied a drunken Saben and I noticed Amcheck wagging his head in disapproval. "Anyway, the Hindu archer shot high. The arrow hung for a long time before it dropped and struck your friend in the back, cutting right through his cape. The Romans thought they had him except he stayed on his mount and continued to ride away. I would say he must have died later, but there is no proof. The Romans said the Hindu placed his arrow right between the shoulder blades, not a good place to have an arrow strike. They did find a blood trail but still lost him in the desert. He just kept outdistancing them, and the patrol said he was heading toward Egypt when they gave up the chase. That is all we know of him."

"What is Herod's plan for us here in Sychar?" asked Amcheck, lifting his cup to Euna and smiling a lopsided smile, something I had never seen before from Amcheck. Euna smiled back while filling his cup. I decided I was going to have a private moment with Amcheck and ask him what was going on between him and Euna.

"Now for all your futures," declared Saben lifting his cup for a refill. After Euna topped his cup, Saben took a long drink before continuing. "These are my orders from Herod. Cata and Amcheck are to return to duties in Jerusalem now that you are both healed from your wounds. However, Herod has one small task for Cata before his return to Jerusalem." I now noticed a downcast look pass over Amcheck's face. I looked to Euna; and she hurried out of the room with the empty silver pitcher, also looking somewhat disturbed by this news.

"Since when does a member of the Sanhedrin get ordered about by Herod?" asked a feisty Nicodemus.

"Herod only believes it would be best if you accompany Amcheck back to Jerusalem, for the Sanhedrin is starting to ask questions. Some are even saying Nicodemus has disappeared only to follow Jesus. It will be best to distance yourself, Master Nicodemus, from this holy man if you are right about his soon demise by the Romans. And I can be sure that Herod does not want a noted member of the Sanhedrin connected to Cata. Therefore, you, Nicodemus, would be wise if you do accompany Amcheck back to Jerusalem without Cata."

Nicodemus blurted, "Connected! I was connected when the Romans fractured Cata's head outside my door. And tell me how Amcheck is going to protect me from the one he whipped who might be returning for revenge?"

"Lord Nicodemus," stated Saben with a wicked smile. "I would say the Parthian did a complete rearrangement of this senatorial pup you seem to fear. I seriously doubt he will be returning this Passover; and I must say, if he does, I wouldn't want to get behind Belkin's *sicarius*."

I decided to ask, "What about Nicodemus's safety from my father's spies? Is Amcheck able to take on more than one assassin?"

"Nicodemus will be safe, for Amcheck will stay with him as his personal guard. Besides, it is out of my hands. Those were Herod's words. It is true that Amcheck cannot walk or run as he once did, but guarding a Sanhedrin elder should be right up his alley. Also, this will give favor to the Sanhedrin if Herod cares enough to protect one of their own with one of his own. If any Roman tries anything like arresting Nicodemus, then Amcheck's death will give a plausible reason for Herod's plans to allow the Zealots and Herodians to come together and attack Pilate and his Romans."

Not wanting to hear any more of Saben's flight of ideas, I felt this was the time to ask a more personal question. "Months ago, when talking at our camp on Mount Gerizim, you shared with us about the Sejanus affair. What has transpired in Rome since we last talked?"

"Good question, my young gladiator, who killed five veteran Romans in classic hand-to-hand combat. That story has placed you in good with Herod as well as Herodias. If you know what I mean."

"No, I don't. Tell me instead about Sejanus and how all of this relates to Pontius Pilate."

"Well then, since the Tiberius-Sejanus purges, Pilate is safe for now. Perhaps that gold present from the rejected shields he placed in Herod's Palace must have worked. As I said months ago, Herod and his brothers should have left the shields hang and later used the gold to pay for Antipas's new mercenaries he has gathered at Machaerus. Nevertheless, I can tell you one of Herod's spies intercepted a letter from Tiberius to Pilate; and its contents are very revealing about the change in Rome, especially regarding the Jews. The letter was an edict with Tiberius's signet, and it declared a complete Jewish policy reversal. From now on, Pilate is to treat the Jews with respect.

Pontius Pilate can no longer officially order any anti-Jewish practices unless he receives orders from Tiberius himself. This is a complete reverse of Rome's Jewish-Sejanus policy. For years Sejanus openly encouraged and applauded every misuse of power over the Jews by Pilate. All of this has now changed if our Roman *prefect/procurator* wants to finish out his term here in *Palestina*. Herod's spies have also learned Pilate needs a few more years as governor to pay off his debt to his *patroni* in *Italia*. Thanks to you, Cata, Herod has now learned the name of Pilate's *patroni*. Your little suggestion has placed you in a new light at the palace in Machaerus. After you return to Jerusalem, you might find Herod giving you a new role over being just a palace guard."

To change the direction away from me I asked, "Will Pontius Pilate obey Tiberius's decree?"

"Herod believes the Roman governor will not be able to kill one more Jew unless he has substantial reasons. Any more adverse reports to Rome and, well, we all know what that means."

Euna was back pouring more wine and gall into Saben's cup. "Herod's spies say Pilate is a mean dog but a dog on a tight leash from Capri. If you ask me, I would say this could be the perfect time for a revolt to place Herod back on the throne in Jerusalem as king of the Jews. The dog can bark, but he cannot bite anymore. Now the only real problem is Jesus of Nazareth. The people want him to be their new king since he raised that dead four-day-old Jew." After seeing the look from Nicodemus, Saben said, "No offense. And, if you are correct and he does show his face in Jerusalem this Passover, there could be bloodshed but not by the hands of Pilate. I predict the preacher from Nazareth will be killed but most likely by a knife in the back while he walks a crowded street in Jerusalem. A larger-than-average crowd is expected this year, much more than usual. More than half are coming from all over the Empire to see this prophet from Galilee who does miracles like raising the dead. Pilate is planning on bringing most of his legion from Caesarea to the Castle of Antonia. Besides, like I said, there might be a second legion marching toward Jerusalem as we speak. The war Herod fears against Aretas is frozen for the moment because Rome is signaling the king of the Nabateans with the appearance of a new legion in Jerusalem. I am sure Aretas understands he would be a fool to attack Herod now. Besides, let it be known by us alone that Herod has been secretly giving a significant amount of gold and silver to the king of Petra for the insult he placed upon him by marrying Herodias. Aretas seems satisfied for the time being."

Nicodemus lifted his right elbow waving his hand toward Saben, "Does this mean Herod plans on attending the Passover feast in Jerusalem?"

Chapter Twelve

"For the second time in years, Herod will be present. He is also bringing a substantial force with him when he comes. Think about it for a moment. In a few weeks, there will be over a thousand mercenaries at Herod's palace in Jerusalem; and the Romans might have close to ten thousand men at the Castle of Antonia. It will be like when Caesar crossed the Rubicon with his legion to meet Pompey in Rome."

"More like Sulla and Marius," I added. "It could get bloody."

"Bloody indeed," commented Saben in a clear drunken slur. "Everyone knows what happens when two armies are together in the same city at the same time. The Zealots also have over a thousand warriors in the hills, and their leader is in contact with Herod. This information is not to be shared with anyone. Do I make myself clear?"

This last statement revealed my plan of using gall in Saben's drink was working. Saben's tongue was now wagging freely. Praetorian Felix would be proud.

"Who might that Zealot leader be?" probed Nicodemus.

"A Zealot hothead named Jesus bar Abbas. Yes, there will be two Jesuses if the pseudo-prophet shows up along with this Jesus bar Abbas," laughed Saben. Once again I caught Euna's eye and lifted two fingers for Euna to see. She lowered her eyes to the silver picture and smiled.

With all this drunken jollity, Nicodemus began showing a bit of anger when he asked Saben: "Why did you use the term pseudo when referring to Jesus?"

"So it is true. You are a disciple of this Nazarene. I will inform Herod of this, which, I am afraid, will distance you from the unified Sanhedrin who all fear the man from Nazareth. Now you, Master Nicodemus, High Priest Caiaphas has already declared before witnesses that Jesus is to die this Passover. Caiaphas has a plan in place to have Jesus arrested if he shows. The high priest wants to have a show trial to reveal to all Jesus's religious infractions. Then, once Jesus is convicted of blasphemy, Caiaphas will deliver Jesus to Pilate before the Passover to do the Sanhedrin's dirty work."

I could not contain myself any longer. "If Pilate has received a letter from Tiberius not to kill any Jew without the emperor's permission, how is this going to happen?"

Saben threw up his right arm in frustration; and Nicodemus now was visibly angry and tabled my question by saying, "I do not deny my association with Jesus; he very well could be the promised Messiah as he claims. Nevertheless, why would the Sanhedrin want him dead? This is the first time I have heard this."

"I am just reporting the facts, Master Nicodemus. High Priest Caiaphas has issued orders to have Jesus arrested. That is a fact. His father-in-law Annas still runs the temple ropes up and down behind the scenes like a skilled *gypsy* stagehand. Antipas, too, wants Jesus dead and wants it done before Passover ends this year. And if Pilate won't do the deed, Herod just might."

"What is the Sanhedrin saying about Jesus's new miracle of raising a man after being dead for four days?" asked Nicodemus, showing a bold and open stink eye toward Saben. I did not want to look to see if Saben saw the look.

Saben's voice did not betray any hostility toward the old scholar, "The Sanhedrin would like to tell everyone it did not happen, but there are too many witnesses. Therefore, the Sanhedrin is on the record saying the miracle happened by the power of Beelzebub."

"What?" retorted Nicodemus. "Are they insane? Why would the 'lord of flies' heal the blind, cure lepers, give legs back to the lame, and cast out evil spirits possessing people? Besides, why would they invoke the name of the pagan god of the ancient and dead Philistine city of Ekron? I ask you, would a general kill his own soldiers before a battle? Would he?"

I jumped in to spare any nasty response from Saben. "The problem is simple. The Sanhedrin refuses to believe this man from vile Nazareth is the God of Israel. I would not be surprised if they were planning to murder this man raised from the dead."

Saben ignored my comment and looked over at Nicodemus and asked, "Is not the Sanhedrin on record saying this to you a few years ago when they suspected you were a secret disciple of Jesus?"

Nicodemus did not answer at first. I assumed it was because he was correct in his original argument. His high points made complete sense, but I was thinking about Sun Tzu killing the king's concubines. Master Sun achieved a great deal by killing only two of the king's concubines; therefore, why wouldn't the Evil One use the same tactic and kill one or two of his own men?

Finally, Nicodemus had had enough. "Well, this is the polemics of all controversies. Jesus said if anyone says or even believes the miracles are done in the power of the Evil One, then that is a sin against the Holy Spirit. And, such a person can never be forgiven."

I began to feel uneasy and silently asked Yahweh to excuse me for any of my past drunken thoughts. When Euna came to fill my cup, I put my hand over the top to signal I had enough.

"Understand one thing," continued Saben. "I personally would never, ever, say such a thing, just in case he is who he thinks he is. I believe that the Sanhedrin is following their own evil desires; but I am just an old soldier who

Chapter Twelve

follows orders, no matter what they are. This God of the Jews cannot condemn me since I am a non-Jew in the middle of this mess."

Surprised by Saben's words, I asked, "Why would you believe that?"

Looking now in my direction with glazed eyes he started to slightly slur his words. "What I am about to tell you happened before you became a guard. John the Baptist told some of my soldiers who went to him for baptism out in the desert – and understand these men were not even Jews – that they should remain soldiers but not to steal and use their power for evil. It looks like John knew soldiers are victims of their masters even if their masters order them to murder innocent people."

Nicodemus was even more disturbed but held his tongue from what he really wanted to say. I, too, was bothered by Saben's conclusions. First of all, I didn't know of any soldiers in Jerusalem who submitted to John's baptism. Second, I wanted to tell Saben I would never follow any order that went against my conscience. I might even decide to kill Saben if he gave me an immoral or wicked order such as killing innocent people. This was the moment I decided being a soldier was not going to be my career choice. However, sometimes these decisions are not ours to make. All I wanted was to get out of *Palestina* with Messina and to find Hector. If Grillius survived the arrow strike, I was sure he would be with Hector and Anab right this moment. The only good news out of this visit from Saben was Nicodemus was going to be in Jerusalem by Passover. When Nicodemus asked Saben about Euna and me going to Jerusalem, I at first did not understand his dissipated demeanor. When I did comprehend, it touched my heart to think he was doing what my mother told me: "Think of others above yourself." Nicodemus was, indeed, a selfless man. He wanted to make sure I was in Jerusalem to be on the Mount of Olives when the Messiah declared himself. His eyesight was weak, but his heart was rich. Besides, I also had an appointment to meet Messina, which I could not miss.

"Herod wants his money back for the gimbals," declared Saben to Nicodemus's query. "The only way is to sell the gimbals or maybe sell your slave woman Euna," laughed Saben. I noticed Euna was out of the room and most likely did not hear this hurtful statement made by a drunk, drugged Saben. I hoped Amcheck could protect her tonight from the likes of a man with the name Saben. Of course, if he couldn't, I would. "Herod has instructed Cata to take the woman and that monster cart to Tyre or Sidon. Two large Gentile trading ports will provide the perfect place to sell the entire lot of gimbals along with the wagon. Now mind you, I argued with him that it was excessively dangerous to put that wagon back on the road for any of the thousands looking to make an easy four million *sestertii*." Saben stopped and took a drink, and everyone waited until he finished his thoughts.

"Herod has changed for the worse since you all last saw him. This Jesus has him unhinged, to put it mildly. He really thinks Jesus is John the Baptist returned from the dead to torment him. Could that not be true? I think not. Jesus and John were alive at the same time, so how could Jesus be John. Try telling that to Herod. It is like asking that wall painting over there to speak. Never going to happen."

I looked over to where Saben had waved his right hand and thought maybe the painted figures could if God wanted it to be so. Nicodemus threw up his right hand. "Herod does not care about Cata! All he wants is the return of his investment, and that means selling that huge wagon in one of those pagan cities. I will not be surprised if Herod betrays Cata to get that heavenly reward for himself. All the mercenaries he has acquired are not cheap, and four million *sestertii* is a fortune even for a king."

The gall was now doing its work, even on Nicodemus. This is what I was waiting to hear. I looked at Saben and gave him a sideways look of disbelief to show him my obedience to his drunken words. Saben smiled back after he gave me his quick glance.

"The truth is I like you, Cata," Saben declared. "At Bethel and here at Sychar, you, Cata have actually and not virtually but literally saved the best soldier with whom I have ever served. I will do my best to warn you if Herod tries to turn his back on you. Besides, Herodias still favors you; but this could also be dangerous for other reasons. The only safe thing will be to follow orders, sell the gimbals, and give back to Herod all his money. It should be safe if Euna dresses like a wealthy woman and you, Cata, act as her bodyguard. Always wear your helmet with the face shield closed. Once the gimbals are sold along with the wagon and horses, you both can return to Jerusalem; and you should do it as quickly as possible. Herod explicitly told me he wants you, Cata, in Jerusalem before the Passover begins. That gives you fewer than three weeks to sell the wagon and gimbals and get back to Jerusalem. When you return, Cata, Herodias wants you as her personal bodyguard." Saben smiled and looked at me for a long moment before he began laughing as a fisherman would do when gaffing a prized fish with his trident spear. This performance of love and loyalty to me had only been an act. For my own safety, I laughed with him.

After sounding like a couple of silly horses, I said with false amusement in my voice, "This plan is insane, but I will obey."

Chapter Twelve

"It is not so bad, Cata. This new job when you get back to Jerusalem guarding Herodias will be the safest job in the world. Who would ever think Herod Antipas's wife has the most-wanted man in the Roman Empire defending her?" Again, Saben lapsed into a bout of hilarity that reminded me of a gush of water going down a drain. This time, I did not comment or laugh. My mind was on my return to Jerusalem. I told myself I would not return to guard Herodias; instead, I would find Messina and run. It was then when I realized Saben had said Passover began in fewer than three weeks. I remembered that I had to be in Jerusalem a good week before Passover since Jesus presented himself on the Mount of Olives a year ago at least six days before the Day of Unleavened Bread began. Did I have time to sell the gimbals and return in fewer than two weeks? I decided to just dump the wagon before reaching Tyre and return to Jerusalem and get my stash of money from the wall in my barrack's room. Perhaps, if I did sell the gimbals, wagon, and horses, I could skim some of the money for myself, considering I was not going to get my wages from Herod before I bolted with Messina. Actually, money was the least of my problems since I still had a good horde of what was left from the bag Grillius gave me in the meadow before we parted. During this time of running my future plans through my mind, I decided to keep Zeus just in case I needed to exit Jerusalem quickly. A pleasant feeling came over me when I realized I would soon be leaving this troubled land as soon as Jesus returned as he promised a year ago on the Mount of Olives, only a few weeks away if Saben was correct about the date. Nothing was going to keep me from being on the Mount of Olives in a few weeks. I would be with Nicodemus and then make my escape as soon as I spotted my dog and Messina. It could be accomplished if I moved quickly, but time seemed to be my only enemy. A final thought passed my mind. Maybe, Jesus might be accepted at the king of the Jews and die much later. Anything could happen since no one could put God in a box.

Late on Sol Day or Sunday, Saben left Photina's home telling me to be in Jerusalem and standing before Herod at least five or six days before Passover began with Herod's money. Amcheck and Nicodemus were to leave as soon as possible for Jerusalem. I would come later with Euna after I sold the gimbals and the wagon in Tyre or Sidon.

Not long after Saben rode out of the back gate of Photina's home, Amcheck cornered me napping in the *stabulo*. "What are you doing on your cot?" barked the old assassin.

"What is the problem? This is where I do my best thinking!"

"You were asleep and not thinking!"

"That is right, and you just disturbed a pleasant dream where I was sitting on the side of a green grassy hill with Messina watching Zoe running after a zigzagging hare."

"Do you love Euna?" Amcheck asked with his eyes drilling into mine.

To break his stare, I sat up slowly before I responded, "What are you saying?"

"You heard me. Now, what is your answer?" I noticed Amcheck's hand move to the hilt of his *sicarius*. Was he going to fight me, or was it just a reflex?

"Euna is a sweet lady; but she is a little old for me, don't you think?"

"Do you love her?"

"I have loved only one woman, and she is somewhere with Jesus and his disciples. At least I hope that is the case. What is all this about?"

Amcheck looked more and more like he was going to fight me over Euna; but, after I had said what I felt about Messina, he seemed relieved. He tried to talk but struggled with the words he wanted to use. I sat quietly allowing him to gather himself. His vocabulary and his demeanor were much different from a few years back when I first met him. Perhaps we all change over time. "Euna says she is your slave for life."

"She is not my slave. Why do you ask?"

Amcheck turned and walked to the entrance of the *stabulo* and looked across the yard to the house. When he turned back toward me, he confessed he and Euna wanted to get married.

"How is that going to work?" I replied. "She is a Samaritan-Hebrew, and you are a pagan-whatever. Anyone who believes in only one God will have nothing but difficulties if he or she espouses with someone who does not accept the idea of many gods."

"I am going to be like you. I have talked to Nicodemus; and he says, as long as I believe in the Scriptures as the inspired words of Yahweh and that Yahweh is the only true God, I can become a proselyte Jew. I will need to be circumcised, which you can do, and then be baptized. Nicodemus will officiate a wedding before I go to Jerusalem. When I leave with Nicodemus for Jerusalem, you will protect my wife until you return her to me in Jerusalem, safe and unmolested!"

I was stunned but began grinning. I stood and slapped Amcheck on the back. "If you want to be circumcised and baptized, you can have my slave as a wedding present." However, I am not sure that was my real feelings. But, to be selfish, if I gave Euna to Amcheck, then I could stop worrying about him selling me out for that stellar reward. She just might be my insurance under such an act. But, if Euna and Amcheck married, I realized there would be a

Chapter Twelve

delay of reaching Jerusalem by a few days. I lowered my head and realized that I needed to start living under a new rule: you take care of Yahweh's business – He will take care of yours.

Within an hour I had circumcised Amcheck in the main house, who moaned more than when I put my hot knife into his infected hip wound. A few days later he baptized himself in the center of Photina's villa by dipping his entire body in the atrium pool that was full of rainwater. That same hour Nicodemus conducted the ceremony of marriage with Euna and Amcheck becoming man and wife.

The next day after the wedding Nicodemus entered the library where I was reading and announced that Saben had the days wrong. "I learned from people in the street that Passover begins in three weeks from today. That gives you two weeks to get your business completed in Tyre before you need to meet me on the Mount of Olives."

"Are you sure about the number of days until the Unleavened Festival begins?"

"Last night I noticed the moon was waning. You see, in a few days we will have a dark moon. Then begins the waxing until it is full on Nisan 14. From today, we should have three weeks before the start of Passover."

"Maybe a few days less, but that is great news. Do you think Saben was lying to get us moving sooner than later?"

"I want to think the best of people and not the negative. However, just remember, when the moon is in its first quarter, we will need to meet Jesus upon the Mount of Olives. Can you remember?"

"I will, but I have a question about what Saben said concerning the Tiberius letter sent to Pilate. How is Pilate going to crucify Jesus if Pilate now has orders from the emperor not to do such an act?"

Nicodemus frightened me with his answer. "Did not Saben say a second legion is coming to Judaea? He also said that it most likely would be stationed in Jerusalem." I indicated with a nod that was what I remembered. "Well, did you know that each legion is led by an appointed *legate* who is lower in rank from provincial governors, but still holds the rank of a *legate*?"

"I did not know this, but why is that important?"

"All *legates* have *imperium* power. If Pilate does not crucify Jesus, Satan can use this new *legate* to kill the Messiah on a cross." Now I was beginning to fear Nicodemus and his thoughts.

The second morning after Euna and Amcheck's wedding night, we all knew we had to leave. Euna and I waved to Amcheck and Nicodemus as they departed by foot for Jerusalem. We both watched an old and younger man both walking the same way and using a staff. "What a pathetic sight. My old roommate will never be the soldier he used to be."

"True, but he will be happier."

It was only a few hours later when I drove the wagon out of the gate of Photina's home toward Tyre with Euna sitting next to me. The plan was to go north on the Ridge Road until we reached the Caesarea cutoff near the Galilee border. From there we would go east through the Jezreel Valley, eventually passing Nazareth upon its northern rise; and later we would transit past the citadel of Megiddo up high on the southern side of the road when we passed the ancient battle valley of Megiddo or as some called it Armageddon. I had guaranteed Amcheck I would protect his new wife. I also told him, now that he was a proselyte Jew, and he better start praying to Yahweh three times a day for a wagon load of gimbals to be quickly sold so he could see his new wife without much delay. A changed Amcheck had agreed to pray three times a day on his knees. Before they left, I said in front of Nicodemus that he should get the old sage to instruct his newest student on the finer points of his new religion. Besides, I told Amcheck he was blessed if he did become Nicodemus's bodyguard; there would be ample time to learn more than what I did over the past nine months.

The things a man does for the love of a woman is one of the great mysteries of this world. I can no more explain it than I can understand how a snake moves on its belly across a hot rock or how ants all work together without officers, generals, and kings telling them what to do.

As the huge wagon with its four horses and Zeus tied to the back left Sychar, I began thinking about the words from Nicodemus concerning *legates* having *imperium* power. I absently looked at a field next to the road ready for its first harvest and smiled thinking about the Feast of First Fruits that was only a few weeks away. If my memory served me right, it would fall on the first Sun Day after Passover and that is when a loaf of bread would be offered to Yahweh by the high priest at the Temple. I re-calculated the days in my head and figured Passover most likely would land on Frigg's Day or the sixth day this year or very close to it. I looked at Euna sitting next to me on the Parthian wagon, and she smiled back the most pleasant smile. Birds were singing, and wildflowers were beginning to pop here and there. It all seemed like the most peaceful spring I could remember; but little did I know before the next third quarter moon, the world would never be the same again. A cataclysmic shift was soon to occur, and I was going to be in the center of it.

TO BE CONTINUED IN VOLUME III

CPSIA information can be obtained
at www.ICGtesting.com
Printed in the USA
LVHW022048230719
625065LV00006B/9/P